Self and Nation

Self and Nation:
Categorization, Contestation and Mobilization

Steve Reicher and Nick Hopkins

SAGE Publications
London • Thousand Oaks • New Delhi

SAGE Publications Ltd
6 Bonhill Street
London EC2A 4PU

SAGE Publications Inc
2455 Teller Road
Thousand Oaks, California 91320

SAGE Publications India Pvt Ltd
32, M-Block Market
Greater Kailash – I
New Delhi 110 048

We are grateful to David Godwin Associates, on behalf of Ben Okri,
for permission to publish an extract of his poem *Soul of the Nation*.

British Library Cataloguing in Publication Data

A catalogue record for this book is
available from the British Library

ISBN 0 7619 6919 5
ISBN 0 7619 6920 9 (pbk)

Library of Congress catalog card number available

Typeset by Keystroke, Jacaranda Lodge, Wolverhampton
Printed in Great Britain by Athenaeum Press, Gateshead

Contents

Preface

Proverbs for Paranoids, 3. If they can get you asking the wrong questions, they don't have to worry about answers

Thomas Pynchon

Nations, nationalism and national identity are all around us. Finding evidence is no more difficult than finding sand on a beach. For those who investigate the more arcane aspects of the world this might seem to give us an envious advantage. But there is a major cost. Because nationhood constitutes such a central aspect of our social world, there is much at stake when one comes to trying to understand it. No one who wishes to comment on the relevant phenomena can expect to find a hushed and pliant audience waiting for enlightenment. Quite the opposite in fact. We must try and raise our voice above a Babel of voices. We must contend with a welter of preconceptions. We must be aware of the considerable personal and political investments which buttress those preconceptions and make them hard to challenge.

Both the positives and the negatives of studying nationalism are exemplified in the following passage. It is taken from a column by Douglas Alexander in the *Glasgow Herald* entitled, 'Old national stereotypes should be cast aside', which we came across not as part of our study but rather when taking a break from our work. Alexander (2000) writes:

> National identity seems to be the political equivalent of internet shares at the moment. So popular is the issue that last week alone saw a much-reported interview on Englishness by Jack Straw [Home Secretary in the British Government], a major article on Britishness by Gordon Brown [Chancellor of the Exchequer], and suggestions of a shift in Alex Salmond's thinking on Scottish independence [Salmond being the leader of the Scottish National Party]. For all the talk of focus groups and poll-led politics, this interest is a heartening instance of political dispute mirroring intellectual discussion. Over the past year such discussion about the 'new Scotland' seems to have been never-ending. With Tom Devine's *The Scottish Nation* adding a welcome historical perspective, acres of newsprint have been given over to discussions of the character and characteristics of post-devolution Scotland.

So, even when you try and get away from nationhood, you can't help running slap bang back into it. On the surface, what Alexander does is confirm our claims concerning the omnipresence of questions about national phenomena. However, of equal importance is his illustration of the ways in which these questions are asked and the presuppositions that allow them to be asked in this way. The most common question takes the form: What is the character of the nation? What does it mean to be Scottish or to be English, or to be German or Latvian or indeed of any nationality? Alexander may question the particular terms in which the national identity is characterized. He may feel that old national stereotypes need to be discarded for new ones. To be more specific, he may wish to make tolerance a central value when it comes to determining 'what is a Scot'. But he takes it as a non-negotiable given that there is a singular and distinctive national identity which is lying out there just waiting to be discovered. It is this general presupposition which we aim to challenge.

Perhaps, though, Alexander is atypical. Perhaps his presupposition that we can find a singular national identity stems from his concern with the break up of the British state and the creation of devolved parliaments in Scotland, Wales and Northern Ireland. Such a context of division is bound to lead to a focus on difference and hence a need to identify exactly what it is that renders any one nation different from others. If we looked at a context which involved bringing nations together in supra-national Union rather than a context where a supra-national state was being divided into constituent nations, we might find less credibility given to the idea of the singular national identity. So consider the following. It is taken from a book called *We Europeans* (Hill, 1997), which is promoted by an organization called 'Understanding Europe' whose aim is to promote a joint European future. Hill states his purpose as to discover the 'cultural ids' of different European nations – that is the deep characteristics which drive the actions of each population. However, he wishes to discard 'the ethnic folklore that has clouded Europeans' perception of one another for far too long: the rude frivolous Frenchman, the idle pretentious Spaniard, the dull humourless German (not forgetting his archetype, the bull-headed sabre-scarred Prussian) and so on' (1997: 12). The reason is that such 'one-liners' are inevitably simplifications and distortions, but not that the notion of a single national character is a problem. Hill therefore goes on to state that:

> I feel the attempt to correct some of the most pernicious deformations of national character, in more than a single phrase, can serve some purpose. The fact that the French may seem rude to many foreigners may in fact . . . conceal a much more subtle complex of characteristics: self-absorption (my favourite), directness, eagerness to spark a response and *desinvolture*. (p. 13)

It is clear, then, that the assumption of national singularity is not affected by whether one champions international disintegration or integration. However, if we pursue Hill's argument just one step further, we can see that national singularity is not entirely unrelated to the opposition between disintegration and integration. He writes:

> If the generalizations in this book do something to correct the folkloric stereotypes of the past, they will have served their purpose. In any case I offer no excuse. It seems to me that there is no better combination than British inventiveness, French wit, Slav music, Italian cuisine, German perfection, Spanish reality, Dutch decency, Scandinavian fairness . . . in short, the best combination in the world. (pp. 13–14)

What Hill is doing, then, is to substitute definitions of identity which characterize other nations in such terms as to render contact (let alone integration) as undesirable with a new set of definitions which render integration both possible and mutually advantageous. So, at the same time as claiming to discover the single authentic identity which accurately describes what people are like in the here and now, it could be argued that what Hill (and Alexander) unwittingly demonstrate is that there are multiple competing definitions of national identity and that these are as much orientated to sustaining different projects for the future as to describing the present state of the nation.

That is precisely what we will argue. We want to create a shift from questions of the type: 'what does it mean to be Scottish' to questioning the different consequences of the different ways in which Scotland is defined. In other words, we wish to move from a view of national identity (and social identity more generally) as solely about *being* and start investigating the way in which it is also related to the process of *becoming*. We intend to examine how identity is used to mobilize people in support of, or in opposition to, different forms of political project and is thereby instrumental in directing the evolution of our social world. For us, the link between identity and mobilization must be moved centre stage.

This is easy to state, but far more difficult to fulfil. Firstly we must work against the weight of political interests. If a particular political project is underpinned by a particular definition of identity, then political ascendancy can be guaranteed by mythologizing that definition as the sole authentic definition (we shall see much evidence of such activity in the following pages). The ability to mythologize particular definitions of a particular identity is, in turn, aided and abetted by the general myth that there is always a single valid definition for any given identity. Our attack on that myth would therefore (if, by any chance, it were successful) constitute a blow against ideological domination – and it is unlikely that those interested in domination would take such a blow lying down.

Secondly, we must work against the weight of popular preconceptions and thirdly – as Alexander accurately observes – we must equally work against the weight of intellectual assumptions. In talking about identity as a matter of becoming, we are breaking with the perceptualism that has dominated social psychology for half a century and more. We are suggesting that human mental life does not derive from a passive contemplation of the world but from active engagement in the world – from the ways we are, we want to be and are capable of being. Social psychology needs to relate human understanding to the structure of human action. More specifically, we need to relate national identity to the structure of national action.

But, as we shall shortly see, even the most cursory examination of nationhood reveals that this is a two-way relationship. Certainly, national identity may shape collective movements, which create national structures, but equally national structures are crucial in shaping the way people identify themselves. In the terms we have used above we are not simply proposing that a focus on *becoming* supplants the focus on *being*, but rather that we must examine how the one supplements the other. The task of a fully rounded social psychology is to help explain the dynamic and evolving relationship between the way in which our self-understandings create the world and the way in which the world creates our self-understandings. We consider that an examination of national phenomena can help us to develop such a rounded psychology. Conversely, such a psychology is necessary to understand the complexities of nationhood. To put it in a phrase: our ambition in writing this book is to use nationhood in order to develop psychological understanding and to use psychology in order to develop our understanding of nationhood.

In order for the reader to understand how we have sought to realize these ambitions, it may help to give some background concerning the way in which this volume came about. The book is, in fact, one of two books that started life as one book. By the time we had written the original draft it was clear that the thing was neither fish nor fowl – or rather, it was both fish and fowl, which made for a rather unappetizing combination. It started with some two hundred pages in which we engaged with the dominant traditions in social psychology in order to explain and position our own approach. It then continued with a further three hundred pages in which we used nationhood as an exemplary case through which to validate this approach. However, as both our editors and their reviewers pointed out, the theoretical discussion was rather arcane for many of those interested in nationhood and the issue of nationhood may not have been of major concern to all those interested in the theoretical controversies. So we decided to separate the package, to create one book which was mainly theory (perhaps still with a hint of nationhood in some of the examples) and another – this one – which summarizes the theory but then concentrates on illustrating and applying it through a study of the relationship between national identity and national being. Each book stands alone and there will be more than enough theory in the following pages. However should anyone wish to examine the roots and the justification of our model, and if they would like to consider the more general implications of this model for an understanding of the human social subject, we would refer them to the other volume (Reicher, in press).

There is another significant manner in which this book has changed in the re-writing. At first, our argument was based largely on the analysis of how Scottish politicians and the Scottish media and activists in the various struggles around the formation of a Scottish parliament used and contested the idea of Scottish nationhood. While this debate may have seemed of almost unsurpassed importance to those living in Scotland, we fully recognize that it may have seemed far less significant to those living further away. However, our aim was not to be parochial. Our logic was based on what Clifford Geertz has had to say about the relationship of culture to human nature and hence of particularity to generality.

Geertz notes how, for many, the hunt for human nature involves looking for that which everybody shares in common and hence ignoring what is specific to different groups. He describes this 'stratigraphic' approach in the following terms: 'At the level of concrete research and specific analysis, this grand strategy came down, first, to a hunt for universals in culture, for empirical uniformities that, in the face of customs around the world and over time, could be found everywhere in about the same form' (1993: 38). In contrast, Geertz himself advocates a synthetic approach. Because it is in the nature of human beings to be cultural, we can only discover that nature by paying close attention to its manifestations in the details of a culture. In other words, generality is to be found by respecting, not by denying specificity: 'If we want to discover what man amounts to, we can only find it in what men are: and what men are, above all other things, is various. It is in understanding that variousness – its range, its nature, its basis and its implications – that we shall come to construct a concept of human nature that, more than a statistical shadow and less than a primitivist dream, has both substance and truth' (1993: 51–52).

Following Geertz, we wished to explore the general relationship between the ways in which identity is constructed and the ways people act through a detailed appreciation of the Scottish case. But this wasn't appreciated quite so much by our editors and our reviewers. They were concerned that, however valid our argument, it might be ignored as being 'only about Scotland'. So, in the re-written text, we use examples from all around the globe as evidence of the identity–action relationships which we are claiming. We show that they don't only obtain in one small part of one small island on the north western periphery of Western Europe. However we do still tend to follow through our analysis of these relationships by focusing on Scottish examples – and that for the simple reason that our evidence is so much richer, so much more direct and frequently so much more eloquent when it comes from Caledonia. It is therefore worth saying a few words about this evidence and about the context to which speakers were referring.

Scotland's history, especially in relation to England and to Great Britain, is long and complicated. After an enduring period of feudal domination by English kings, Scotland finally won its independence after the Battle of Bannockburn in 1314. Independence lasted until 1707 when union was declared between the two countries and the Edinburgh parliament was dissolved, although Scotland retained a separate church, as well as separate legal and educational systems. Initial opposition to the Union soon died down. However, throughout the second half of the twentieth century, support for some measure of renewed Scottish autonomy grew. This blossomed dramatically in the 1970s with the capture of parliamentary seats by the Scottish National Party (SNP), a party based on the call for Scottish independence. In 1979, a referendum on the issue of devolution (that is, a separate parliament for Scotland within an overall UK framework) was narrowly lost. In fact, more voted for than against, but a clause had been inserted to say that, as well as a majority of those voting, 40 per cent of the entire electorate must support the measure before it could be enacted. That threshold was not reached. By the 1990s, the question of Scotland's constitutional status in the UK had again risen to the fore and, in the 1992 general election, formed the major issue in Scotland and, to some extent, in the UK as a whole. Within Scotland, there were four major parties. Labour and the Liberal Democrats supported a devolved parliament. The SNP supported independence. The Conservatives supported the status quo. The contest was fought with passion and seriousness and continued to reverberate throughout Scotland long after the Conservatives (having won a majority of the seats throughout the UK as a whole) were returned to power. If their UK majority ensured the temporary survival of the status quo, the Labour victory of 1997 brought a referendum on devolution, which was soon followed by the re-establishment of a Scottish parliament in 1999. Of course this is not the end of the matter.

The 1992 election lies at the heart of the analysis developed throughout this book. Over the period before and after the election date we interviewed 52 candidates and senior activists spanning all the parties (20 of whom were MPs). We attended and recorded 16 election meetings, some by a single candidate, some involving all the candidates in a constituency. We also recorded 12 public rallies, demonstrations or fringe meetings organized at the parties' annual conferences and connected with the election and its aftermath. So too we recorded meetings or rallies organized by non-electoral groups (five) and several events as diverse as demonstrations in support of sacked Scottish workers and the annual commemoration of the Battle of Bannockburn. Finally, we continued to collect major public speeches and statements on the matter. In the case of public statements we have identified the speaker. In the case of private interviews we have respected the anonymity of the speaker and only identified him or her by a number, political party and by political position. The one exception, in this as in so many other things, is the late Conservative MP, Sir Nicholas Fairbairn. He was more than happy to be identified and so we have done so.

We are particularly grateful to all of those who gave us their time, who agreed to long interviews and who provided us with so much material. There are others who have given us a great deal, but in different ways. We owe much to those who read the original text in various forms and provided us with helpful comments, which we have tried to take on board. We are also grateful to those who have discussed the ideas in this book and given us cause to think and sometimes to reconsider. It is always hard to remember all those who are included in these two categories, but they include Mick Billig, Susan Condor, Alex Haslam, David McCrone, and Jonathon Potter. We owe a particular debt of thanks to Ziyad Marar at Sage who was more than an ordinary editor, who encouraged us and who made a crucial intellectual input to the shaping of the book.

We also depended on several other forms of support. The research was conducted without an external grant. This meant that we ourselves conducted the interviews, attended the meetings, joined in the rallies and demonstrations – but we would have had it no other way: we wanted to be there! However, it also meant that in addition to accumulating a growing pile of audio-tapes we incurred all sorts of expenses. We are indebted to Dundee University's Psychology Department (especially Nick Emler and Alan Kennedy) for tolerating (and subsidizing) such behaviour and to the University's own Research Initiatives Fund for a small grant towards the transcription costs. Over a number of years, the Dundee Department's secretaries – especially the remarkable Liz Evans, Linda Fullerton and Lynda McDonald – and a number of others outwith the Department (most notably the equally remarkable Carol Larg) spent many hours carefully transcribing our tapes (and providing us with their own thoughtful insights on what they had heard). To all of these, a genuine thank you.

Most importantly, we would like to thank our partners, one teenager, two cats and one dog for putting up with our moods. They have had much to endure but now the pain is over. Or rather, it is now the reader's turn.

But there is one final point we wish to make before we get down to business. This book has been a genuinely collaborative effort. Neither one of us would or could have done it without the other. However, unfortunately the linear nature of text means that one name has to come first and the other second. So we tossed a coin. It came down tails and the book was authored Reicher and Hopkins. It could as easily have been Hopkins and Reicher.

1 The National Question

Psychology in a world of nations

We have said it before, but let us say it again: the aim of this book is to use social psychology to answer some questions about national phenomena and to use national phenomena to pose some questions about social psychology. This might seem an obvious task, and one might reasonably suppose that it had been undertaken with such frequency that any new attempt would be jostling for room in a very crowded space. Yet, on closer inspection of that space, one finds a remarkable absence – or rather, a remarkable pair of absences.

For all the huge and burgeoning literature on nations and nationalism, there is virtually no explicit consideration of the psychological mechanisms which mediate between structural, cultural and ideological considerations on the one hand and action on the other. Even more notably, psychology is frequently excluded from the family of disciplines that are invited to discuss the nature of national phenomena. For instance, in his review of explanations of nationalism, John Coakley (1992) provides a taxonomy based on the definition of the phenomena to be explained, the disciplinary approach to be adopted and the ideological approach that is taken. Under 'disciplinary approach' he lists:

> political science; philosophy; sociology; anthropology; geography; sociolinguistics (history has been omitted on the assumption that the contribution of many historians who have addressed this subject on a theoretical level will fall under the heading of one of the above disciplinary perspectives, all of which, in any case, tend to adopt an historical approach to the topic). (pp. 2–3)

Just as the study of nations is booming, so social psychology is a growth area covering an increasing number of topics as reflected in a diversifying array of journals. What is more, after prolonged neglect (cf. Steiner, 1974), group and collective processes are receiving renewed attention. Between 1974 and 1989, 5.9 per cent of articles in top mainstream social psychology journals were concerned with some aspect of group processes or intergroup relations. Between 1990 and 1995 the average grew to 10.6 per cent, with the figure for 1995 alone standing at 14.9 per cent (Hogg & Moreland, 1995; Moreland, Hogg & Hains, 1994). Further, two new journals have started in the last couple of years alone: *Group Dynamics* and *Group Processes and Intergroup Relations*. As these titles would suggest, their remit is limited exclusively to collective phenomena. Yet, for all this interest, nations and nationalism have received scant attention.

In the first two volumes of *Group Processes and Intergroup Relations*, not a single article has been devoted to such phenomena. Looking at an admittedly non-random sample of social psychology textbooks on our bookshelves (Baron, Byrne & Johnson, 1998; Brewer & Crano, 1994; Brown, 1965, 1986; Forsyth, 1987; Hewstone, Stroebe & Stephenson, 1996; Hogg & Vaughan, 1998; Levin & Levin, 1988; Moscovici, 1972; Pennington, Gillen & Hill, 1999; Sabini, 1992, 1995; Wrightsman & Deaux, 1981) only two contain any mention at all of anything to do with nations and both of these are limited to passing reflections covering no more than a single page: one on whether we have clear stereotypes of different nations (Brewer & Crano, 1994); the other as to whether different nations have different values (Wrightsman & Deaux, 1981). This isn't because textbooks are somehow atypical. A computer search of psychology journal articles over the period 1987–1994 reveals eight articles on nationalism and 11 on national identity. This compares with 485 articles on a specific personality characteristic (neuroticism) and 3174 on rats!

This is not to deny that there are many papers in which national identity is employed as a dependent or independent variable, but these are cases where the nation is not of interest in itself, nor are the particularities of national categories a focus of study. Indeed these are glossed over since the nation is only employed as a convenient domain in which to study more general phenomena – stereotyping, intergroup comparison or whatever (cf. Billig, 1995; Condor, 1997, in press). There are, of course, some exceptions to this sorry picture and there are incipient signs that psychologists are beginning to treat the nation more seriously. We shall be dealing with these exceptions in the next chapter. Nonetheless, in broad terms, there is little doubt that students of the nation have ignored psychology and that students of psychology have ignored the nation. If this double absence is remarkable enough in itself, it becomes even more remarkable when one considers the extent to which the issues and the concepts used by each are so inhabited by the other. It is as if, on each side, a central member of the family had been banished to the nether regions and, while never spoken of by name, still haunted each and every conversation.

This is, perhaps, most obvious in studies of nations and nationalism. If the revival of peripheral nationalisms in Western Europe sparked the new wave of study and if the emergence of nationalisms following the break up of the Soviet Union only added to the impetus, the most acute concerns accompanied the periodic upsurges of violence, most notably around the break up of Yugoslavia. To quote from the back-cover blurb for Michael Ignatieff's account of his journeys into the new nationalism: 'modern nationalism is a language of the blood: a call to arms that can end in the horror of ethnic cleansing' (1994). Such concerns lead to a frequent definition of nationalism as a psychological category (Giddens, 1985) and, more particularly, an equation of nationalism with the psychological categories of passion and of sentiment (Hooghe, 1992). The combined taint of extremity and irrationalism also leads to a widespread suspicion concerning all manifestations of nationhood. In Kitching's delightful phrase, 'son, when they raise your flag, raise your eyebrow' (1985: 116).

However, there is a danger in reducing nationalism to its most intense manifestations. As Gellner (1994) observes, nationalism may be an important and pervasive force, but it rarely leads to violent disruption. If we limit our concern with the phenomena to those moments when people are preparing to die, or else to kill, in the nation's name, we would conclude that, however spectacular, nationalism is generally of little relevance to the way in which we live our everyday lives. Gellner's own description of nationalism is revealing in this respect. He likens it to gravity – a force that exerts its pull upon us in both spectacular and mundane ways. Sometimes it may cause things to crash to the ground, or apples to drop on our heads. But it also shapes the way we act in less obtrusive ways. To borrow Billig's term, it is banal nationalism – the way we presuppose a national frame for everything from what counts as 'the news' to what we understand as 'the weather' – that may ultimately have the greatest impact upon us (1995). By focusing on the periodic explosions of nationalist fervour we miss the fact that nationalism is the ideology through which people act to reproduce nation-states as nations (Billig, 1996).

But even in these banal forms, where national identity is not overtly asserted but rather taken for granted and where a national frame of reference does not lead one to kill but shapes the way one scans and understands a newspaper, one is still invoking a psychological category. One is dealing with the ways in which people understand who they are, the nature of the world they live in, how they relate to others and what counts as important for them.

It is not only nationalism and national identity that invoke psychological constructs. Increasingly, the very concept of nation has come to incorporate a psychological dimension. Perhaps the two most famous quotations in this regard are from Rupert Emerson and Benedict Anderson. Emerson states that: 'the simplest statement that can be made about a nation is that it is a body of people who feel that they are a nation; and it may be that when all the fine-spun analysis is concluded this will be the ultimate statement as well' (1960: 102). Anderson defines the nation by saying that: 'it is an imagined political community' (1983: 15). However, these two are not alone. Walker Connor states that: 'many of the problems associated with defining a group are attributable precisely to the fact that it is a self-defining group. That is why scholars such as Ernest Baker, Rupert Emerson, Carleton Hayes, and Hans Kohn have consistently used terms such as self-awareness and self-consciousness when analysing and describing the nation' (1994: 104).

To introduce a psychological dimension to the definition of nations does not mean ignoring other dimensions. In Anderson's case, quite the opposite is true. His analysis centres on the material conditions of national subjectivity and may best be seen as contributing to a materialist theory of consciousness (Kitching, 1985). We will consider these conditions in more detail later in this chapter. For now we simply want to stress that, even if psychology must not be allowed to supplant other social scientific analyses, an understanding of nations and nationalism requires it to be re-admitted to the debating table.

To try and address the conditions of national imagination without considering the nature of human imagination will be a futile exercise. To analyse the cultural battles over the definition of national identity without understanding how people come to assume and inhabit such identities, and how the identity then shapes what they do, may be an interesting exercise in its own right, but it does not get us very far in understanding nationalism. How can nationhood come to be so important to people and have such an impact on their actions? Why and when will national identity lead to violence against members of other nations? How is it that the Serbians of 1999 can be so moved by the Battle of Kosovo in 1389 and the slights or triumphs of the distant past can exert such influence on present-day behaviour? Without finding a way of articulating the social and the psychological rather than subsuming one under the other, we will be left, like Paul Valéry, simply wondering at the nation as 'something unquantifiable, an entity which cannot be coldly defined, that is determined by neither race, language, land, interests nor history: that analysis can deny, but which nonetheless resembles, as by its proven all-powerfulness, passionate love, faith, one of those mysterious possessions which lead man there where he did not know he could go – beyond himself' (quoted in Privat, 1931: 3; translated by the authors).

Having looked at social psychology in the study of nationhood, let us turn to nationhood in the study of social psychology. The first and most obvious point is that, if this latter study is concerned with the understanding of behaviour in social context (cf. Israel & Tajfel, 1972) then the context in which we act is a world of nations. For Eric Hobsbawm, the twentieth century both began and concluded as an era of nationalism. The national conflicts that tore Europe apart in the 1990s were the old chickens of Versailles once again coming home to roost (Hobsbawm, 1994). We are, to use Balibar's phrase, *homo nationalis* from cradle to grave (1991b: 93). Castells (1997) goes yet further and argues that it isn't just that the nation is the predominant form of collective being in the contemporary world. Rather, nationalism has re-invigorated the very possibility of collective identity in an age of individualism.

The apparent ubiquity of nations has led to claims that there is something eternal and necessary about them. Smith (1986) refers to the widespread assumption that nations were as natural as the human body itself – an assumption that bridges popular, political and academic divides. According to the South African Broederbond intellectual Nico Diedrichs, nations are of divine inspiration: 'God does not only work through men, but also through nations . . . An effort to obliterate national differences thus means more than collision with God's natural law. It means an effort to shirk a divinely established duty or task' (quoted in No Sizwe, 1979: 23). According to Regis Debray, they embody a natural logic: 'We must locate the nation phenomenon within general laws regulating the survival of the human species' (1977: 28). However, the most developed expression of this viewpoint is to be found in the work of Friedrich List (cf. Gellner, 1994). List argued for a nationalist ontology: people may not always construe themselves in terms of nationhood, but national divisions are the motor that drives history forward. The political task is to turn the nation 'in itself' into the nation 'for itself'. If this is reminiscent of Hegelian–Marxist language, that is because List was involved in a direct polemic with Marx and Engels over the issue of whether class or nation should be given ontological priority. There are those, such as Gellner, who have declared List the victor: 'The supposition that [nations] will be dismantled, anticipated by Marxism, is the *real* chimera – and not ethnically defined protectionism, as Marx thought. In all this, List was superior to Marx, and much more prescient' (1994: 19; emphasis in the original).

Irrespective of whether Gellner, List, Debray and Diedrichs are correct, the very fact that their views have such currency is evidence in itself of the predominance of national consciousness alongside national forms throughout the world that we live in. So whether spoken of or not, it is often the nation that frames the concerns that guide social psychological research, it is often the nation that social psychologists have in mind when they address collective phenomena and it is often through the contemplation of national phenomena that social psychologists frame their core concepts. It may help to provide a concrete example of each.

Genevieve Paicheler (1988) illustrates how the emergence of social psychology as a distinct discipline in the USA during the 1920s was bound up with the concerns of nation formation. The growth of Fordism and of mass production demanded a mass market in which the new volume of products could be sold. The division of a population into separate groups – German Americans, Italian Americans, Anglo-Americans and so on – with different tastes was an obstacle to the emergence of this market. What was needed was a new and singular national consumer with unified tastes. The task of psychology, as clearly enunciated in the editorials of new social psychology journals, was to help in fitting the individual to the needs of the nation.

In such a context, hostility between groups of different national backgrounds became a serious issue. The perception of others as different and as negative required urgent attention, and it received such attention in the form of stereotype research. The pioneering study of Katz and Braly in 1933 presented college students with a list of adjectives and asked them to indicate which were typical of ten groups. While the groups included 'Negroes' and 'Jews' and while the paper was entitled 'Racial Stereotypes of 100 college students', it is notable that most of the groups chosen were nationalities and that the paper is generally described as concerning nations. For instance, Brewer and Crano (1994), in one of the two references to nationality that we found in recent text books, present the Katz and Braly results in a three-quarter page box under the heading 'National Stereotypes in the United States' and they then ask 'following are the four characteristics most frequently assigned to ten nationalities by US college students in 1933. How many of these stereotypes do you think would still be held today?' (p. 463). Katz and Braly's actual discovery of considerable consensus about the nature of particular groups and the differences between groups led them to express strong fears about the breakdown of community.

It continues to be true that nations are used by psychologists as exemplary instances of stereotypes and stereotyping processes (see Spears, Oakes, Ellemers & Haslam, 1997, for a recent overview of the literature) and indeed of many other group processes besides (Condor, in press). It is also true that the very concept of a group in social psychology has been defined in relation to the nation. Work on groups and group processes in psychology has, over recent years, become increasingly dominated by the social identity tradition (Tajfel, 1978, 1982; Tajfel & Turner, 1986). Part of the appeal of the theory is that it seeks to explain the behaviour of large-scale collectivities and not just the small groups of traditional laboratory research. So, when Tajfel seeks to define the social group in such a way as to understand how people who are not co-present and have no personal acquaintance can come to act together, he states that: 'We shall adopt a concept of "group" identical to the definition of "nation" proposed by the historian Emerson' (1978: 28) and he then provides the famous quotation reproduced above.

All in all, social psychology is as thoroughly haunted by the nation as the nation is haunted by psychology. In consequence, just as our understanding of national phenomena will gain by addressing the psychological dimension, so our under-standing of social psychology will gain by an explicit consideration of national phenomena. To understand how people assume and act in terms of national identity, when national identity leads to international conflict, and how distant pasts can shape present actions, not only demands a psychology but also makes severe demands of psychology. These demands have already been expressed in their most general sense: we need a psychology that articulates with the social world – the world of nations – rather than one that subsumes it. We need to elaborate psycho-logical constructs that act as a pivot between structure, culture and ideology on the one hand and understanding and action on the other. To ask of psychology that it helps us to understand the complex realities of national phenomena and to test it against this ability is to set a very stern test and to risk some painful discoveries for social psychology as a discipline. However, if we, as social psychologists, are demanding a seat at the table of social sciences it is incumbent upon us to prove ourselves.

It is best to acknowledge openly and from the start that this proof is all the more necessary because of a sorry history. If the other social sciences have tended to ignore social psychology as a discipline and have tended either to gloss over psychological concerns or else develop their own psychologies, it is largely because the discipline of social psychology has tended towards intellectual imperialism and to proceed as if all could be explained by psychology without the need for sociologists, political scientists, anthropologists or whoever. That is, the social was indeed subsumed under, if not obliterated by, the psychological. From the very start, on those occasions where psychology did address nations and nationalism it was to explain them as the reflection of an irreducible psychological essence (e.g. Le Bon, 1894). If the disciplinary sleight is bad enough, the politics are even worse. There is a tragic tale, frequently told (e.g. Billig, 1978, 1979; Hopkins, Reicher & Levine, 1997; Kamin, 1977; Richards, 1997; Rose, Kamin & Lewontin, 1984), of how psychology has portrayed the consequences of social inequality as the reflection of set group characteristics and then used these characteristics to justify further oppression. Lest we take comfort in the notion that these are past sins from which a painful lesson has been learnt, it is worth quoting from Anzulovic (1999) who notes how the idea of Croatians as murderous and incurably dangerous was inculcated by the Serbian intelligentsia in order to create the conditions for ethnic cleansing: 'Psychoanalysts explained why, thanks to the specific character of certain peoples, things had to happen that way. Poets added a few poems about the calvary of their own people, regarded as heavenly, and the atmosphere of hatred – which became a way of life – started from there' (pp. 140–1).

This is the background against which we will address what sort of psychology is needed to be fit for the nation. If it indicates how far there is to go, it also indicates how important it is to undertake the journey. The first step is to investigate the world of nations in a little more detail, for we can only assess the adequacy of our explanations by grounding them in a thorough knowledge of what we seek to explain. This might seem self-evident. However, sadly, Herbert Blumer's concerns of over thirty years ago still ring true today, if not truer than ever (at least in psychology). He noted that there was 'an astonishing disposition in current social science to identify methodology with some limited portion of the act of scientific inquiry, and further, to give that portion a gratuitous parochial cast' (1969: 24). In other words, investigation is equated with hypothesis testing and hypothesis testing is largely equated with quantitative sophistication. There are obvious advantages to such sophistication but the obvious disadvantage is that both the questions one is asking and the way one seeks to answer them may have little to do with the phenomenon one purports to explain. We therefore intend to take Blumer seriously when he enjoins us to 'respect the nature of the empirical world' (1969: 60) by starting off with a closer look at the phenomena of nationhood. Later on, when it comes to our psychological analysis of these phenomena, we hope to live up to the second part of Blumer's injunction '. . . and organize a methodological stance to reflect that respect' (ibid).

Defining issues

Let us start off by noting what looks alarmingly like a paradox. On the one hand, one cannot miss the clear and concrete traces of nationhood. On the other hand, whenever one turns to grasp whatever it is that produces these traces, the thing seems to slip away and one is left wondering at the chimeric quality of nations and nationalism themselves (cf. Anderson, 1983). Nationhood seems to exemplify the old rhyme: 'I saw a man on the stair and when I looked he wasn't there'. Given our fears, the rest of the rhyme seems equally pertinent: 'He wasn't there again today, I do so wish he'd go away'.

In one sense, our entire argument will be devoted to showing that this is no paradox at all and that, far from being contradictory, these two sides of the phenomenon are interdependent. However that is to get far ahead of ourselves. The more obvious and immediate reactions are either to dismiss the validity and legitimacy of dealing in nationhood or else to try and give sufficient substance to the idea of nation that it seems capable of bearing the load placed upon it.

Many theorists have noted how hard it is to define terms in this area. Seton-Watson (1977) finds himself driven to conclude that, despite its unquestioned consequences, no scientific definition of the nation can be devised. Lofgren (1989) refers to the concept of nationalism as possessing a 'chameleonic vagueness' (p. 9) and then goes on to state that the concept of national identity is even more ambivalent! In the political domain, Rosa Luxemburg drew on these difficulties to argue against those of her fellow Bolsheviks who supported the right of nations to self-determination. She argued that such a slogan sounded fine, but in practice it proved empty and meaningless. It is worth reproducing her argument at some length:

The 'nation' should have the 'right' to self-determination. But who is that 'nation' and who has the authority and the 'right' to speak for the 'nation' and express its will? How can we find out what the 'nation' actually wants? Does there exist one political party which would not claim that it alone, among all others, truly expresses the will of the 'nation' whereas all other parties give only perverted and false expressions of the national will? (1976: 141)

The oldest, and probably the most popular attempt to answer Luxemburg's questions derives from German romanticism and, more particularly, from idealist philosophers such as Herder and Hegel (Guibernau, 1996; Jurt, 1992; Llobera, 1996). For them, the nation is formed out of people who share a common spirit (*Volksgeist*) which manifests itself in their language, their customs, their myths and their culture. In its romantic guise, the idea that nations represent a trans-historical spirit is primarily intended as a moral imperative. According to Herder, if nations are sacred they must be worshipped rather than destroyed (Guibernau, 1996). However, perhaps more prosaically, there are many who have drawn on such ideas in order to posit a list of objective criteria in order to determine when a nation exists.

Of all these various lists, perhaps the best known is that produced by Stalin in 1913. We can use this list in order to evaluate the general viability of this approach, firstly because Stalin covers most of the criteria advanced by others and secondly because his list so clearly echoes the romantic position. Stalin asserts that 'a nation is a historically evolved stable community of people based on a community of language, territory, economic life and psychological make-up manifested in a community of culture' (quoted in No Sizwe, 1979: 181).

Like the romantics, then, Stalin starts with language. Certainly, the issue of language is central in many national movements. To quote the Moldavian Dabija writing in 1989, 'language is the soul of the people. It resembles those who speak it. Our language resembles the shepherds who have spoken it for millennia, it resembles each of us' (translated from Seriot, 1992: 206). Or, to borrow an example from Connor (1994), the Ukrainian struggle for independence was waged around the right to employ Ukrainian, rather than Russian, in all oral and written matters. However, as Connor asks, 'is the language the essential element of the Ukrainian nation or is it merely a minor element which has been elevated to *the symbol* of the nation in its struggle for continued viability?' (1994: 44; emphasis in the original).

The idea that a nation needs its own language doesn't live up to even the most superficial scrutiny. Passing aside the thorny issue of how to categorize languages (as Seriot notes, languages exist on a continuum of dialect and there are no formal criteria for placing the breaks in one place rather than another) the problem is twofold. On the one hand, one can think of multi-lingual nations. Belgium and Switzerland come easily to mind. Even though the latter includes at least four language populations, there is little difficulty in recognizing it as a nation. Indeed, in his study of collective sentiment, Privat (1931) uses the Swiss, in contrast to the League of Nations, to show what a nation is: the one is ancient and has forged its soul in the course of time, the other is recent and has no soul. More seriously, perhaps, the use of language to define nation can be used to stand in the way of building national unity in a multilingual country such as South Africa.

On the other hand, many nations share the same language. Repeatedly, in South America and in Africa, nation-building goes on in the language of the old colonial administrators and without the question of a national language even being an issue. (Anderson, 1983; Schlesinger, 1987). As Anderson argues, Ghanaian nationalism is no less real than Indonesian nationalism simply because the national language is English rather than Ashanti. None of this is to deny that a nation needs language. Indeed, as will emerge later, we see language as absolutely central. However, it is to deny that nations need their own language or even a single common language in order to define themselves.

Stalin's second criterion is territory. Once again, it may well be true that many national movements organize around the issue of land. It may also be true that territory is seen by nationalists as an inalienable aspect of their identity (Grosby, 1995) – the conjunction of 'blood' and 'soil' in defining the essence of the nation is painfully familiar. But, as with language, we have to ask whether territory is more a symbolic means of mobilization than essential to nationhood. To claim that the nation needs to be contained in its own territory is to exclude at least two types of nation and probably a third. The first are Diaspora nations where groups are scattered across different territories: the Jews and the Palestinians are examples. The second are irredentist nations where the nation is seen as extending beyond the boundaries of the existing state: thus at least a third of Somalis live in Ethiopia, Kenya and Djibouti (James, 1996) The third are multi-territorial nations where the nation is divided up into multiple territories: Indonesia, for instance, is formed of literally thousands of islands.

If a nation needs no territory, the converse is also true. Territories rarely correspond to nations. Thus, in a survey of 132 entities considered as states in 1971, Connor (1994) estimates that only 9.1 per cent correspond to a single nation. Multi-national states, immigrant states and mestizo states (those in Latin-America where a grouping of joint European–Amerindian ancestry are in the ascendancy) are the rule rather than the exception. Thus, while territory, like language, is plainly important to an understanding of the nation, it is simply wrong to consider it as a necessary criterion for the existence of a nation.

Similar points could be made about the economy and national character. After all, if a separate economy were the criterion of a separate nation, then there would be no basis for nationality or for the resurgent nationalism in the countries of the old Soviet Union. We will address the thesis of national character in the next chapter. Suffice to say here that the term is more normative than descriptive. That leaves culture.

In 1926, Prime Minister Stanley Baldwin answered the question 'what do I mean by England' in the following terms: 'The tinkle of the hammer on the anvil in the country smithy, the corncrake on a dewy morning, the sound of the scythe against the whetstone. The sight of a plough team coming over the brow of a hill . . .' (quoted in Osmond, 1988: 158). In 1949 T.S. Elliot sought to pin down the key elements of English culture: 'Derby-day, the Henley regatta, Cowes, August the 12th, a cup final, the greyhound races, the Fortuna game, the dart board, Wensleydale cheese, cabbage boiled in cloves, pickled beetroots, churches in nineteenth-century Gothic and Elgar's music' (quoted in Lofgren, 1989: 13–14).

The one, a rural version of a country landowner, the other the vision of a middle-class intellectual. As Lofgren argues of the Elliot example – though it is applicable to both – these are attempts to capture the essence of Englishness but: 'they reflect *one* version of or perspective on what constitutes the typical or essential in the national culture' (1989: 14; emphasis in original). Neither version would have much resonance for the urban working-class.

One by one, Stalin's criteria have to be discarded – certainly if they are meant to constitute either necessary or sufficient aspects of nationhood. However, a defender of the romantic position might well argue that these are merely the signs of the *Volksgeist*. They might emanate from the national spirit but they don't constitute the essence of the nation. In more modern terms, this translates into the argument that language, character, culture and so on are consequences of common ethnicity. To take the argument in its crude form, the existence and the membership of nations can be identified through a common ethnic or even racial heritage (Balibar, 1991a; Mosse, 1995). Such claims have tended to be associated with the rejection or even the annihilation of those who are positioned as ethnic outsiders and, in consequence, have not so much fallen from favour as achieved pariah status. Even in societies such as Nazi Germany and Apartheid South Africa, which went furthest towards defining the national community in ethnic or racial terms, it has been shown how the idea of an ethnically homogenous nation was largely fictitious and how the criteria for inclusion or exclusion were largely arbitrary – at least in a cultural or biological sense (Cornevin, 1980; Peukert, 1987). As Cornevin (1980) says of South Africa:

> Although the specificity of each of the nine South African ethnic groups is presented as self-evident, the foreign reader cannot help wondering about the obvious advantage to the white minority of dividing the black majority into nine separate groupings. Isn't this division of the blacks into nine 'emergent nations' simply a pseudo-scientific way of camouflaging the principle common to all colonial powers, namely divide and rule? (p. 70)

Even if one rejects the idea that nations are constituted out of ethnically homo-geneous communities, there are two other ways in which one might defend the idea that ethnicity remains central to nationhood. The one is to argue, like Anthony Smith (1986, 1991, 1995), that while the nation is based upon a pre-existing ethnic community (which he terms an 'ethnie'), this heritage has to be discovered and interpreted before it is used for nation-building. Thus ethnic homogeneity cannot be equated with nationhood, however it facilitates the process of nation-building.

Smith's argument is part of a larger debate concerning the antiquity of this world of nations. It is, in effect, a reaction to the so-called 'modernist' position according to which nationhood is a phenomenon of the last two centuries (e.g. Balibar, 1991b; Gellner, 1983; Minogue, 1967; Nairn, 1977; Poole, 1994; Wallerstein, 1991). Most famously, Kedourie (1960) declared nationalism to be a doctrine invented in Europe at the beginning of the nineteenth century.

For the modernists, the nation is a new form of social organization. It arises out of the economic, social and political change wrought by the Industrial and French Revolutions. This had two sets of consequences. The first had to do with developments within the major industrial powers such as the break up of self-enclosed communities, the break down of old cultural differences (including linguistic differences) between the elite and the populace, and the rise of the modern state with its attendant institutions and processes of social control. This allowed for the emergence of a new form of community which transcended traditional parochial loyalties.

The second set of consequences had to do with the relationship between centre and periphery. Essentially, those elites on the periphery needed to mobilize the population in their locality in order to resist the crushing weight of metropolitan imperialism. In Nairn's words, the middle classes needed 'to invite the masses into history; and the invitation had to be written in a language they understood' (1977: 340) – or rather, a language in which they were included. That language was nationalism. Indeed, the very terms 'nationalism' and 'nation-state' have only been in common usage since the mid-nineteenth century. The term 'nation' may seem much older, being traceable to the Latin *natio*. However, in its early usages, 'nation' denoted such things as the communities of foreigners in universities, monasteries and the Reform Council of the church; as 'uncivilized' peoples, and, somewhat later, as the ruling classes in opposition to the *Volk* or *peuple*. Only in the late seventeeth century did 'nation' come to denote the entire population living in a country (James, 1996).

Smith does not dispute the importance of recent developments, but he criticizes the notion of a complete discontinuity between the nineteenth century and all that went before – as if the nation and nationalism was created out of nothing. Along with others (e.g. Colley, 1992; James, 1996; Poole, 1994), he argues that we need to look back further in history if we wish to understand why certain communities emerged as nations and that it is possible to find traces of national consciousness amongst earlier 'ethnies'. In Smith's own words, which we will have occasion to revisit, 'perhaps the central question in our understanding of nationalism is the role of the past in the creation of the present' (1995: 18).

Apart from the controversies surrounding the historical evidence, there is a conceptual difficulty at the heart of Smith's argument. If nationhood depends upon the mobilization of an ethnic past, then it becomes necessary to define ethnicity in such a way as to determine whose history belongs to whom. That is to say, before one can even interpret a particular discovery as 'our history' one has to agree on what constitutes 'us'. Yet, to presuppose commonality on the basis of ethnicity is to ignore the fact that ethnicity is no less troubled a concept than nation (Connor, 1978; Poole, 1994). While it may appear to be based on the solid ground of relatedness, Weber (1968) notes that ethnic ties cannot be directly traced to kinship, but rather depend upon a presumed identity. Indeed, as a number of authors have noted, the notion that we, along with those in the past, form part of a common ethnic group, and that the history of our ancestors serves to define us in the present, is as much a consequence of nation-building as its precursor (Balibar, 1991b; Lofgren, 1989; Poole, 1994). In other words, to try and fix the concept of nation in the notion of ethnicity is akin to fixing shifting sands on running water.

So, if there are problems in defining the nation as an ethnic community, there are related problems in defining the nation as based on the invocation of ethnic community. This leaves one further possibility. It might still be argued that all nations need to be conceptualized in ethnic terms even if that ethnicity is fictitious. This represents an empirical claim about the nature of national consciousness rather than a theoretical model concerning the conditions of national consciousness. The distinction between the two is illustrated by Max Weber who rejected the notion of ethnicity as objectively determining the nation but still claimed that any concept of the nation depends upon a sense of common descent (Weber, 1968). To put it somewhat differently, even if nations are not necessarily ethnic, they are ethnocentric and even if they are not racial they are racist.

Since this is an empirical claim it is open to empirical disconfirmation. And since it is a claim of necessity, it is only necessary to find exceptions in order to challenge such a viewpoint. Consider, then, what Julia Kristeva has to say in the context of a debate with Harlem Desir, the leader of France's largest anti-racist group 'SOS Racisme'. She pleads that the idea of nation should not be abandoned to those who have made a racist appropriation of it: 'I am among those people who dread and reject the notion of *Volksgeist*, "spirit of the people", which stems from a line of thinkers that includes Herder and Hegel' (1993a: 53). Kristeva contrasts the German romanticist view to another tradition, based in Montesquieu's notion of the *esprit général*. According to Montesquieu, the national whole has a three-fold nature: it is historical, it is a layering of diverse causalities, and it provides the conditions for its own transcendence into more inclusive categorizations. So, rather than emphasizing totality within the category and exclusion of those beyond it, Montesquieu sees the nation as a series of differences and it embraces otherness. On this basis, Kristeva expresses a clear preference: 'I would choose Montesquieu's *esprit général* over Herder's *Volksgeist*' (1993b: 33).

If Kristeva pleads for the possibility of constituting actual nations in terms of an alternative to the ethnic tradition, there is also evidence of nations in which such alternatives are the actuality. Thus, in his history of the National Association for the Vindication of Scottish Rights (NAVSR), Morton (1996) quotes from a public meeting held in Glasgow in 1853 where Patrick Dove defined the Association's understanding of the Scottish nation: 'Whoever – whatever man – whether he be black, white, red or yellow, the moment he identifies with the institutions of Scotland, that moment he becomes a member of the Scottish nation, and Caledonia must throw around him the mantle of protection. (Applause)' (p. 270). Of course, there may have been other understandings of Scottishness. Indeed, it may be wrong to suggest too stark a dichotomy between 'civic' and 'ethnic' conceptions of the nation. Poole (1994) notes that while most countries allow people to naturalize, they also have a strong and rooted sense of themselves as a people. Thus, both between nations, and even within the same nation, ethnicity may simply be one means of defining boundaries amongst many.

To re-label these arguments about nationhood in national terms, it could be said that the French tradition, in which the nation is seen as a contract between free and equal individuals, provides the final nail in the coffin for the German tradition, whereby nations are seen in ethnic terms. At this point, it is hard to disagree with Connor when he states 'comparative analyses establish that no set of tangible characteristics is essential to the maintenance of national consciousness'

(1994: 73). Moreover, the continued failure to find such characteristics might lead one to echo Seton-Watson's despair at ever finding a viable definition of nationhood. However the seeds of a new way forward are already present in the argument. They exist within the French tradition, but they depend upon a more positive interpretation than that employed so far.

Just as ethnicity can be used as a theory of nation formation or else an empirical claim about national consciousness, so the same can be said of the civic approach. Hitherto we have used this approach simply to rebut ethnic empiricism. However, viewed on a theoretical level, the civic view points to a way of conceptualizing nationhood that is rooted neither in ethnicity nor in any set of objective criteria. This can be seen by considering the work of Ernest Renan who, despite Kristeva, is the figure most often used as the standard bearer of the French tradition.

As happens so often, the impact of Renan results less from the full body of his work than from the impact of a single phrase. In his essay of 1882, 'What is a nation?', Renan asserts that 'a nation's existence is, if you will pardon the metaphor, a daily plebiscite' (1990: p.19). It is worth quoting the passage that precedes the famous epigram:

> A nation is . . . a large-scale solidarity, constituted by the feeling of sacrifices that one has made in the past and of those that one is prepared to make in the future. It presupposes a past; it is summarized, however, in the present by a tangible fact, namely consent, the clearly expressed desire to continue a common life. (1990: p.19)

If this is read on the empirical level, it is clearly partial. Just as Morton's civic Scotland can be counterposed to Nazi Germany, so Nazi Germany can be counterposed to the Scottish example. Any Jewish person in the Third Reich who had expressed the desire to be part of the common German life would have received an all too tragic awakening. But Renan can be read in another way. What is important in this second reading is process rather than content. Thus, Renan argues that the nation is dependent upon an act of imagination in which people see themselves as having something in common with their compatriots. By this reading, the content of their imaginings – what it is that they have in common – is left open. It could be adherence to institutions, it could be a sense of descent. So ethnicity is not ruled out, but what is important is the way ethnicity is imagined rather than its facticity.

This shift of perspective is particularly clear in Renan's use of history. Certainly he considers history to be central to nationhood, however its relevance is mediated by a double act of imagination. Firstly, subjects need to imagine themselves as part of a national community before national history is of any relevance. Secondly, that history itself is imagined rather than experienced and what is more it is selectively imagined. Renan's renown was such that he has been remembered for not one, but two aphorisms. The second reads: 'The essence of a nation is that all individuals have many things in common, and also that they have forgotten many things.' He continues, 'No French citizen knows whether he is a Burgundian, an Alan, a Taifale, or a Visigoth, yet every French citizen has to have forgotten the massacre of Saint Bartholomew or the massacres that took place in the Midi in the thirteenth century' (1990: 11). But the historical imagination does not just stretch backwards to the past but also forwards to the future. As the earlier quote reveals, Renan views both visions of history as important to the nation.

This takes us very close to the definition of a nation as an imagined community, which we encountered above in the work of Emerson and, particularly, of Benedict Anderson. However it is important to see this definition as a point of departure rather than a point of arrival. As we have intimated, it is necessary to delineate the conditions of national imagination or else one runs the risk of being branded 'subjectivist' and 'voluntarist'. Certainly such charges have been laid at Renan's door (James, 1996; Smith, 1995), though perhaps a little unfairly since he undertook detailed historical analyses of the historical contexts which made the principle of nationality possible. It is also necessary to clarify what makes the imagination national or else one can be accused of blurring an account of nationhood into a general model of collective forms.

Nation, imagination and contestation

For Anderson, the national imagination is only possible when three conditions are fulfilled. Firstly, it is necessary to have a concept of time which allows the different constituents of a community to be imagined as acting in the same way at the same moment in time and also acting together through time. This concept is termed 'homogeneous empty time' in contrast to classical concepts whereby events are linked through divine providence rather than a neutral temporal dimension. Secondly, it is necessary to have a print language accessible throughout the community and through which the national idea can be communicated. For instance, newspapers allow events to be brought together because of their relevance to the nation. In reading them, each individual is aware that many other members of the national community will simultaneously be doing likewise. The print language need not be particular to the given nation, nor need it be the first language of all members of the nation. Rather than being an emblem of nationality, it is a means of imagining. Thirdly, the boundaries of social opportunity need to be coterminous with national frontiers. Especially in the colonial setting, if functionaries can move freely across territories and prosper anywhere then national allegiances are unlikely to develop. If, however, mobility is blocked once one moves beyond a prescribed territory then functionaries are liable to become the intellectual instigators of national–popular movements.

Rather than dwelling on the details with which Anderson describes each of these three conditions, some of which may be open to historical challenge (Poole, 1994), it may be better to regard them, respectively, as representing three more general classes of condition. The concept of time is an instance of the representational conditions for nationhood. The emphasis on print languages has to do with the technological conditions under which people can imagine themselves as a single community partaking of unified experiences. The limits to the mobility of functionaries can be seen as introducing a stress on the practical–experiential dimension of the nation. That is, the use of national categories becomes viable and meaningful when it corresponds to and makes sense of the ways in which one's activities are structured and the way one is treated by others. To view Anderson's arguments in this way is to open up fields of investigation in which disagreements over detail facilitate rather than stymie the more general intellectual achievement. Indeed a number of Anderson's critics recognize that they are charting domains which his work made possible (e.g. Alonso, 1988; James, 1996).

It is also important to bear in mind the limits to Anderson's project. His concern was with how the general pre-conditions that make it possible to imagine the national form originally emerged. Clearly, these pre-conditions have changed over time. Most obviously, things have moved on since the advent of newspapers. Nowadays it is as much through the radio, through the television and increasingly through the internet, that we share the simultaneous experience with millions of others of consuming national sporting triumphs (and failures), royal weddings and even soap operas (cf. Schlesinger, 1987).

It is also clear that, as nations become more entrenched, so the practical–experiential dimension of nationhood is not simply a matter of constraints upon the professional trajectories of functionaries. Rather, it comes to structure our everyday social reality on both an institutional and face-to-face level (James, 1996). Balibar (1991b), for instance, insists on the way in which the nation affects seemingly private and personal domains such as the family and affects such things as procreation, discipline and education. These are regulated as much in terms of their implications for the health of the nation as the well-being of individuals. Even the collection of family heirlooms can be equated with the preservation of national heirlooms (Lowenthal, 1985). Lofgren (1989) also argues that the nation exists in the way we spend our leisure visiting national sights or watching national sports, the way we share jokes, peddle stereotypes and discuss the character of our (national) selves and others. Thus, the nation is not an abstract idea but rather 'a cultural praxis in everyday life' (p. 23).

It is important to stress that this relationship between the nation and the structure of everyday life is a two-way street. While it is important to acknowledge how the structure of experience affects the possibility of a national imagination and the likelihood of seeing ourselves in national terms, the more usual stress is on the way in which the national imagination leads to the creation of new social structures and new experiences. Anderson himself virtually equates nations with nationalism and nationalism principally with the move to create nation-states (although he also considers 'official nationalisms', which emanate from the state and serve to protect state structures).

The relationship between nationalism and the nation-state is, in fact, an issue of some controversy, though many of the disagreements can be put down to a confusion over the use of terms. For some, nationalism is defined as a form of social movement which is organized around the claim to a nation-state. Any movement which eschews such a claim is formally denied nationalist status. Thus, in a well-known definition, Gellner (1983) refers to nationalism as a political principle which holds that the national and political unit should be congruent. This is tied up with a model that holds that nationalism is a force which creates nations where they did not previously exist (Gellner, 1964; Hobsbawm, 1990).

For others, however, nationalism is defined as a theory about the proper functioning of the state (Parekh, 1995) or even as any form of action related to national consciousness. Kohn (1965) sees nationalism as simply meaning loyalty to the nation-state and Giddens (1985) sees it as meaning an affiliation to a set of symbols expressing the commonality of members of a political order. However, perhaps Hroch (1996) is most insistent in arguing for a wide use – which he claims to be the original use – whereby nationalism simply means a state of mind in which the interests and values of one's own nation are prioritized above those of other nations. What others term nationalism in the sense of a political project he prefers to call a 'national movement'. What he calls nationalism, others refer to as 'national identity' or 'nationality' (James, 1996; Parekh, 1995; Shils, 1995).

If one uses these wider definitions then it becomes a matter of empirical evidence rather than of logic as to whether nationalism always involves a claim for national statehood. The evidence suggests that there are many movements rooted in national consciousness which are either agnostic or even actively opposed to the idea of a state for the nation (Morton, 1996). There are also many movements, such as anti-foreigner or anti-immigrant movements, that have no interest at all in whether the state should be national or not, although they may agitate for whatever sort of state exists to support their cause (Hooghe, 1992; Shils, 1995). However, for our purposes what is interesting are the commonalities rather than the differences between those who relate nationalism more or less closely to the nation state. Whether those acting on the national imagination seek to create a new state, defend an existing state, re-order state structures, oppose the existence of a nation-state, seek to ban immigrants, boycott foreign products or whatever, in each and every case, the way in which the nation is imagined underpins forms of social action which (re)shape our social being. It therefore becomes a matter of some consequence to turn from the pre-conditions for a national imagination to the ways in which a given nationality is imagined. However, before we can do this it is necessary to address the dimensions through which nations in general are imagined. Or, as we put it above, what do we mean by a national imagination and what is it that makes this imagination specifically national? In order to provide a response, we shall re-visit Anderson's definition of the nation, but this time we shall provide a little more detail.

After his assertion that the nation 'is an imagined political community', Anderson continues that it is 'imagined as both inherently limited and sovereign' (1983: 15). He then elaborates on the various terms of the definition. The reason that a nation is imagined is that in even the smallest country one will never know, meet, or even hear of most of one's fellow members. But each member can imagine him or herself to be in communion with all the others. While this is a necessary part of the definition, it is plainly not sufficient since the nation is not the only community that exists despite the impracticality of bringing all its members together – what Webber (1967) has called 'community without propinquity'. As a result, large communities in general depend upon acts of imagination, indeed Balibar (1991a) makes this claim of all communities.

What is important, then, is not simply that the nation is imagined but the style in which it is imagined. The nation is imagined as limited because even the largest nations have boundaries. No nation is coterminous with humanity as a whole. It is part of a system of nations. The nation is imagined as sovereign for historical reasons. Nations emerged as divinely inspired, hierarchical dynastic realms declined. Aspirants to a universal religion were confronted by a pluralism of faiths confined in distinct territories. Nations dreamed of being free and independent under their own God. The emblem of this freedom was that nations should have their separate states. Finally, the nation is imagined as a community because, whatever divisions may actually exist, 'the nation is always conceived as a deep, horizontal comradeship' (1983: 16). That is, all members stand as interchangeable equals, at least as far as their nationality is concerned. Hence it is 'the man on the Clapham omnibus' who is able to speak for the nation as much as the Prime Minister and the unknown soldier who stands as a symbol of the nation as much as, if not better than, the most distinguished Field-Marshal. It is this comradeship which, for Anderson, is the basis for nationalism's power – in particular, the fact that the imagined community can lead innumerable unknown soldiers to kill and be killed in its name.

Anderson is not entirely explicit about why this should be so. However, one reason may be found by asking why every nation has its tomb to the unknown soldier, but that to suggest a tomb to the unknown marxist or unknown liberal would seem absurd. The answer alerts us to one further dimension of the national imagination. As Anderson puts it, nations have a central concern with immortality which is absent in other ideologies. They are seen as communities moving together through time. As nationals, we are in contact with people who died before we were born and with those who will be born after we die. Being part of a nation confers immortality upon us. It allows us to share in the glories of past generations and to feel their pain. Dvornikovic provides a dramatic example of how twentieth century Serbians relate to their ancestors who fell in the Battle of Kosovo of 1389: 'A few peasants, usually in a tavern, put their heads together and let their sorrowful modulations sound for hours, which constitutes a very grotesque sight for a European. And if they are asked why they sing like this, they give the answer: the lament for Kosovo!' (quoted in Anzulovic, 1999: 1).

The importance of history is becoming a leitmotif. It is stressed by virtually all theorists of nationhood, even if they disagree on all other matters. It is as important to Anderson as it is to Smith. However, it is important not to be beguiled by this apparent consensus. Beneath the agreement lie very different views of how history relates to the nation. At one extreme lies the claim that nations have actually existed since time immemorial and are perennial features of our social landscape (which Smith, 1995, unsurprisingly calls perennialism). At a slight remove lies the claim that the existence of a common history is necessary to the emergence of nations. Here, however, the argument is not so much as to whether nations have history or not, but rather about the ways in which nations use historical themes as part of the national imagination. Whether nations are recent or ancient is not the point, what counts is that they are always imagined as ancient. According to Lowenthal (1985) 'most peoples exaggerate their cultural antiquity or conceal its recency. The English used to date Oxford from Alfred the Great, Parliament from the Romans and native Christianity from Joseph of Arimathea. Olof Rudbeck's Atlantica established ancient Sweden as the fount of modern culture; Germans and then the English and

Americans ascribed the roots of democracy to early Goths; African arts are said to antedate the Assyrians' (p. 336).

The significance of these formulations is that they formulate historical continuity in order to place the nation outside history. If the nation has always existed then it becomes something eternal and necessary rather than temporal and contingent. As Anderson puts it: 'it is the magic of nationalism to turn chance into destiny' (1983: 19). This argument does not only apply to the fact of national existence but also the form it takes. History establishes how we must always be by virtue of how we have always been. Or rather 'the sureness of "I was" is a necessary component of the sureness of "I am"' (quoted in Lowenthal, 1985: 41).

The converse of this argument is that to obliterate a nation's history is to undermine its very ability to be imagined as a distinct community – that is, its ability to exist. Lowenthal quotes a seventeenth century Welsh chronicler who laments that the loss of Welsh history 'hath eclipsed our Power and corrupted our language, and almost blotted us out of the Books of Records' (1985: 44). He also notes how the Nazis sacked historic Warsaw in order to cripple the will of the Poles and how the Poles rebuilt the centre in exact replica form as a key step in rebuilding post-war Poland. According to the head of conservation: 'we wanted the Warsaw of our day and that of the future to continue the ancient tradition' (1985: 46). The continuing stakes involved in the way we conceptualize even the most remote past is well-illustrated by the arrest, in December 1992, of a Greek youth for distributing leaflets claiming that Alexander the Great was a war criminal (Morelli, 1995).

Given this power of history in relation to the present and future, it is not surprising that new interests should be formulated in terms of ancient claims and that recent developments should be portrayed as the result of long-standing processes (Blommaert & Slembrouck, 1995). Nor is it surprising that, the more we dig for distant relics, the more we uncover contemporaneous concerns. Whether it is a matter of uncovering Masada in Israel or Greater Zimbabwe in, significantly, Zimbabwe, the pursuit of history helps define a people as distinct and allows it to lay claim to particular territories (Kohl & Fawcett, 1996). It can also define how a people should live within those boundaries. For instance, Spanish archaeology under Franco stressed the unity of the Spanish people in order to legitimate strong, centralized control and deny claims for regional autonomy (Diaz-Andreu, 1996).

There are two further points to be made about the relationship between nations and antiquity. First of all, it isn't simply that existing historical disciplines were adapted to the needs of the nation. Rather, it can be argued that these disciplines emerged as the handmaiden of nationalism. Pearton, for instance, argues that 'historians had, in the most literal sense, nationalized the culture. In doing so, they had fixed the way of defining the nation, determined its characteristics – what are the essential properties of being Ruritanian? – and provided criteria for citizenship' (1996: 7–8). Hobsbawm encapsulates the relationship in terms of a powerful image: 'historians are to nationalism what poppy-growers in Pakistan are to heroin addicts; we supply the essential raw material for the market' (1992: 3). When it comes to archaeology, Kohl and Fawcett (1996) go even further. They note not only that the discipline emerged in the nineteenth century as a means of creating a national history that legitimizes the existence of a nation and its right to an independent state (and also, we might add, its claim to ancestral lands) but also that many nationalist movements are actually led by archaeologists, philologists and ancient historians. Rather than being mere producers of raw materials, they suggest that such intellectuals are also the pushers and mob capos directing operations on the streets.

The second point is that there is more to the relationship than a nationalist appropriation of historical discovery. As well as creating historical disciplines to serve the nation, there is also an active process of creating particular histories to fit national needs. This is encapsulated in the title of Hobsbawm and Ranger's influential book, *The Invention of Tradition*. In the Introduction to this edited collection of essays, Hobsbawm writes, 'it is clear that plenty of political institutions, ideological movements and groups – not least in nationalism – were so unprecedented that even historic continuity had to be invented, for example by creating an ancient past beyond effective historical continuity, either by semi-fiction (Boadicea, Vercingetorix, Arminius the Cheruscan) or by forgery (Ossian, the Czech medieval manuscripts)' (1983: 7).

Perhaps the two most famous essays concern, respectively, Scotland and Britain. Trevor-Roper (1983) argues that those supposed ancient symbols of Scottishness, the kilt and the clan tartan, were respectively invented by an English Quaker industrialist in order to facilitate the assimilation of Scots into the factory system and through an imperial review in order to assimilate Scots into the armies of empire. Cannadine (1983) argues that the supposedly ancient ceremonials of the British monarchy were invented in the late nineteenth century in order to consolidate the hegemony of the British imperial vision. Thus, when Richard Dimbleby's reverential coronation commentary included the assertion that 'I might be watching something that happened a thousand years before. In all that time there has been no change in our coronations' (quoted in Lowenthal, 1985: 337) he was actually describing ceremonies that had been invented in the last 50 years.

In recent years, the idea that national pasts are constructed, that traditions are invented and that 'time immemorial' refers mainly to the span of social memory, have all assumed the status of orthodoxies. Indeed, the main controversy surrounding the work brought together by Hobsbawm and Ranger is not that they went too far but that they didn't go far enough in their emphasis on construction. While they attend to the constructed nature of certain versions of the past, they presuppose their own background version to be neutral and unproblematic. It provides a factual benchmark against which those caught in the critical spotlight can be measured and found wanting. However, in what sense can they protect themselves from the treatment they mete out to others?

This point can be illustrated by reference to the treatment of Scottish history and the assault that is mounted upon the antiquity of Ossian's poetry, of kilts and of clan tartans. While Hobsbawm suggests that the works attributed to the ancient bard were in fact a latter-day invention by James MacPherson, others have claimed that MacPherson simply transposed old Irish works to Scotland where the boundary between Irish and Scottish was itself ambiguous (James, 1996). While Trevor-Roper delights in the irony that Scottish dress was invented by the English in order to impose the structures of British industrialism and British imperialism, others accuse him of deliberately over-playing his hand. Even if Quaker industrialists and imperial reviews had some part to play, they didn't create highland culture anew but rather worked upon existing clan differentiations and existing patterns of dress (James, 1996; McCrone, 1989; Telfer-Dunbar, 1981).

These arguments are not matters of truth and lies but of interpretation and emphasis. On a logical plane, any issue of temporal continuity turns on a definition of categories. It is only by identifying the characteristics which define an object as such (whether it be a kilt, a clan tartan, a tradition or whatever) that we can determine when it exists and hence how old it is. For instance, if the short kilt is a development of existing forms of plaid, how do we decide whether its antiquity is authentic or not? It comes down to deciding on the essential features that make a kilt a kilt. Or again, whether the Ossian story is regarded as an invention or not depends on whether one thinks the essential significance of the story lies in the figure of Ossian himself or in the establishment of a Scottish literary antiquity and, if the latter, where one locates the roots of the Scots – many of whose early settlers were Irish and whose Gaelic speakers saw themselves as linked to the Gaels of Ireland (Broun, 1996).

So, while there is no doubt that the antiquity of Scottish culture is a construction and that this construction was put to use by Scottish nationalists, it is equally true that the denial of Scottish cultural antiquity is a construction and that it too advances a nationalist agenda. McCrone points clearly to Trevor-Roper's British nationalism in referring to him as 'that arch-enemy of Scottish Home Rule . . . a.k.a. Lord Dacre' (1989: 164). The implication of this is that there is little use in trying to distinguish between invented and authentic versions of the national past and hence of national identity. It is more useful to consider how any version of the national past and of national identity serves contemporary interests. White makes the point clearly in his account of Australian histories:

> There is no 'real' Australia waiting to be uncovered. A national identity is an invention. There is no point asking whether one version of this essential Australia is truer than another because they are all intellectual constructs, neat, tidy, comprehensible – and necessarily false . . . When we look at national identity, we need to ask, not whether they are true or false, but what their function is, whose creation they are, and whose interests they serve. (1981: viii)

While these points still relate to history, they do much more than simply illustrate the existence of a historical dimension to the national imagination. They also show, in some detail, the ways in which specific versions of history serve to underpin specific ways of imagining specific nations. Throughout the discussion it has either been implicit or else explicit that the importance of these ways of imagining lies in the way that they relate to the practical creation of particular forms of national being. Because of this link, we find multiple historical versions and multiple versions of identity being advanced, each of which relate to a different set of practical ambitions and interests. This being the case we need to address the process of contestation between versions as well as the link between any one version and any one interest. In so doing, we need to acknowledge that history is not the only means of anchoring the national imagination. This can be done through the use of cultural icons, through the employment of symbols, by reference to the built environment and even to the physical environment. In all of these domains, one can find different versions of the phenomena used to support different visions of national identity.

As an example of how icons are used, Sinko (1989) shows how those who wished to shape Hungary in different ways variously prioritized either Saint Istvan or Arpad as a national symbol. He also illustrates how the meaning of each was contested. Istvan, for instance, went from being a passive and merciful figure to a Christian warrior in order to mobilize the population against the Ottomans. Hungary also provides a good example of the symbolic battleground. After the fall of communism, one of the first tasks facing the newly elected legislative assembly was to restore the emblem of the nation. The key question was whether to include the historic crown in the new republic and those with different versions of society debated the issue fervently (Kiss, 1992). In Australia the national flag has created equal controversy. When the Australian Commonwealth was first formed in 1901 and a competition was set up to design the Commonwealth flag, the criteria for selecting the winner were 'loyalty to the Empire, federation, history, heraldry, distinctiveness, utility and cost of manufacture' (quoted in Foley, 1996: 77). More recently, those who are critical of these values – especially the first – have called for a new design. The two major issues are whether any vestige of the Union Jack should be retained and the extent to which Aboriginal imagery should be included. Monarchists and republicans, multiculturalists and conservative nationalists remain at loggerheads over the answer (Foley, 1996).

Moving on to the environment, national identity can be read from the design of buildings and the layout of cities. Disputes over national identity are expressed in controversies concerning the buildings that should be preserved or else left to rot (Kohl & Fawcett, 1996). Similarly, different interpretations of landscape can be used to underpin different claims about national identity and different claims about national identity underpin different views as to whether and how the countryside is conserved and managed or else handed over to various forms of development (Lofgren, 1989). In the attempt to portray versions of the nation as natural, nature itself becomes an arena of intervention. Our constructions of nationhood are built in earth and stone as well as in words. There is virtually no domain which has not been enlisted in the contest to fix our national identity and thereby chart our national trajectory.

Whichever domain we look at, we find a space of argument and each argument is an argument about the true identity of the nation. Therefore, we need to examine how a given notion of the nation is advanced through the singular and combined use of different domains. Equally, in studying the process of contestation, we must be alert to the possibility that the argument between those supporting different notions of identity may occur simultaneously in a number of different domains. An excellent case in point is provided by the dispute between the Congress Party and the Muslim League over the partition of India.

The demand of the Muslim League for a separate Pakistan was articulated around the claim that there were separate nations in the sub-continent. The first explicit assertion of this 'two-nation theory' was made in Jinnah's presidential address to the League's Lahore conference of March 1940. Jinnah declared that:

> The Hindus and the Muslims belong to two different religious philosophies, social customs and literature. They neither intermarry, nor interdine together, and indeed they belong to two different civilizations which are based mainly on conflicting ideas and conceptions. Their aspects on life and of life are different. It is quite clear that Hindus and Musulmans derive their inspiration from different sources of history. They have different epics, their heroes are different, and they have different episodes. Very often the hero of one is a foe of the other, and likewise, their victories and defeats overlap. Musulmans are a nation according to any definition of a nation, and they must have their homelands, their territory and their state. (1993: 55–7)

Jinnah uses multiple dimensions – culture, custom, history and others besides – in order to advance his argument. The retort came from Abdul Azad, another Muslim, in his Presidential address to the rival Indian National Congress later that year. His construction is almost the mirror image of Jinnah's. It also uses multiple dimensions and in each case argues for similarity rather than difference:

> Eleven hundred years of common history have enriched India with our common achievements. Our languages, our poetry, our literature, our culture, our art, our manners and customs, the innumerable happenings of our daily life, everything bears the stamp of our joint endeavour. There is indeed no aspect of our life which has escaped this stamp. Our languages were different, but we grew to use a common language; our manners and customs were dissimilar, but they acted and reacted on each other and thus produced a new synthesis.

In his turn, Azad concludes that:

> these thousand years of our joint life has moulded us into a common nationality. This cannot be done artificially. Nature does her fashioning through her hidden processes in the course of centuries. The cast has now been moulded and destiny has set her seal upon it. Whether we like it or not, we have now become an Indian nation, united and indivisible. (1993: 67–8)

If these two extracts clearly demonstrate the link between versions of reality and versions of national identity and also between versions of national identity and the interest of the speakers in mobilizing people to support their (or rather their party's) political project, the latter point is made even clearer by adding some further words of Jinnah's. In this context he was promoting the inclusion of the whole of Bengal and the whole of the Punjab in Pakistan. Both regions had mixed Hindu/Muslim populations and therefore a construction of nation as based on religion would foster division and hence undermine his project. Hence Jinnah uses a construction that is completely at odds with the 'two nation theory'. Addressing himself to Mountbatten, he argued that 'the Punjab is a nation. Bengal is a nation. A man is a Punjabi or Bengali first before he is a Hindu or a Muslim. If you give us those Provinces you must, under no condition, partition them. You will destroy their viability and cause endless bloodshed and trouble' (quoted in

Khan, 1988: 65). If the different speakers differ in their construction of the nation within the same context, and if the same speaker differs in his construction of the nation across different contexts, what remains ever constant is the relationship between the construction of nationhood and the project for which support is sought.

All of this forces us irresistibly towards two further questions. If versions of identity are contested through contesting versions of history, culture and custom, and if these contests are important since the outcomes will determine how people act together to structure the social world, what determines which version will be victorious and what are the processes through which these versions shape mass action?

As concerns the first question, studies of nations and nationalism provide a number of pointers. First of all, those who are able to communicate their views most widely, most insistently and most early will have an obvious advantage. Thus there has been particular attention paid to histories which achieve textbook status and through which children acquire an understanding of their national past – or rather, of their past as national. Smith (1995) describes the role of the Lavisse textbook in France which invoked the idea of an immemorial French nation through repeated use of the catechism '*nos ancêtres les Gaulois*'. Similarly, Morelli quotes from Theodore Juste's nineteenth century text *Histoire de Belgique depuis les temps primitifs jusqu'à la fin du règne de Léopold 1er*, which traces Belgium back beyond Julius Ceasar. Despite subsequent subjection to, amongst others, Spain and the Dukes of Burgundy, Juste declares that 'all these disasters destroyed the ancient power in Belgium, but they didn't destroy national feeling, something inalienable that generations handed down religiously even though ten different flags floated over our conquered cities' (1995: 16; translation by the authors). Not surprisingly, he sees the creation of an independent Belgian kingdom in 1830 as the natural reemergence of the old country.

These textbook narratives are instructive in a second sense. Although they may be constructed histories, they do not present themselves as such. Indeed, they are presented more as revelations than as interpretations. More generally, it can be argued that the success of a given construction will depend upon its ability to conceal all traces of construction and to present itself as the only story that could be told (Alonso, 1988; Balibar, 1991a). In Alonso's terms, historiographies must hide their hermeneutics and thereby transform partiality into totality. They do this by a series of narrative techniques including the language in which accounts are written ('scientific' rather than figurative, scholarly rather than vernacular) and the effacement of the writing subject.

What Alonso says about giving authority to versions of history can equally be said about custom, culture, nature or any of the other domains through which national identity is defined. It is worth adding what should be clear by now: the very use of custom, culture, nature and, particularly, history is important in giving authority to versions of national identity. However, it is not just a matter of invoking history in general terms. Successful accounts are those which weave the best known moments of the national past or the national iconography into their accounts of identity. Conversely, where there are no obvious historical referents for one's account, it is less likely to persuade. This third point can be illustrated by contrasting the attempts to construct nationality in the two South African bantustans of KwaZulu and the Ciskei. Whereas moves by Chief Gasha Buthelezi to construct a Zulu nationhood were at least partially successful in mobilizing a constituency (Mare, 1993), parallel moves by President Lennox Sebe to establish a Ciskei national identity largely failed. The anonymous analyst notes that the various attempts to build a national shrine, a 'historical' capital, a legitimate leadership all went against existing traditions rather than re-modelled them. It is concluded that 'Sebe's appeals to a Ciskeian national consciousness will not take root because they refer to something that is simply not there' (Anonymous, 1989: 410). Thus, while nationalists may be creative writers, their creativity does not have entirely free play. Their ability to construct national stories is dependent upon the materials that are available to them.

This argument may look dangerously close to contradicting our earlier discussion of history. Whereas we previously dismissed the argument that the construction of nationhood depends upon the existence of a common past, it may now appear that we are starting to sneak it back in. However there is an important difference. We are not suggesting that it is the past in itself which provides the material for nationalist narratives. Rather, it is the contemporary store of historical icons, historical myths and historical images which provides the building blocks. To continue with our metaphor, it is not impossible to create new blocks to fit one's uses, but it will be a far more cumbersome, a far more difficult and a far more time-consuming exercise than adapting ready-made resources. Hence it will start from a strong disadvantage.

Perhaps Reichler's concept of a 'symbolic' reserve is of use here (1992). He suggests that, just as nations have gold reserves to guarantee the value of their economic currencies, so they use their symbolic reserves in giving sense to situations, in legitimating their actions and in designing their futures. Of course, these symbols only gain meaning through their usage in specific fields of social relations and in being used their meanings are ever shifting. However, equally, the sense-making process is facilitated by the existence of symbolic resources and the creation of the new meanings is affected by their relation to the old. Where these resources are either too scarce or else so vast that it is hard for people to claim them as their own – which, for Reszler (1992) is the case in Europe – then the possibilities of nation-formation become severely curtailed. In sum, the relationship between the national past, the national present and the national future is not simple and one-way, but rather multiply mediated and reciprocal. In the words of Christopher Hill: 'We ourselves are shaped by the past; but from our vantage point in the present we are continuously reshaping the past which shapes us' (1974: 284).

We have one more point to make and it can be introduced by considering the way in which Masada has acquired such importance to modern Israel as a symbol of how the Jewish people have always been surrounded by a hostile and numerous enemy, but have always emerged victorious against the odds (Kohl & Fawcett, 1996). Masada has not always had this importance. It gained prominence only as the Israeli state emerged. Its prominence depended upon construing a link between modern Israelis and ancient Palestinians, upon the excavation of Masada and its interpretation as a heroic triumph as opposed to futile self-destruction. However, its power as a symbol also depended upon its material reality as a site of pilgrimage and a location where pilgrims could connect with an experience of Jewish martyrdom through the ages. To put it in more general terms, the creation of spaces in which versions of nationhood are matched by practical experience is likely to enhance the effectiveness of those versions – and hence their subsequent ability to shape reality still further in their image. As with the relationship between past, present and future, so the relationship between identity and experience is a reciprocal one.

These four factors – dissemination, totalization, symbolic capital, and practical resonance – are all important elements in explaining why one way of defining the nation should prove popular and prevail over any other. However, once we move from studying how the nation has been represented to asking how these representations might shape human action, we are inevitably shifting from an analysis of those national phenomena that require some psychological explanation to the psychological explanation itself. What is more, the question of why some representations might predominate over others is obviously bound up with the issue of how constructions of nationhood move human actors. This takes us back to the second of the questions posed above. It is one on which the literature on nations and nationalism has been almost completely silent. It seems to be assumed that our psychology is entirely transparent and that we will act as ciphers of any construction that is offered to us. It is time to move on and foreground these psychological issues.

Conclusion

In this chapter, we have argued for psychology to be involved in the explanation of national phenomena and then we have sought to outline the phenomena that need to be explained. At the outset, we referred to an apparent paradox between the ephemerality of nationhood itself and the solidity of its effects. In regard to the former we quoted Rosa Luxemburg to the effect that it is meaningless to base policies and rights on the nations when one cannot specify what a nation is in any definitive way.

Luxemburg is undoubtedly right in her premise. Those, like Stalin, who have sought to resolve the paradox by outlining the objective characteristics of nationhood find themselves involved in a frustrating exercise. Like Tantalus, each time they turn to satisfy their quest it slips further away from them. In practice, however, Stalin was well aware of the flexibility of the national construct and he made full use of this flexibility in asserting the right to national self-determination while refusing to allow any of the Soviet republics to secede.

Stalin's lieutenant, the leader of the Communist International, Dimitrov, was explicit about the importance of taking advantage of such flexibility, though more in the context of claiming the mantle of accepted nationhood for oneself than in deciding on the existence of nations. In justifying the strategy of the Popular Front he declared that 'the fascists are rummaging through the entire history of every nation so as to be able to pose as the heirs and continuators of all that was exalted and heroic in the past'. It was therefore up to the Communists 'to link up the present struggle with the people's revolutionary traditions and past' (quoted in Schwarz, 1982: 55). Schwarz goes on to quote James Klugman in order to show what this meant for British Communists: 'We became the inheritors of the Peasants' Revolt, of the left of the English revolution, of the pre-Chartist movement, of the women's suffrage movement from the 1790s to today' (p. 56).

For Dimitrov, as for so many others that we have encountered in this chapter, the flexibility with which the category 'nation' can be applied and defined represents an opportunity rather than a problem. It provides a means of appealing to a group of people – those scattered across different territories or all those within a given territory. However seizing this opportunity depends upon shifting from an attempt to define the character of nations to a focus upon the uses of national categories. It may be futile to seek uncontroversial answers to such questions as 'does this population constitute a nation?' or 'what is the identity of this nation?' However there is much to be gained by asking 'what are the consequences of constituting this population as a nation?' and 'what is achieved by defining national identity in this way?'

In an ever-shifting world, it is absolutely crucial to be able to define the boundaries of social inclusion or exclusion in shifting ways, and equally to define appropriate forms of social action in a flexible manner. Immanuel Wallerstein makes precisely this point when he argues that the nature of capitalism makes the malleability of nationhood and like communities a necessity rather than an aberration. He is therefore worth quoting in full:

> The very inconstancy of peoplehood categories of which we have been speaking turns out to be crucially important. For while capitalism as a historical system requires constant inequality, it also requires constant restructuring of economic processes. Hence what guarantees a particular set of hierarchical social relations today may not work tomorrow. The behaviour of the work force must change without undermining the legitimacy of the system. The recurrent birth, restructuring and disappearance of ethnic groups is thereby an invaluable instrument of flexibility in the operation of the economic machinery. (1991: 84).

In short, the social power of nations comes because of, and not despite, their ephemerality.

But that social power is based upon a psychological power – one that is often noted, frequently taken for granted and never explained. Throughout this chapter we have repeatedly pointed to the psychological issues that inhabit the study of nationhood. Like Billig (1996) we note that nation is understood as imagination, but little attention is paid to what is involved in imagining ourselves as a national community. We have also noted that it is not enough to analyse the construction of national identity without any regard to the ways in which such constructions come to shape what people think and what they do. An account of these psychological mediations is essential to understanding what types of narrative will prove effective and which aspects of any narrative are most important in the creation of national mobilizations.

However, as well as raising psychological questions, there is much in this chapter to indicate what sort of psychology will – and will not – do. Firstly, and most obviously, it must be a psychology which does not take national categories and national characteristics for granted. It must allow that these categories are not fixed in advance either in the social or the psychological domain, but rather are a focus of argument. Hence, the explanation must concentrate on the relationship between these arguments and their outcomes.

Secondly, a psychological account of nationhood must be able to account for the reciprocal relationship between national categories and action. Our focus has undoubtedly been on the way in which definitions of national categories shape what people do; after all, the interest in these phenomena has been largely concentrated on the way in which nationalism makes nations. However, equally, the ways in which action is structured, and the constraints upon the way we can act, have been shown to be crucial in shaping the use of national categories.

Thirdly, our psychology must be sensitive to the particular ways in which the nation is imagined. It must address the importance of seeing ourselves as part of a horizontal community, it must take into account the significance of history in the national imagination and the uses of historical and cultural icons. It might even ask whether and why we are willing to invest more in communities imagined in these various ways and whether there is any psychological basis to the particular power of nationhood in our lives. This is not to reify the nation as a necessary consequence of the human psyche but rather to address the ways in which we may need to imagine alternatives if we wish to supersede this world of nations.

This takes us a to a fourth and rather more general criterion. We must buck the trend which leads so many in the social sciences to make a vampire sign when the name of psychology is mentioned. We must not reify social contingency as psychological necessity. Rather, the ultimate aim of any psychological input must be to facilitate our ability to have choice over the social forms which constitute our world.

2 Psychology and Nationhood

On the character of nations

In this chapter we shall outline a psychological model which addresses the way in which constructions of nationhood affect the structure of our actions while at the same time addressing how the structuration of social action affects our construction of nationhood. To be more specific, we will suggest that identity constitutes the mediation between these two orders. Hence we will address the reciprocal relationship between construction, identity and action.

In developing our position we will draw heavily upon psychological models of social identity processes (Tajfel, 1978, 1982; Turner, Hogg, Oakes, Reicher & Wetherell, 1987) and also upon psychological analyses of national identity (Billig, 1995, 1996; Condor, 1996, 1997, 2000a, in press). However it is necessary to start off by acknowledging that psychological work on nationhood has, at least in its more traditional forms, served more as a hindrance than a help to our enterprise. Rather than providing insights into the way national identity is constructed and how these constructions relate to social action, this work serves to naturalize national identity. It does so both in the sense of representing national identity as a natural aspect of a people rather than an aspect of its social practices, and also in the sense of presupposing that each nation has a single authentic nature. One could say that such psychologies have been more a part of the process of constructing the nation than an analysis of these processes. This is most obvious in relation to the concept of 'national character'.

The idea that national populations display distinctive characters is both older and goes wider than the discipline of psychology. David Hume was only one of many to provide a descriptive sketch: 'We have reason to expect greater wit and gaity in a FRENCHMAN than in a SPANIARD; though CERVANTES was born in SPAIN. An ENGLISHMAN will naturally be supposed to have more knowledge than a DANE: though TYCHO BRAHE [a famous astronomer] was a native of DENMARK' (Hume, 1748: 197–8; emphasis in the original). Such has been the popularity of this notion that the major issue has been less whether it makes sense to talk in terms of national characters than where national character comes from.

When psychologists got hold of the idea, character was firmly rooted in nature rather than in society. Gustave Le Bon, author of an early and influential text (*Les Lois Psychologiques de L'Evolution des Peuples* (1894)), summarized his argument in a book of aphorisms: 'The ancestral soul of a people dominates the entirety of its evolution. Political upheavals can do no more than alter the expression of this soul' (1917: 59). Or again: 'The civilization of a people is the external clothing of its soul, the visible expression of those invisible forces that direct it' (1917: 64).

Thus, far from being a social product, inbred national character determines the social circumstances in which we live. Each nation can be defined in terms of a single and distinctive character type, which is the root of differences between national societies.

Such ideas never went entirely unchallenged, yet they were clearly in the ascendancy in the first half of the twentieth century. However, their greatest triumph was also their greatest tragedy, for it was the association of ideas of inherent national differences with the propaganda and practice of Nazism that caused them to fall into disrepute. The revulsion against traditional notions of national character both within and beyond academia is well illustrated by Hamilton Fyfe's popular volume, *The Illusion of National Character*, which was first published in 1940 as part of the 'Thinker's Library'. In the book, described on the frontispiece by George Bernard Shaw as 'a righteous piece of work', Fyfe sets himself the task 'of proving national character to be an illusion, and one that is doing great harm in the world' (1946: 2).

This Nazi association led to two responses. On the one hand, where the notion of national character was retained, it was heavily reformed and its more objectionable aspects – the idea that differences are innate and the idea that all members of a nation reflect a single 'type' – were discarded altogether. If the people of a nation did have a character this was put down to the history, culture and institutions of that country, which was a return to what Hume had to say two centuries earlier when he put the various national characteristics he had described down to 'the nature of the government, the revolutions of public affairs, the plenty or penury in which people live, the situation of the nation with regard to its neighbours' (1748: 198). Thus, when Inkeles and Levinson wrote a chapter on national character for the 1954 *Handbook of Social Psychology*, they argued strongly for a view of national character as deriving from sociocultural forces although they acknowledged that this viewpoint had primarily been advanced by anthropologists and that extraordinarily few psychologists had contributed to such an enterprise.

Inkeles and Levinson also acknowledged that psychologists provide no adequate account of how cultural patterns might create personality structures. The consequence was a tendency to draw naive and unsubstantiated parallels between national character and sociocultural phenomena. These could be explained as easily in terms of culture reflecting character rather than the reverse. For instance, Gorer describes the relationship between the Senate and the House of Representatives as reflecting the relationship between older and younger brothers in American families, whereby the latter may behave irresponsibly, secure in the knowledge that the former will always get him out of scrapes (1948). Inkeles and Levinson therefore talk of 'a tendency to reason by analogy from the assumed personality mode to the structural pattern or functioning of institutions. Probably no other aspect of these studies has aroused as much criticism or as much intensity of feeling among critics from other disciplines' (1954: 1015).

This observation may be getting on for half a century old but it still has force today. Psychologists may no longer embrace Le Bon's confident innatism, but their silence on the matter of causality allows such ideas to survive by default. Indeed the very use of the term 'national character' carries the danger of mistaking description for explanation, for its meaning is marked by its origins. In psychological discourse, it is hard to escape the trappings of a term like 'character' which points to intra-psychic structures as the basis for public behaviours. It is a problem that afflicts all those who use such language, whatever their disciplinary origins and whatever their intentions. As Richards (1997) points out, Ruth Benedict's 'culture and personality' school, which was developed in order to counter the racism of the late 1930s and 1940s (and which Inkeles and Levinson draw upon heavily), slipped all too close to the positions it sought to criticize – especially in the way that German and Japanese wartime behaviour were ascribed to a pathological national character (Benedict, 1946a, b).

This pattern of explicit repudiation and implicit reproduction is equally applicable to the idea that all members of a nation reflect a single character type. Inkeles and Levinson (1954) condemn such a notion as a sweeping generalization that says more about the stereotypes and personal motives of its proponents than about the phenomena they purport to study. Instead they define national character in statistical terms. It is the distinctive distribution of personality characteristics in the country. To use their own words: ' "national character" refers to *relatively enduring personality characteristics and patterns that are modal among the adult members of the society*' (1954: 983; emphasis in the original). It is now generally accepted that the uniqueness of each country relative to others must be balanced by a respect for variability within all of them (Peabody, 1985). Such balance represents an important corrective to the idea of a national type. However, in the form of its corollary, it has also been crucial for salvaging the notion of national character from its critics.

As Peabody (1985) insists, if national character represents a distinct pattern of variability, then the widespread evidence of differences amongst members of a single nation presents no threat. At the same time, the very fact of concentrating analysis at the national level and aggregating the data from all members of a single nation gets rid of more troubling forms of variability. It suppresses evidences of variability between members of different groups within the nation as defined by class, gender or whatever. It also takes evidence given by individuals at one point and place as an indication of 'relatively stable' personality characteristics and therefore obscures contextual and temporal variations. As various authors have suggested, one of the most difficult issues for any proponent of national character is the fact that populations may change their modes of behaviour very dramatically over very short time periods (Altemeyer, 1988; Billig, 1976). Equally, as the literature on nationhood shows, at any given time there may be multiple competing models of the values and norms which should guide national action. But perhaps most troubling is the fact that, since analyses of national character are usually undertaken in order to make comparisons between nations, even such variability as is acknowledged within any given country tends to come second to a focus on differences between the modal positions of different countries. That is, intranational variability succumbs to international variability. Once again, and despite all the attempts to put distance between them, the newer and more subtle accounts of national character can all too easily slip back towards the older and cruder versions. Those who sup with the devil risk damnation however long their spoon.

For these reasons, the major response of post-war social psychology has been to reject, not to reform, the idea of national character. Indeed if one were to characterize the last half-century of the discipline in a phrase, it would be in terms of a shift from the study of group differences to the study of why people perceive others to be different. The classic expression of this shift is Gordon Allport's 1954 text *The Nature of Prejudice*. Allport concedes that there may be some genuine differences between groups: Hollanders speak Dutch while most others do not and Scotsmen wear kilts while few other men do. He is far more circumspect as to whether there are personality differences or moral differences between groups, although he does not rule out their existence. However he concludes that 'any stereotype concerning any people is usually thought to mark the entire group . . . but the ascription is an exaggeration, and may be wholly false' (1954: 104). What requires study, then, are not the facts of (national) difference but rather the process of stereotyping.

In order to understand the consequences of this shift, one must note that it is a matter of level of analysis and not just the topic of analysis. That is, the stress has gone from a description of specific national differences to an analysis of general group processes. Hence, even if concerns about national phenomena and the ways in which they were analysed have been of fundamental importance in the rise of stereotyping research, the nation itself no longer gets a mention. Even where studies concern national stereotypes, the national dimension is treated as almost irrelevant – merely as a convenient domain in which to look at something of relevance to all groups. To take just one of many possible examples, Poppe and Linssen (1999) start off by noting that psychologists have studied the stereotypes of national groups for over 60 years. However, they rapidly note that interest has moved from the content of these stereotypes to the study of cognitive biases in stereotypes and further to the issue of how stereotypes relate to social reality; they pose their own study as addressing the latter issue. This is reflected at textbook level by the fact that one can find volumes that are replete with studies of national stereotyping, but the 'national' is so incidental that the term does not appear in the index. Rupert Brown's *Group Processes* (1999) is just one case in point.

As we intimated in the previous chapter, this is not only true of the stereotyping literature but of group psychology in general. Brown himself has conducted studies concerned with such issues as the nature of international comparisons (Brown & Haegar, 1999) and the effects of international contact (Brown, Vivian & Hewstone, 1999). These are quoted in his text, and yet still nation is absent as an indexed topic. Indeed, virtually every aspect of group psychology is both informed by the nation and ignores the nation. If we want to understand what social psychology might have to contribute to the study of nationhood it is therefore necessary to address the broad theoretical approaches rather than hope to find a dedicated literature. It makes sense to start off by concentrating on the social identity approach as developed by Henri Tajfel and his colleagues – particularly by John Turner.

In the first place, this is probably the dominant paradigm for the study of group processes within contemporary psychology. In the second place, as we have seen, Tajfel's very concept of the group was taken from Emerson's definition of the nation. Thirdly, when social psychologists study national groups they are most often doing so in the context of addressing some aspect of social identity processes. Fourthly, and finally, since those concerned with nationhood return repeatedly to the importance of the way in which national identity is defined, it makes sense to explore how psychology has studied such collective identities and whether it can help us understand the relationship between identity and action.

Social identity in social psychology

Tajfel's ideas on social identity were deeply influenced by two sets of social concerns and intellectual preoccupations. Ironically, the more immediate social influence gave rise to the broader intellectual framework, while distal social influence gave rise to the specific questions guiding his work.

Tajfel's work was undertaken amidst the social turmoil of the late 1960s and the 1970s. Even within psychology, it became clear that one could no longer take the status quo as a given and therefore ignore the social contexts which frame behaviour (Israel & Tajfel, 1972). Rather, Tajfel argued that psychology has to focus on those contexts, on how they influence behaviour and on how they are changed through behaviour. On both intellectual and moral grounds, psychology had to be concerned with movement. The key issue was not simply to document the reality of discrimination and oppression between groups but to examine how such realities could be challenged. As Tajfel (1978) put it himself, he was only concerned with social identity as an intervening causal mechanism in the explanation of social change. It is worth dwelling on this point. Tajfel was not concerned with the issue of what social identity 'is', rather he was concerned with the dynamics of identity processes.

Tajfel's personal and intellectual formation was also deeply marked by the Nazi era. His work forms part of the general intellectual reaction to the experience of Nazism. It was intended to help explain how people could hate, fight and even exterminate others simply because of the groups to which they belong. More particularly, it built upon the work of Muzafer Sherif. Sherif (1966) had demonstrated that collective aggression cannot be explained in terms of the predispositions of individuals, but rather depends upon intergroup dynamics. He had shown that even the least disturbed people can be induced to act with extreme aggression if they are divided into groups and set in competition against each other. Yet even in Sherif's own studies there were signs that competition may not be necessary for intergroup hostility since there was evidence of intergroup hostility even before one group was set against the other. The particular question which Tajfel set out to answer was this: What are the minimal conditions that are necessary for the creation of intergroup discrimination? The quest culminated in a series of studies which, unsurprisingly, became known as the 'minimal group studies' (Billig & Tajfel, 1973; Tajfel, 1970b; Tajfel, Flament, Billig & Bundy, 1971).

In these studies, individuals are told that they belong to one of two groups: where the criteria for categorization are either trivial or explicitly random. That is all they are told. They don't know who else is in their group or who is in the other group.

There is no interaction or interdependence between the groups. All that happens is that the subjects are required to divide monetary values between two others of whom all they know is that one is a member of the ingroup and one is a member of the outgroup. The characteristic finding is that people will not only favour the ingroup over the outgroup, but that they will show a tendency towards sacrificing absolute levels of ingroup award in order to ensure that the ingroup gets more than the outgroup. The result is disturbing since it seems to suggest that mere categorization – the logically minimum condition for the existence of a group – is sufficient to produce outgroup discrimination. Indeed this conclusion is often drawn from the studies. However that is not the conclusion that flows from social identity theory which Tajfel and Turner elaborated in order to explain what happened (Tajfel, 1978; Tajfel & Turner, 1979, 1986).

Social identity theory suggests that the behavioural shift from interpersonal to intergroup behaviour is underlain by a psychological shift from personal to social identity. Personal identity refers to the idiosyncratic characteristics which distinguish us from other individuals. Social identity derives from our knowledge of our membership of social groups and the meaning that such memberships have for us. Particular individuals will have a variety of social identities corresponding to the different groups which they see themselves as belonging to: for instance, I am a worker, I am a Catholic, I am a Scot and so on. For the moment, the important thing to note about social identity is that it is simultaneously something that is deeply personal and profoundly felt while also being something that is irreducible to any individual. What it means to be a worker, or to be Catholic or to be Scottish is an ever shifting product of social processes. When we act in terms of social identity we act as socially defined subjects.

It is also true that social identities are defined in terms of difference from the other. What any category is can only be understood by reference to what it is not. Thus social identification necessarily involves social comparison. These comparisons occur at a collective, not an individual level. Group members are not assessing how they stand in relation to other individuals but in terms of where their category stands in relation to another category. It matters not that a privileged member of an oppressed nation is better off than many members of the oppressor nation if the nation itself remains under the yoke.

However, social identity theory assumes that the comparison process is not simply a neutral search for meaning. There is an evaluative dimension to the quest. People seek to achieve a positive understanding of who and what they are. However, since the self is defined at a collective level, this can only be achieved by establishing the ingroup as better than the outgroup on the things that matter. Hence group members will seek to differentiate themselves positively from outgroups on valued dimensions of comparison. The whole process can be summarized by saying that social identification entails social comparison and that social comparison entails social differentiation insofar as people seek positive social identities.

It is easy to mistake the differentiation for discrimination (in the sense of negative behaviours towards the outgroup), but the two are not the same. Social identity theory will be profoundly misunderstood and misrepresented if one forgets the key proviso: differentiation occurs on *valued dimensions of comparison*. What is valued depends upon the specific category that one is dealing with. It is a function of cultural and not of psychological factors. It may well be true that in many cases group culture prioritizes such things as dominance, affluence and aggression such that differentiation from the outgroup entails negative and discriminatory behaviours towards them. However, one could also differentiate oneself by being more charitable or more generous or more caring towards the other. Differentiation is a process. The behavioural consequences of that process depend upon the cultural parameters that feed into it. Discrimination is one class of behaviour which is dependent upon particular cultural definitions of certain categories. Therefore, in order to understand how groups behave towards each other one cannot be content with looking at psychological process in the abstract. Rather, one must look at how general processes manifest themselves within the specific context of concern. This is not just true in relation to the issue of differentiation but to all aspects of the social identity tradition. The point was made forcefully by Tajfel (1979) and is echoed with equal force by Turner twenty years later: 'process theories such as social identity and self-categorization require the incorporation of specific content into their analyses before they can make predictions either in the laboratory or the field, and are designed to require such an incorporation' (1999: 34).

The conflation of differentiation and discrimination might first appear like a minor matter and it might initially seem something of a distraction from our general argument to insist on the difference between the two. However, by now it should be apparent that it raises issues which go to the core of how social identity theory should be understood – quite apart from the fact that to see discrimination as inevitable has profoundly dangerous social and political consequences. Any attempt to go directly from group processes to group behaviour without considering the mediation of social context violates the meta-theoretical concerns which led to the development of social identity theory. It uses the general to sideline the specific rather than looking at how psychological processes manifest themselves in context and at how it is essential to pay attention to the context in which human behaviour occurs. More concretely, such a tendency has meant that insufficient attention is paid to the specific meanings associated with different category memberships and how these are quite central to the ways in which social identity processes play themselves out. Even less attention is paid to the ways in which these meanings form a field of cultural and political contestation and the ways in which that contestation affects what groups come to do – issues which we have seen to be so important in the case of nationhood. If those who invoke social identity theory always give a nod to the importance of cultural context, it is all too often bracketed off, pushed into the background and ultimately forgotten as allegedly universal cognitive processes take the foreground and are used to advance universal claims about the character of intergroup behaviour.

This is not to suggest that the meanings of specific identities have been altogether ignored either in social identity theory or in relation to the question of national identity and international relations (cf. Breakwell & Lyons, 1996). Indeed there is one issue of meaning which has received as much attention within psychology as in the other social sciences. It concerns the distinction between two faces of nationalism: the one benign and associated with pride in one's country; the other pernicious and associated with hatred of foreigners. Kecmanovic (1996) provides a long list of different terms which have been used to capture this distinction, including those introduced by Hayes (1931) who wrote of 'humanitarian liberal nationalism' versus 'Jacobin integral nationalism'; by Royce (1982) who distinguished 'open' from 'closed' nationalism; by Griffin (1991) who referred to 'liberal' nationalism as against 'illiberal' nationalism; and by Tehranian (1993) who made the division into 'democratic–benign' nationalism and 'totalitarian–aggressive' nationalism. However, perhaps the most pervasive way of talking about the distinction, in much popular as well as academic discourse, is to pit positive 'patriotism' against negative 'nationalism'. Psychologists have sought to show that these are independent factors and not simply two sides of the same coin, such that love and pride of one's own country is inevitably matched by hatred and denigration of foreigners (Bar-Tal, 1993; Bar-Tal & Staub, 1997). They have also sought to show that the two forms result from different psychological processes (Mummendy, Klink & Brown, in press).

The difficulty, however, is that such a dichotomy is far too simple to capture the many variants of national ideology and the multitudinous forms of action which stem from it (Hopkins, in press). It suggests that tolerance is all or nothing rather than acknowledging that certain things may be tolerated and not others and that tolerance may take certain forms and not others. Indeed, the dichotomy is often less an analysis of national ideology than an instance of it in which the phrase 'we are patriotic, you are nationalistic' conceals much (Billig, 1995). A simple division between beneficent and hostile stances does not only misrepresent differences between nations in terms of what they tolerate and how. It also misrepresents the complexities of how those from one country view those from different nations. Hostility may be targeted at some and not others as a function of particular histories. Indeed, as the meaning of particular identities is bound up with contrasts from others (with the selection of these 'significant' others depending on history: Triandafyllidou, 1998) it follows that there is a need to move beyond such global schemas and analyse how particular self- and other identities are constructed. All in all, the 'patriotism/nationalism' distinction is more like a cup half-empty than a cup half-full. It does not impel the analyst to relate ideological specificities to general processes. Rather, it reduces the subtle play of meaning to a crude metric which obviates the need to look at the understandings associated with any given national category as they relate to any given national other. Similar observations may also be made in relation to other schemas often found in the nationalism literature. One of the most frequently encountered categorizations seeks to differentiate between 'civic' and 'cultural' nationalism (with this latter being characterized as intrinsically illiberal). However as D. Brown (1999) argues, such a categorization is too simplistic and fails to capture the complexities of different forms of nationalism. In turn he argues that it is more appropriate to attend to the specificities at hand and investigate the ways in which political elites depict 'nationalist goals, and the insecurities, threats or enemies which inhibit their attainment; and also at the receptivity of the wider populace to those nationalist visions and threats' (Brown, 1999: 298).

This tendency to ignore the particular is even more obvious when it comes to the question of how to reduce hostilities between groups in general and between nations in particular. This has been one of the key questions for those who study intergroup relations, including those who work within the social identity tradition. One of the main ways in which it has been addressed is in relation to the effects of contact between groups (Allport, 1954; Amir, 1976; Hewstone & Brown, 1986; Miller & Brewer, 1984). In recent years, this debate has focused on the structural conditions under which contact ameliorates intergroup relations and the issue has been whether it is best for those in contact to be treated as individuals or as group members and, if collective identities are stressed, is it better to stress the subordinate or superordinate categories? Social identity theorists have argued that, if positive effects of encounters are to generalize beyond the immediate context and have an impact on general intergroup attitudes, it is essential for participants to be seen in terms of their group memberships (Hewstone & Brown, 1986). This has been supported by studies of inter-national relations: when Britons meet Germans, they will only extrapolate from a positive encounter to a positive view of the other country when national as opposed to personal identity is salient (Brown, Vivian & Hewstone, 1999). It may help still further to stress both national and supra-national identity: we are fellow nationals within Europe.

But once again the question arises as to whether one can understand the processes of contact in general terms without referring to the specific meaning of contact and of what the presence of particular others implies for the self: is it an act of invasion, of pollution, of defilement, or of enrichment and support (cf. Dixon & Reicher, 1997)? Does being in Europe mean domination by the 'other' or does it limit the ability of the other to dominate? Is Europe itself something which infringes on the national identity or something which allows it to thrive? In Britain it may be the former, in countries such as Spain and Italy it may well be the latter (Cinnirella, 1996, 1997; Torregrosa, 1996). As Ortega y Gasset once observed, 'to grieve for Spain is the will to become Europe' (quoted in Torregrosa, 1996: 112).

The point of this argument is not to deny that national identity is central to the way in which individuals react to others. It certainly is. People embrace or reject 'foreigners' and endorse or excoriate Europe because of the way they are seen as impinging on the national 'we'. However, the attempt to find generic relationships between the level of identification (at whatever level, personal, national or supra-national) and behaviour will fail if, as happens all too often, the situated historical and cultural context is ignored and specific meanings are not incorporated into analyses of process. To reiterate Turner's words, social identity theory was designed to facilitate the articulation of specific content and general processes (Turner, 1999). Forget that, and the theory becomes more of an encumbrance than an asset – certainly when it comes to understanding the many facets of nations and nationalism.

There is another way in which social identity theory has been taken out of context, leading to equally profound distortions in how the theory is understood and proving equally fatal to any possibility of addressing the several sides of nationhood. For Tajfel, the minimal group experiments and the process of differentiation used to explain them were points of departure, not points of arrival.

He sought to examine how the process operated within the complexities of real-life intergroup relations in socially stratified societies, as Turner (1999: 8) puts it. Tajfel was not interested in making generic statements of the sort that those with lower self-esteem will differentiate more. He was interested in the structural and ideological conditions under which people will act to challenge their social and psychological degradation. That is what he meant when he indicated that his concern was with social identity in relationship to the explanation of social change.

Consequently, there was always a two-sidedness to Tajfel's work: how does context frame the operation and consequences of social identity processes but also how do social identity processes help explain how and when people act to challenge the status quo and to reorganize the contexts in which they live? As we have seen, this two-sidedness is an essential part of nationhood – where nationalism makes nations as much as nations make nationalism. However, while Tajfel may have stressed the importance of addressing both concerns, his writings – especially on the matter of change – are better seen as programmatic than as fully realized. He sketched out some of the considerations that need to be included in a model of change but he died in 1982 without having produced a model. As a consequence, those who employ the ideas of social identity theory all too rarely address the issue of change. What is more, as we shall shortly argue, an account of change cannot simply be tacked on the top of social identity theory. Rather, it requires a thorough re-evaluation of the fundamental concepts and methods which guide our studies. Since change has been such a marginal concern, these concepts and methods have developed in a way that is inimicable to understanding the two-sided relationship between social categorization and social context – and hence to an understanding of nationhood. Those who wish to revisit the issue of change are forced to consider far more radical transformations than they may have realized at first.

These problems are further exacerbated by the fact that, in attempting to address the impact of context on categorical processes and the impact of categorical processes on context, there is always the danger that a focus on the one will lead to the other being eclipsed. In the period since Tajfel's death, self categorization theorists (Turner, 1991, 1999; Turner, Hogg, Oakes, Reicher & Wetherell, 1987; Turner, Oakes, Haslam & McGarty, 1994) have done much to deepen our understanding of social identity processes and to broaden their application from intergroup processes to group processes in general. In the face of influential schools who suggest that categorical perception and collective action are based on cognitive errors, they have insisted that categorization relates to social reality and that all group behaviour can only be understood in context (e.g. Oakes, Haslam & Turner, 1994). This perspective has much to offer in developing a psychology for the nation. In particular it orients us towards an examination of how category definitions relate to collective action. However, there is a danger that the intellectual guns have been so arranged to fire at those who ignore the social structuration of categories that there is nothing left when it comes to those who ignore how categories create social structure.

The starting point for self-categorization theory lies in an increasing emphasis on the cognitive aspect of social identification. While there are many and various antecedents to collective action, the point at which people begin to act as group members is the point at which they categorize themselves in terms of the group. We all have a number of self-categories, but in different situations different categories will be more or less important to us. Acting as a member of a given group is therefore dependent upon the contextual salience of the relevant self-category. I may be a Scot, but if I am in Church what counts is that I am a Catholic just as I am a Catholic, but, in front of the flag, what counts is that I am a Scot.

In general terms, what is being proposed is that self-categorization is the psychological process which makes collective behaviour possible. People act together because they are acting on the basis of a shared social identity. They expect agreement and they seek agreement with others who are included within the collective self-definition. In specific terms, members of any given group will behave in the terms on which the relevant self-category is defined. Self-categories provide the values, norms and understandings that guide what members do and don't do. Two things flow from this. First of all, in different contexts the same people may behave in fundamentally different ways, depending on which of their several self-categories is salient. Secondly, the way in which the members of any given group behave depends upon the way the associated self-category is defined. This latter point is of fundamental importance for what we have to say in this book and therefore needs to be specified in some detail.

If members of a common social category seek to act together on the basis of their shared social identity, then three things follow. First of all, the extent of co-action will depend upon who is included as part of the category. The more widely the category boundaries are defined, the greater the extent of collective action. More people will act together as Scots than as Glaswegians and even using the category Scottish, more people will be available for co-action if the category is defined as including all those living in the country as opposed to those born and living in the country.

Secondly, the direction of co-action will depend upon the content ascribed to the category and whether particular proposals for action are construed as consonant or dissonant with that content. Since category members seek to act in terms of category identity, then only those actions which are seen as the concrete enactment of that identity are liable to become normative and to elicit collective support.

Thirdly, the ability of any individuals to influence collective action will depend upon the extent to which they are seen as able to define category content. Individuals who are unambiguously representative of the category are more likely to be perceived as able to determine what category identity means for action in context. In other words, those who are more prototypical of the category are more able to speak for it.

If we combine these three elements, it is clear that category definitions are not simply a matter of how individuals understand themselves and how they should act. Category definitions shape collective actions and mass-mobilizations. They determine how wide those mobilizations go, where those mobilizations are aimed and how those mobilizations are directed. How, then, do these category definitions come about? For self-categorization theory, the categories through which we choose to define ourselves and others are a joint function of our general pre-disposition to think in terms of different categories and the actual structure of our social worlds – with the emphasis, at least in terms of research, being decidedly on the latter. This factor is encapsulated in the concept of 'fit', which has two aspects. 'Comparative fit' can be conceptualized in spatial terms. We use those categories which best match the clumping of instances in the world – that is, those that maximize inter-category differences compared to intra-category differences. Thus, if all the men in a situation are saying one thing and all the women another, we are liable to see people in terms of gender categories. Moreover, if what the men are saying matches our expectations of masculine behaviour and the same goes for women, the probability of categorizing in terms of gender is further enhanced. That is the second aspect of fit: 'normative fit' (Oakes, 1987; Oakes & Turner, 1990). A key implication of this is that categorization depends upon who is present in context. For instance, if radical feminists were in debate with moderate feminists, then the differences between them might seem large and they might well categorize themselves as being in opposition to each other. However, if some anti-feminists were to enter the debate, the differences between factions would become comparatively small in relation to the differences between both and those who supported traditional gender relations. Hence salience would change from 'moderate' vs. 'radical' to 'feminist' vs. 'anti-feminist' (cf. David & Turner, 1996).

The same basic logic is used to explain how we define what is prototypical and who is prototypical of a given category. The category prototype is that position which best differentiates the ingroup from the outgroup or, to be more exact, which again maximizes inter-category differences compared to intra-category differences. As before, this also means that the prototype will vary as a function of comparative context. What makes the Scots distinctive compared to the Greeks will be different to that which renders the Scots distinctive compared to the English (Hopkins, Regan & Abell, 1997). Far from being fixed and insensitive, our stereotypes of groups will be a flexible representation of the comparative context (Haslam, Turner, Oakes, McGarty & Hayes, 1992; Haslam & Turner, 1992; Hopkins & Murdoch, 1999; Oakes, Haslam & Turner, 1994). To put it slightly differently, stereotypes constitute contextually valid perceptions.

This is a radical step. It undermines one of the key assumptions which is used to assert that stereotypes are distortions of reality, namely, that they are fixed and insensitive to social reality. For self-categorization theory, group-level categorization is an accurate perception of a world organized into groups. When people are organized into categories it would be no less a distortion to see them as individuals than it would be to see people as group members when they are organized as individuals (Oakes, Haslam & Turner, 1994). To see individual-level perception as always superior to collective perception is simply an ideological preference masquerading as a cognitive hierarchy. These are powerful arguments, and they constitute a crucial corrective to the prevailing anti-collectivism of social psychology. Our concern is that, in order to make the relationship of categories to the social world seem absolutely self-evident, the nature of that world has been made too transparent and categories have been mapped on to it in a way that overplays their neutrality.

Self-categorization theory tends to treat context as if it were a given and categories as if they are largely read off from this context. This has two consequences. First of all, although stereotypes vary between situations, in any particular situation all group members should share the same stereotype. This argument has undergone important refinement in recent work by Alex Haslam (Haslam, Oakes, Turner, McGarty & Reynolds, 1998). The achievement of agreement amongst group members is not an automatic product of group member-ship. Rather, those who share a common salient self-categorization expect to agree and enter into a process of interaction on this basis. They emphasize similarities rather than differences and perceive commonalities rather than differences between members. Thus consensus is not an immediate consequence of self-categorization, rather it is the outcome of a process of consensualization. As we shall soon see, this distinction between process and outcome is of major significance. However, while Haslam allows for an analytic separation between consensualization and consensus, substantively the two collapse back into each other. Consensualization always leads to consensus. Even if discussion and debate are brought into the picture, they always lead in time to a single outcome. The possibility that people may contest and continue to contest the meaning of a single identity – as is so often the case of national identity – is all but excluded.

The second consequence is that stereotypes are tied so rigidly to existing reality that their role in changing reality is all but forgotten. The image is of a world of constantly shifting contexts and constantly varying self-categories, but of no systematic movement. People may find themselves in new social relations and compute new categories from those relations. But they do not act in order to restructure their social relations nor are their stereotypes intended as part of the process of realizing such restructuration. Such a model explains how contexts make categories but has a harder time of explaining how categories make contexts.

In order to understand how this one-sidedness has been sustained – and therefore how it might be transcended – it is helpful to consider the research practices through which self-categorization theorists have arrived at their conclusions. Let us look in some detail at the studies of category salience (e.g. Oakes, 1987; Oakes & Turner, 1990; Oakes, Turner & Haslam, 1991). In the typical experiment, subjects watch a video showing a number of men and a number of women expressing their opinions and are then asked to describe these people using rating scales. The study manipulates the extent to which all the men are saying one thing and all the women are saying another thing and also the extent to which what they say matches gender stereotypes. The aim is to measure how these manipulations affect the extent to which subjects employ gendered descriptions of those in the video. Three features of the study concern us here.

First of all, the experimenters impose a very clear and a highly specified frame of reference. It is the frame of the video which provides an unambiguous definition of who and what belong in the context. In addition, all those in the context provide an explicit expression of their position and they do so before subjects have to make judgments. These things are not problematic in themselves, unless one forgets that such pre-specification of context is a function of the particular power relations of experimentation in which subjects enter into the laboratory on the experimenters' terms, accept the definitions set by the experiment and either agree not to contest any of these terms or else find themselves excluded from the study.

Secondly, the subjects are separated from the reality which they are required to judge. There is no way in which they can act upon that reality or that their judgments can have any effects upon those who are judged. This separation is exacerbated by the fact that the studies are ahistorical. Subjects see people in a video. They rate those people. The study ends. There is no possibility that judgments can be oriented to the future since there is no future in these studies. There is only a certain preset reality and subjects can only view it passively. They cannot alter it.

Thirdly, the manner in which subjects make judgments is constrained by the experimenters in order to fulfil the pre-requisites of producing quantitative values which are amenable to statistical analysis. Characteristically, subjects have to tick which of a list of trait adjectives apply to those who are being rated, or else they have to indicate the extent to which the adjectives apply using five- or seven-point scales. One then has a clear measure and can tell if there are statistically significant differences between conditions, although for this to follow it has to be assumed that one is measuring different amounts of the same quality in different conditions and therefore that traits always carry the same meaning. Moreover, there is again the danger of forgetting that the nature of the responses is a product of experimental constraint. Any such amnesia may lead the analyst to conceive of identities in trait terms as if that is how people see themselves rather than it resulting from what the experimenters imposed in order to meet the requirements for conducting analysis of variance.

The combined effect of these three features is to create a situation in which the role of categories in creating social structure cannot be addressed. The relationship between context and identity is frozen at one moment in time whereby context is predetermined and category judgment is an outcome. The study exists in space but not across time. Just as the abstraction of experiments from the synchronic cultural context is fatal to any understanding of social determination (Israel & Tajfel, 1972), so we would argue that the abstraction of experiments from their diachronic context is fatal to understanding change. If the context–category relationship is frozen in practice, how can it be otherwise in theory?

The first step in unfreezing this relationship is to acknowledge that the nature of social reality is rarely as self-evident as it appears in experimental studies. For instance, during the Gulf War it was unclear as to who belonged in the frame: was it just a matter of Iraq and Kuwait? Was Saudi Arabia a relevant player? What about other Arab and Western countries? And where did Israel stand? What is more, even once one had decided on the players, how did one define their positions? Was Morocco pro- or anti-Saddam Hussein? Did one pay note to the position of the King who supported the anti-Iraqi coalition or the crowds demonstrating against this policy outside the King's palace? Finally, it was frequently necessary to take action prior to knowing the positions of all the actors or even if they were relevant actors: one could not wait to see if Iraq would invade Saudi Arabia before deciding whether Saudi Arabia was part of the frame.

If social context is a matter of debate rather than something that is self-evident, a perceptualist understanding of the categorization process begins to unravel. One can no longer view categories as simply 'read off' from context. Rather one must look at the way in which both context and categories are contested. Equally, one can no longer assume that everyone in a given context will share a common view of categories. Even those sharing a common salient self-categorization may differ profoundly about how their group should be defined. What is more, the basis on which they differ may be related to the future and not only to the present. Category definitions are not simply a perception of what is, but an attempt to produce what should be – and those who wish to produce different futures will need to produce different definitions of context and categories. Our Gulf War example can be used again to illustrate this point. The definition of Morocco and Egypt and other Arab countries as sharing a common position with the USA and Britain and other Western nations was not the reflection of a pre-existing coalition but part of the drive to produce such a coalition. Conversely, the portrayal of Iraq along with other Arab countries as suffering from a common domination by America and its clients, such as Israel, was intended to break that coalition and recruit Moroccans, Egyptians, Jordanians and others besides to Saddam's cause (Hiro, 1992; Reicher, 1991).

What we are suggesting is akin to the philosophical distinction between being and becoming (cf. Heidegger, 1991). Categorical understandings should not be judged for their accuracy in depicting a static world. Rather they should be understood in terms of their role in directing the constant flux through which our world is produced and reproduced. In Heidegger's own words:

> If the world were constantly changing and perishing, if it had its essence in the most perishable of what perishes and is inconstant, truth in the sense of what is constant and stable would be a mere fixation and coagulation of what in itself is becoming; measured against what is becoming, such fixating is *in*appropriate and merely a distortion. The true as the correct would precisely *not* conform to Becoming. Truth would then be incorrectness, error – an 'illusion,' albeit a perhaps necessary one. (Heidegger, 1991: vol. 3: 64; emphasis in the original)

Tajfel himself made similar points. It is no coincidence that they appear in one of his early papers on images of the nation and that they flow from his recognition that national stereotypes are employed in the process of creating nation-states as much as the reality of nation-states serves to create national stereotypes. As Tajfel puts it, such images are 'often endowed with the magic of self-fulfilling prophecies' (1970a: 130). He goes on to note that, insofar as they make future realities as much as reflect present reality, then 'the issue of the "core of truth" in stereotypes loses much of its true–false simplicity' (ibid.).

It may seem ironic to employ Tajfel in order to sustain a critique of developments in the social identity tradition. This is not a reflection of the fact that these developments have distorted the original work. Rather, it reflects the fact that there was a tension within Tajfel's own work which made it impossible to develop these insights to the full. To do so requires us to take some further steps which he was not prepared to take. To begin with, an understanding of how category definitions can be involved in shaping the nature of our social relations requires us to re-conceptualize the character of these definitions. Whatever advantages trait ratings have in terms of experimental convenience, it is hard to see how our world can be modelled by reference to such a simple list of characteristics. It therefore becomes incumbent upon us to investigate the precise ways in which people conceptualize the categories of self and other and how these relate to the shaping of social practices. It also becomes necessary to analyse the particular forms of identities that serve to create particular forms of social reality. In the present context, we must ask about the precise contours of those identities which are implicated in organizing our world of nations.

Next, it becomes necessary to elevate the process by which people negotiate and debate their identities from an epiphenomenon on the road to consensus to a central concern which has an independent and determining role in the shaping of collective action. We must consider how versions of identity relate to the prophecies that they are designed to fulfil, how different versions of identity seek to fulfil different prophecies and how the different prophets seek to establish their words as the truth about identity and the words of others as false.

Lastly, we need to adjust our methodologies to the nature of the phenomena we wish to investigate rather than vice-versa. This is not a call for or a rejection of any particular methodology. While we may have criticized certain aspects of the salience experiments we are certainly not advocating a rejection of experimentation per se. Indeed, elsewhere we have argued that experiments are particularly powerful techniques for imposing particular constructions of reality and examining the consequences (Reicher, 1997). In the context of social identity research, they allow us to investigate how different aspects of the definition of context and of self-categories affect the character of collective understanding and collective action. However, experiments are not appropriate for looking at complex structures of meaning, at processes of construction and at processes which relate to inter-actions over extended periods of time. That is, experiments simply cannot address the slippery process of identity construction. A one-sided reliance on experimental methodologies will therefore inevitably result in a one-sided view of identity processes whereby the emphasis is on how social givens produce psychological and behavioural consequences but where those social givens remain inviolate. Along with others (e.g. Condor, 2000b; Wetherell, 1996), we would argue that it was the refusal both of Tajfel and of those who followed him to countenance anything other than experimentation that limited the extent to which his theoretical insights about the future orientation of category definitions, and about change more generally, could be followed through.

For all these reservations, and despite our sense that there is still some way to be travelled, it would be a serious misrepresentation of our position if we were not to stress how far the social-identity tradition has taken us towards a psychological understanding of nations and nationalism. The very concept of social identity, and particularly the cognitive redefinition of group membership offered by self-categorization theory, provides a means of understanding how people can act in terms of a collective, such as the nation, which is too large to be encompassed by their immediate experience. It also provides a bridge between the cultural and the personal by indicating how people can take the understandings and values associated with large-scale social categories as their own. Furthermore it specifies in some detail how these category definitions may affect collective action. It points to the determining importance of how category boundaries, category content and category prototypes are defined. The route from cultural definitions of nationhood (or indeed any other category) to mass-behaviour is therefore complete. Finally, by showing the practical consequences of category definitions, self-categorization theory raises the importance of understanding their antecedents. This becomes a matter of societal as well as psychological importance since the way in which we understand our social categories is not simply a matter of clarifying the sense which individuals have of who they are and how they should act. It is also a matter of raising the mobilizations through which our world is made and unmade. Our concern is that, while this account of consequences has raised the question of antecedents, more needs to be done in order to settle that question. We need to develop our conception of identity and develop the ways in which we study identity in order to understand how self-categories shape national realities as well as being shaped by them.

Social identity in practice

Many of the points that we are making here, both as they relate to the general issue of social categorization and to specific issues of nationhood, echo those made by others. The work of Michael Billig is particularly pertinent as it relates to both issues. However, as we shall see, there is an important difference of emphasis between Billig's critique of the categorization literature (Billig, 1987) and his analysis of nationalism (Billig, 1995, 1996).

In the former, Billig challenges the view that human beings have a natural tendency to categorize and that categorization reflects a cognitive imperative. He suggests that human understanding always occurs in a context of argument. Even our private thoughts arise out of an internal dialogue in which we pit different positions against each other. Indeed we only take positions to the extent that there are counter-positions. We may have attitudes towards abortion because that is controversial. But, in the contemporary world we would look askance if someone asked us our attitude as to whether the world is flat. We don't have an attitude because we don't see there being any alternative.

This principle of argumentation can be applied to the various facets of human understanding in two ways. On the one hand it should lead us, as analysts, to beware of one-sided claims. Whenever such a claim is made we should immediately invoke its opposite. In the case of categorization and the claim that individuals have an inherent tendency to ignore differences by putting things together under the same label, Billig insists that we are equally skilled in finding ways of distinguishing instances as special cases and as exceptions to the general rule. All of us, even the fiercest bigots, are as adept at particularization as at categorization. On the other hand, we need to approach all aspects of understanding as domains of argumentation. Categorization is an excellent example of this. We can contest the nature of categories in a number of ways and nothing is immune from that contestation. Thus we might contest the nature of the category itself and hence which particular instances belong within it. Or else we can agree on the category but contest the nature of given particulars and whether they meet the criteria of inclusion. Frequently we can go to a second order level and argue over where the argument properly lies. As Billig puts it, there is no final full stop to this process.

Billig's work on nationalism might be seen as turning the principle of argumentation onto argumentation itself, insofar as it stresses how national categories are taken for granted in our understandings of ourselves and our social world. As we have previously seen, he argues that the power of nationalism lies not so much in its occasional spectacular manifestations – those which grab the headlines and the attention of so many commentators. It lies in the way that we presuppose nationhood in talking about the banal phenomena which constitute our everyday lives. So, when we talk about 'the' weather or 'the' economy we presuppose the reference is to whether it will rain or shine in our country and whether our national economic performance is close to boom or bust. In order to understand the banal power of national categories we need to look more closely at what makes these categories specifically national.

Billig argues that, while social identity theorists may stress the importance of incorporating the specific nature of different identities into their analyses, in practice their concern with general relationships such as that between categories and comparative context has precluded any attention to this specificity. They look at nations only insofar as they are like any other cognitive self-category – or, to use Anderson's language, like any other imagined community. Social identity theorists do not look at what makes such imaginings national or at what else one has to imagine in order to see oneself in terms of nationality. For Billig, this is to 'close down analysis at precisely the point when it should begin' (Billig, 1995: 68).

Condor (1996, 1997, 2000a, in press) echoes this point, and her studies of English national identity provide some of the most detailed analyses of the national imagination, certainly within the psychological literature. Her investigation of how people articulate their national belonging provides a very different view of identity to that presupposed in experimental investigations. Most starkly, there is very little evidence that people imagine their national identity in terms of a set of individuals sharing common traits. In one set of interviews (Condor, in press), only 70 out of 298 (23.5 per cent) references to national identity touched upon anything that people had in common. Even when people were explicitly questioned about national character, a mere 25 out of 186 (13.4 per cent) references involved trait ascriptions. Most referred to customs, to appearance or even to diet.

Condor acknowledges that such reluctance to talk in terms of national character may be culturally specific to the English. Indeed she finds her respondents markedly resistant to talk about national identity at all (Condor, 2000a). One simple response to this would be that national identity was not salient amongst the sample – and that also explains the lack of homogeneity in trait ascriptions. However, such an interpretation would be overly simple because, at the same time as they disavow their nationhood, respondents repeatedly talk in terms that presuppose a national frame of reference. In a manner that is akin to Billig's concept of banal nationalism, they use terms like 'we' and 'here' which imply a national population and a national territory. Condor (1996, 2000a) therefore argues, firstly, that the nature of

Englishness lies in distinguishing the vulgar nationalist foreigner from the measured and mannered self. Paradoxically, English identity is asserted by denying English nationalism. Secondly, respondents are alive to the dangers of being labelled as prejudiced, intolerant and irrational if they are seen to believe in national character and to endorse nationalist sentiment. They are therefore wary of expressing such positions to the researcher.

This work provides a number of salutary lessons for the student of national identity and of social identity more generally. It warns us to guard against drawing direct conclusions about internal mental states from expressions of national identity. We need to look at what people are doing when they express (or don't express) national identity: how they are attempting to manage their relationships with others and manage how others are able to position them. We also need to take the culture of the specific national group into account before we draw conclusions about the psychological significance of what is said. It may be that in some cases a disavowal of national identity violates cultural norms and therefore may indeed signify a rejection of national categories. However, where such disavowal reflects the national culture we have to be more wary. But Condor's analyses also force us to reassess our understanding of national identity, and even social identity, more generally. They show us that it is untenable to presuppose that social categories are defined in terms of common traits or indeed any commonalities between category members. They may just as easily refer to the ways people exist within common institutions or within a common territory. They have to do with how we live together as much as who we are.

Billig also stresses that there is much more to the national imagination than traits in common. He writes:

> As far as national identity is concerned, not only do the members have to imagine themselves as nationals; not only do they have to imagine their nation as a community; but they must also imagine that they know what a nation is; and they have to identify the identity of their own nation. (1995: 68)

He goes on to stress that, in the same way as Balibar (1991c) argues that there can be no racism without theories, so nationalism involves a more general representation of how the world is organized (Billig, 1996). To adopt a national identity requires that we see it as self-evident that we live in a world of nations. It leads us not only to see subjects as nationals but also to see the nation as a subject with its own rights and its own value – one which all too frequently transcends the value of individual citizens. Thus, while international intervention is sanctioned (or even required) if the sovereignty of one nation is violated by another, little or nothing tends to be done when nation-states do terrible things to their own populations.

For us, this emphasis on theories of social relations provides the basis for an understanding of the reciprocal relationship between national categories and national structures and, indeed, between categorization and social reality more generally. This is because it is not only national identities which should be seen as involving theories of social relations. If defining oneself in terms of 'race' depends upon seeing oneself as part of a world organized by 'races' and with particular relationships obtaining within and between different 'races', and if defining oneself in terms of nationality is part of seeing oneself as living in a world of nations with its corresponding sets of rights, values and relationships, so the same could be said of class, of gender, of age and in fact of any category.

This point was brought home to us in the first study that we ever conducted on social identity processes (Reicher, 1984). The study arose out of the St Paul's 'riot' which occurred in Bristol on 2 April 1980. The aim was to show that the pattern of crowd action was not random or meaningless but rather made sense in terms of the collective identity assumed by crowd members. If this aim was, to some extent, fulfilled, the study also raised a question mark over what was meant by identity. In defining themselves as St Paul's residents, participants in the events did not refer to traits or attributes. Rather they described a set of social relations: to be from St Paul's was to be subordinated and oppressed. It was to be kept in poverty by a nexus of financial institutions, to be denied jobs by prejudiced employers and, above all, to be kept in one's place by oppressive policing. If this sounds familiar, the connection was made by the participants themselves. As one put it, 'politically, they were all black' (quoted in Reicher, 1984: 15).

By tying St Paul's experience to black experience, there is a clarification of what sort of social relations are implicated in this identity. What is interesting, however, is that such a clarification is necessary to make sense of what the identity means. It is also worth noting that when anything akin to traits were expressed, they only made sense when interpreted within the relevant social relations. Thus, when Desmond Pierre, Chair of the St Paul's Defence Committee, was asked to tell a television audience why the committee was set up, he replied 'we are defending ourselves on a lot of issues, but the main one is the right to lead a free life' (Reicher, 1984: 14). One might infer from this that St Paul's people are 'freedom loving', but in this context such an attribute meant fighting the police and destroying financial institutions, since these were seen as the source of oppression. In other contexts, say when we are told that the English are 'freedom loving', it means very different things, including respect for the law and the state. But even the attribution of 'freedom loving' to Englishness will vary depending upon the social relations in which the English are embedded. As Schwarz (1982) points out, the notion of the freeborn Englishman acquires a very different meaning according to whether one is preparing to fight the Nazis or to stop a Pakistani family moving in next door.

This ambiguity of trait terms is not only a theoretical problem for the analyst. It is also a practical problem for actors. Self-definitions in terms of traits are simply too vague to tell one what to do. What does it mean to be freedom loving or courageous or careful or whatever? How does it tell you what to do in any situation? However, a self-definition which provides a model of social relations, which maps out the nature of the world in which we live, which gives us the grounds on which to recognize people as similar or other, which tells us what the other will do to us and respond to what we do, thereby provides a guide to action. The social identity of St Paul's placed the police as an oppressor and was the basis on which 59 out of 60 police officers who were present received injuries but virtually no one else was attacked. The relational sense of self also accounts for why those properties housing financial institutions were burnt and other properties were collectively defended. The general point is that, by knowing where we stand in a system of social relations, we not only know what is important (whether that be the sovereignty of nations, the purity of races, the achievement of liberty) but we also know what is possible. Putting these various aspects together, we conceptualize social identity as an understanding of one's place within a system of categorical social relations along with the proper and possible actions which flow from such a position.

Such a definition implies that identity not only relates to the organization of action but is necessary for actors to be able to pursue desired ends. On the one hand, it determines the values and beliefs which define what counts as a desirable end. On the other hand, it provides a map of the social topography which shows one how to reach that end. Another way of putting this is to say that any definition of self-interest or interested behaviour needs to take the self term seriously rather than take it for granted. One can only have an interest or pursue an interest in one's capacity as a particular sort of subject. Different identities (or different definitions of the same identity) will lead to different interests and different ways of pursuing them. One implication of this, about which we will have much to say in the next chapter, is that the way to get people to act in a given way is by providing a definition of the self that makes such action seem self-evidently in their interests.

Our definition also implies a relationship between identity and social reality that is necessarily two-sided. We may define social identities in order to shape collective practices and to bring about a world in the image of our categorical understandings. However, the world is not a passive medium that we can shape at will. There is always resistance from the nature of the institutions people have built and from the actions of others who seek to shape collective practices in different ways. If the resistance is such that it is impossible to enact alternatives, then our categories will reflect the structure of the social world rather than vice-versa. Three points are worth noting here. First of all, the world in which we live is always organized by the activity of human agents acting on categorical understandings. However, it may not necessarily be *our* activity but rather that of other agents at other points in history and sedimented into institutional forms. If it appears to us as external and objective that is because it is not a product of *our* subjectivity and not because it is independent of any human subjectivity. Secondly, the balance between our categories determining the world and our categories being determined by the world is actually the balance between our agency and that of others – both past and present. The issue is settled by whether 'we' are able to prevail over 'them' or they over us. The third point is that the process of category argumentation will have an independent determining weight in shaping this process.

Category definitions shape collective mobilizations, on that we are in agreement with self-categorization theory. Where we differ is that, for us, these definitions are not only perceptions of the present, but also attempts to make the future. The success of one definition over others does not so much depend upon the extent to which it accurately represents the present but in the extent to which it is successful in ordering the future. Following from our argument, there will be a number of elements which contribute to that success. At one level, one can distinguish between the power of the collective to shape the social world and the resistance offered by the social world. The power of the collective can likewise be divided into a number of factors. Some will have to do with the ability to reach people, others will have to do with the ability to shape their activity into the most effective forms. However, the ability to get people to imagine themselves as forming a given community and to envisage specific forms of social relation as proper and possible is essential in getting them to initiate actions that are aimed at realizing this reality. It is in this domain that psychological factors are crucial to an understanding of collective action. It is by reference to these factors that those who wish to shape collective action – those we shall refer to as the 'entrepreneurs of identity' – will gain effect. Their skill lies both in defining categories as such that they entail the form of mobilization necessary to realizing the desired future and in making these definitions seem so self-evident that they are immune to counter positions.

The first of these relates directly to the consequences of category definition as outlined by self-categorization theory. If the boundaries of categories determine the extent of collective action, the content of categories defines the direction of collective action and the category prototypes determine who can speak for the nation, then the probability of success for any given attempt to move a given collectivity towards the realization of a given end will depend upon the extent to which all those in the collectivity are defined as part of a common category, to which the forms of action necessary to reaching this end are seen as an enactment of category identity, and to which those offering these definitions are seen as prototypical of the category.

Once these consequences of categorization are freed from a perceptualist account of the antecedents of categorization, we can see both how constructions of categories are relevant to the process of becoming and why they should be such a focus of controversy. The crucial link, for us, is between category construction and the shaping of mass action. We need to investigate how the various aspects of category construction relate to the various dimensions of mobilization. We need always to ask how a particular account of boundaries, of content or of prototypes, leads to one or another form of mass action. It is because of these links and these consequences that identity becomes such a key battlefield for all those interested in shaping action to shape the future. It is because category definitions serve to position all members of the categories which constitute our social worlds (rather than being simply a private psychological matter of telling individuals their place) that they are characterized by argument.

It is in this respect that the distinction between consensualization and consensus, which we noted above, is so important. Members of common categories expect to agree. By seeking to define the category, we are not saying what we alone think or what a sub-set of members think, but rather what all members of the category should think and do. Were it otherwise, then category definition would be an idiosyncratic exercise with little collective import. So it is precisely because group members expect to agree that it is worth devoting such attention to what such agreement should actually consist of. It is another reason why different versions should exist in such abundance. In a phrase, the process of consensualization can co-exist with the empirical reality of dissensus (cf. Reicher & Sani, 1998; Sani &

Reicher, 1998, 1999). Not only that, consensualization provides the impetus towards dissensus. And it is because there is such an impetus towards dissensus that it becomes so important for any given version of identity to put its competitors into the shadows.

The success of any given construction of identity over its competitors depends upon hiding all traces of construction and making the definition of identity that is present seem self-evident. This is akin to the process of reification which Thompson describes as:

> representing a transitory, historical state of affairs as if it were permanent, natural, outside of time. Processes are portrayed as things or as events of a quasi-natural kind, in such a way that their social and historical character is eclipsed . . . or, to borrow a suggestive phrase from Claude Lefort, it involves the re-establishment of 'the dimension of society "without history" at the very heart of historical society'. (1990: 65)

Thompson describes various modes of reification, and we would argue that the modes through which identity is reified will vary as a function of the categories themselves. This is our cue to move on from a general discussion of the relationship between social identity and collective practice and to conclude with a consideration of what all this means for the phenomena of nationhood.

Conclusion: social identity and the nation

In the previous section we argued that identities both organize and are organized by practice, the balance between the two depending on whether particular forms of social organization are too entrenched to be overcome through collective action. In the previous chapter we argued that nationhood is the predominant form of social organization in the contemporary world – so entrenched that it is easy to take it for a natural rather than a social fact. So many forms of activity are organized by reference to nationhood and so many institutions exist at a national level that it is often hard to envisage alternatives. Moreover, as Giddens (1985) stresses and as Billig (1995) affirms, the nation is a container of power. If one wants power to affect institutional structures and patterns of activity it needs to be sought at a national level. Even if one wants to shape international realities – including attempts to transcend the nation – this still depends upon nationally bounded activity. For instance, the attempt to create a European currency in Britain will depend upon victory in a national referendum.

The upshot of all this is that we would expect, as indeed Billig (1985) has shown, that national categories will be taken for granted, especially in regard to practices that are oriented to contesting power and shaping institutions. If one wishes to mobilize all those subject to these institutions in order to determine their nature, then nationhood is the way to do it. The most obvious example of this is the electoral process. Especially in a mediatized world where what one says in one locality will be broadcast to the entire territorial population, the construction of a majority will depend upon being seen to speak on behalf of the nation and upon one's policies being seen to represent the national interest. Of course, the corollary of this is that where one seeks to mobilize different types of constituency and seeks to gain power through winning specific groups to direct action rather than through a general appeal to the population at large, then different categories may be used. We are not suggesting that national categories are in any way necessary. Rather we are drawing a link between types of category and forms of mobilization, or, to be more specific about this particular case, between the extent of mobilization that is sought and the types of categories which include all the relevant constituency within their boundaries. Our point is simply that national categories are particularly useful in achieving the particular types of mobilization that happen to predominate in the contemporary world. In particular, electoral politics under (relatively) universal franchises will tend to be conducted with reference to the national interest.

Having said that, the banality of nationalism does not exclude argumentation. It simply means that different political perspectives, different policies, different ways of envisioning institutional practice, will be conducted by arguing over the meaning of nationhood rather than through the counterposition of one set of categories to another. If politicians are likely to agree in basing their arguments on the national interest, they are all the more likely to disagree on the nature of national identity and therefore whether any given proposal is an expression of the national interest. We would expect them to seek support for their party positions by presenting these positions as the enactment of national identity, to present their policies as distinctive in this respect and to present the positions of their rivals as subverting national identity and hence being against the national interest. An implication of this is that there will be highly different versions of any national identity both between different politicians and parties seeking to mobilize the population in support of different projects and also from the same politicians and parties as their projects differ over time.

Likewise, we would expect intense argument over category prototypes as those who seek mass support would have it that they speak for the nation. They will seek to present themselves alone as prototypical while their opponents by their person or their acts place themselves outside the national community or even set themselves against the national community. Again, the versions of prototypicality will vary across different politicians at the same time and across the same politicians at different times. But always, the more successful politician will appear as an icon of the nation.

With so many versions of so many things, the question of making the contingent seem necessary becomes all the more important. As we previously noted, there are many ways of doing this. However, the particular way in which nationhood is theorized as a category – in terms of a territorially bounded community moving together through time – gives priority to some over others. Most obvious is the use of history. We have seen how central historical studies have been to nationhood. We know how important it is to find some silver thread which stretches back to time immemorial and can therefore be used to trace the national essence. Now we are suggesting that, if national mobilization depends upon national identity, then establishing identity depends upon embedding it within an essentializing historical narrative. Different histories will be invoked to essentialize different versions, which is why history itself is such a domain of argument. What is important, and what may advantage one version of history and hence one version of identity over another, is the skill with which certain iconic moments of national history are incorporated into the narrative and used together to exemplify the visions of social relations which are being promoted.

If history is of undoubted importance in this regard, it is not the only such domain. There may be other artefacts which are commonly agreed to be national icons and which provide powerful support when interpreted in the terms of a given version of identity. These include both the person and the works of national bards, they include institutions which are held up as exemplifying the national spirit, they even include the landscape in general, as well as particular natural features. All of these things are open to interpretation, all of them provide fields of argumentation, the argumentation provides a key ground in which battles over national identity and hence over national mobilization are fought.

In the following chapters we will investigate the manifold forms of argumentation we have identified here. However, as we go deeper into these matters it is important not to lose the wood for the trees. We have set out to demonstrate the importance of psychology to an understanding of nationhood and, more particularly, to develop an understanding of identity which can act as a pivot between the world of nations and what individuals do and think. We have argued that social identity exists in relationship to the categorical organization of action. The two key relationships which we are constantly seeking to illustrate by illustrating the details of argument are, first, how the organization of people in a world of nations gives rise to the use of national categories; secondly, and most prominently, we are concerned with the ways in which the specific definitions which are given of national categories relate to the mobilization of collective action and collective support. National identity has to be malleable in order to support an ever changing array of mobilizations. It has to be portrayed as fixed such that any given mobilization may succeed in shaping our world of nations.

3   Nation and Mobilization

Invoking the nation

It is the best of beliefs and it is the worst of beliefs. For many there is nothing nobler, indeed nothing more sacred, than national identification. For others, there is nothing heroic about the love of nation and nothing to sing about. Tom Nairn (1997) describes the cover of *Time* magazine from 6 August 1990. It shows a death head across Europe whose mouth splits the continent and dribbles venom over Yugoslavia and Romania. The message is made clear by the fact that the teeth are lettered so as to spell the word 'nationalism' and the whole image is crowned by the title 'OLD DEMON' in scarlet 72-point lettering. More generally, and more succinctly, Einstein declared that nationalism was an infantile disorder, the measles of mankind.

In this and the next chapter we shall come to address the question of whether nationalism is indeed a blessing or a poison – or, at least, we shall address a narrower issue which is often used as the basis of moral judgment: does nationalism necessarily conflict with more inclusive identities and does it inevitably lead to distance, if not outright hostility, towards those who are not members of the national category? But there is another matter which must be settled first. The fact that the champions of nationalism are matched by its detractors might seem to undermine our claims concerning the general usage of national categories and of self-categorization as national. Rather than a world in which people embrace national identities, we would seem to have two large and opposed camps. However, such a conclusion depends on equating nationalism with national identification. Or rather, to be more exact, it depends upon the assumption that nationalists identify deeply with the nation and anti-nationalists do not.

In one sense, such an assumption is easy to challenge. It could simply be that the anti-nationalists are not attacking nationalism in general but rather attacking one form of nationalism the better to defend another. By pathologizing one set of enthusiasms as nationalism they undermine challenges to another, taken for granted, form of nationhood. Thus those who deplore the conflicts in the former Yugoslavia as exemplifying nationalism tend, at least implicitly, to accept the nationalism which supported and sustained the idea and practices of a Yugoslavian national identification.

There is, however, another way of challenging the assumption that nationalists have a monopoly on national identification, one with potentially more far-reaching consequences. As we argued in Chapter One, the term 'nationalism' has been used to denote a range of phenomena with some usages implying quite specific political projects (e.g. the pursuit of statehood). One problem with adopting a definition which reserves 'nationalist' for those advocating the establishment of such state structures is that analysts are led to underestimate both the scope and the significance of national identification. Thus, in her study of centenary and bicentenary celebrations in Australia and the USA, Spillman (1997) warns against too simple an association between political sovereignty and national identity. She shows that, in the case of the Australian centennial of 1888, 'a language expressing distinctive "Australian" national identity was considered entirely consistent with and even dependent on British attachments' (p. 26). For instance, Sydney's festivities began with the unveiling of a statue of Queen Victoria in the city, attended by a crowd of 50,000 people. Spillman also uses this centennial to show that 'it is possible to create expressions of national identity with neither unified sovereignty nor much of an oppositional nationalist political movement' (p. 26).

This uncoupling of movements based on national identity and the nation-state (either as goal or indeed as origin) requires a clarification of terms and we will henceforth use 'nationalism' to refer to any form of collective action in which people are mobilized and hence define themselves in terms of national identity. We would suggest that the form that such action will take depends upon how the national category is construed, how particular actions are construed and hence whether the relationship between them is constituted as consonant or dissonant. More generally, we could say that the form of action pursued will depend upon the ways in which the 'interests' of the nation are defined, and that national identity and national interest can be invoked to argue against, as well as for, nation-state status. What we are suggesting is that even 'anti-nationalists' act in national terms.

This is but one example that illustrates our more general inversion of the usual approach to nationalism. Rather than seeking to uncover generic relationships between nationalism and particular action outcomes – nationalism and the nation-state, nationalism and chauvinism, nationalism and parochialism and so on – our aim is to show how differing forms of action can be pursued through invoking the name of country. Rather than suggesting that nationalism necessarily leads to one outcome rather than another, we seek to demonstrate that outcomes are dependent upon the situated definition of national identity. Rather than seeking generality in terms of the actions that flow from nationalism, we pursue generality in terms of the process which relates specific identity definitions to specific forms of national mobilization. Furthermore, rather than conceiving of the term 'nationalism' as an index of categorization, it may be better viewed as a rhetorical device which is used to disqualify one form of national project to the advantage of other, equally national, projects.

In order to explore these points in more detail, let us turn to the Scottish case. More specifically, let us examine the ways in which the moral dimension features in characterizations of nationalism and how such characterizations are organized to facilitate particular political projects as against others. So too, let us explore the construction of the national interest and whether this interest is best served by statehood or not. Once these issues have been addressed we will be better placed to proceed to the broader issue of whether action in terms of one's national identity inevitably entails distance from and hostility towards those who are not members of the national category.

It is time to visit the first in our cast: Michael Heseltine, the then Deputy British Prime Minister, speaking just prior to the 1992 election at a venue in Edinburgh:

Extract 1

They tell me that nationalism is on the march – that all over the world, suppressed instincts are striving to burst forth. They imply that it's a virtue. Extremism in France. Riots on the streets of Marseilles. Fascism on the rise in Germany. Eastern Europe convulsed by the ethnic hatred, racial bitterness, social turmoil that nationalism has always brought in its wake. It's about yesterday. The hidden warning. The slaughtered generations. It's about the young people sent to tear each other apart. That's what nationalism has always been about. We put all that behind us hundreds of years ago. Let no one pretend that we've never been through it. The Kingdoms of England fought each other – to obliteration. The Wars of the Roses still strike a nerve in Yorkshire and Lancashire. But Wales joined with England – and prospered. The Act of Union between Scotland and England has brought prosperity, peace and strength to both nations over 300 years. Nationalism nearly destroyed it – German nationalism – three times in three-quarters of a century. Scotland couldn't have stopped Hitler alone. But nor could England. Or Wales. Or Ireland. None of us. Together we did. This Union of ours did. Alone, and together – in the greatest trial of armed strength in human history – we held that most fragile of lines which separated freedom from tyranny.

(Michael Heseltine, Conservative MP, speech, Edinburgh, 7.4.92)

This really is double jeopardy. On the one hand, nationalism is denounced as an atavistic evil, something that has been overcome in Britain if not in Europe. On the other hand, a nationalist dissolution of the UK is not only an evil in itself, but makes it impossible to fight similar evils elsewhere. It is not only the overt nationalists who stand condemned, but equally those, like Labour and the Liberal Democrats, who, wittingly or unwittingly, would condone the break up of Britain.

If Labour is on the receiving end of Conservative anti-nationalism, they are equally adept at handing it out. In doing so, they draw on a long tradition on the left. Most pointedly, Isaac Deutscher warns that socialists must 'understand the nationalism of the masses, but only in the way in which a doctor understands the weakness or the illness of his patient' and that 'socialists should be aware of that nationalism, but, like nurses, they should wash their hands twenty times over whenever they approach an area of the Labour movement infected by it' (Isaac Deutscher, cited in Beveridge and Turnbull, 1989: 53). For Labour, as for Conservative, the most obvious example of such 'infection' is wartime Germany and thus a Scottish Labour MP duly warned against the 'siren voice' of nationalism. It was, he said, something that 'you can only fight on the basis that you're being discriminated against and whatever failings there may be, either as a group or as an individual, is because it is somebody else's fault. And the parallel, I don't want to make it too strong, but the parallel, I mean with Germany it was the Jews'. (Labour MP, interview 32). In a public speech to a conference on nationalism organized by the 21st Century Trust, George Robertson – then Scottish MP and member of Labour's 'shadow cabinet' and now NATO's Secretary General – spelt the point out at greater length:

Extract 2

Nationalism used to be unfashionable and unrespectable. It is time to make it unfashionable and unrespectable again. Nationalism is possibly the worst danger to stability in the world today and in its many different manifestations it is among the most malign forces challenging international order.

(George Robertson, Labour MP, Frankfurt, 2.8.94)

Robertson went on to argue that racism and ethnic hatred were 'only the superficial sores on the body politic', the source of which was the 'cancer of nationalist extremism . . . deep inside and eating away relentlessly'. In some cases, nationalism is used deliberately as 'the tool of the unscrupulous and the desperate and the calculating'. However, sometimes it develops its own momentum, which goes well beyond what was originally intended: 'The momentum of the case, starting with the first boast, the next scapegoat, the next blame allocated can effortlessly go on to worse and worse excesses . . . The slippery slope to the worst extremes has all too often become very slippery indeed'. In either case, nationalism remains an evil and the nationalist is either a dupe or duplicitous – hardly an appealing choice!

Of course, in the hands of Labour, attacks on nationalism constituted a double-edged sword for not only did Labour support devolution, which could be constituted as validating a certain form of national self-expression, but in addition there was a wing of the Scottish Labour Party which was considerably more sympathetic to radical forms of autonomy. One response was simply to plead pragmatism. To paraphrase an interview with a Trades Union leader (interview 30), if the left leaves the mobilization of nationalist sentiments to small-business people and populists, it is in danger of going down a 'very unhealthy road'. Implicit in this is the notion of good and bad (or, at least, better and worse) nationalisms. The point is amplified by another Scottish MP:

Extract 3

Nationalism is like electricity. It can be a good or a bad thing. It can electrocute someone in the electric chair or it can heat and light the world. The point is what use is the electricity being put to, by whom, and I think nationalism is the same. Nationalism can be an exhilarating revolutionary force for progress as it has been in places without number, from Nicaragua to Palestine to South Africa, to Britain and the anti-fascist war. Many, many places. But we only have to open our newspapers today to areas where nationalism becomes in the wrong hands a primeval force for darkness and reaction. A kind of throat-cutting nationalism and ethnic-cleansing nationalism like we are seeing in some parts of east/central Europe and will see much more of in the former Soviet Union and elsewhere. So it is a volatile mercurial thing which is why I argue the socialist

> *movement should be the leading force in the national struggle here and elsewhere and that we ought to utilize, I can say cynically, we ought to utilize the potential revolutionary force of nationalism and by our leadership, ensure that the dark side of the beast does not emerge.*
>
> (Labour MP, interview 36)

If there are different nationalisms, then Scottish nationalism can be tentatively placed in the camp of progress rather than that of genocide, dependent of course on who leads it. The involvement of progressives therefore becomes a form of opposition to the 'dark side' rather than a capitulation to it as others would allege. The argument can be taken a step further by suggesting that the accusers themselves adopt a nationalist position – that of British nationalism – and therefore are in no position to criticize. Thus one Labour MP (interview 38) argued that defenders of the Union are supporting a British nationalist concept and therefore, in attacking Scottish nationalism, are endorsing British nationalism. That, he suggests, is ridiculous. It is only a short step from here to argue that the opponents of Scottish nationalism are attacking a progressive concept in the name of a pernicious nationalism. This is a step rarely found within the Labour Party, whose devolutionism implies a commitment to the Union of Scotland and England. Such restraint does not apply to the SNP.

There is a considerable overlap between the SNP and Labour devolutionists in responding to attacks on nationalism. First of all, they suggest that there are different forms of nationalism. For instance, in its second issue, the left-leaning nationalist quarterly *Liberation* bemoaned the fact that, although the people of Greenland have twenty words for snow, there is only one term for national awareness: nationalism. Then, Scottish nationalism is differentiated from negative instances. For instance, the SNP's long-standing MEP Winnie Ewing (affectionately known as 'Madame Ecosse') argued, 'We are nationalists in the Scandinavian mould. We are not nationalists in the Serbian mould and no serious observer believes that we are' (SNP MEP, Winnie Ewing, speech, annual conference, Perth, 26.9.92). Elsewhere, the SNP activist and candidate, Ian Hamilton, speaking on the occasion of his installation as Rector at Aberdeen University, sought to differentiate between 'the virtue of nationalism' and 'the vice of racialism' and defined the latter as having no place in Scottish national identity:

Extract 4

Did you know, as I hope every Jew here today knows, that Scotland is the only country in Europe which has never had a pogrom of your race? Race after race has come in peace, and mingled its blood with those who were already settled here. There is no such thing as a pure bred Scot. We are all mongrels, and perhaps it is our mongrel breeding which gives us our restlessness, our curiosity, and our sheer damned bloody-minded intransigence. No Scot would win a prize at Crufts.

(Ian Hamilton, rectorial address, 'On the virtue of nationalism and the vice of racialism', Aberdeen University, reprinted in *The Scotsman*, 3.2.94)

The essence of Scottish nationality, then, is ethnic pluralism, it therefore cannot be the basis of ethnic exclusivism. What is? Hamilton goes on to provide an answer: 'I come now to isolate the cause of racialism, and to distinguish it from nationalism. It is empire, the dominion of the few over the many, which causes racialism'. This argument provides a hinge that allows the charges levelled at Scottish nationalists to be turned round. For empire and imperialism – the dominion of large nations seeking to dominate others rather than small nations seeking to resist domination – can be used to characterize English and British nationalism (the two being seen as equivalent by the SNP and many other Scots besides). Thus one senior SNP activist and election candidate described how he had taken a Labour opponent's jibe that 'nationalism had died with Hitler' and turned it back on the accuser:

Extract 5

Sorry, Hitler was on your side not mine. He wasn't in favour of freedom for small nations. The problem is not nationalism, the problem is Imperialism. Imperial people want to tell other people how they should live, where they should live. As nationalists, as we use the word, we are not wanting anything for ourselves that we don't want for everybody else.
(Contribution from floor at a fringe meeting held at the SNP annual conference, Perth, 23.9.92)

So far we have weakened the counter-position between anti- and pro-nationalists by showing that members of all parties – the SNP as well as Labour and the Conservatives – repudiate forms of national feeling which lead to hostility and worse against 'ethnic', 'racial' and 'national' others. The distinction can be weakened still further by showing that everybody – Labour and Conservatives as well as the SNP – claims a deeply felt national identity. However, as we observed in Chapter Two, if the enthusiasms of others are branded as nationalism or imperialism, one's own tend to receive more benign labels such as patriotism. Far from being 'irrational, surplus and alien', the national sensitivities of the ingroup are 'beneficial' or 'necessary' (Billig, 1995: 55). This difference between 'our' flagging of the nation and 'their' flag-waving is well illustrated by reading more from George Robertson's speech to the 21st Century Trust's 1994 conference. Having castigated nationalism at some length, he paused to observe that: 'it's not the flags which are draped on victorious Olympic athletes which exploit the base instincts – there is a natural patriotism in all of us which is warmed by the success of fellow countrymen and women'. The warmth in our national feeling could not be further from the coldness of their hatreds.

In similar vein, a more recent Conservative Party newspaper advertisement entitled 'THE DARK SIDE OF NATIONALISM' featured a sketch of a brick wall bearing the graffito 'ENGLISH GET OUT'. The text to the advert carried the slogan 'Be a patriot not a nationalist' and declared that 'Patriotism is about the love of your own country, not the loathing of someone else's' (advert appearing in *Scotland on Sunday*, 10.11.96). This contrast echoed one more fully developed by a senior Conservative activist and candidate in the run up to the 1992 election:

Extract 6

I think that patriotism is something that's outward-looking. It's the sort of expression of pride in one's country. The feelings of pride that one has in the history that's brought you to where you are. I suppose in a funny old way, the sacrifices made in the past to make the future, make the present what it is and the responsibility of us as trustees to provide something better for the future. Pride in the achievements of the Scottish people, over the ages and currently. Pride when one in contemporary economic terms can export more per capita and can achieve things in a competitive world. I see nationalism as being something with a destructive potential where you are pitting one off against the other. I find that sort of thing ugly. I find it threatening. I think it's very undesirable. I think nationalism can be an ugly force if the lid's not kept fairly well screwed down.

(Conservative candidate, interview 7)

By now, it should be clear that the distinction between supporters and opponents of nationalism does not lie in the extent to which they endorse identification with certain visions of the nation and repudiate identification with others. All praise and condemn in equal measure; it is simply that they claim the noble identifications for their own and attribute pernicious identifications to their opponents. Moreover, for anti-nationalists as for nationalists, the claim to national identity is not voiced in the abstract, as something that is allowable in general. Rather it is voiced as a personal and deeply felt claim. As the following quote from a Labour MP makes clear, for many non-nationalists in the narrow sense, there is some resentment at the implication that their Scottish identity is somehow the less:

Extract 7

One of the things which irritates me about the Scottish National Party is that they try to say they will, exclusively, represent nationalism in Scotland and of course they don't. They are only one wing of the nationalist movement in Scotland, and there are many nationalists in the Labour movement, many nationalists in the Liberal Democrats, even within the Conservatives. I mean there are many Conservatives who will regard themselves as Scottish nationalists in the extent that they believe themselves to be Scottish and want what is best for Scotland and recognize Scotland as a nation.

(Labour MP, interview 38)

Lest it be thought that such protests are unsurprising amongst supporters of devolution, consider the following two quotations from confirmed Conservative unionists, the one in a private interview and the other at a public meeting:

Extract 8

It seems to me, our political opponents are trying to render artificial Scottishness by seeking to attach some political or structural or administrative label to the name. And apart from finding that politically unacceptable, personally, I find it rather offensive because to me, my Scottishness in fact, transcends all other considerations. I just feel that it is of paramount importance and every other influence is subsidiary. And I think that is why being a Conservative, wanting to be part of a Union within the United Kingdom, is a very natural corollary of my personal feelings as a Scot . . . I think the other political parties are, as I say, artificially trying to tilt that philosophy on its head and say that you can't be Scottish unless we can stick up a whole lot of labels and signposts saying for example, 'this is an independent country', or 'here we have a parliamentary administration in Edinburgh'.

(Conservative candidate, interview 19)

Extract 9

Advocates of change have in the past been inclined to claim the emotional high-ground about the future of Scotland. They parade their Scottishness as unique to their cause. I yield to no one in my Scottishness and I believe that I do have some understanding of the needs and aspirations of the people of Scotland. I therefore yield that emotional high-ground to none. It is not anti-Scottish to be for the Union rather it is anti-Scottish to put the future of Scotland at risk . . . There is an argument which is constantly put these days that one can only be emotional about Scotland and express one's Scottishness by espousing the case of constitutional reform. I believe this to be deeply insulting to those of us who are proud to be both Scottish and British. I am proud that Scotland has played such an important role in shaping and influencing the history of the United Kingdom . . . For all of us who love Scotland, let us ensure her continuing place as a full partner within the United Kingdom. I believe our destiny must be to continue our role as a positive influence in shaping the future direction of the United Kingdom.'

(Lord Mackay, Conservative peer, speech, Bearsden, 6.3.92)

Despite the difference in rhetorical contexts the similarity between the two is striking. These characters deny being anti-Scottish because they oppose a Scottish nation-state. Rather, they claim to be against a nation-state precisely because they are and care about being Scottish. That is, their political positions are based on the claim to be Scottish and act in terms of the Scottish interest. Independence is opposed on the basis of this interest. Similar opposition can be found amongst devolutionists. To quote from Labour's George Robertson one more time:

Extract 10

But when nationalist pride spills over into ethnic superiority then it becomes ugly and dangerous and we should all beware. Across Europe today we are seeing the dark side of nationalism; the hatred, the paranoia, the racialism. Grievances dressed up as national identity. Grudges disguised as patriotism. Scotland deserves better than the slogan 'blame the English'.

(George Robertson, Labour MP, speech at annual party conference, Dundee, 12.3.94)

Here, the SNP's opposition to being part of Britain and to what it sees as English domination is construed as an anti-Englishness which demeans Scotland. It is therefore against the Scottish interest to support independence. The true Scot can have nothing to do with it. Hence, whether unionist, devolutionist or separatist, whether Conservative, Labour or SNP, all make equal claims to national identity and to act in its terms. This evidence indicates that the scope of nationalism (in the sense of basing one's claims and seeking support on the basis of national categories) cannot be limited to the political nationalists (in the sense of those who support the foundation of a nation-state). Indeed, nationalism in the latter sense can be as easily opposed as supported on the basis of nationalism in the former sense. Our first conclusion, then, concerns the ubiquitous use of national categories across the parliamentary political spectrum (and the qualifier 'parliamentary' has an importance that will become clear by the end of the chapter). As Billig (1995) puts it, if nationalism is only used in relation to separatists and to 'an extraordinary, emotional mood striking at extraordinary times' (p. 44), then we will fail to grasp the significance of the national in our everyday lives. Further, and as a corollary, people need be no less passionate about their own nationalism simply because they oppose national self-determination.

Our second conclusion concerns the manner in which national identity gains its social significance. Again, we would agree with Billig when he says that, far from constituting a particular political strategy, nationalism constitutes 'the condition for conventional strategies, whatever the politics' (Billig, 1995: 99). More specifically, all our speakers use national identity to provide the values on which 'interests' are based along with the understandings by which those interests are pursued. All equally root their appeals in the national interest.

These may seem weighty conclusions to mount on the flimsy edifice of just a few quotations. However, we would stress that this is just a starting point. Throughout this chapter and those that follow, we shall see national identity and national interest being used as the basis for appeals and arguments. In looking at how these appeals and arguments are conducted, how national identity and national interest are construed and used, it becomes easy to be dulled by familiarity and lose sight of the fact that the omnipresence of the national within our data is of significance in itself. For now, though, let us pursue the question of how national identification relates to international relations. Does love of country necessarily imply hatred of others and, if not, what does determine the relationship between different national groups? These are complicated issues and our answer must necessarily span this and the following chapter. The issues we address are under a long shadow, cast first by Nazism and, more recently, by conflicts in the former Yugoslavia. The question, already voiced by our speakers, but which will also be in the mind of the reader, is whether those who endorse national sentiment thereby bring the horrors of Sarajevo and Tuzla and Kosovo closer to fruition. Once we praise the nation, whatever nation, what stops us acting towards others as Serb towards Croatian, Bosnian Muslim or Albanian? There is, however, a dangerous assumption in this question which may, paradoxically, constitute part of the problem. It is the assumption that we start off knowing who is national and who is other and need only ask about how the one relates to the other. Such an assumption resides on the premise that nations are easily defined by reference to a set of objective, or at least consensual, criteria. Yet, as Bauman puts it, this is to end up 'deproblematizing . . . the very elusiveness and contingency of the nation's precarious existence which nationalisms try hard to conceal' (1992: 677).

Nations and others: identifying the other

Rather than asking one question about how nationals relate to others, we need to ask two. The first is how we constitute people as national or as other. Only then can we go on to ask about how 'we' relate to those constituted as other. Before Serb could turn on Croatian the notion of the two as separate had to usurp the idea that they were fundamentally similar within a single southern Slavic nation (Wachtel, 1998). Serbian and Croatian or Yugoslav? The issue of international relations clearly turns on the definition of nationhood: which national categories are used for self-definition?

The argumentative resources available for constructing a 'nation' are many and varied. The history of argument concerning the number of national categories to be found in the Iberian Peninsula illustrates something of their range and the manner of their deployment. Throughout the nineteenth century liberal politicians struggling against the overthrow of absolute dynasties construed Spain as a nation in which 'the people' were defined in terms of a common identity, a national character and soul (Alvarez Junco, 1996). Indeed, nineteenth century Spanish nationalists retrospectively construed the Peninsular War (1808–14) as the 'War of Independence', characterizing it as testimony to a Spanish love of independence which ran back two thousand years to the Celt–Iberian towns of Numantia and Saguntum and their resistance to Carthage and Rome. However, this definition of Spain as a nation was faced by another – or rather, by many others. In Andalucia, Galicia, Catalonia, the Basque country and elsewhere, alternative definitions of the national make up of the Iberian Peninsula were advanced by ideologues who provided what Smith and Mar-Molinero (1996) rather judgementally refer to as 'an exotic cocktail of racial nationalistic theories and historical exegesis which were meant to provide the passport to nationhood' (p. 7). For example, Andalucian ethologists claimed that Andalucians were an amalgam of Arab and Christian blood and so were different from their neighbours. Galician nationalists claimed a Celtic–Swabian descent and characterized themselves as a subgroup of a superior central European 'race'. Likewise, Enric Prat de la Riba (1906/1986), a leading Catalonian nationalist, argued that Catalonia deserved statehood. Accepting the argument that the nation and the state should be coextensive, he claimed that Catalonia was a nation and Spain was not. Inevitably such arguments did not go unchallenged. For example, Conservative Spanish nationalists constructed a unitary Spanish nation around the history and experience of Catholicism. In the words of one such Spanish nationalist, 'Christianity gave its unity to Spain . . . Thanks to it, we have been a Nation, even a great Nation, and not a multitude of individuals' (cited in Alvarez Junco, 1996). Under Franco the argument as to the existence and distinctiveness of the Spanish nation was given concrete expression through all manner of vehicles, including the words on the 'national' currency: coins minted in the Franco era read *'Espana: una, grande y libre'* ('Spain: one, great and free') (Williams, 1994). At the same time the status of those criteria used for defining alternatives to the Spanish nation was challenged. For example, given the importance of language in many of the nationalisms referred to above, it should come as no surprise to find that these minority (i.e., non-Castilian) languages were proscribed and ridiculed. Indeed, whereas some construed these languages as 'passports to nationhood' (Smith & Mar-Molinero, 1996: 7), the Spanish centre often characterized them as 'dialects' rather than languages. Along with 'non-standard' varieties of Castilian, these languages were dismissed as merely the speech of the uneducated and the peasantry (Mar-Molinero, 1996).

Moving closer to home, consider the complex case of Ireland. Gallagher (1995) identifies six broadly discernible positions concerning the national groupings that exist there. One of the rarest was put forward by a group calling itself the Revolutionary Marxist Group, which argued that there was no discernible national community in Ireland. Others identify an 'Irish' nation but disagree on how to conceptualize the inhabitants of Northern Ireland. For some they are Irish. For others they are British. For still others it is more complicated. Not only is the identification of Northern Irish Catholics complex, but so too is the identification of Northern Irish Protestants. Indeed, the lack of homogeneity amongst the Ulster Protestant Community (cf. Finlayson, 1996; Gallagher, 1989) suggests that whereas some 'Loyalists' conceived of Britain as the relevant 'national' category, others promoted a nationalism based on a separate Ulster.

Ulster as a nation? Loyalism as nationalist? This might seem like an Alice through the Looking Glass world, since according to popular, media and even academic understanding, the Irish conflict pits loyalists against nationalists. Yet, given the flexibility and creativity of national definitions, it only provides a dramatic case for abandoning normative uses of nationalism in favour of a more analytic investigation of the ways in which national categories are construed and used.

From such a perspective, there is much to be gained through viewing Ulster Loyalism as an instance of nationalism. Most obviously, our attention is drawn to the processes whereby a distinctive collective self-definition is advanced through all manner of media so as to mobilize those so constituted to realize certain 'historic' rights and interests. Thus Finlayson attends to how a Loyalist publication claims to document 'the historical points that give the Ulsterman his separateness and the facts that make Ulster a separate cultural and political entity – The Ulster Nation within the British Family of Nations'. He also describes how this construction of national community was literally inscribed into the physical fabric of housing estates in the form of the giant murals for which Northern Ireland is famous: one striking Belfast wall mural portrayed Cuchulain (an historical character construed as an ancient leader of the Ulster people) alongside the twin slogans 'Defender Against Irish Attacks for 2000 years' and 'The Ulster Struggle Is About Nationality' (cited in Finlayson, 1996).

A short step across the Irish Sea and one finds similar debates in relation to the national status of Scotland, England and Britain, especially (but not exclusively) in Scotland. In order to understand these debates, it is necessary to look at their historical development and the way in which a sense of Britishness came into being. According to Colley this sense gradually developed after the Union of 1707 through a series of contrasts with Catholic France, the population of which was imagined to be 'superstitious, militarist, decadent and unfree' (1992: 5). Britishness did not emerge through a blending of different regional or older national identities and a homogenization of disparate cultures. Instead, Colley describes how Britishness was 'superimposed over an array of internal differences in response to contact with the Other, and above all in response to conflict with the Other' (1992: 6).

How this emergent sense of Britishness should be conceptualized has provoked considerable debate. For example, Crick (1993, 1995) questions whether there was much evidence of the development of a sense of Britain as an imagined national community. According to Crick, Britishness did not (and need not) entail a common culture but only 'a common allegiance and a pragmatic utilitarian sense of obligation . . . there is no British way of life, only a common political culture, or that the way of life is the political culture' (1995: 173). Implying that the 'passion' of one's identification is a criterion of national identity, Neal Ascherson once put it in these terms: Britain is 'not so much a nation as a sort of authority, a manner of speaking rather than a matter of weeping' (Ascherson, 1988, cited in McCrone, 1992: 211). Indeed, the Scottish academic, commentator and activist Tom Nairn (author of *The Break-up of Britain*) is even unwilling to talk of 'Britain' and advocates the term 'Ukania' as an alternative so as to highlight the non-correspondence between state and nation and hence the category's 'artificiality' (Nairn, cited in McCrone, 1992: 210). In this it is undoubtedly successful; this 'bureaucratic gobbledegook' has, as Marquand observes, 'about as much resonance as an income tax form' (Marquand, 1995: 188).

These debates about the degree to which 'Britain' was ever, and is now, experienced as a genuinely 'national' imagined community (rather than merely as a political category) are complicated by the potential for 'Britain' to have different meanings in different locations. A respondent in Edinburgh is quite likely to differentiate between Scottishness and Britishness allowing as a possibility a duality of identification as well as identification as either Scottish or British. Indeed, a common research tool in Scottish political science is to ask which of five labels best describes the way in which respondents define themselves (i.e. 'Scottish not British', 'Mostly Scottish sometimes British', 'Scottish and British', 'Mostly British, sometimes Scottish', 'British not Scottish'). Data gathered in this manner provide ample evidence of the potential for a duality of identification. However, a respondent in London may be tempted to use 'English' and 'British' almost interchangeably, for Englishness and Britishness tend to be fused (Osmond, 1988; Taylor, 1991).

If Englishness and Britishness are sometimes fused, then it follows that when 'Britain' is said, it is often 'England' that is meant (Marquand, 1995). Marquand illustrates this slippage through reference to Mrs Thatcher's address to the Conservative Women's Conference at the height of the Falklands War in 1982. First she referred to 'we' and then to 'Britain' but then as Marquand notes the final peroration gave the game away: 'And let our nation, as it has so often in the past, remind itself and the world: 'Naught shall make us rue/ If England to herself do rest but true'. A more recent example may be found in the words of Mrs Thatcher's successor, John Major. In a speech delivered to the Conservative Group for Europe (22 April, 1993) establishing Britain's distinctiveness in relation to Europe, Major argued that: 'Fifty years from now Britain will still be a country of long shadows on county grounds, warm beer, invincible green suburbs, dog lovers and pool fillers and as George Orwell said "old maids bicycling to holy communion through the morning mist" and – if we get our way – Shakespeare still read even in schools. Britain will survive unamendable in all essentials'. As Billig observes, all such metonymic stereotyping is partial and involves exclusion. In this case, the 'evoked nation is empty of motorways, mine-shafts and mosques' (Billig, 1995: 102). Furthermore, as Billing continues, the exclusiveness of this definition is particularly striking in Scotland: the imagery of 'long shadows on county grounds' evokes the cricket pitch – a common enough sight in England but rather rare in Scotland. So too, the imagery of the 'invincible green suburbs' has much more of an English resonance than a Scottish one.

Inevitably this fusion of Englishness with Britishness by those south of the border has a series of corollaries that are of relevance for political argument amongst those north of the border. Most obviously, it threatens to undermine the willingness of the latter to define themselves as British instead of, or even as well as, Scottish. For, if 'British' is seen as merely a device to impose a hegemonic Englishness in which Scottish reality is obliterated, then it becomes a mode of domination rather than a possible form of identification. One can therefore find a tension between different formulations of nationality within the Scottish debate. At one extreme, there is an attempt to formulate Britishness as an inclusive nationality, within which the distinctions between Scottish, English and Welsh are entirely secondary. Its most passionate advocate in the 1992 election campaign was the Prime Minister, John Major.

In a speech delivered in that most English of English towns – the south coast English holiday resort of Torquay – Major argued that the question of Scotland's future 'is more than a Scottish concern. It matters in Gloucester as it matters in Glasgow' (John Major, speech, Torquay, 14.3.92). In the English midlands he defined the maintenance of the constitutional status quo as 'quite literally the national issue' (Birmingham, 30.3.92). In London, Major made his strongest plea against constitutional change:

Extract 11

There is no division in the British flag between red and blue. In it, and under it, we are one people. . . . Let me therefore speak to you simply, directly and, through you to every part of the country. As your Prime Minister, yes, but as a Briton, too . . . If I could summon up all the authority of this office I would put it into this single warning – the United Kingdom is in danger. Wake up, my fellow countrymen, wake up now, before it is too late.

(John Major MP, Conservative Prime Minister, speech, Wembley, 5.4.92)

Major's symbolic reference to the red of the English flag of St George and the blue of the Scottish flag of St Andrews construes 'Britain' as a genuinely superordinate category in which all are represented. Further, this collective self-definition is construed as a non-contingent given (it is 'the birthright of us all') and, in using the classic nationalist rhetoric of 'awakening' (cf. Gellner, 1964, 1997), he implies that this 'British' nation is an eternal being.

An associated position is to insist on Britishness as an authentic nationality (and one under threat from constitutional changes) but to place it alongside Scottish national identity.

For example, at a pre-election public meeting, the Conservative MP, Bill Walker, argued that Britishness as well as Scottishness was a personally valued identity. He confessed to his audience:

Extract 12

Now ladies and gentlemen, I get a little emotional at this point in my speech. I yield to no one in my support for Scotland and things Scottish and equally I yield to no one in my support for things British. I can get just as emotional about my Britishness as I can about my Scottishness. The two are not in opposition, they are in fact complementary. Nearly 300 years ago our ancestors created a unique combination of peoples . . . They wish to stop you being British. Whatever happens, you won't stop being Scottish, we retain that and everything else that's Scottish, we keep it forever, but what we would not keep is being British and that's why at this election you must vote Conservative.

(Bill Walker, Conservative MP, speech, Glamis, 23.3.92)

Far from merely being 'a manner of speaking', Britishness is here explicitly defined as more akin to 'a matter of weeping'. That he gets 'a little emotional' is testament to the reality of Britishness. Or to put it another way, it passes the 'passion' test. Of particular importance is the way in which Britishness is defined as compatible with Scottishness and how this is used to shape the audience's understanding of itself and its interest. If one is both Scot and Briton, one does not enhance the former by losing the latter, one merely sees part of one's being destroyed. Moreover, if identity is the basis of all one's interests then the destruction of identity undermines one's interests in general.

By contrast, the notion of complementarity often forms the focus of sustained attack, especially amongst those advocating constitutional change, by constituting Britain as England in flimsy disguise. As one SNP activist stated in interview: 'I'm a Scot and a European. "British" I really see as being English' (interview 46). Another claimed that: 'the United Kingdom is a fiction. It is in fact England with Scottish and Welsh appendages. It's the state of England' (SNP MP, interview 9). The implications of the essentially English nature of Britishness were drawn out by the former MP and prominent SNP activist, Gordon Wilson, speaking at an election meeting in St Andrews:

Extract 13

We've got to ask ourselves what is our identity. Now if you're British, that is fine you are British. You haven't yet tumbled to the fact that the rest of the world has that you're English, because they don't recognize the term British very much these days. If you're British, you're English as far as they are concerned. Being British is English and they're not terribly bothered about it. If however you are Scottish and British, then you are suffering from a bad case of schizophrenia. You can't be both, not when it's the turn of loyalty and so forth.

(Gordon Wilson, SNP activist, speech, St Andrews, 31.3.92)

For Wilson, the adoption of a British identification is deeply problematic. Not only is Britishness equated with Englishness, but the language of mental health and the popular imagery of schizophrenia is used to imply that Britishness and Scottishness must necessarily pull one in different directions. Others, drawing on more radical nationalist traditions, explained the opposition between Britishness and Scottishness in terms of political oppression. Britishness is the form taken by English colonialism. Thus, a visiting Plaid Cymru speaker addressing the 1993 SNP annual conference was well received when he characterized the Scots and the Welsh as struggling 'for self-determination' – 'the most basic of all human rights' in the 'dying years of the final two British colonies'. He continued:

Extract 14

Let us work together to free our nations from the imperialist shackles. We've both had enough of colonial government and its abhorrent paternalism and denial of democracy. The democratic deficit, as it is known, has never been so great as the present time. But the important point is that people in Scotland and in Wales are realizing it. Our countries are witnessing the dying embers of the Raj in the British Isles.

(Elfyn Llwyd, Plaid Cymru MP, SNP annual conference, Dunoon, 25.9.93)

Thus, in Scotland, as in Ireland, as in Spain, as in Yugoslavia and many other places besides, the question of who is other (and hence of how we relate to the other) cannot be settled in advance. The issue of international relations cannot be addressed until the identity of the nations in question has been settled. Whether the Scottish–English relationship is inter- or intra-group obviously depends upon whether one accepts or repudiates a British identity. Having said that, the definition of national categories may be necessary but it is clearly not sufficient to determine international relations. Given a division into national and other is accepted, what then determines how one relates to other categories and other category members? This is the question to which we address ourselves in the next chapter.

In this chapter, our focus will remain on the prior question of how – and when – we see ourselves in terms of national identities along with the way in which national identity underpins all manner of political projects. Yet, as always, phenomena are best understood by reference to their limit conditions. We understand how national identity is used by examining when it is not used. In this context we can now redeem a pledge made earlier. In stressing that the use of national identity and national interest was general across the parliamentary political spectrum, we promised to draw out the significance of the term 'parliamentary'. It has to do with the relationship between politics, mobilization and the conditions under which different types of category are used. So before we close this chapter let us consider a rather different sort of politics: the politics of class. On the one hand, this should illustrate something of the degree to which the categories relevant to self-definition, the identification of 'interest' and the determination of political action, are contestable. On the other hand, the mere fact that national categories are not the only politically significant categories highlights the importance of analysing nationalism as an ideological process in which the adoption of national categories is contingent upon particular sorts of argument and particular sorts of project in particular structural contexts.

Non-national politics

In a context where 'the nation' is so familiar, those who propose alternative self-categories and alternative constructions of 'interest' must, of necessity, seek to problematize 'the nation' at the same time as advancing their preferred alternative. This is a task which is not only faced by those on the left inspired by *The Communist Manifesto*'s dictum that the working class has 'no country'. Feminists too have sought to develop alternative categories of belonging. In this many have no doubt been inspired by Virgina Woolf's declaration that 'As a woman I have no country. As a woman, I want no country. As a woman, my country is the whole world' (1943: 197). Certainly the diverse contributions to the Scottish feminist magazine – *Harpies & Quines* – illustrate something of the challenge to the relevance of national identity. As one woman put it: 'national identity is much over-rated . . . I am a feminist first, not a woman, and a socialist first, not a Scot . . . Unite with the people who share your ideas not your accent or your genitals' (*Harpies & Quines* no. 6 April/May, 1993: 45). However, many other contributors disagreed. Even here the national imagination had considerable purchase.

This purchase is exemplified by the personal trajectory of Regis Debray, which, in some measure, mirrors the ideological trajectory of the late twentieth century. In his youth he followed, and was even imprisoned with, Che Guevara. Debray later moved to a position he himself describes as 'left-wing Gaullist' in what is close both to a personal apologia and a hagiography of the General (Debray, 1994). In it, Debray writes that 'Che's defeat made me understand that the World Revolution is not a mother country, that in the long run national connections count for more than class or ideological commitments' (p. x). And then, later on: 'At the heart of every historic gamble lies a decision on what is and what is not useful to define as real. A separation of the absurd from the serious stuff. De Gaulle opted for the spirit of peoples: we chose legal conventions and programmes based on *isms*. He won his bet; we have lost ours' (p. 63).

There are two aspects to Debray's claim. The first is that politics and mobilization are as much a matter of creating reality as a response to reality. Nation is not a place but a call, as Debray – interpreting De Gaulle – puts it. This is true not only of the nation but of any collectivity. There is no human grouping and no attendant set of practices that exist automatically without being brought into being. So, as Przeworski (1980) makes clear, a similarity of class position does not necessarily entail any sense of class solidarity or collective identity as 'workers' with 'workers' interests'. Indeed, the logic of capitalist social relations is that individual workers are positioned so as to compete with each other and it is only through adopting a collective identity as 'workers' that certain conceptions of 'interest' are possible. 'Class interest' is therefore 'something attached to workers as a collectivity rather than as a collection of individuals, their "group" rather than "serial" interest' (Przeworski, 1980: 37).

The second aspect of what Debray says has to do with the concept of 'useful'. For Debray, 'use' is principally to do with spiritual qualities of memory and imagination and hence engagement. We would not deny that there may be certain features of the national imaginary that are particularly adept at engaging us as subjects; the linkage between ourselves and both previous and future generations may articulate with a variety of desires for rootedness and immortality. However, it must be stressed that national identities are constructions. In addition, we must not dismiss the possibility of other categories partaking of the dimensions that facilitate engagement. Most importantly, we would stress that 'use' is principally related to practical rather than metaphysical matters.

If categories are the tools of mobilization, then what is useful resolves to what categories will achieve the form of mobilization necessary to the ends in view; what categories will move the people who need to be moved and move them in ways they need to move. In the former respect, if not in the latter, all parliamentary politicians and all those who pursue an electoralist strategy have much in common. As we have argued, in an era of universal suffrage, this strategy is entirely dependent upon winning over the largest possible section of the electorate as a whole. If one appeals to only one section at the expense of others, failure is almost inevitable. One cannot, for instance, use class categories and address oneself to concerns specific to 'workers' as a collectivity. Rather one must use more general categories and appeal to what such workers 'share as individuals with members of other classes' (Przeworski, 1980: 43). The most obvious category, which addresses all the actual and potential voters in a territory, is nationhood. In this sense, nation is not so much a call rather than a place, but a call to all those in the national place.

It follows from this that, when one seeks to mobilize a constituency which transcends national boundaries then supra-national categories will be employed, and when one seeks to mobilize specific categories within the nation, then sub-national categories will be used. A graphic example of the former comes from the Gulf War of 1990–1. On 20 August 1990, shortly after Iraqi forces had moved into Kuwait, George Bush, then the American President, declared that 'we need the oil. It's nice to talk about standing up for freedom but Kuwait and Saudi Arabia are not exactly democracies'. Yet, on 16 October, the President was complaining that 'some people never get the word. The fight isn't about oil, the fight is about naked aggression'. This perspective had been presaged in Bush's famous 'new world order' speech to the United Nations on 1 October. In the speech, he characterized the nature of the conflict as follows:

> The present aggression in the Gulf is a menace not only to one region's security but to the entire world's vision of our future. It threatens to turn the dream of a new world order into a grim nightmare of anarchy in which the law of the jungle supplants the law of nations. [Bush went on to define more explicitly the sides in the conflict] Our quarrel is not with the people of Iraq. We do not wish for them to suffer. The world's quarrel is with the dictator who ordered that invasion. (Reicher, 1991, 1993)

The rhetorical shift from August to October makes sense in terms of the emerging American strategy. To define the issue in terms of oil implies a distinction between an 'us' who need oil and a 'them' who produce it. In other words it places the Western industrialized countries in opposition to the Arab world. However, the Americans quickly decided on the need to mobilize an international coalition, including Arab countries, which would sanction sending American troops to the Middle East in order to drive the Iraqis out of Kuwait. It would be plainly impossible to mobilize an ingroup including the Arab countries using a rhetoric which cast them as part of the outgroup. Hence the shift to a more inclusive rhetoric where Arabs were part of the global ingroup and Saddam Hussein alone formed the outgroup.

To use supra-national categories may be possible for elected politicians as long as it subsumes the national interest. Using sub-national categories is more difficult since, in seeming to support one section of the population, one may lose others. Hence, rather than seeking to find electoral politicians switching from the national to sub-national categories we may instead expect to find the latter usage amongst those pursuing non-electoral strategies.

Consider the case of the British Miners' Strike of 1984–5. In this, possibly the most significant trade union dispute of post war British history, one might expect to find a wealth of class constructions amongst Labour, if not Conservative politicians. True to form, Conservative Prime Minister Margaret Thatcher turned the nationalist rhetoric honed against Argentina in the Falklands War two years earlier into an onslaught on the so-called 'enemy within' – the leadership of the miners' union. They, the perpetrators of the strike, were portrayed as an alien, undemocratic and un-British influence who deserved the enmity rather than the solidarity of others.

But, when Neil Kinnock (Labour's leader) dealt with the strike in his address to the 1984 Party Conference, he did more to match than to contest Thatcher's categories. In Kinnock's account, the strikers were representative of ordinary people under attack from privilege and arrogance as personified by Thatcher herself. Hence, rather than being targeted by the strike, strikers represented the entire people who were being targeted by Thatcher and her government. While 'Britishness' was explicitly referenced only occasionally, there were indications that, in what Billig (1995) calls the deixis of small words, 'the' people were not just any people but that the reference was to those in Britain. For instance, at the start of a long list of examples of how Thatcherism constituted an attack on people,

Kinnock mentioned that 'this was the year, too, when tax was introduced on fish and chips' (Kinnock, 1992: 60). Kinnock is referring to the introduction of a sales tax on take away foods of all sorts, but he chooses to describe it in terms of the nearest thing to a national dish – kebabs or chop sueys would have had less of a symbolic resonance!

Even Tony Benn MP, Labour's most prominent left-winger and most vocal supporter of the miners, sought to use similarly generalized categories. Although he employed the language of class solidarity at one level, addressing the conference as 'comrades', he declared that 'I believe that the miners are fighting for us all' (Labour Party, 1984: 44). He then explained that what he meant by this was that the miners were fighting 'to defend democracy . . . to defend the jobs and services that parliament created for us . . . to defend civil and human rights' (ibid.). This may be a radical–democratic vision, but it is hardly a class one since it is relevant to all the population.

In sum, there is a similarity in the scope of the categories used by all the parliamentary speakers despite the political gulf between them, despite the fact that they characterized the category content in different ways and despite their differences with regard to who represented the category and who stood against it. More or less explicitly, the category is always national and the argument concerns how that category should be used, not whether it should be used. Contrast this with the speech to Labour's Conference given by the leader of the National Union of Mineworkers, Arthur Scargill. He stated that his union was 'not fighting for the NUM, not fighting for jobs of miners, but fighting against the whole concept of this government's economic policy which is designed to destroy jobs and wreak havoc amongst the British labour and trade union movement'. He went on, rather poignantly in retrospect, to assert that 'the miners union is winning this fight and it is not only winning for miners, but for you and the entire Labour and trade union movement' (Labour Party, 1984: 34). Here, the category is class. Scargill was concerned with winning a dispute not winning an election, and he saw the route to success as lying in sympathy action by other unions. Those that he sought to mobilize to action were workers in other industries and the categories he employed were designed to achieve just such a mobilization.

If a pursuit of politics by means other than election could entail the rejection of national categories in the case of the Miners' Strike, the same is true in relation to Englishness and Scottishness more generally. The largest non-electoralist party of the left in the UK is the Socialist Workers Party (SWP). The Party did not itself put candidates forward for office, but promoted a politics of industrial and collective action. Although, in the 1992 election, the SWP did call for a Labour vote, it saw this as a means of raising class consciousness and class confidence and so coupled its electoral advice with a call to 'build a socialist alternative' which would realize workers' interests. The party sought to mobilize action at a class level and likewise constituted social reality at a class level. If, for the parliamentary parties, the election was about the Union or about Scotland, the SWP demurred. According to Chris Bamberry, one of the Party leadership, speaking at a pre-election rally in Dundee, it was about one word: 'one word which Margaret Thatcher certainly thought was a word that had ceased to exist anymore during the

1980s. One word which you wouldn't have heard Neil Kinnock or John Smith uttering just a few weeks ago. One word which most of us, the people in the left, had given up using. And that word is very simply CLASS' (Chris Bamberry, SWP activist, speech, 26.3.92). Moreover, he sought to characterize the category as not something dreamt up for himself, but as something characterizing the understanding of voters themselves. If Labour saw support for themselves as a vote for devolution, for social justice or whatever, Bamberry claimed that it was plain to employers as for workers that a Labour vote was a class act. In short, 'the bosses' knew that:

Extract 15

When people vote Labour they actually are identifying themselves as being working class. They are identifying themselves. There's them. We're pro-Labour. We're pro-trade union. We're working class. And there's us. That divide's there and it's something that worries the ruling class'.

(Chris Bamberry, SWP, speech, Dundee, 26.3.92)

If class was the issue, and if it was an issue recognized by all, the nation must be an epiphenomenon. Time and again the speech and ensuing discussion returned to the issue of Scotland's relationship with England, and whether the analysis offered by the SNP captured 'reality'. For example, one member of the audience argued that the SNP's characterization of the context in terms of national categories was wrong because voting patterns of northern England were much the same as in Scotland. He concluded that political difference was not a matter of Scotland and England. Instead, there was 'a North–South divide'.

Bamberry countered: 'I don't think the divide is North and South'. For him, the real division was class. Rather than the Scots having something in common in contrast to the English, Scotland like England was riven by class divides. Scotland was described as particularly polarized: 'within the British state, I think Scotland is actually one of the places with the most naked open class divisions. You know people go on about the South East of England. I think a walk through Edinburgh teaches what naked class division is'. However, England too, including those areas often portrayed as particularly prosperous at the expense of Scotland, was polarized. Thus the South East was characterized by 'massive obvious class divisions' and London was described as 'a seething bloody cesspit of class divisions and again poverty and wealth side by side'. Even where there appeared to be territorial homogeneity, and stereotypes of people from particular areas, this was merely an artefact of a particular class composition and associated class prejudices. Thus Bamberry complained that:

Extract 16

People go on about Essex-man and Essex-woman. It makes me bloody annoyed. Essex is the county of Dagenham, Tilbury – the Docks. It is the county that saw the Colchester,

> *the upheavals in Colchester about the Poll Tax. The people that make these jokes about the people they call Sharon, you know the high-heels, the typists and all the rest of it that come from Essex into the city of London to do shit, low-paid work, low wages as alienating as Timex. It is anti-working class. Essex is populated by those people.*
>
> (Chris Bamberry, SWP, speech, Dundee, 26.3.92)

In this, Bamberry not only stresses class differences within the same nation, but also the fundamental commonality between those of the same class in different nations. Essex workers have the same experience as workers in Dundee's Timex factory, later to be subject to a major strike. For him, then, all talk of territorial identities in general and national identities in particular was a distraction from real similarities and differences of class. But the point is that, for all that class was regarded as the reality, it was far from self-evident. Class practices had to be brought into existence in part at least through the use of class categories. People had to be urged to combine according to class and to resist combining with those outside their class. Apparent differences of nation had to be recast as real similarities of class (and vice versa).

If the SWP's rhetoric provides a particularly stark reminder of the danger in taking nation for granted, there is also a danger that we fail to represent the complex articulations that are possible between class and nation. While the SWP scorns the parliamentary and council chamber and restricts its actions to the street and the factory floor, there are others who have a foot in both electoral and activist politics. Similarly, while SWP speakers portray class and nation as polar opposites there are others who see them as intertwined.

One SNP MP, who defined himself as a socialist, squared his nationalism with support for working class politics through arguing that class and nation were not orthogonal. More specifically he declared that his ambition was:

Extract 17

To liberate the Scottish working class from the constraints that there are upon them. I have no animus against the Scottish middle class. You see Scotland is a very peculiar society. We are an egalitarian people. I mean the whole atmosphere is infused with that basic idea and that affects other folk outside the working class . . . We just feel working class very very naturally.

(SNP MP, interview 9)

Now consider a speech by Harry McLevy, a prominent trades union activist, but also a leading supporter of a Scottish parliament. From the other side of the fence, here is an organizer of workers' action who is also an advocate of nationalism. He is speaking to a large rally gathered in support of sacked Timex workers. In this context the tension between class and nation might seem even more acute. McLevy however, argued that the Timex struggle was representative of a wider struggle for the 'restoration of democratic rights to the British people. And part of those democratic rights is to end the democratic deficit here in Scotland and have a Scottish Parliament here in Scotland elected by the Scottish people'. Given the values of Scottish people, this meant that:

Extract 18

a Parliament reflecting the reality of Scottish politics would be on our side, and if I was a Timex worker or a miner or a steel worker or any other worker calling for the right to work I'd sleep sounder in my bed if I knew if we had that type and that character of a Parliament here in Britain. To our friends who have come from all parts of Britain and to those of you who think that such a Parliament or development would divide the British Labour movement, I say to you that if that were true the Tories would have granted one decades ago. The opposite, the opposite is true: that such a Parliament would be on the side of workers everywhere in Britain that were fighting for their democratic rights.

(Harry McLevy, speech, demonstration in support of sacked Timex workers, City Square, Dundee, 20.3.93)

For both speakers, then, one might say that there is working-class hegemony in Scotland. The category may be national but it is defined by working-class values of solidarity, equality and support for the weak. Thus expressions of Scottishness are expressions of working-class interest and to achieve parliamentary status on the basis of Scottish identity would constitute a defence of working-class interests. The categories of nation and class are complementary not contradictory. Where McLevy goes further than the SNP MP cited in Extract 17, possibly because his audience includes activists who have travelled up from England, is in arguing that a Scottish parliament would not only defend Scottish workers, would not abandon English workers, but rather would serve to advance the interests of all workers throughout Britain.

It is important to note how McLevy describes the Timex struggle as well as the nature of a Scottish Parliament such as to achieve a consonance between the two (and more widely, between workers' action and the fight for national structures). For him, Timex was a struggle for the restoration of democratic rights in the workplace. It therefore fits easily with the general fight for democratic rights in the form of the Parliament. Equally, McLevy like the previously cited SNP MP defines Scottish values as workers' values – although this is implicit in the former and explicit in the latter – and therefore the struggle for the Parliament is entirely germane to a demonstration in defence of workers. Thus, the relevance of national categories in this context is achieved through a particular characterization of Scottishness. An understanding of how workers are mobilized in support of constitutional change and how Scots are mobilized in favour of strikers depends upon the ways in which the values and norms that characterize Scotland are defined. However, this is beginning to stray on the subject matter of Chapter Five.

Before concluding this chapter, there is one more point that we need to underline. In demonstrating the articulation of nation and class, the examples of

Extracts 17 and 18 also show that it is possible to support workers' interests and to solicit workers' support without necessarily using the category of worker or class. Thus, our argument cannot be dismissed as a truism – that class politics demands class categories. That plainly isn't so. Rather, the choice of categories relates to the nature of the mobilization through which class politics are to be pursued. Nation is therefore crucial to politicians not because they are right or left but because they use an electoral strategy, just as alternatives to the nation don't depend upon the rejection of any particular politics but upon strategies which require an alternative constituency.

Conclusion

The point of departure for this chapter concerned the nature of nationalism and the question of the implications of national identification for action. As we proceeded to address this issue we found ourselves forced to widen our focus and query assumptions which would otherwise inhibit and constrain our progress. Most obviously we saw that, even before we investigated how nationals relate to others, there was a need to interrogate the manner in which people were constituted as fellow nationals or as other. More specifically we saw that there was argument and counter-argument concerning the existence and relevance of Britain as a national identification.

Yet, if our progress has necessarily entailed a somewhat circuitous route, there are a series of interim observations that may be noted. Perhaps the most obvious constant in the extracts we have provided is the ubiquity of identity talk. When proposals are made and interests either stated or implied, it is always in relation to some sort of subject. We have just stressed that this might not always be a national subject, but if it isn't, it is a class subject or a gendered subject or some other alternative. So, while the nature of the category may be open to argument and the definition of a given category may be open to argument and while the impact of events or others upon the category may be open to argument, identity occupies a pivotal role in all the arguments. Empirically, as well as theoretically, it seems that one cannot suggest or advance an interest without, implicitly or explicitly, having a subject of interest.

Another constant lies in the relationship between identity, interest and mobilization. Again it may be obvious, but it is nonetheless worth stating that there is a consonance between the nature of the categories used by a speaker and the constituency that the speaker is attempting to mobilize. There is also a consonance between the definition of category values and hence category interests on the one hand and the ends to which category members are being mobilized on the other. It seems fair, on these grounds, to stick with our notion of politicians as entrepreneurs of identity and to persist in investigating the link between identity and mobilization.

With regard to the more specific issue of nations and nationalism there are several points to emphasize. One has to do with our constant theme that nations both make and are made by nationalism. Often both are true but in different places and at different times. In Scotland, in the period we were studying, both are true in the same place and at the same time. This was a period when many national institutions and practices organized everyday life but a national parliament was lacking. The existing structures underpinned the clamour of nationalist talk. At the same time, certain specific constructions of Scottishness and its disadvantage in the Union were used to mobilize a movement that sought constitutional change, whether that was devolution or independence.

In relation to the clamour of nationalist talk, there are two further points to be made concerning the way that nationalism is conceptualized. The first is that there is a danger in equating particular political projects with the importance of national identity. It is not just the advocates of independence who assert the value and importance of Scottishness. Political separation is just one way one can invoke the nation and its interest. One can just as well use that interest to oppose statehood. Indeed to suppose that national identity is only satisfied through particular forms of arrangement is to reify a specific understanding of the nation. It is thereby to lose our ability to analyse the ways in which different definitions of nation can be used to advance different types of arrangement.

The second observation is that, because so many invoke the nation, it becomes difficult to make general statements about how national identity has consequences for the treatment of others. With every additional extract showing the centrality of the nation, a paradox grows. On the one hand, the popular image of nationalism is of something which is extraordinary, unsavoury and disturbing. Yet on the other, the routine invocation of the nation evidenced in our extracts confirms Anderson's (1983) argument that the 'nation' is one of the most universally accepted categories for political action. The point of course is that when academic analyses define nationalism in terms of particular characteristics (such as a dislike of foreigners) they fail to consider the specificity of national identity and the contingent nature of specific identity definitions, and so lose the plot. Debray puts the point trenchantly when he insists that different constructions of the national lead in entirely different directions. While it might be true that 'nationalism is a hideous evil which, since its appearance two centuries ago, has disfigured mankind and the planet', nonetheless 'those who attack nationalism at random are like experts on the Dreyfus affair who use the same word to describe the pro-Dreyfus and anti-Dreyfus camps. Hardly the best way to clarify things' (1994: 75).

This brings us back to the issue of 'interest'. If all those pursuing electoral success define interest by reference to national identity, then the way events and people are evaluated will be in relation to their impact on this identity: do they enhance it or do they threaten it? In consequence, do they promote or endanger our interests? And therefore are we to view them as a good thing or a bad thing? To take one specific issue, and hence to introduce the topic of the next chapter, international relations will depend on the way in which the national other is seen to impact on the national self.

4 National Identity and International Relations

National identification and intergroup relations

For many nationalism 'builds its love with hate, its solidarity with exclusiveness, and its intensity of feeling with a narrowness of sympathy and understanding' (Kitching, 1985: 116). Such a characterization of the relationship between ingroup identification and outgroup derogation would certainly be familiar to many in social psychology. Although not concerned with the specifics of national identity, psychologists often proceed on the assumption that it is possible to discover generic relationships between group membership and treatment of the outgroup and between ingroup identification and intergroup tension. Indeed, in Chapter Two we observed that there is a danger that social identity theory may be read so as to imply that ingroup identification inevitably leads, via social comparison, to discrimination against the outgroup. On this basis, psychologists with an interest in nationalism are then led to ask such generic questions as whether individual identifications with regional, national and supra-national categories are positively or negatively related (cf. Breakwell & Lyons, 1996). Or else, to return to contact theory (Hewstone & Brown, 1986) they wonder whether contact between group members that stresses the group dimension is more or less likely to enhance intergroup relations than contact where the individuality of participants is stressed.

Our argument throughout is that all depends upon the specific meanings accorded to specific identities and to the encounters between those of different identities. Since identity provides the norms and the values which determine what is valuable to the subject (in other words, what is in their self-interest), we would expect identity definitions to relate to the treatment of others in two ways. In certain cases, the category may be construed in such a way as to invoke certain general values about the treatment of others – we are a tolerant nation; we are a nation which embraces otherness; we are above prejudice – as, for example, in George Robertson's claim that Scotland deserves better than the slogan 'blame the English' (quoted in Chapter Three, Extract 10). More directly, however, one can manage orientation to the other by defining their impact upon one's collective interest. If say, they enhance the national interest, they are to be embraced; if they threaten the national interest they are to be rejected. This means that one can view others positively as well as negatively and also that one can view some others positively while viewing different others negatively. All depends upon the way in which the national interest is construed, the way the other is construed and hence the nature of the relationship between the two of them. We would therefore expect those who wish to manage the orientation of a national audience towards others to do so by defining such relationships. Let us look at some of the ways in which this is done, specifically in relation to Scottishness.

The most obvious way is to take the nature of the national interest for granted and simply to stress the benign or else pernicious influence of the other. As we might expect, unionists – those who make claim to Scottish identity but also promote Britishness – argue that being part of Britain has allowed Scottishness to flourish. We will use John Major to make the point, but first it is necessary to allay a possible criticism. In using Major here, we may appear to be self-contradictory. After all, we used him in the previous chapter to show that Britain (rather than Scotland) can be used as the appropriate national identification (Chapter Three, Extract 11). How can we now use him to argue that Scotland is the nation but that its interest is facilitated through the British union? The answer is simply that the contradiction lies in the nature of argument itself rather than in the nature of our argument (cf. Billig, 1987). If identity arguments, like other arguments, are used strategically, they will vary as a function of audience and of project. It is, perhaps, significant that Major was in Edinburgh rather than London when he declaimed:

Extract 1

No one asked in those years whether the statesmen, the administrators, the men and women of industry and the arts, the writers and the law-givers who came from these shores were Scottish, English, Irish or Welsh. It was enough that they came from this United Kingdom. It was enough that they carried our language, our laws, our principles, our civilization. Together our nations have been far, far greater than the sum of their parts. Separate, we could never have changed the face of the half the world. But together we did. Although we achieved this together, no one, once they set foot on these islands, could doubt that the identity of each of our nations persisted and thrived.
(John Major MP, Conservative Prime Minister, speech, Edinburgh, 25.3.92)

The term 'nations', as used here, clearly puts national identity at the level of being Scottish, English, Irish, Welsh (Scotland notably given first place). It is through their alliance in Britain that each identity thrived in itself and that the enterprises of each flourished. The implication, of course, is that, if Britain promotes the Scottish interest, devolution or independence would undermine it.

Others are more explicit on this point. Mary Scanlon, a Conservative candidate speaking in our own home village, asserted the support of her party for Scottish identity and rejected the notion that SNP leaders in an independent parliament could promote it to any greater extent: 'We believe in Scotland, we believe in the character, the identity, the legal system, the culture of Scotland and everything that's Scottish. We believe we're born Scottish, live Scottish and die Scottish and we'll be no more Scottish with Jim Sillars and Alex Salmond sitting in a Scottish parliament' (Mary Scanlon, Conservative candidate, speech, Newport-on-Tay, 20.3.92). Or again, a Conservative peer stressed how Scottish institutions had been guaranteed by the Union and would be undermined by any form of Scottish parliament, devolved or independent: 'I do not believe that the development of these or their continued success, depends on having another layer of government in Scotland. Indeed, I believe the talent of the Scottish people is fostered better the less legislation there is' (Lord Mackay, Conservative peer, speech, Bearsden, 6.3.92). Indeed, referring to the so called Scottish enlightenment of the eighteenth century – the period of David Hume, John Stuart Mill and Adam Ferguson – he went on to suggest that Scotland began to thrive precisely when the Scottish parliament merged with Westminster: 'It may be interesting to note that our academic institutions flourished and received much worldwide acclaim when the politicians left Edinburgh and went off to London leaving the intellectual brilliance of the Scots to shine out across the world!'

However, it was the maverick Conservative MP Nicholas Fairbairn who put the point most colourfully. He too invoked the enlightenment as a measure of how Scotland flourished in Britain, and then invoked the symbolism of diet to describe what Scotland had been before the Union and would be again were independence allowed to turn the clock back:

Extract 2

Once again we would be a state in ruin. An oatmeal republic. And that's what our national foods are: oatmeal, oatcakes, porridge, broth, haggis, bagpipes, and whisky. They're all made out of the waste grain and the bits of animal you cannot sell. They are the symbols of a peasant economy which Scotland was before the Union. And that's what we would be again after it if lunacy enabled this country to be smashed to pieces and rent asunder.

(Sir Nicholas Fairbairn, Conservative MP, speech, Longforgan, 2.4.92)

The historical importance of oats in the Scottish diet has often been observed (for example, the English satirist Samuel Johnson (1979) had once defined oats as 'a grain, which in England is generally given to horses, but in Scotland supports the people') and is here used to offer a striking re-characterization of such celebrated Scottish symbols as haggis, bagpipes, and whisky. From such a position there is no tension at all between stressing one's Scottish identity (Fairbairn, for instance, was well-known for his self-designed tartan dress) and stressing one's attachment to Britain and other Britons. Even if the English, Welsh and Irish have different national identities, these others allow one to be, to express, and to have pride in, one's Scottishness. Otherness does not equate to foe, but to friend. If a contrast is needed, we have already seen it in the previous chapter where a 'colonial' construction was used by a Plaid Cymru MP addressing the SNP (Chapter Three, Extract 14). These words merely echoed a construction frequently used amongst SNP sympathizers, members, activists and representatives. We encountered many references to the Secretary of State for Scotland as the 'Governor General' and it was not uncommon to hear Scotland being described as one of the last colonies of the British Empire.

For example, Billy Kay, a well-known author and broadcaster active in the campaigns for constitutional change, argued that the 'the Scots aren't any different from other culturally colonized peoples' and that the Scottish psyche was damaged by the Union. Speaking at a public meeting he argued:

Extract 3

Franz Fanon always described the North Africans as 'The Wretched of the Earth', and to a lesser extent, but in some ways in a more insidious way, we are 'The Wretched of North Europe', because if you live in a culture where in a couple of centuries your education system hasn't taught you your own history, your own literature, your own language and taught you to think of them as inferior, then you've got big problems. The Catalans have got the same problem, they recognize it'll take generations of them empowering their people to get rid of what they call the 'slave mentality'.

(Billy Kay, speech, Newport-on-Tay, 1.9.92)

Kay's argument, and his use of Fanon, echoes Beveridge and Turnbull's influential text *The Eclipse of Scottish Culture* (1989) in which they invoke the process of 'inferiorization' to characterize the English–Scottish relationship as one in which the Scots psyche has been progressively colonized by a powerful metropolitan centre. Yet, Kay's characterization of the Scots as 'The Wretched of North Europe' is particularly striking and, along with his reference to a 'slave mentality', works to define the Union as undermining the Scots' self-belief and ability to perceive that which is in their national self-interest. The power of the formulation is that it suggests not only that the British connection subordinates Scottish to English interests but it also deprives Scots of the ability to resist. It is an account of utter degradation.

Our argument, much like that in the previous chapter, is that both unionist and separatist speakers make equal claim to Scottish identity and that they equally base their positions on the Scottish interest. What is novel is the demonstration that their pro- or anti-Britishness cannot be traced to whether Scottishness is invoked or not. It is more convincingly traced to their specific constructions of the way in which Britain impinges on Scottish interests. While the evidence we have produced may be compatible with such an argument, the sceptic could easily retort by challenging our assumption of equivalent identification. Even if unionists protest their national allegiance, it is clearly more important and more passionate for the separatist. All we have shown is that as national identification increases, so the call to reject others and the opposition to wider identifications also increases. Such an objection may have some plausibility based on unionist and separatist views of England. However, it clearly falls on the issue of Europe.

Whatever the term 'Europe' refers to, it is undoubtedly undergoing change. The social transformation of the old Eastern bloc has entailed a re-definition of the national categories that constitute Europe. So too, the activities of the EU have contributed to a changing sense of the social categories that are relevant to self-definition. Whether through the introduction of a single currency, the production of a common European flag, the adoption of a European anthem (taken from Beethoven's 'Ode to Joy'), or through the commemoration of community history in postage stamps, the EU Commission is actively seeking to construct and disseminate a sense of a European identity. Indeed, Shore (1992) describes how there was a proposal that European athletes in the Olympic games should wear the EC logo on their tracksuit sleeves so as to create, in the words of one official, 'a double sense of belonging; being British and being European.'

As the very public arguments within the British Labour and Conservative Parties demonstrate, there has been considerable debate about the degree to which a European identification is compatible with a national identification. Much of this debate has taken as its reference point a specific identity: Britishness. However, the relationship between Europe and Scottishness has also received much attention. Inevitably this debate has been shaped by developments which have changed Britain's relationship with Europe. For example, as the development of the very concept of 'Britain' was so closely linked to a contrast with a predominantly Catholic Europe (Colley, 1992), it was inevitable that changes in Britain's relationship with Europe would have far-reaching implications for people's understandings of the social relations within Britain. As the concept of a 'Europe of the Regions' (Harvie, 1994) developed, the question of Scotland's relationship with Europe became inextricably linked with arguments about the meaningfulness and political significance of Britain. The potential of these debates for shaping self-definition are enormous. In the words of a representative from Wales, 'there is the opportunity to pull Wales out of a British way of thinking. We are no longer obliged to think of ourselves as a minority within Britain, but as part of the varied pattern of Europe' (1989 European Election address from the Welsh 'nationalist' Plaid Cymru MP, Dafydd Elis Thomas, cited in Bowie, 1993: 191).

Inevitably the evolution of the debate concerning Scotland's relationship with Britain and Europe has been gradual. In the 1975 UK referendum on membership of the 'Common Market', the SNP campaigned against the UK's continued membership, but subsequently was won over to championing 'Europe'. Indeed, at the 1988 SNP Conference, the party voted for the policy of 'Independence in Europe' as its main election theme (Marr, 1992). For our purposes here, it is important to note that this pro-European stance – proposed by the leadership and endorsed by the membership (by an overwhelming majority of eight to one) undermines the notion of generalized 'nationalist' exclusivity and chauvinistic intolerance of others. Indeed, it was argued that the policy of 'Independence in Europe' would mean that 'We'll be in a NEW Union . . . with the whole of the EC. Giving us a place at the top table. And we'll have a stronger friendship with England as EQUAL partners in the EC' (SNP election newsletter, Scotland First, 1992. Emphasis in the original). Moreover, it is equally important to note that the support for Europe was premised upon the way it was construed as compatible with, if not necessary for, the pursuit of Scottish interests. Thus, some SNP speakers were at pains to stress that their embrace of Europe reflected a characteristic internationalism. In other words, the national identity included a general value which governed their view of alliances with others. Andrew Welsh MP, addressing an eve of poll rally, argued that Scots were temperamentally unionist, the only question was which Union: 'Scotland has always had an internationalist outlook. I mean sovereignty is actually a problem for the English. It's not a problem for us.

We pooled our sovereignty with the English in a common market three hundred years ago and what we are now saying is we wish to regain that sovereignty to once again pool it in a wider three hundred million European community' (Andrew Welsh, SNP MP, speech, Arbroath, 8.4.92).

Another SNP MP, Winnie Ewing, likewise stressed Scotland's ingrained internationalism, but went further in suggesting why the European Union should prevail over the Union Jack. That is, because Europe shares more of what makes Scotland Scottish than England, not only in terms of values and spirit (notably, internationalism itself) but also in terms of institutions and experiences:

Extract 4

The view of the UK is that they are half-hearted. De Gaulle said years after UK entry: 'England has not yet joined the Community'. For once I don't mind the misuse of the term 'England'. Scotland on the other hand is a European nation in spirit and history. Bruce's first act was to join the Hanseatic League. Our students went regularly to Leiden, Paris, Bologna, Vallollidad. We have a Euro system of law. We had an Alliance with France for 800 years, with joint citizenship – a forerunner of the EC itself. In 1707 we got England and lost Europe. It was not a good bargain!

(Winnie Ewing, SNP MEP, speech at SNP annual conference, 25.9.93)

The significance of these references to similarities of constitution (in the various senses of the word) is that they represent the preconditions for working together to promote the common interest. Only if the larger body values the same things as the nation can the enterprises of the one constitute goods for the other. The corollary is that, where constitutions differ, the successes of the former are either irrelevant to, or else actively negate, the interests of the other. That is why getting England at the expense of Europe is considered, in Ewing's terms, to be a bad bargain.

Lest this be seen as inferring too much from the extract provided, consider another extract from an influential separatist pamphlet. Here it is spelt out quite clearly that, because Scotland and England are so different in terms of both physical and social landscape, they cannot work together for the common interest. Inevitably one set of interests prevail over another and Scotland, for reasons of size if nothing else, is equally inevitably the loser:

Extract 5

The UK delegation is the voice of the UK Government. For more than a decade it has been formed by a party which has been rejected by the Scottish electorate. It follows an ideology and carries out policies of which we disapprove. Whenever the views of the interests of Scotland and England differ, as they frequently do, a government of the UK must give preference, for good democratic reasons, to those of England. We are different in climate, geology, systems of law and education, industrial structure, the nature of our

> *farming, the relative importance of fishing. For most of the time, therefore, Scotland under the present arrangements is either misrepresented or not represented at all.*
> (Paul Scott, SNP activist in *Scotland in Europe. Dialogue with a Sceptical Friend*, 1992: 44)

This is a powerful argument, and so it is only to be expected that others will use a similar form of argument but to different ends. Sir Nicholas Fairbairn provides just such an instance:

Extract 6

Scotland finds Westminster, which speaks the same language and has a homogenous population in Britain, difficult to accept. On what possible basis is it going to accept orders from Mr Delors, who's never been to Scotland, will never come to Scotland, from Brussels, who don't speak the same language?
(Sir Nicholas Fairbairn, Conservative MP, interview)

For Fairbairn, as for Scott and Ewing and Welsh, the argument is about difference, but this time the key differences are not between Scotland and England in Britain, but between Scotland and the rest of Europe (personalized as the Head of the Commission, Mr Delors). Indeed Fairbairn minimizes the Anglo-Scots differences compared to the Scottish–European gulf. Not speaking the same language can be taken literally or metaphorically. Either one cannot understand the concerns and hence the interests of the other or else one has different concerns and interests. In both cases, it is impossible for Europe to represent a Scottish interest. So, rather than Scotland 'returning' to a familiar European 'home', Scotland is in danger of being subjected to the misunderstanding of an alien other.

The notion of Europe as the other can be achieved not only by re-evaluating 'difference' but also by substituting histories; rather than Ewing's benign account of Scottish experience abroad, an altogether more sinister set of references can be used to suggest that other European countries are marked now, as ever, by their tendency to dominate and destroy small nations. Perhaps one shouldn't mention the War, but there are subtle ways of doing so which allow one to introduce the topic while simultaneously defending oneself against the accusation that one is the sort of old-fashioned and bigoted person who rakes up past hatreds (cf. Potter, 1996)

Extract 7

Now what they mean when they say Independence in Europe is they don't mean an independent Scotland in Europe. They mean a Scotland independent of the rest of the United Kingdom in Europe. Now that's a subtle distinction but it's a terribly meaningful distinction, because the Scots, or a Scottish Parliament would be more subsumed within a huge Europe than it is at present within the United Kingdom . . . I'm not convinced about the ability of a Scottish Parliament or a Scottish Assembly to protect themselves in the same way within a Europe which you know has a capacity frankly for – I almost said 'goose-stepping' that would be a frightful Freudian slip – walking over national interest.

(Conservative candidate, interview 11)

Of course, this isn't just an argument against Europe, it is an argument for Britain. We are back to our very first extract in the previous chapter, to Heseltine's invocation of Britain as a bulwark against the goose-stepping hordes across the North Sea – only here represented as a present not just a past threat. If small nations will be crushed by Europe, the only way for a small nation like Scotland to defend its distinctive interests is as part of the Union:

Extract 8

If you like, we use a pneumatic drill to break the ground and then we allocate the gravel, if you like, to the individual parts where it is needed. And I think that it would be very difficult for us on our own to wield that pneumatic drill. I just don't think we would break the ground because we would be one of numerous little pneumatic drills all trying to be heard. And I think that it is the bigger clout, the bigger crunch of the UK which takes us forward but allows us as integral parts to derive undoubted benefit from that.

(Conservative candidate, interview 19)

In sum, there is a compelling symmetry between these separatist and unionist constructions. For the former, Britain threatens domination over the Scottish interest and it can only be defended as part of Europe. For the latter, Europe threatens domination over the Scottish interest and it can only be defended as part of Britain. If the SNP see England for Europe as a bad bargain, the Conservatives warn that Europe for England would be worse. The more general point is that neither those who promote or those who oppose a separate Scottish state are generically pro- or anti-supra-national entities. The orientation towards others cannot be settled by reference to the salience of the national issue in and of itself. As we have argued, it is necessary not only to look at the specific definition of the national identity in question, it is also necessary to look at the specific orientation towards particular others in relation to that national identity. What is more, it seems clear that these orientations are not atomic but molecular: they are inter-connected as part of an overall construction of the relations in which the nation is embedded.

At this point, our sceptical friend might substitute indifference for dissent: so, people are enjoined to embrace Britain if it is good for them or to eschew Britain if it is bad for them, and likewise for Europe. So what? Worded in this way, our argument does indeed seem like a profound glimpse into the absolutely obvious.

Our first response would be to accept the charge of obviousness, but to view it positively rather than negatively. If we measure psychological (or indeed social) theories against the phenomena they purport to address, and if we see that our theories in fact fail to address obvious elements of these phenomena, then it is a powerful argument for theoretical change. If our position is accepted as self-evident (we need to look at the ways that others relate to ingroup interests if we want to know how group identification will affect our orientation to those others, and hence the way to affect these orientations is through the way we construct such relationships), then all attempts at generic theories of intergroup relations must be scratched from the start. That is far from a trivial consequence!

Our second response would be to argue that the validity of the charge is dependent upon its wording and that, as so frequently, what is interesting lies more in what the words conceal than in what they reveal. All the work is done in the terms 'good for them' and 'bad for them'. These both presuppose who 'they' are and what is good or bad for them. In other words, both identity and interest are taken for granted. Since the whole thrust of our position is to argue that interest is contingent upon identity, that the nature of our interests depends upon the definition of identities and that people are mobilized through the construction of identity, such that the positions being advocated represent the interests of the subject, then it is little wonder that the position seems trivially obvious when these issues are concealed. That is why it is so effective an argumentative ploy to promote British or European Union (or indeed, anything else) by taking national interest for granted, as occurs in so many of the extracts we have provided. Thus, the fact that it seems obvious is not a sign that nothing of significance is going on, but rather the success of that double activity: of construction and a simultaneous covering of the traces. However, in a number of the extracts, the fact that interest relates to the construction of identity has been a little easier to glimpse. These are the occasions where a difference of values and concerns between self and other is used to imply the impossibility of simultaneously serving the interests of both (for instance Extracts 4 and 5 above). This indicates that one will not seek to maximize just any asset, but rather those assets that are of value (in terms of national identity). In other words, orientation to the other can be managed through explicit reference to the interest term in 'national interest' with which that other is (or is not) at odds.

National values and international relations

Before continuing with the Scottish example, and in order to add some perspective, consider again the Spanish case – another state which has been riven by debates over constitutional arrangements and the ability of all the people to coexist under a single constitution. Catalan nationalists argued not only that the state is a Castilian creation, but also that there are a series of fundamental differences between the Catalan and Castilian national identities. According to Llobera (1983), Valenti Almirall, one of the key figures in the movement for Catalan autonomy, used these differences to question the very possibility of harmonious coexistence within a unitary Spanish state through identifying a series of binary oppositions.

For example, whereas the Castilians were authoritarian, the Catalans were freedom-oriented. Perhaps the most potent contrast was established through defining Catalans as '*particularista*', by which Almirall meant that they see and are tolerant of differences. As Williams puts it, Almirall saw the Catalans as having 'a tendency to see the trees rather than the woods, to see the member rather than the category and therefore, to be federalist rather than centralist in their view of government' (1994: 44). In contrast, the Castilians were construed as '*generalitzador*', by which Almirall meant that they do not see, and are intolerant of differences. In other words, the Castilians were characterized as having 'a tendency to see the woods rather than the trees, the category rather than the member' (Williams, 1994: 44) and were, therefore, 'prone to absorb and assimilate'. How can such different people live together? On the one hand, Castilian hegemony meant that the Catalan character was in danger of degeneration (Llobera, 1983). On the other, the expression of Catalan identity demanded autonomy and power sharing.

One might paraphrase Almirall by saying that Catalans and Castilians are as alike as sheep and wolves and that, put together, the one will inevitably devour the other. These are precisely the terms used in the anonymously authored *Complaynt of Scotland*, written so as to rebut and oppose the English Henry VIII's 'rough wooing' of the infant Mary of Scots on behalf of his young son Edward (although, in the uncertain spelling of the times, they are written as 'scheip' and 'wolvis'):

> There is nocht tua natiouns under the firmament that are mair contrar and different fra otherirs nor is Inglis men and Scottis men, quhobeit that thay be within ane ile and nichtbours and of ane langage. For Inglis men are ambitious in prosperity, and Scottis men are humain in prosperity. Inglis men are hummil quhen thay are subjeckit be force and violence, and Scottis men are furious quhen they are violently subjeckit. Inglis men are cruel quhen thay get victory, and Scottis men are merciful quhen they get victory. And to conclude, it is unpossibile that Scottis men and Inglis men can remane in concorde vnidr ane monache or ane prince, because ther naturis and conditiouns ar as indefferent as is the nature of scheip and wolvis. (cited in McLaren, 1961: 101–2)

It is not only Scottish opponents of the Union who have employed such arguments. In the eighteenth century, an English opponent – the Bishop of Bath and Wells – compared the Union to 'the mixing together strong liquors, of a contrary nature, in one and the same vessel, which would nigh to be burst asunder by their furious fermentation' (cited in Faber, 1985: 55). Whilst we are now more used to hearing constructions of category difference articulated by Scottish voices, the eighteenth century witnessed many English-accented voices characterizing the Scots and English as being fundamentally different in nature. For example, the cross-eyed English Parliamentarian, John Wilkes (characterized by Colley (1992) as a 'rake on the make') was damning in his definition of the Scots' differences from the English and vitriolic in his characterization of the consequences of the Union for the expression of Englishness. A strong advocate of the idea that England was an elect nation blessed with a tradition of struggle for 'liberty', he took the fact that the Stuart dynasty came from Scotland as proving that the Scots had, as

Colley puts it, a predilection for arbitrary power and a willingness to cringe before it. Indeed, the Wilkite press was to be found attributing the American War of Independence to the pernicious influence of the Scots upon England's relations with the Colonies. Apparently, the 'ruin of the British Empire is merely a SCOTCH QUARREL with English liberty, a SCOTCH SCRAMBLE for English property' (cited in Colley, 1992: 116). Reviewing these sentiments Colley observes that they held that 'alien men and alien attitudes from North Britain had finally succeeded in infecting the seat of power in London, forcing those other Englishmen across the Atlantic into righteous rebellion' (1992: 116).

In a period when the Union was coming into being as, nearly three centuries later, when the Union is again in question, opponents use difference to imply that the interests of either Scotland, England or both must suffer if they are yoked together. That is, it is not difference per se which leads to the rejection of the Union. It is the character of the differences which mean that both cannot flourish under the same system. Paul Scott links the two periods together by invoking Jonathon Swift's description of the eighteenth century Irish to describe the plight of the twentieth century Scot. They are, he suggests, akin to: 'patients who have physic sent them by doctors at a distance, strangers to their constitution, and the nature of their disease' (1992: 16).

If there are commonalities between the discourse of the early eighteenth and the late twentieth centuries, there is nonetheless an important difference. For the former, as we have just seen, the problem for the Scots lies in the character and actions of the English people, and vice versa. It is the cruel Englishmen who conflict with merciful Scots or else the cringing Scot who impedes the English-man's pursuit of liberty. For the latter, a post-holocaust sensibility renders the public expression of prejudice problematic and it is important to avoid the charge of chauvinism or racism (cf. Wetherell & Potter, 1992). Hence it is stressed by contemporary separatists that the problem lies not so much in the different constitution of the other as in the political constitution that binds them together. There is no quarrel with the English people but rather with the British state. Indeed it is often argued that independence will improve relations between people. Take for example the argument of one SNP MP:

Extract 9

The trouble with the Scots is that without their own government they therefore don't have a political system which actually reflects the true nature of the Scottish psyche. What I mean by that is that now we have policies in education, in law, which are based on alien English ideas which are being imposed. For example, the Poll Tax which is a very good example, and privatization of water are two issues being imposed upon Scotland by a minority Tory government on a basically English philosophy.

(SNP MP, interview 47)

It would be hard to create a clearer account of different identities. Yet the critique is not of the English psyche in itself, but rather of a single government pursuing policies that cannot reflect the Scottish psyche. Thus the policies are described in national terms: the Poll Tax (a regressive scheme of local taxation) and privatization are characterized as reflecting English concerns rather than, say, representing class interests and hence disadvantaging most English people (and advantaging not a few castle-dwelling Scots).

As we have seen in Chapter Three there are those outside the parliamentary spectrum who oppose independence and argue that the notion of national difference is a distraction from class solidarity. Obviously conservative unionists cannot deploy such arguments against the SNP. They have other ways of denying national difference and defending the possibility of advancing a common interest. However, as well as advancing their own arguments, Conservatives would find it hard to simply ignore the complaints of their opponents. In late twentieth century Scotland, the chorus crying 'domination' is simply too loud to ignore. One Conservative MP grasps this sizeable bull by the horns. He states that: 'one of the things I find offensive today is this business that's constantly suggesting that the Scots are downtrodden, the Scots are backward, are taken advantage of. That's absolutely nonsense' (Conservative MP, interview 18). Why, then, are there such constant suggestions? The above account makes use of that which minority influence theorists term 'psychologization' (e.g. Mugny & Papastamou, 1980). That is, what is said reveals more about the nature of the speakers than the nature of the world. Scots, he argues, are naturally contrary:

Extract 10

I recognize that there is another quality the Scots have, we are in there pushing for what we believe in. We're not reluctant to stand and say, 'Look we think that this should be done'. A Scottish voice is always heard . . . Scots love to debate and often this is misunderstood. That's why we make good trade union leaders, politicians and all the rest of it. Why we contribute more to the cabinet than anyone else, because we love to debate, we love to talk about things. But it doesn't mean that we're against, you know, [the status quo]. *This is often what's not understood.*

(Conservative MP, interview 18)

Such an argument goes further than merely denying that complaint constitutes evidence of disadvantage. It suggests that complaint is noticed only because Scots have the positions of influence from which to utter it. Thus complaint is actually evidence that Scots have thrived in Britain. They have done disproportionately well in competing for the power which all, English as well as Scottish, desire. Another of our Conservative interviewees develops this claim. His argument, the mirror image of SNP claims, is that those throughout the British Isles are fundamentally concerned by the same things. He too acknowledges that there are differences which might mislead the casual observer into assuming fundamental tensions. However these differences are portrayed as secondary compared to the similarities. Moreover, the differences are largely personal or symbolic and hence beyond the political domain. They are therefore irrelevant to political arrangements, just as political arrangements do not constrain their expression:

Perhaps the most interesting thing about this extract is the use of the phrase 'We're all Jock Tamson's bairns'. This is a common Scottish saying which conveys the view that, underneath surface differences, all people are basically the same. Normally it is used to refer to something distinctive about Scottish sensibilities (although, as we will see in a later chapter, exactly what it says is open to some debate). Here, however, the 'we' refers to what all Britons share together rather than what distinguishes Scots from the rest. All those in our small island share a common humanity which is equally served by the Union.

It may be tempting to suppose that a defence of union must always be based upon the denial of the significance of political differences between England and Scotland. However, it bears repeating that the issue is not difference per se but relates to the impact of the other for ingroup identity. Thus, one Labour MP took a construction of category difference widely used by SNP spokespeople to advance the argument for independence and employed it to the opposite effect. More specifically he took the argument that the Scots were more progressive than the English but used this to argue that Scottish interests, far from being furthered by independence, would be compromised:

Here, rather than the differences between Scotland and England demanding independence, such differences demand union for it is through union that the deleterious consequences of England for Scotland are attenuated and countered.

More specifically, the Union is construed as working to restrain (English) Tory impulses and so constitutes a first line of defence which facilitates the Scottish goal of building a just, high-skill, high-wage economy. In other words, independence could only worsen the Scottish position because the social relations that would ensue would pit a progressive Scotland against a polity in which 'the Tories rule without check'.

So far, we have shown that the management of orientations to the other is mediated through invoking the national interest. This can be done by taking the national interest for granted and asserting that relationships with the other will (or won't) undermine that interest. It can also be done by problematizing the interest term and making explicit whether the bases for interest (e.g., the nations' values) allow joint action or not. Let us conclude this section by drawing attention to a third form of management in which the other term of 'national interest' is problematized – namely, the national.

Even if one agrees on what constitutes the group interest, the application of that interest (and an evaluation of whether any concrete measure realizes it) depends on determining who or what constitutes the group. If a measure is not applied to the Scots then, whether or not it is consonant with the Scottish interest, it cannot realize that interest. To be more specific still, the issue of whether the Scots interest is served by a separate state becomes redundant if the proposed state is not of the Scots. For Nicholas Fairbairn, the dispersal of the Scottish people makes a nonsense of proposals for a territorial state. Addressing a pre-election meeting in the village of Longforgan, he declared that: 'all Scotland is, is one eleventh of the British people. It's not, the Scots do not live north of the border. The majority of Scots live south of the border and the majority of Scots in the world don't live here at all' (Sir Nicholas Fairbairn, Conservative MP, speech, Longforgan, 2.4.92). Fairbairn expanded on these sentiments in an interview. Over a drink or two, he argued that the SNP's claim that winning a majority of the 72 Scottish seats would constitute a mandate for independence was false; it was not for 'the people who live in Scotland to decide':

Extract 13

if there's going to be a referendum, it must be the British people, the 80 per cent of Scots who live in Britain in England must decide, and the English must decide and the mixed Scots and English and Irish and Welsh all mixed up in marriages. I mean, I'm a twelfth English. Em, we must all have the right, not just because we happen to be resident above a certain parallel like the 48th Parallel in Korea. See before the Union, the Scots lived north, you know the milk chocolate lived one side and the plain chocolate lived the other. Now it's liquorice allsorts in the whole jar. You can't just draw a line in the jar and say the liquorice allsorts above it are Scots liquorice allsorts and the ones below it are English liquorice allsorts. They're not.

(Sir Nicholas Fairbairn, Conservative MP, interview)

As so often, this is a hybrid argument – a sort of rhetorical belt and braces to hold up the case against independence. On the one hand, Fairbairn implies that the existence of distinctively Scottish people is in question. Even he, tartan garb and all, is partly English. On the other, even if there are Scots, they are (according to a mixed set of metaphors of mixture) equally spread throughout Britain. A constitutional dispensation north of the border would abandon the great majority of Scots – four out of every five – who are south of the border. It would also include the many English people in Scotland. The moral is stated by one of Fairbairn's colleagues. An intermingled people can only be served by a composite state:

Extract 14

Britain is now totally intermingled. It doesn't matter where you go in England or in Wales or in Northern Ireland or Scotland, you'll find English, Welsh, Irish and Scottish all working there and getting on well together. So we've got the perfect federal system you could say with only the one government looking after the federal state.

(Conservative MP, interview 20)

All these arguments depend upon a particular construction of nationality. They are based in what we have previously referred to as an ethnic (as opposed to a civic) model. To be Scottish is a matter of descent. If your ancestors came from Scotland, you are Scottish even if you live and have always lived elsewhere. Conversely, living in Scotland is not enough to make you Scottish, even if you have always lived there. Elsewhere, we will analyse in some detail how and to what ends this matter is debated. For now, it is sufficient to note that such constructions do not go unchallenged. For instance, the SNP stress that those not born but living in Scotland are 'New Scots' and are welcomed as members (and occasionally, even as candidates) of their party. At a meeting prior to the 1997 General Election held for all the candidates at St Andrews University, an ancient Scottish institution noted for its high intake of students from English schools, one such student asked the SNP representative if an independent Scotland would discriminate against those like himself. The SNP speaker responded by stressing that his election agent was born in England, was a new Scot and was obviously an SNP member; his wife was also born in England, was also a new Scot and was another SNP member. He concluded, to loud applause, that the position suggested by the questioner represented the policies of the British National Party (the major fascist group in Britain) not the Scottish National Party.

The contrast between Conservative and SNP positions on this matter serves to deepen the paradox with which we started. Earlier, we stressed that unionists, devolutionists and so-called nationalists in fact all make equal claims to national identity and all equally ground claims in national interest. Here we show that, contrary to what is often supposed, it is the so-called nationalists who appeal to a more civic and inclusionary model of national identity whereas the so-called anti-nationalists are nearer to a classic ethnic and exclusionist model. This should serve as further warning against making general claims about the substantive nature of national identities and alert us rather to their construction and strategic usage.

The important thing, which should by now be a familiar refrain, albeit sung in a slightly different key, is how speakers seek to show that their party position concerning relations with supra-national entities serves the national interest. We have analysed some of the levels on which this demonstration can take place, including the values which characterize national identity (category content) and the criteria for national inclusion (category boundaries). In so doing, it has been apparent that these various aspects of identity are open to argument and that, occasionally, one has not only to advance one's own arguments but also undermine those of one's opponents. At this point, it should be clear that there is one basic aspect of our position which has not yet been touched upon. To recap, if identity is so variable and so consequential at the same time, one must not only make one argument amongst many, but also seek to make one's own position seem the only possible position. For the first time (but not for the last) we shall address the means by which this can be done – in this case, through the use of figurative language.

Metaphors and relations

Time and again, in the interviews that we conducted and the speeches that we recorded, political activists were found applying terms or phrases to an object or relationship for which such terms and phrases may not seem literally applicable. However, when Conservatives talk of Europe 'goose-stepping' over small nations (Extract 7), or talk of using a 'pneumatic drill' in Europe (Extract 8), or even characterize Britain as a jar of 'liquorice allsorts' (Extract 13), there is no confusion as to what is being said. Nor are we confused by an SNP MP's characterization of Scotland as a 'tartan' in which 'so many different, very brightly coloured parts of the whole merge together as a pattern' (SNP MP, interview 47). As soon as we know that it was produced in the context of a discussion concerning divisions within Scotland and whether it was possible to speak of a 'national character', the speaker's meaning is clear. The reference to fabric design produced an image of harmony in which quite distinctive elements complement each other and allow a higher-order unity to be realized from rich diversity. Thus, instead of undermining the whole, internal diversity is reconstrued as that which makes the whole a possibility.

Far from sowing the seeds of misunderstanding, such figurative language typically conveys meaning 'above and beyond the surface form of what has been said' (Wilson, 1990: 115). Because of this, there has been much analysis of analogies, synonyms and particularly of similes and metaphors. Indeed, the interest in metaphor can be traced back to Aristotle and adds up to a huge literature. We will not attempt to summarize this literature, partly for reasons of space and partly because much of the interest, particularly in recent linguistics, has been to do with the pragmatics which allow the speaker's intended meaning (located beyond the surface structure) to be communicated (e.g. Wilson, 1990). We would also heed Edwards' (1997) warning that in acknowledging the constructive power of metaphor one should beware of assuming that non-metaphorical language is somehow literal and non-constructive. Our own interest is in showing how metaphors may serve as a particularly powerful way of characterizing the nature of social relations, in particular that between national categories.

We would suggest that such figurative terms serve three functions in this regard. The first two correspond to what social representation theorists term 'concretization' and 'anchoring' (Farr & Moscovici, 1984). Concretization refers to the means by which an abstract concept is made material, the better to imagine and understand it. Relations between nations are largely abstract. They occur on a scale that is hard to see directly, hence if they can be represented in a form that is directly observable and directly experienced they are rendered more self-evident. Anchoring means the making of something unfamiliar into something familiar and well understood. Once again, metaphor may represent the rarefied world of (inter)national politics in everyday terms. The third process is naturalization (cf. Thompson, 1990). Where one thing is likened to another in which certain features, properties, behaviours or relations are seen as natural, then acceptance of their linkage serves to naturalize these things for both.

Perhaps this is why animal metaphors are so popular in politics. Whatever we think of humans, animals are seen as living in the realm of the natural rather than the social. Their properties are unquestioned givens and therefore to liken friend or foe to an animal is to suggest that the humans in question are naturally gifted (or cursed) with the relevant properties. Of all the animals in the bestiary, perhaps that most replete with symbolic significance is the lion: king of the jungle, noble and powerful; it is hardly surprising to find many groups and nationalities employing leonine metaphors. Perhaps the first that comes to mind is the British lion, much used by nationalist politicians in general and by Margaret Thatcher in particular. Thus, in her keynote address to the Conservative Party Conference in 1984, in the midst of a year-long miners' strike, Thatcher dealt with the accusation that those miners who continued to go to work were scabs: 'Scabs?' she retorted, 'they are lions'. In so doing she represented these men as brave and strong rather than as cowards who betrayed their fellows. Moreover, she constituted them as prototypically British and thereby buttressed her overall construction of the conflict as the British people under attack by the leadership of the National Union of Mineworkers (Reicher & Hopkins, 1996).

Thatcher was far from alone in invoking the noble lion. By way of contrast, consider the following characterization of Muslims living in a non-Islamic state. Speaking at a conference in South Africa on the eve of his death in 1996, a key figure in the Muslim Parliament of Great Britain and a keen advocate of a politically active Islam – Dr Kalim Siddiqui – argued that 'if we live outside the state of Islam, we are like the African lion living in the zoo in London . . . Of course the lion is still alive, it lives in the zoo. But it does not have the liberty of killing its prey: it is thrown dead meat. And this is the state of the Muslims today. We are thrown dead meat to eat. Yes, we can pray, yes we can fast, yes we can go to Hajj.'

Siddiqui's topic is of great complexity and considerable abstraction. Yet, in the space of just a few short sentences, a clear analysis of the contemporary position of Muslims and their relationship with others is constructed. Siddiqui's concrete and familiar image of the lion in the zoo allows us to proceed from the known to the unknown and so impose a recognizable shape and order on a topic that is otherwise difficult to conceptualize. More importantly, though, we all know the lion as 'king of the jungle': an animal that is noble and powerful, a natural predator whose essence is expressed in the freedom to hunt and kill. Consequently, there can be nothing more unnatural than denying a lion the liberty of the kill and throwing it dead meat instead. The simile serves to constitute Muslims as similarly constrained, as living in an equally unnatural state. So, although they are given the means of religious survival – they can pray, fast and go to Hajj – that which is central to the essence of the Muslim identity is denied expression. Siddiqui goes on to argue that only through changing their context and establishing 'the state of Islam' can Muslims be true to Islam and to their real nature.

Siddiqui uses metaphor principally to characterize the ingroup and the relations in which they are embedded. In other accounts the focus is more upon the characterization of the other. For example, throughout Spain's war with the USA (culminating in Spanish defeat in 1898), the Spanish press characterized Spain as a lion and the US as a pig. The lion was an ancient symbol of the kingdom of Leon and the Spanish monarchy and so conveyed both strength and nobility. The choice of the pig over the 'official' (i.e. US) symbol of the eagle had obvious advantages in building mass support for the war. Whereas the eagle would construe the opposition as similarly strong and noble, the pig rendered them 'plebian, gluttonous, dirty, cowardly and mercenary' (Balfour, 1996: 111). Moreover, the contrast between animals helped naturalize a portrait of the war as pitting greedy commercialism against the nobler values of the traditional '*ancien régime*'.

For all the advantages to be gained from the metaphorical employment of lions and other beasts, there are also disadvantages. While there may be consensus as to the qualities associated with the animal, it is obvious that the identity between mineworkers, Muslims and Spaniards and lions is figurative rather than real. That provides a space to challenge the metaphor. Other metaphors, in which the comparison object is also human, may therefore have an advantage, if only one can find examples where the qualities concerned are widely perceived as natural. Of all human qualities, perhaps most work has been put into naturalizing those associated with gender and with the relationship between men, women and children within the family unit. Moreover, gendered and family metaphors can pass almost without noticing that they have been used, for example when we talk of 'sister organizations', when ingroup members are referred to as 'brother' and so on. We might therefore expect gender and family metaphors to have a particular resonance. Certainly a metaphorical gendering of identity is widely used to construe human relationships. To continue with our example of the Spanish–American War, the lion was often accompanied by a woman who also represented Spain – often a virgin lusted after by a lecherous Uncle Sam (Balfour, 1996: 111). A similar metaphor has also been very important in Muslim rhetoric, especially amongst important Muslim clerics in pre-revolutionary Iran. According to Thaiss (1978) these clerics sought to mobilize opposition to America and the Shah's pro-American regime through invoking a sexualized metaphor which implied that the 'female' Muslim community was being penetrated and violated by a non-Muslim 'male'. Obviously, the power of this imagery is in part based upon a conception of heterosexual female sexual identity as involving a foreign (i.e. masculine) body entering one's own. However, it was particularly potent in a religion that preaches involvement in the world but rejects that which is worldly and material. Further, Thaiss observes that, because the Islamic word for Muslim community ('Umma') is etymologically derived from 'Umm' or 'mother', the sexualized metaphor may be a uniquely powerful vehicle with which to construe the relationship between the parties in terms of violation and pollution (Thaiss, 1978).

The important thing about gendered metaphors, then, is that they don't simply tell us about one protagonist or the other. Rather, they tell us about relations between protagonists, for what tends to be naturalized about gender is the relationship between men and women. The same is equally, if not more, true about families. However, families involve more than two people and hence more than one set of relations: that between husband and wife; that between parents and children; that between mother and daughter; that between husband and mother in law and so on. The consequence is that family metaphors are particularly useful because they can be used to so many ends. This is well illustrated in Jensen's (1977) analysis of the speeches and pamphlets of the eighteenth century concerning the question of the British Government's relationship with the thirteen colonies on the North American coast. Many of the debate's protagonists were to be found characterizing the relationship as one between parent and child. However, as Jensen observes, the complex of rights and responsibilities to be found in families meant that all could use the parent–child metaphor so as to construct quite contrary characterizations of the rights and responsibilities of the British 'parent' and the American colonial 'children'. In Jensen's words, it was as if looking at Paul's letter to the Colossians, the one party had focused on Verse 20 ('Children, obey your parents in all things') whilst the other had focused on Verse 21 ('Fathers, provoke not your children'). The important corollary was that each side was able to use an image of 'the family' to present the other as somehow having failed to live up to their duties and obligations (Jensen, 1977: 30). As Soame Jenyns, a stern critic of the colonies' opposition to taxation, enquired: 'Can there be a more proper time for this mother country to leave off feeding out of her vitals these children whom she has nursed up, than when they are arrived at such strength and maturity as to be well able to provide for themselves and ought rather with filial duty to give some assistance to her distresses?' (pamphlet, 1765; cited in Jensen, 1977: 46). Yet where this pamphleteer implied that Britain's fulfilment of its parental obligations justified taxation, Edmund Burke's defence of the colonies used the child–parent metaphor to characterize the colonies as having fulfilled their duties to Britain: 'At the beginning of the century, some of these colonies imported corn from the mother country. For some time past the old world has been fed from the new. The scarcity which you have felt would have been a desolating famine, if this child of your old age, with a true filial piety, with a Roman charity, had not put the full breast of its youthful exuberance to the mouth of its exhausted parent' (speech, House of Commons, 1775; cited in Jensen, 1977: 46).

The range of metaphors apparent in past and present characterizations of the Scottish–English relationship is enormous. For example, sexual metaphors were particularly prominent in the past. Colley (1992) describes how the old belief that Scottish Highland men were unusually 'well-hung' provided a vehicle to express

English concerns that the Scots were gradually taking over that which was not rightfully theirs. This characterization of the Scotsman's 'tackle' was probably linked with the popular image of the Highlander as primitive and threatening, but may have been boosted by the rumour that the Scotsman Lord Bute was bedding George III's mother. As Colley observes, the many ribald prints of the pair testify to the way in which English concerns were given concrete expression through reference to sex. In one, Bute had a set of bagpipes placed suggestively close to his body. Colley describes how, in another, the princess had her hand under Bute's kilt whilst observing that 'A man of great parts is sure greatly to rise.' Even more dramatically, when crowds gathered in support of Wilkes they took to the streets with a woman's petticoat and a boot (to represent Bute). In all this imagery the message was clear. In Colley's words, the Scots were 'penetrating England itself, compromising its identity, winning access to its riches and cutting out English men' (1992: 122).

By the 1990s such flippant and explicit use of sexualized metaphors was out of favour. However, the use of family metaphors was not. Unionists frequently construed the relations between Scotland and England as family-like: intimate and essentially harmonious. For example, one Conservative representative argued that 'at the end of a day, it's like a family. We can fight and squabble as much with each other, but don't anybody else try to mess with us or we pull together' (Conservative MP, interview 14). Another used a more specific aspect of the family structure in order to argue that Scotland and England exist in:

Extract 15

an almost brother–brother relationship. It's a sort of England–Scotland rugger match or rugby or whatever. It's almost two brothers playing each other. They'd rather anybody else won apart from the two sides, because we're so close. Yet we sort of, we have that love–hate relationship. And you know I feel sure that if there was a common enemy we would unite together as never before. But it's when everything is going quite rosily that perhaps we choose to sort of bicker amongst ourselves and make an issue of it.

(Conservative candidate, interview 22)

As with some other examples we have seen, these extracts demonstrate argumentation and counter argumentation. They do not only use the metaphor to insist on the harmony in Scottish–English relations, they also use it to recuperate apparent counter-evidence. Thus others might point to fighting, squabbling and bickering; however if they think it indicates real opposition they are sadly mistaken. It is precisely because, as brother nations, the Scots and English get on so well and are so secure in their relationship that they can afford the luxury of surface differences. Similarly, in the same interview, the candidate argued that if Scots often complained, that is because such behaviour is typical of younger brothers. The behaviour is naturalized and dismissed as another epiphenomenon of sibling relations. Thus, the metaphor accomplishes in a phrase what took a considerable amount of work to achieve in Extract 10.

Yet another Conservative MP used yet another aspect of the family metaphor to make his point. For him, the Union was a marriage and independence would destroy the marriage. It was, he argued 'a great institution' from which Scotland 'has benefited beyond comprehension'. Indeed, they had benefited to an extent that 'Miss Scotland and Mr England would never have done before they became Mr and Mrs Britain'. By now the style may be familiar. This was Nicholas Fairbairn in full flight (first interview).

The argument for constitutional change was advanced through constructions of the relationship as much less intimate or harmonious. On the one hand we found very different metaphors. Rather than construing Scotland and England as bound by intimate familial bonds, the SNP MP Andrew Welsh, speaking at an eve-of-poll rally, described Scotland as 'a disgruntled lodger in Westminster' (speech, Arbroath, 8.4.94) and so implied that the Scots were outsiders in an institution that was not of their own making, not under their control, and which had no affection for or commitment to them. In a similar vein, an activist speaking at a post-election rally to protest at the election results argued that 'we do not want to be meagre tenants in other people's houses' ('Democracy For Scotland' Rally, Calton Hill, Edinburgh, 19.4.92). On the other hand, we found 'family' metaphors deployed in very different ways. One nationalist activist and pamphleteer argued that Scotland and England as man and wife was a far from nurturant relationship:

Extract 16

I think maybe he's just a put-upon husband who, for years and years and years he's been working away; he's been bringing home his pay and giving it to his wife, which is England, and the wife has been spending it on everything for the house and everything else and then giving him his pocket-money, okay? Well, that's still going on but I think the husband is so knackered now, he's been working himself to the bone and he's working harder than ever but he doesn't seem to be getting any more pocket-money, you know? And the house seems to have everything, actually the house has too much and the wife is starting to go out to the dancing and stuff, on her own or with her friends or having parties and everything else and the husband is still out working every day. He's not getting any time to enjoy himself, he's not acquiring any wealth, he's still got one pair of shoes and maybe, in part, that's the way I look on it and it's a case of, perhaps, friends of the husband, places like Norway and Sweden and Denmark, who are sort of saying, 'Hey wake up guy. This wife's taking you to the cleaners you know. Isn't it about time you divorced her?

(SNP supporting pamphleteer, interview 48)

This draws upon all too common sexist constructions of the marriage relationship as exploitative: the cuckold, the hen-pecked husband and so on. The Scottish husband is exploited by the shameless English wife to the extent that he is almost unaware of it and needs to be awakened to his plight by friends. An alternative metaphor, drawing on the more progressive discourse of sexual abuse, was used by Irvine Welsh, author of the best-selling novel *Trainspotting*: 'It's perverse. With the two countries, it's like this wife-beating thing [makes fist], "Bang, bang, bang," then, "Oh darling, I didn't mean it, I was drunk at the time" [makes smooching shapes with arms]. It's unhealthy. It's not as simple as the English just exploiting Scotland, otherwise we'd have broken away a long time ago' (Irvine Welsh, interviewed in *The Face*, no. 93, June, 1996).

In this extract, as in the previous one, England and Scotland are partners in a marriage, the marriage is unhealthy and abusive, and what is more, the abused partner is psychologically trapped into the relationship. Thus, just as Unionists turn evidence of complaint into an indication of the fundamentally harmonious relationship between nations, so separatists use absence of complaint to indicate the fundamentally destructive nature of the relationship. These metaphors constitute arguments and counter-arguments at the same time. Indeed, as we have seen, metaphor and simile provide a rich and fertile field for argument. It is possible to differ over which metaphors and similes are used; it is possible to dispute the relations implied by a given metaphor or simile; it is even possible to differ over who has what role within those relations.

All this may appear to sit uneasily with our claim that metaphors, similes and other figurative devices serve to naturalize a construction and to make it seem the only possible account rather than just one amongst many. However, it will be recalled that our argument was not that naturalization is in contradiction to argument. Rather, we argued that there will be a variety of contingent constructions of categories (and category relations) each of which is presented as non-contingent. It follows that, the more any particular form of usage serves to render constructions self-evident, the more it will be appropriated in different ways to different ends by those advancing different projects. It is because metaphors serve naturalizing functions *within* accounts that they are all the more disputed *between* accounts.

Conclusion

In Chapters One and Two we have seen the ubiquitous flow of argumentation and the constant attempts to freeze it. In Chapter Three we saw arguments over whether national categories are relevant and, if they are, over which national categories are relevant. In this chapter we have shown that one can argue about international relations and supra-national bodies and how these impinge upon national interest. We have also seen that the terms of national interest – what are the elements that define the nation and underpin interest, who or what is a national – are disputed. As we looked at attempts to naturalize particular versions and as the stakes are thereby raised, we found that the argument became ever deeper and more multi-faceted. In short, we have replicated Billig's arguments about the importance of a rhetorical approach to all constructs of understanding. We would only add, again, that arguments over identity seem particularly significant and this makes sense in terms of their link to collective action.

In these two chapters a constant theme has concerned the treatment of others. Nationalism has had a bad press and social psychological analyses have tended to contribute to it. Sometimes this contribution is specific. Although social psychologists have rather little to say about nationalism per se what little there is typically associates it with an ethnocentric chauvinism (see Bar-Tal & Staub, 1997). Sometimes the contribution is rather more general as when social identity theory is read so as to imply that intergroup discrimination is a necessary corollary of group identification. Our data suggest that the relationship between national identification and the characterization of others is much more nuanced than all this implies. Certainly entrepreneurs of identity can argue that others inherently threaten the nation and thereby justify their elimination in more or less brutal ways. But equally they can argue that it is not individuals but structural arrangements which are the problem and therefore oppose superordinate identities without attendant individual prejudice.

People can also identify passionately with the nation but believe that one's connection with others facilitates national identity. They can further believe that certain links facilitate while others atrophy the nation. Nothing is settled *a priori* but rather depends upon the process of identity construction and argument. To search for a general link between identification and ethnocentrism is yet another example of psychology seeking to ignore the ideological character of identity definitions and thereby look for generality in the wrong place. Generality there is, and we have pointed to various forms of it. However, generality in human social action is to be discovered in the processes that mediate between specific ideological formulations and specific forms of action, not by excluding ideology and ignoring the specificity of behaviour.

5 In Quest of National Character

A singular quest

There are times when politicians couldn't illustrate your points more perfectly if you had scripted them yourself. In March 1999 the UK Labour Prime Minister, Tony Blair, came to his party's annual Scottish Conference in order to launch their campaign for the first Scottish Parliament since 1707. With his SNP rivals firmly in mind, Blair declared that he was in Glasgow: 'because I care about Scotland, care passionately about the future of Scotland, and I want that future to be based on the politics of ideals not identity, of principles not of passports. Our creed is solidarity not separatism and it will always be' (5.3.99). Unsurprisingly, his speech drew the ire of the SNP and its supporters. George Kerevan, writing in *The Scotsman*, objected that the oppositions were entirely false. The SNP did indeed have ideals, it did have policies, and its creed was sovereignty rather than 'Blair's misleading *separatism*' (*The Scotsman*, 8.3.99). We too would want to contest the opposition, but from the other side. It is not just that the SNP have ideals as well as identity, it is also that the Labour Party have identity as well as ideals – or, more accurately, that it had to have identity in order to have ideals.

That much was clear within Blair's speech itself. He defined the election as 'the battle for the future of Scotland'; he promised that 'we're going to fight this campaign appealing not to the worst but to the best instincts of the Scottish people'; and he insisted that 'the principle of solidarity' – that self-same solidarity which is 'our creed' – 'is what this election is about'. To put it slightly differently, he claimed to be advancing the Scottish interest, to be doing that through mobilizing the Scottish psyche and to be basing his appeal on the distinctive collective value of solidarity. There is some ambiguity as to what that collective value is: does 'our creed' refer to party or national identity? As we will later show, the important thing is that it is seen as both. For Labour, the ideal of solidarity is held to be a Scottish ideal which is how Labour policies based on solidarity are made to appeal to a Scottish electorate. The ambiguity of Blair's reference helps him to achieve such a valuable conflation.

In a sense, these few words from Blair summarize much that we have been arguing in previous chapters, the last one in particular. 'Nationalism' and 'identity' are terms that are reserved for particular 'hot' forms of action that challenge and disrupt the status quo. However, those who repudiate such concepts, and who even castigate their very usage, often still base their arguments and their appeal on national identity. To use a commercial metaphor, those such as Blair are no less entrepreneurs of national identity, they just want to rebrand the product. His versions of national values and of national interests don't lead to independence but they are no less central to the selling of his political project. Thus we can see that national identity is as much implicated in 'banal nationalism' as in 'hot nationalism'. It structures our on-going day-to-day reality as much as it organizes disruptions of that reality. The question then arises as to exactly what is this thing which has such power that it can both make and break our social world. Surely, to move now to a physical metaphor, something which can exert such material force must itself be a large and solid object?

On 20 January 1999, the feature supplement of the *Guardian* newspaper (G2) was devoted to the question: 'Which is the real Britain?' The question was posed on the front page of the supplement under four images: of a man drinking beer; of a masked black face at a multi-cultural carnival; of a rural game of cricket; and of the stars of a popular television programme devoted to home improvements. Inside, spread over two pages were the responses of 'a selection of influential Britons (and a Canadian)' to a slightly elaborated query: 'What does Britain mean in 1999?' The subsequent quotations are testimony to a profound sense of confusion. On the one hand, there is a long selection of attempts to list prototypical traits or events or sights which define Britain. These vary from Orwell's 'old maids bicycling to Holy Communion through the morning mist' (quoted by the former Prime Minister, John Major), through 'tolerance, decency and determination to talk about the weather on all occasions' (according to the anti-corruption campaigning MP, Martin Bell), to 'looking out of a bus window, seeing sexy stylish people laughing' (from the artist, Tracy Emin).

On the other hand, a whole swathe of commentators argue that there is only individual and local difference, but nothing common that might be called Britishness. There are variants who claim that such commonality once existed but is now lost (the broadcaster Jon Snow states: 'When I was a child it was Winston Churchill, beefeaters and lots of pink on the globe. Now it's an irrelevant concept. Personally, I'm a Londoner living in Europe'); there are populist versions (the 'agony aunt' Claire Rayner complains that 'People define themselves as coming from Yorkshire or Lancaster or as being cockney, like I am, rather than coming from Britain as a whole. There is a certain snottiness in trying to define Britishness'); and then there are elitist versions (for the art critic, Brian Sewell: 'what an idiotic Yorkshireman thinks is Britain is not what some cultured Southerner thinks. There is no one type of Britishness'). However, for all, diversity rules in the place of uniformity.

Finally, the feature contains a poem by the writer Ben Okri who combines the two tendencies using an image of surface and depth: if there is an appearance of diversity, it only serves to conceal an underlying and continuous imperialist ethos:

> The souls of nations do not change; they merely stretch their hidden range.
> Just as rivers do not sleep
> the spirit of empire still runs deep. . . .
> Accents diverse ring from the land's soul
> a richer music revealing what is whole; new pulsings from abroad shake the shores,
> troubling the sleep of the land's resident bores.
> But the gods of the nation do not change, their ways are deep and often strange.
> History moves, and the surface quivers, but the gods are steadfast in the depth of rivers.

For us, all of these positions miss the point, because they start from the assumption that singularity and diversity are empirical opposites such that one has to favour either the one or the other or else reconcile them as different levels of description. We have argued at some length that it is because of the assumption that all category members should act in terms of a common social identity that it is worth struggling over the nature of that social identity. That is, there is a process whereby group members seek to reach consensus (which Haslam, Oakes, Turner, McGarty and Reynolds (1998) call 'consensualization') which is the basis for differences over where that consensus should come to lie. So, whereas consensus and dissensus (or singularity and diversity) would necessarily be opposed if they were both state descriptions, the process of consensualization and the state of dissensus are entirely compatible – more than that, they are interdependent (cf. Sani & Reicher, 1998). Lest this sound rather arcane, it can be put in simple, commonsensical terms: we only bother arguing because we expect to agree. Why would rival politicians and other would-be mobilizers put so much effort into proposing their version of identity unless it were to form a basis on which all should behave?

With this in mind, it becomes obvious that our physical metaphor, whereby the consequences of identity point to its solidity, does not apply. Rather, the fact that identity is so effective means that all entrepreneurs, whatever their hue, will want to harness it. Identity will be fragmented, contested and variable, as we have described. Different projects will be grounded through different descriptions of what the category means and different electoral projects, which seek to mobilize all within a bounded territory, will seek to make principles and policies the expression of national identity. To take just one example, Montesquieu argued in his *De l'Esprit des Lois* (Book XX) that government should be in accordance with nature and hence the 'general spirit of the nation' which was seen as arising from a complex of climate and customs. According to the degree to which the nation's distinctive qualities are realized, situations are experienced as tolerable or intolerable and political demands articulated (Montesquieu, 1977). When, for instance, the Levellers championed constitutional reform in seventeenth and eighteenth century England, it was on the grounds that England was an elect nation, possessed by a special love of liberty and these were rights due to *Englishmen* (Finlayson, 1996).

More recently, in the aftermath of the 1992 election, the Conservative Secretary of State for Scotland, Ian Lang, justified the social and economic changes implemented by successive Conservative governments, in terms of the degree to which they were consonant with Scottishness and indeed allowed Scottishness to be more properly realized. Reviewing the recent years, Lang argued:

Extract 1

Many of the old orthodoxies have gone. Others are on their way out and Scotland has profoundly changed. Policies and ideas that were described just a short time ago by our opponents as alien to Scotland and her people are now becoming part of the fabric of Scottish life. In truth, it was not the policies that were alien, but socialism. Those distinctive Scottish qualities, so compatible with Conservatism, are finally re-emerging from the long shadows of socialism. And the political culture of Scotland is changing as a result. Slowly but surely the increase of home and share ownership, the extension of rights in housing, health and education and greater personal prosperity than ever before, are all beginning to make their impact felt. This process will go on and it is this party which will have changed Scotland for the better.

(Ian Lang, Conservative MP, speech, Brighton, 7.10.92)

So we see not only those supporting independence in the SNP and those supporting devolution in the Labour Party, but even Conservative unionists promoting their policies as reflecting the authentic content of Scottish identity and transforming Scotland through ridding it of 'alien' ideas. Indeed, so ubiquitous was the claim to reflect the true identity of contemporary Scotland and the desire to re-establish a lost Scottishness that we found ourselves reminded of the film producer responsible for the Hollywood classic *Brigadoon* (where, in a timeless and magic village that appeared for one day every hundred years, the unlikely hunter, Gene Kelly, fell for the even more unlikely Scottish lass, Cyd Charisse). After visiting many potential locations in Scotland the producer returned to Hollywood complaining that although he had gone to Scotland he 'could find nothing that looked like Scotland' (cited in McCrone, Morris & Kiely, 1995: 49).

There was a similar sense of exasperation in the voice and demeanour of Sir Nicholas Fairbairn as we conducted an interview in a rather upmarket Glasgow lounge-bar. Contrasting contemporary Scotland with a 'real' Scotland of past glories in the arts, sciences and industry, he lamented that all this was now 'replaced by the football league and the Cup which I do not take to be of quite such cultural value'. Declaring that the nation was currently characterized by 'a total lack of painters, architects, writers, poets, people who write music, composers of any worth, of any kind at all,' Fairbairn continued, 'so all you're left with is football and complaint . . . the absolute reverse of what Scottishness is about. Iris, we'll have the same again please.' (To which a good-hearted Iris replied: 'Right you are sir.')

Faced with a Scotland that was insufficiently Scottish, *Brigadoon*'s producer returned to produce a more authentic location in his American studios. Such an option was neither available nor of interest to our interviewees. Rather, they were concerned to mobilize action that would transform the contemporary reality of Scotland into their image of a real Scottishness. In order to do so, they had to convince their audience not only that their interpretation of what national identity means was a reasonable interpretation and their claim to instantiate that meaning through their principles and policies was a reasonable claim. That would merely put them in the race against all their rivals who also might be said to have reasonable claims. The important thing is to win the race by debarring entry to all others. That is, as we emphasized in Chapter Two, it is not enough to construct a version of national identity, it is crucial to cover all traces of the constructive process such that one's version becomes the one and only possible version.

This provides a second sense in which singularity and diversity are complementary rather than contradictory. Because there will be so many competing versions of (national) identity, each will need to present itself as singular – as the sole legitimate or authentic version of what it means to be British or Scottish or whatever. Singularity will feature prominently as an aspect of each construction, even if it is a poor description of the field.

This chapter, then, is divided into two broad halves. In the first half we seek to show how speakers construe the content of national identity so as to make their policies be seen to reflect the priorities of a national electorate. To translate this into a more orthodox psychological language, we want to show how national stereotypes are argumentative devices for mobilizing specific types of social action and thereby for realizing specific forms of social reality. They are as multiple as are political projects and as variable as is political strategy. Any conceptual or methodological approach to stereotypes which abstracts them from their argumentative context is likely both to obscure our understanding of the phenomenon and to reify particular political dispensations. This half of the chapter can therefore be read, at least in part, as a critique of the psychology of stereotyping.

The second half of the chapter is then devoted to the way in which speakers themselves seek to reify their national stereotypes. There are a whole series of ways by which contingency can be obscured and by which one of many versions of national identity can be made to seem as natural as the fields and mountains, as solid as cathedrals, as ubiquitous as bardic sayings and as timeless as the ages. Indeed, environment, institutions, and culture will all feature prominently in the account. History is of sufficient importance to deserve a more extended treatment in the next chapter.

Forming the national character

There are a number of ways of referring to the distinctive identity of a nation. Fyfe (1946) refers to such terms as 'national soul', 'national spirit' and 'national genius' in his book on the subject. Perhaps the concept of character is the most common way through which the content of national identity is understood, both in public discourse and in psychology. From the earliest work of Katz and Braly (1933) to the present day, stereotypes in general and national stereotypes in particular are operationalized by providing lists of traits which respondents are invited to select. Yet, as we noted in Chapter Two, Fyfe's volume invoked the idea of character in order to attack the concept of ingrained national difference. First published in 1940, the book maintains that 'the idea that nations have different characters still prevails. It has been one of the most potent of the elements making for war' (1946: 2). Later, in a chapter called 'A hindrance to the good life', he concludes yet more forcefully that 'there are no "national character types". It seems to me that the duty of everyone who understands this is to make it known, and so to help in removing the most dangerous of the myths which in our time prevent the nations from settling down to make the best of life' (p. 21).

If Fyfe decries any usage of national character, there were and there are many who continue to employ such language. However, while the language is held in common, the precise usage is rarely shared. Consider the following characterizations of Scottish identity, one from an SNP activist followed by another from a senior member of the Conservative Party.

Extract 2

The Scot would hate to be wrong. That's why he sometimes doesn't offer opinions when asked. In case there is something risible in the opinions. So he keeps his mouth shut and looks at less inhibited people, like the English, who will give opinions on any damn thing it seems to him and don't care whether they're right or wrong. Now, he wouldn't expose himself to that sort of thing – he might be laughed at and oh! you can't have that.

(SNP activist, interview 42)

Extract 3

And I think you will find that whereas, perhaps unkindly, non-Scots will accuse us of being girners and moaners and groaners, really what I think they are saying is, they are commenting on the Scots' natural desire to express themselves and to express himself in the knowledge that he may hold a view differing from those held by other people . . . I think it is a manifestation of a national characteristic that we like to have an opinion and to express it.

(Conservative candidate, interview 19)

Were this data to be obtained using trait-rating scales, it would reveal highly different scores on the dimension of 'self-confidence'. The nationalist rates Scots as lacking in such confidence. The Tory rates them as exemplifying the characteristic. From a conventional perspective it would therefore be tempting to conclude that the dimension was of little theoretical interest. At best, the lack of consensus might be taken as evidence that students of identity should look elsewhere if they wish to say anything meaningful about that which defines Scottishness. We should reserve our attention for those traits that are characterized by consensus. However to dismiss such dissensus as theoretically uninteresting is too hasty. When viewed as arguments about identity which serve to ground distinctive political projects as against possible rivals, the variation becomes both explicable and highly significant. Thus when the former defines the Scot as silent in the face of English loquacity, it serves to develop a view of the Scots–English relationship as asymmetric and hence to justify the SNP call for independence. When the latter redefines Scottish complaint as assertiveness, it is in the context of rejecting a frequent attack on Scots by fellow Conservatives (they are 'subsidy junkies' always wanting more), which might play well in Westminster but would be fatal to their chances north of the border. It also serves the purpose of arguing that the Scots are fully able to hold (and get) their own in the Union.

Of course it could be objected that this initial selection of extracts is unrepresentative, so consider another pair.

> ### Extract 4
>
> *I don't know whether it's some, I'm almost scared to say this, some form of idealism which clouds, or if you like, it's where maybe Scots allow their hearts more to rule their heads perhaps more than people in England do. People in England are perhaps more taken with, 'we've got to balance the books', 'we can do what we can, but we have to balance the books'. In Scotland, no, we give to those who have not got and to hell with balancing the books.*
>
> (Conservative candidate, interview 11)

> ### Extract 5
>
> *Incorporated or encapsulated within the Scottish psyche is a degree of carefulness, carefulness about money for example, not frugalness, perhaps in some senses, carefulness about being able to balance the budget, an absence of any sort of liking for debt.*
>
> (Conservative candidate, interview 11)

Here as before the extracts could be summarized in terms of opposed trait scores: the Scots either are or are not concerned with 'balancing the books'. So, here as before, this dimension could be dismissed as irrelevant to the national stereotype and the search for relevant dimensions could be continued in different quarters. Such a conclusion may even be reinforced on learning that both extracts came from an interview with the same senior Conservative activist. To the extent that stereotypes and other forms of representation are taken as the expression of relatively fixed internal cognitive constructs, then within-individual variability of this type can be dismissed as measurement error. Just as a quantitative test that yields poor test–retest reliability will be rejected as a poor measurement instrument, so it could be argued that qualitative material is generically imprecise and therefore liable to yield different responses at different times.

However, if a conventional critique of Extracts 4 and 5 would mirror and extend that of Extracts 2 and 3, so would our retort. Viewing them as strategic constructions oriented to shaping collective action rather than as cognitive representations of collective action makes it essential to analyse the argumentative purpose and the argumentative context in which the words were produced. When related to purpose and context, variation ceases to be random error and begins to reveal a systematic pattern. So, while Extract 4 was produced in the course of explaining why the Tories had experienced less electoral success in England than in Scotland, Extract 5 was a response to the interviewer's suggestion that this performance might point to a fundamental contradiction between contemporary Conservativism and Scottish identity. Past failure can therefore be explained not as a flaw in the party but rather as a flaw in the national psyche – a romanticism which can cloud the nation's better judgment. However when it comes to the prospect of future failure, it becomes important to stress that the Conservative ideology of financial prudence is in tune with the fundamental traits of Scottish identity.

But the critic might still persist: yes there is variability between speakers and even variability across the pronouncements of the same speaker, but this doesn't mean that one cannot find consistency. Perhaps our view has been distorted by looking at a disputed periphery. Were we to turn our attention to the core, we would find more consensus. Certainly some trait terms do seem to be seen as more applicable to the Scots than others (Cheyne, 1970; Hopkins, Regan & Abell, 1997; Lindsay, 1997). Perhaps here at last we will discover clearer evidence for the singular national character posited by the ideology of nationalism and implicitly assumed by the methodologies of quantitative social psychology. The next two extracts, the one from a left-wing member of the Labour Party and the other from a right-wing member of the Conservative Party, might seem at first sight to bear witness to a consensus that runs right across the political spectrum as to the character of the Scots.

Extract 6

[The Scots have] *a healthy kind of cynicism for hierarchy and authority. Like, for example, the Monarchy is not held with the same devotion in Scotland as it is within the UK as a whole and when indeed we had our own Monarchy before 1603, if you go back to that time and read the old records, then again there was a healthy, it was much more a people's monarchy with a kind of healthy disdain. . . . And there's a famous line that Scott does in his novels about the Union of the Parliaments, where a woman says standing outside the Scottish Parliament building after the vote for the Union and she says in Scots, 'Well, at least when tha wi' here, we could pelt 'em wi' stanes when they were nae good bairns but nobody's nails can reach the length a' London.' And that's another example – there was a great practice of mob riots outside the Scottish Parliament building when folk were nae passing laws that the people wanted. So there's a kind of healthy disdain, I think, for authority.*

(Labour activist, interview 34)

Extract 7

I mean it's, it has a national identity. It has no reason to have a governmental identity. And the Scots resent authority. They don't like being talked down to and told what to do and therefore, now, I've never found anybody who thought governments were better if they were closer. I mean if you think you'd like your income tax inspector living next door and your VAT collector on the other side and your social security chap opposite, I've never met anybody who wanted that. . . . And the Scots, as I say, resent authority. You know the great characteristic of Burns – people don't understand Burns – his great characteristic was he couldn't bear people who were pompous or authoritarian, and thought a lot of themselves and not much about other people: that was his, he couldn't stand bogusness, that was his philosophy. Well now the last thing we want is a whole lot of apparatchiks in government offices with tartan on ordering us about. Bad enough having people doing it from miles away. Don't want 'em any closer and double the number. And I think it would sour Scotland and divide it as Scotland was soured and divided before the Union with England.

(Sir Nicholas Fairbairn, Conservative MP, interview)

Both these extracts could be summarized by saying that the Scots are anti-authority. Given a trait rating scale, both speakers might circle the same point on this item. Left at that, a victory of sorts could be claimed for the traditionalist. However, it would be a most pyrrhic victory. The symmetry only appears by reducing a rich argument to a single characteristic. On reading the extracts in full, it is patently obvious that they carry very different – even opposed – meanings. In the former, the Labour activist is talking about a collective desire to hold authorities to account and his argument is for a Scottish Parliament that will be more immediately accountable to Scottish people. Fairbairn, on the other hand, evokes an individual desire to be left alone by authority and uses this to argue against authorities in general and a Scottish Parliament in particular. Thus, the same term, when viewed in its broader context, reveals two quite different notions of the types of social relations Scots value and the type of institutional arrangements that serve their values.

This is a crucial point, and so to reinforce it, consider another pair of extracts, one from the left and one from the right, which might be taken as indicating a consensus around another core attribute: the caring qualities of Scots.

Extract 8

I think we have a long history in Scotland of saying – of not saying – 'I'm all right Jack';
we are far more caring about those that aren't, for whatever reason, are less fortunate,
in inverted commas, than ourselves. We care more about the poor, we care more about
the disabled, we put our caring into operation and this is reflected I think in voting
patterns, it is reflected through religious medias, it's reflected through the media itself,
it's reflected through our culture in Scotland. Robert Burns after all, with many of his
poems [was] trying to expand on that about with 'a man's a man for a' that' etc. And a
lot of his works went down very well with socialist, in inverted commas, countries and
I think that again epitomizes our attitude towards the corporate community which is
Scotland.

(Labour candidate, interview 52)

Extract 9

We are different. I think we have a number of aspects about Scotland and Scots and the
way that they think that are much better than what I perceive to be the case elsewhere.
I think that we're more community minded. I think that we care about our neighbours
more so than do people – particularly in urban England. Perhaps it's wrong to draw
that conclusion but I think about my neighbours in my flat in London. I hardly know
them. I'm not there very often, but I hardly know them. But if you move to a new area in
Scotland, you'll quickly know your neighbours. Your neighbours will quickly make a
point of knowing who you are. There's a, Robert Burns expressed so very many things
about Scottish culture with his poetry, 'a man's a man for a' that': we may be achievers,
we may get here and we may get to the top, but there are these quintessentially human
characteristics that the Scot does not lose sight of. . . . My mother lives in a small village

in Fife. There's a fantastic system of informal social support. They care for one another and it's very much, you know, 'do unto others as you would have done to yourself'. And I've seen her as a both a giver as well as a recipient of that informal social support which I happen to think is infinitely better than anything that would be provided by the regional council's social work department.

(Conservative candidate, interview 7)

Both speakers might well endorse the notion that Scottish people are very caring (they also both use the same famous words of Robert Burns to support this ascription, a point we will return to later), but to see this as indicating consensus would be as misleading as to put the collectivist cited in Extract 6 and the individualist Fairbairn (Extract 7) in the same boat. The collectivism/individualism distinction likewise distinguishes between the candidates cited in Extracts 8 and 9. The former sees caring as embodied in a corporate community, socialist values and (by implication) welfare provision. It is a form of caring which is realized by Labour policies. The latter sees caring as a matter of interpersonal relations which is embodied in voluntary action. It is a form of caring which is realized by Conservative policies. Here, even more obviously than before, a reduction which skated over all these differences, would be more than a little misleading. Let us, therefore, reiterate the three key points which emerge from the material we have covered thus far.

First, these examples illustrate something of the contestation surrounding the elements which serve to constitute national identity. Different people invoke different qualities, the same person invokes different qualities at different times and, even when the same terms are used, this cannot be taken as evidence of any consensus as to the nature of national identity for they can obscure quite different analyses of valued social relations and desired institutional relations.

Secondly, these examples illustrate the strategic dimension to identity construction: the definitions of Scottishness advanced in the above extracts are organized so as to recruit Scots to realize the speaker's political project. This explains both the commonality and the variability between them. Those who share political projects tend to advance similar constructions even if different terms are used: Extract 6's depiction of the Scots as 'anti-authority' and Extract 8's 'caring' might appear to have nothing in common, but both relate to a supposed collectivism at the core of Scottish identity which coincides entirely with the Labour project. Those who are divided by political project advance different constructions even when sharing terms. Thus Extract 8's 'caring' relates to Labour welfarism, while Extract 9's 'caring' relates to Tory small-state politics.

Thirdly, these examples illustrate the inadequacy of traditional notions of stereotypes, not only in terms of process but also in terms of content – and, indeed, the two problems go together. As long as stereotypes are conceptualized and measured in terms of sets of trait terms, it will be impossible to appreciate their dynamic relationship to social reality – not only reflecting particular forms of social reality but also being invoked in order to reshape the relations and institutions within which we live. If, in our introductory chapters we provided a theoretical critique of trait approaches, in this chapter we have provided empirical evidence as to how misleading such an approach can be. We have made the point twice now in relation to two pairs of extracts: 6 and 7, 8 and 9. That such opposites might be rendered identical is such an obvious distortion as to render any repetition of the point superfluous.

This is not to say that we consider trait terms to be irrelevant or uninteresting. However, that interest has less to do with their value as explanatory concepts for the analyst as with the ways they are used by participants. That is, we see them as vehicles for reification. They serve to take social relations (which by their very nature are contingent and hence open to alternatives) and turn them into invariant characteristics. The role of trait terms in the grounding of constructed models of social relations is evident in all manner of identities. Yet, the prominence of a discourse of 'character' in the ideology of nationalism gives trait talk a particular potency in relation to national identity. However, it does not follow that 'character' is the only means of reifying national identity. Indeed the ideology of nationalism is particularly well endowed with resources which naturalize and essentialize contingent constructions. Penrose, for instance, argues that one has only to look at advertising billboards to see this in action. One of her examples is very close to our tastes – not only academically. It features an advertisement for Whyte & Mackay's Whisky (circulating in 1993) which read: 'An Englishman's taste for Whyte & Mackay is acquired. A Scotsman's is hereditary' (cited in Penrose, 1995: 413). If consumer products can be grounded through reference to such an essentializing discourse of nation, so too can political projects. In the next section, we examine the various means by which speakers seek to hide the contingency of their constructions and to remove choice from their audience.

Covering the tracks

Identity and environment

There is a long history of theorizing about the relationship between the physical environment and a nation's identity (Lowenthal, 1994; Penrose, 1995). Book VII of Herder's *Reflections on the Philosophy and History of Mankind* is entitled 'National Genius and the Environment'. According to Herder,

> Nature has sketched with mountain-ranges which she fashioned and with streams which she caused to flow from them the rough but substantial outline of the whole history of man . . . One height produced nations of hunters, thus supporting and rendering necessary a savage state; another more extended and mild, afforded a field to shepherd peoples and supplied them with tame animals; a third made agriculture easy and needful; whilst a fourth led to fishing and navigation and at length to trade. The structure of the earth and its natural variety and diversity, rendered all such distinguishing conditions inescapable . . . Seas, mountain-ranges, and rivers are the most natural boundaries not only of lands but also of peoples, customs, languages, and empires, and they have been, even in the greatest revolutions in human affairs, the directing lines or limits of world-history. (cited by Penrose, 1995: 415)

For Montesquieu the connection between the environment and national character was even more direct. He claimed that, whereas cold weather made the nerves less sensitive to stimulation, warm weather allowed the nerve-endings to be more sensitive to such stimulation with the consequence that those in warmer climates were more impulsive, pleasure-seeking and lazy. The importance of environment was such that, for many, it was not just one amongst many influences upon character, but rather the pre-eminent influence. Fyfe records that: 'Buckle, in his vast fragment which was to have been a *History of Civilization in England*, classified the physical agents by which the human race is most powerfully influenced under the heads Climate, Food, Soil, and the general Aspect of Nature' (1946: 16).

Whereas some social psychologists have sought to investigate the degree to which character and climate are correlated (Pennebaker, Rime & Blankenship, 1996) our concern is with the way in which talk about aspects of nature is used to naturalize definitions of identity. Undoubtedly, the physical environment occupies a central place in the nationalist imagination. As Schama observes, national identity would lose much of its 'ferocious enchantment' without the mystique of a particular landscape tradition in which its topography is 'mapped, elaborated, and enriched as homeland' (1996: 15). In a similar vein, Lowenthal comments that landscape features occupy a central place in national self-definition with national anthems typically praising the homeland's 'special scenic splendours or nature's unique bounties' (1994: 17). A good example of this is provided by Ostergard (1992) who notes how a characterization of Danish identity as communitarian and egalitarian was grounded through the invocation of peasant experience and interaction with the land in all manner of media including song. He notes how the words of the popular song (and unofficial national Danish anthem) 'Far Whiter Mountains Shine Splendidly Forth' eschew the 'aggressiveness' of other national anthems, and portray a gentle landscape which serves to characterize the Danish people as equally gentle and peaceful and disposed towards an egalitarian ethos. This is apparent from the anthem's opening lines:

> Far whiter mountains shine splendidly forth
> Than the hills of our native islands
> But, we Danish rejoice in the quiet north
> For our lowlands and rolling highlands
> No Peaks towered over our birth
> It suits us best to remain on earth
> (cited in Ostergard, 1992: 14)

If the contrast between the Danes' lowlands/rolling uplands and their neighbours' more mountainous terrain was important in grounding a vision of Danishness which had strategic significance for a range of nineteenth century popular movements, the Scots have more typically been defined through reference to the wild character of the Scottish Highlands. However, the history of popular conceptions of the Highlands shows that the meanings ascribed to landscape are neither fixed nor singular (Horne, 1984; McCrone, Morris & Kiely, 1995). Rather, as Schama (1996) observes, 'landscapes are culture before they are nature . . . constructs of the imagination projected onto wood and water and rock' (cited in McCrone, 1998: 56). Schama's words could have been written with Scotland specifically in mind. Thus Horne (1984) documents changing conceptions of the Scottish landscape (and its inhabitants) through reference to the contrast between two paintings of the same scene by the same painter. In the second, dated 1780, the same mountains are depicted as higher and more rugged than in the first, dated 1747. The shift is intimately bound up with an emerging romanticism about the tough and rugged highlander (McCrone, Morris & Kiely, 1995).

This example points to the fact that our conception of landscape and environment is itself constructed in and through argument – a point made more generally and passionately by Macnaghten and Urry (1998) who commence their extended discussion by writing that: 'In this book we seek to show that there is no singular 'nature' as such, only a diversity of contested natures: and that each such nature is constituted through a variety of socio-cultural processes from which such natures cannot be plausibly separated' (p. 1). However, their whole reason for writing the book was to contest the common-sense idea that the natural environment has an inherent reality and significance that is beyond nature. Hence, any successful attempt to describe identity as a function of the environment allows the assumed fixity of the latter to rub off on the former and hence enshrines identity definitions that are far from neutral.

The way this works can be seen from the early days of Franco's Spain. After Franco's victory in the Spanish Civil War, the Spanish state pursued a strategy of economic self-sufficiency and sought to construe liberalism as alien to the Spanish character. Central to this economic and ideological remaking of Spain was the eulogization of the small-holding peasantry (Richards, 1996). The strategic importance of this celebration of the peasantry was that it allowed certain values to be presented as arising out of man's interaction with the Spanish environment and so ground them as indigenous. Sometimes metaphors alluding to environmental processes and the landscape were invoked. Much use was made of the writer Miguel de Unamuno, who claimed that the essences of Spanishness were deposited in men as 'sediments' left by a flowing stream over the centuries (1895, cited in Richards, 1996). On other occasions a more direct link was made between the physical environment and the peasant's character. Here too, de Unamuno was of use. He had described how 'in the interior lives a race of dry complexion, hard and wiry, toasted by the sun and cut down by the cold, a race of sober men, the product of a long selection by the frosts of the cruellest winters and a series of periodic penuries, suited to the inclemencies of the climate and the poverty of life' (de Unamuno, 1895; cited in Richards, 1996: 154). Such arguments were employed to suggest that 'soft' liberalism was an alien import which was quite literally 'out of place' in Spain. They were also used to extract sacrifices from the working population. As Richards observes, the nation could then be addressed and exhorted in terms of its hard-working, thrifty and selfless stoicism (Richards, 1996).

Given our emphasis upon the strategic dimension to category definition it should come as no surprise to find different definitions of the nation's identity being grounded through different conceptions of the same landscape or different conceptions of which landscape was relevant. Indeed, even if there was agreement on the nation's qualities, arguments as to which aspects of the environment were 'responsible' could also have enormous strategic significance. Take for example the environmental determination of the Australian 'digger' referred to in Chapter Two. According to one influential figure (the Official War Historian) writing in the early part of this century, the Australian was, due to his experience of 'the bush', a natural soldier: 'The Australian is always fighting something. In the bush it is drought, fires, unbroken horses, and cattle: and not infrequently strong men . . . All this fighting with men and with nature, fierce as any warfare, has made of the Australian as fine a fighting man as exists.' (Bean, 1907; cited in White, 1981: 126). Bean was later to argue that the environment of the bush 'still sets the standard of personal efficiency even in the Australian cities. The bushman is the hero of the Australian boy; the arts of bush life are his ambition' (Bean, 1921; cited in White: 1981: 132). However, it was also possible to find the same self-sufficient characteristics being attributed to rather different factors, including aspects of city life. Thus, the Melbourne-born businessman and engineer, Sir John Monash, ignored the bush and attributed these qualities to the 'democratic institutions under which he was reared' and to 'his pride in his country' (Monash, 1920; cited in White: 1981: 132).

For our purposes here, the important issue of note is that these differences were far from innocent for they concerned the identification of the nation's social and economic heart. In the context of a political struggle between rural/agricultural and urban/industrial interest groups, arguments about the 'digger's' environmental origins were pursued so as to shape collective understanding of where the true heart of Australia lay and therefore which locale best represented the Australian character. As White puts it: 'In the stress placed in the antecedents of the Anzac, and in the manner in which the returned Anzac was portrayed, vested interests were using the legend and remaking the image along lines congenial to their own interests' (1981: 133).

The grounding of identity in environment, the contested nature of environment and hence of identity, and the strategic significance of such arguments can all be seen more directly in the Scottish case. Take the confident words of an SNP activist. Asked if it was possible to talk of a Scottish national character, he responded:

Extract 10

Yes. I can be more objective than that. I think that because of the topography, because of the geography, because of the history, the Scottish character is a kind of defensive character. Defensive against the weather, defensive against difficult conditions in agriculture. I am thinking back hundreds of years.

(SNP activist, interview 10)

For all his self-assurance that the environment lent objectivity to his portrait of the Scottish psyche, others used the same natural features to paint a different picture.

Consider first, an interview conducted by Michael Ignatieff with a representative from Scottish Watch (a group concerned about English migration to Scotland) as part of the BBC television documentary *A Different Country* (January, 1995). The interviewee described Scottish Watch's task as 'trying to preserve Scottishness, if you like, from it being eroded, if you like, by English values.' Ignatieff then asked if this talk of an 'English threat' could divide Scotland. The response was as follows:

Extract 11

I don't think so because there are certain values I think most Scots have as a result of their inherited social, economic, historical traditions.
  Ignatieff: *Such as?*
  For example, we've always had a very, probably due to the fact that our environment has been a harsh environment, I think that by and large most Scots are a very co-operative people. We tend not to be as individualistic if you like as the English. We tend to hold back much more. We are not as articulate, we tend to hold community values as being important.

  (Ian Sutherland, Scottish Watch, interviewed in *A Different Country*,
  BBC, January, 1995)

Here, then, we see 'nature' being used to suggest a different set of characteristics as inherent to Scottish identity. The Scots are communal, not defensive, due to their harsh environment. However, it is not just that environment can be linked to identity in different ways, it can also be used to directly opposed ends. So, in contrast to the Scottish Watch version, a Liberal Democrat candidate emphasized how living in a tough environment makes people independent and opinionated. For him 'there are probably environmental reasons why we have been traditionally forced by a large part of our environment to be relatively open and relatively self-sufficient' (Liberal Democrat candidate, interview 49). The same reasons made Scots 'opinionated' and 'ready to sacrifice a lot for their opinions'. More specifically he attributed this 'independent and self-sufficient spirit to the widespread experience of needing to leave home at a relatively early age. He also attributed a supposed 'openness to ideas' to the opportunities for communication brought about by opportunities for sea and river-borne communication.

All the examples we have provided so far have used references to geography in order to essentialize contingent constructions of Scottishness. However, in arguing that environment provides a particularly potent tool in this regard, we are not arguing that the environment is always invoked in order to essentialize identity. Sometimes, in fact, reference to the terrain, climate, and social activities that link people to the land may be used to counter the idea of fixity. A literary example illustrates this well. In Shaw's *John Bull's Other Island* (1904), the character Larry Doyle takes strong exception to an Englishman's comment that he has 'the melancholy of the Keltic race'. Declaring that such talk enrages him ('When people talk about the Celtic race, I feel as if I could burn down London'), Doyle goes on to retort: 'Do you suppose a man need be a Celt to feel melancholy in Rosscullen ?' (cited in Faber, 1985: 153). Here, then, geography has not fixed characteristics in the national psyche such that these ingrained traits are manifested wherever the national subject may be. Rather, geography serves as a situational explanation, such that the national subject would behave differently in different climes and the non-national would behave identically when placed in the same location. The important point to be underlined here is that it would be as wrong to see the uses of environment as fixed as it would be to accept the fixed views of identity that flow from certain usages of environment. The way in which environment may be used in relation to identity is complex and it is a matter of argument as to whether it is used to render identity as contingent or as fixed, just as it is a matter of argument as to where, if fixed, it is located. As always, the argumentative and strategic dimension can be illustrated by variation between individuals. However such variation can always be ascribed to differences of cultural exposure and ingrained belief. Hence it is always useful to complement such evidence with instances of intra-individual variation. It is not uncommon to find the same person invoking notions of the environment in rather different ways. For example, one Conservative candidate used climate and topography to ground a construction of the Scots as inherently possessed of 'a sturdy self-reliance, loyalty, commitment, hard-work, thrift':

Extract 12

He's canny and thrifty, he's a sensible man, not mean, not either mean-spirited or mean in terms of money but careful, avowedly loyal and hard-working – perhaps that derives something from the rigours of the climate, the rigours of life and one only needs to look at so many of the great Scottish achievers, they came from a little cottage up a cold glen somewhere, they were probably brought up in considerable privation compared to modern standards and it may be that that was a spur and an incentive to get on and achieve . . . In any area of human endeavour, the Scots have a representation which is out of proportion with their numerical preponderance.

(Conservative candidate, interview 7)

Physical nature has shaped psychological nature so as to make the Scots natural entrepreneurs and to make it natural that they should thrive in the Union. That is, the Scottish people are natural Conservatives. This is an example *par excellence* of environment used as essentialization. What, then, of cases where the Scots might seem to be acting in ways that are un-Conservative? How are these to be explained? When the interviewer introduced this issue by raising the spectre of Red Clydeside (a period of radical agitation in and around Glasgow which reached its climax just after the First World War in the nearest thing Scotland, or indeed Britain, has seen to a socialist uprising) and suggested that it spoke volumes about the nature of Scottish identity, the same speaker replied as follows:

> ### Extract 13
>
> *I think that the Red Clydesiders were a product of that felicitous accident of the discovery of iron ore and coal in Scotland. If the geophysics of this country had been different and we'd found that in London, then I guess Thameside would have had perhaps the same social consequences that Scotland had.*
>
> (Conservative candidate, interview 7)

Here, environment switches from an indication of fixity to being a measure of contingency. It characterizes behaviour not as evidence for an unchanging nature but rather as accidental, strictly tied to time and place and nothing to do with inherent Scots differences from other countries such as England. It could as easily have occurred by England's capital river, the Thames, as by the Clyde as it flows through Glasgow to the sea. The switch is as easy to explain as it is obvious to behold. When it comes to supporting a construction of identity which is consonant with his political project as against that of rivals, environment is used to essentialize. When it comes to undermining a construction of identity that is consonant with rival political projects as against his own, environment is used to render contingent. The variation is transparent when identity constructions are approached through the lens of collective mobilization.

Identity and culture

As with the relationship between environment and character, the relationship between culture and national character has long been debated. Some, especially German romantics such as Herder, argued that a nation's culture gave expression to the nation's character. Others argued the opposite: a distinctive national character was produced through exposure to a distinctive (national) cultural experience. For David Hume, the human mind had a 'very imitative nature' and consequently 'like passions and inclinations . . . run, as it were by contagion, through the whole club or knot of companions'. He observed that 'whatever it be that forms the manners of one generation, the next must imbibe a deeper tincture of the same dye; men being more susceptible of all impressions during infancy, and retaining these impressions as long as they remain in the world' (Hume, 1748).

Although Herder and Hume offer different conceptions of the relationship between culture and character, both assume that there is but one culture and therefore one character. Of course, this should occasion little surprise. The ideology of nationalism characterizes the world as being divided into nations and the assertion of cultural distinctiveness has long been recognized as one of the most potent ways for a collectivity to claim the status of nation (Penrose, 1995). Further, and as we saw at the outset of this chapter, the idea that nations are marked by the possession of a unique and distinctive character and culture which must be expressed if the nation is to be true to itself has considerable political potency. As a corollary, it should come as no surprise to find definitions of national identity and hence prescriptions for collective action being organized through the invocation of such cultural resources.

Cultural resources invoked in this manner (be they narratives surrounding particular figures, social institutions or events) are often described as 'myths'. This is not to judge them as erroneous or distorting 'reality'. Rather, it is to designate them as having crucial importance in defining the way in which a group understands its own identity. Of course the mere fact that particular narratives and cultural products are seen as 'national' may be taken as implying a degree of sharedness and it may be tempting to conclude that this means that there is a shared understanding of what it means to identify with the nation. Yet, a sensitivity to the strategic nature of identity definition suggests otherwise. The very fact that some cultural products are familiar to all and constitute a part of 'what everyone knows' about the nation means that they are particularly powerful argumentative resources with which to ground one's constructions. As a corollary, we might expect that the greater the consensus as to the cultural status of a given artefact, the greater the dissensus as to its actual meaning.

These observations are well made in Tudor's (1972) analysis of myths. He emphasizes that myths are always invoked in the context of advocating a particular course of action and, as different courses of action are advocated, so different meanings may be ascribed to the 'same' product. Indeed, for Tudor, myths only ever occur as arguments which in turn are invariably responses to a particular state of affairs or opposing alternative, with the result that myths are inevitably shaped in accordance with the speakers' presuppositions, experiences and projects. Consequently, any attempt to identify a 'proper' version of cultural myths involves a reification of culture as standing above or outside practical everyday argument. Whenever one attempts to identify a common core which is shared by all, the result is that one distils out the singular meanings from the many versions deployed in argumentation, and so ends up with a product which is so bland and empty that there 'is virtually nothing sensible to be said' about it (Tudor, 1972: 47). A case in point is Hirsch's attempt to pin down the essentials of American culture in his work *Cultural Literacy: what every American needs to know*. As Lofgren (1989) points out, the end result of this project is a 'rather futile' list of 4,500 dates, places, people, events, books, phrases and sayings that make up the American common culture, but no sense of what they actually mean.

Similar observations are made by Holy (1996) in his analysis of political change in Eastern Europe. Writing of Czechoslovakia, he observes that Czech culture 'must be conceptualized not as timeless and unchangeable attributes of the Czech nation, as Czechs themselves conceptualize them, but as constructions perpetually re-created and modified in political practice. Moreover, rather than as a harmonious, singular, and coherent ideational system, they must be seen as a system of competing values and concepts which are internally inconsistent and ultimately irreconcilable' (Holy, 1996: 201). From this perspective, there is no such thing as a singular culture operating apart from individual or collective action and passed down unchanged from generation to generation. Rather, there is much to be gained from viewing culture as a set of resources that can be invoked to make sense of the present but which are necessarily transformed through the process of invocation and application to contemporary debates and social dilemmas.

Of course this re-conceptualization is difficult. As Handler explains, the

> very idea of culture has been elaborated in terms of boundedness, homogeneity, and the idea of immutable natural essence . . . we speak more readily of culture as a noun – 'a' culture, 'this' culture, 'our' culture – than as a verb indicating process, inter-communication, and the ongoing reconstruction of boundaries that are symbolic and not naturally given. (1994: 29)

However, this difficulty is part of the point. As with character traits and as with environment, the power of culture lies in the way in which its usage makes all that is ephemeral freeze into solidity. Yet if each argument is presented as solid, its ephemerality and the contingent nature of cultural usage is evident, especially within diachronic studies which chronicle the changing meanings attributed to particular products over time.

Nothing and no one escapes the ravages of history. Of all cultural icons, none is more iconic than 'the Bard', William Shakespeare, recently voted by BBC Radio 4 listeners as 'Man of the Millennium' and revered all over the world. Taylor (1989) quotes an Englishman from the 1760s who declared that 'a veneration for Shakespeare seems to be part of [an Englishman's] National Religion, and the only Part in which even your Men of Sense are Fanatics' (p. 399). Yet Taylor's point is precisely that Shakespeare was not always accorded such status. Fifty years after his death in 1616 he was almost forgotten. The first academic treatise devoted to him was published only in 1726 and entitled *Shakespeare Restored*. A quarter of a millennium later, in 1976, another analysis was published entitled *Shakespeare Restored – Once Again*. As Taylor puts it, we have been continuously re-inventing Shakespeare since the moment of his death.

Scotland too has its own unquestioned Bard: Robert, or Rabbie, Burns. And Burns, like Shakespeare, has been continuously re-invented to suit the times. According to Wittig's *The Scottish Tradition in Literature* (1958) it is possible to find a 'sturdy individualism' and 'egalitarian' politics in Burns's writing, which whilst undoubtedly influenced by French Revolutionary ideals, was also a manifestation of a distinctively Scottish tradition to be found in earlier Scottish poetry such as Barbour's *Bruce*, or Lyndsay's *Thrie Estaitis* (written in the fourteenth and sixteenth centuries respectively). In Wittig's words, this tradition may be characterized as exemplifying a 'free manliness, a *saeva indignatio* against oppression, a violent freedom, sometimes an aggressive spirit of independence or egalitarianism' (1958: 95). However, the meaning of Burns was heavily dependent upon the context in which he was read.

In the nineteenth century, Scottish society was riven by struggles between the new commercial middle classes and the power of aristocratic patronage. In such a context Burns was used to give credence to laissez faire liberalism (Finlay, 1997). More specifically, the cult of Burns was used to propagate anti-aristocratic sentiments and challenge the exclusion of the middle classes from the traditional Scottish institutions. Burns was described as a 'commoner' who demonstrated that genius was not the sole preserve of the aristocracy. Moreover, he – the voice and the soul of Scotland – had also been let down by the aristocracy. In the twentieth century, as social division shifted so as to become increasingly focused on the struggle between Capital and Labour, a new Burns emerged. This was the Burns inscribed on Trades Union banners and celebrated in the Soviet Union. Interpreted from a socialist perspective, this Burns no longer represented middle-class aspirations. Rather, he represented the struggle against oppression and inequality. After the First World War Burns and his poetry were to be found featuring in advertisements for the Co-operative movement as evidence of the Scottish tradition of anti-capitalism (Finlay, 1997).

Such historical perspectives are illuminating, but they also carry dangers. To adopt such a broad overview can lead one to suggest synchronic consensus in order the better to highlight diachronic dissensus. To describe one era in terms of the middle-class Burns makes the contrast with another era of proletarian Burns all the more stark. However, even within the same period, Burns is a bone which many dogs fight over. By examining these tussles we can get a more intimate view of how cultural resources are contested, appropriated and applied. Perhaps that is best done by examining some of Burns's most famous words, words so famous indeed that they are likely to be known even by those who hadn't realized their provenance. They have become, to borrow Billig's term, a commonplace of Scottish culture (cf. Billig, 1987). We can then also compare Burns's saying with another which has equivalent status in a Scots cultural treasury.

The two sayings we have in mind are 'a man's a man for a' that' and 'we're a' Jock Tamson's bairns'. If the former is recognizable as a line from Burns, the origins of the latter (literally, 'we are all the children of Jock Tamson') are somewhat obscure. However, both convey the idea that beneath the surface of socially created difference, people share a basic common humanity. The frequency of their usage in political rhetoric is hinted at in Eric Linklater's 1934 comic novel, *Magnus Merriman*. The book, which is based on Linklater's own experiences as a nationalist candidate in a General Election campaign, includes irreverent accounts of election meetings. Merriman, the hero of the tale, describes one such meeting where 'it was hardly possible to distinguish one speech from another. Most of them referred to deer-forests, Bannockburn, rationalization, and Robert Burns' (p. 84). He describes another disastrous occasion where the audience included an 'ill-washed, ill-favoured boy', 'an old man with a dribbling nose, an ear-trumpet, a dirty beard and a noisy habit of breathing', and 'a rough sneering red-faced slit-eyed cattle-dealer, all whisky and lechery'. The speaker was little more distinguished than his audience, and he 'concluded his speech by assuring these dismal electors that a man was a man for a' that, and they were a' Jock Tamson's bairns' before sitting down 'in a mutter of apathetic applause' (p. 164–5).

Almost 60 years later the sayings and Burns himself were still being invoked in political argumentation. Indeed, we have already seen, in Extracts 8 and 9 above, how 'a man's a man for a' that' can be used both to characterize the Scots as collectivists who favour welfare provision and as individualists who favour voluntary support. Both speakers seek to invoke the authority of the same cultural figure, both use the same saying, and yet they employ it to exactly opposed ends. Let us now consider the quite contrary definitions of the nature of the social world that may be sustained by 'we're a' Jock Tamson's bairns' and some further complexities in the use of Burns and his poetry.

In the voice of one SNP MP, 'We're a' Jock Tamson's bairns' was used to advance a radical communitarian politics. Elsewhere in his interview, this politician had condemned the policies of the Conservative government, such as the Poll Tax and the privatization of water, as alien to Scottishness (Extract 9, Chapter Four). He continued:

Extract 14

My argument would be that the Scottish attitude to our institutions is fundamentally different from that in England. We still have a sense of community in Scotland. We don't have any fear of the National Health Service or the education system because it is of the people. It belongs to the people. We would look for democratic control of it, more accountability from it. Whereas in England, especially under the Thatcher years, there was a complete contrast, when it was all self, the individual.... It's just the Scottish way. It's very difficult to pin it down to anything, but we do have a sense of community. 'We're all Jock Tamson's bairns'.

(SNP MP, interview 47)

When used by Nicholas Fairbairn, the words assumed a very different meaning. Fairbairn's usage occurred in the context of a suggestion by the interviewer that the Scots were 'inherently egalitarian and left of centre'. In response, he immediately denied the claim: 'Well they're certainly not inherently egalitarian'. He then proceeded to argue that there were actually significant social class divisions within the Scottish nation but that these were quietly accepted and not experienced as problematic or requiring redress:

Extract 15

[Scotland] *is a very small country and everyone knows everyone else. It's only in the larger countries that the Duc de Normandie is not known by the burghers of Calais that you get an aristocratic structure. There is a perfectly good aristocratic structure in Scotland but the, it's rather like a big pub, Scotland, you know, everyone talks to everyone else and nobody minds who you are particularly; 'we're all Jock Tamson's bairns'.*

(Sir Nicholas Fairbairn, Conservative MP, interview)

Here 'Jock Tamson's bairns' is used to promote hierarchy rather than democratic community. It is used to endorse acceptance of inequality rather than action to overcome inequality. Common humanity is a consolation for our different stations in life rather than a platform from which to challenge them. The distinction between the two usages of the same saying is very close to McCrone's distinction between an 'idealist' and an 'activist' interpretation of the notion that all humans have equal worth in an unequal society. In the idealist reading: 'If man is primordially equal, social structural inequalities do not matter, so nothing needs to be done' (McCrone, 1992: 90). However, the activist reading requires the active pursuit of strategies which resolve the anomaly between primordial equality and humanly constructed inequality. It is exactly the same distinction that underlies the different uses of 'a man's a man for a' that'.

Here, then, we see something which will become increasingly familiar over successive pages: the existence of opposing versions of that which our protagonists claim to have a unique and singular meaning. This makes it all the more important to dismiss the opposition as holding a false and inauthentic version of cultural icons. For Fairbairn, it wasn't enough to contest the notion that Scots are egalitarian or to recruit Jock Tamson to the fight against egalitarianism. He also had to rubbish the notion that any cultural icon could be fighting on the other side. This rubbishing came about when we pressed the argument that Scotland could be seen as an inherently radical place. We pushed Fairbairn by raising the examples that had been raised with us by other interviewees, we cited Burns and we cited more of Red Clydeside – especially John Maclean, a Glaswegian socialist, who was elected honorary president of the First All-Russian Congress of Soviets and appointed Bolshevik Consul in Glasgow. Although Maclean's goal of making Glasgow 'a Petrograd, a revolutionary storm-centre second to none' (Maclean; cited in Foster, 1992) was never achieved, he enjoyed a high status with Lenin, and as late as the 1970s, featured on Soviet postage stamps (Marr, 1992). Fairbairn saw little need to respond to Maclean, but he could not let Burns go so easily, as the following extract shows.

Extract 16

Well I think that's rubbish. Let's take the egalitarian generally and Burns. Well, in St Giles' Cathedral they replaced the West Window which was a very grand window of our Lord and Saviour and his disciples, with one of Burns. So this is a great glorification of the greatest unfaithful fornicating drunk that any land has ever produced and he never spent his time outwith the houses of the aristocracy unless he was among the rushes with the lasses. He was a frightful snob. So this myth that we're an egalitarian race which the communists in Russia latched onto, is mythical.

(Sir Nicholas Fairbairn, Conservative MP, interview)

Several features of this construction are of interest. First, the opposition position is dismissed as simply mythical – in this case myth being used in the popular sense of indicating falsehood and fantasy rather than in the technical sense of grounding collective beliefs. Secondly, that position is further discredited by being associated with an alien national outgroup, the Russian Communists, rather than acknowledging it to be an alternative held within the Scottish ingroup. Hence the possibility that there is legitimate difference amongst Scots as to the interpretation of Burns and that he might allow multiple meanings is dismissed. Thirdly, the idea that Burns might be used to buttress egalitarianism and left-wing ideology more generally is ridiculed by portraying him as antithetical not only to equality but to radical principles more generally. Burns was not only a snob but a waster and womanizer. Fourthly, this extract needs to be placed against Extract 7 where, it will be recalled, Fairbairn described Burns as strongly anti-authority in order to argue against bringing authorities (in the form of a Scottish parliament) closer to home. So, when used in support of his own version of identity, Burns is a man of integrity and of principles that just happen to coincide with Fairbairn's own positions. When used in favour of a rival version of identity, Burns becomes a hypocritical snob who isn't much of a foundation for any principles, especially those of the left. What better illustration could be had of the way in which culture does not fix the meaning of identity, but rather is widely and flexibly applied because of the illusion of solidity that it confers? Fifthly, and lastly, Fairbairn's argument is less concerned with Burns's cultural creations than with Burns the man. It is not the poems or songs which preoccupy him, but the living, breathing, fornicating poet and song-smith. It is a short step from using the poetry to using the poet as an icon of national identity. Burns is but one of several individuals who have achieved such iconic status and whose value in defining the nation turns them into resources for identity construction and sources of identity contestation and we will have cause to consider the place of Scotland's heroes in the construction of identity in the next chapter. Before doing so let us look at the one arena of Scottish life which would seem to offer something of a benchmark against which to judge such contrasting characterizations of what it is to be Scottish.

Identity and institutions

If one wanted to find some aspect of reality that would serve to fix the nature of our identities, then the obvious starting point for any self-respecting social scientist would be in the nature of our institutions: the buildings and rules and regulations which govern our social exchanges and in which we live our everyday lives. These institutions differ from country to country and could well explain national differences. At the very least they would seem to offer an opportunity to adjudicate between the different visions of Scottishness advanced by the political protagonists we have studied.

The institutional distinctiveness of the Scottish educational, ecclesiastical and legal traditions was recognized in the Treaty of Union and these institutions are frequently characterized as functioning to reproduce a distinctive Scottish identity. For instance, the Scottish Presbyterian tradition, and the need for the congregation rather than the church hierarchy to interpret the scriptures is seen as linked both to a distinctive emphasis on education for all and to a broad democratic culture – two ideas that fuse in the concept of the Scots 'democratic intellect' (Davie, 1961). One key element of this 'democratic intellect' is the Scottish four-year university degree system where students enter a year younger than in the English system. The argument is that this places higher education within the reach of all, since one is less dependent upon privileged schools to reach a higher entry standard. Correspondingly, recent threats to the four-year degree and to other distinctively Scottish institutions have evoked much concern about the 'Englishing' of Scotland (cf. Beveridge & Turnbull, 1989; Davie, 1961).

Our concern, however, is not so much with the role of institutional reality in the formation of the Scottish subject as in the ways in which institutions are invoked in order to reify contingent versions of the Scottish subject and hence to (re)create social reality in general and institutional reality in particular. If identity can be tied to the concrete reality of churches and universities and law courts, it becomes far harder to be blown away at will.

Since we have started by mentioning the traditional conception of educational institutions, let us continue by examining their rhetorical uses. In the field of political debate, one of the most frequently invoked figures is the ideological hero of Scottish enlightenment: the *lad o' pairts*. This character is an individual who, despite being born into poverty (a poor young crofter or peasant), had the ability to benefit from educational opportunity and so make his (there is no female counterpart) way in the world. As MacLaren (1976) observes, his success was not simply because of an adherence to Samuel Smiles's philosophy of self-help. Although individual effort is important, it is the presence of both the institutionalized means and the social encouragement for individuals to realize their worth, regardless of their material wealth, that is central to the drama. For our purposes the interest of the *lad o' pairts* resides in the way in which he may be invoked to ground quite divergent characterizations of the social relations obtaining in Scotland. Thus, whereas our participants may be found talking of the singular meaning to be ascribed to this character (and hence the Scots' collective identity), close inspection of 'his' invocation shows that both 'radical' and 'conservative' models of social relations may be constructed and grounded through reference to the same character. For example, in the two extracts below, the *lad o' pairts* (and indeed Burns's 'a man's a man') is used to ground the activist model of Scottish identity which places central value on community support for the weak and poor.

Extract 17

I think if you talked to most Scots they would say we are a much, much more egalitarian society, a much more community-orientated society. We are not so thrusting. We don't suffer from the 'me too' or the 'keeping up with the Jones's' em, and that's why I think the Scots rejected Thatcherism in the way that they did because they saw in Thatcher the embodiment of everything that they might have considered English people to be. I think we understood that she was trying to impose upon the Scottish people a culture, an ethos, call it what you will, that was totally alien to what we were. . . . For example, Burns. I think that most people would see a Scottish person as being the Burns, the, caring, 'a man's a man for a' that'. Em, that we should be brothers and sisters or whatever, if anybody no matter where they are in the world and I think you know that runs through Scottish society. I think we still hold on to the belief that while we would like to get on, you know there's the lad o' pairts *who, you know, from a working-class background, who go to university who get on in the world, but they never actually forget where they came from, but they will give a helping hand to somebody else. I think it's the ability to get on, to get on and not at the expense of others, that you would not do somebody down, you would'nae stamp on people in the scramble to get to the top. You would be more likely, I think, to give them a helping hand.*

(SNP candidate, interview 3)

Extract 18

The democracy of the Presbytery spins off and that is that you, this is the questioning view, it's the independence of it. And that is engendered and enhanced by poets, particularly like Burns. It's that view, having an independent view and not thinking you're better than anybody else. You're every bit as good and this is very worrying to me now, these standards of fairness, a great sense of fairness, the concept of justice, 'That's no', one of the things is 'That's no' fair', something isn't fair, and a view you know, that the underdog should be supported, a sense of fairness. Well, fairness – justice is a much more difficult concept – but fairness and egalitarian. Egalitarianism – everybody is as good as everybody else – and that goes through your educational system. The idea of the lad o' *pairts getting his way and make use of the talents. And society had calls and claims on him: very strong. And that's very worrying to me. That's being, you can see it before your eyes, being eroded, day in and day out. And that's throughout the Scottish character and that I think is deep in our history.*

(SNP candidate, interview 41)

For both these SNP candidates, the *lad o' pairts* is the concrete expression of Scottish egalitarianism. His progress is not so much a matter of celebrating individual advancement as the social fact of advancement for all, and his betterment is only celebrated insofar as it allows betterment for all: it leads to him having the ability to help others and it gives others the right to call upon his qualities. In addition, this quality is a distinctively Scottish quality which, explicitly in the former extract and implicitly in the second, is contrasted to English individualism and competitiveness. What is more, in the latter extract it is stressed that the core Scottish character is under attack. In two ways, then, this *lad* serves SNP policy well by the way this *lad* is held to be served by SNP policy. On the one hand, there is a match between SNP social–economic policy and the egalitarianism that he is used to enshrine. On the other hand, SNP constitutional policy becomes the only way of preserving the *lad* and the values that surround him.

In the hands of Conservatives, this selfsame *lad* acquires a whole new character which now enshrines rather than undermines Tory policies towards social provision and towards the Union. The Conservative MP and sometime Secretary of State for Scotland, Michael Forsyth, took issue with activist constructions of Scotland which he characterized as 'propaganda', peddling 'the mythology of class warfare' and which libelled 'working-class values by equating them with those of the under-class rather those of the aspirational majority' (Michael Forsyth, Conservative MP, speech, Stirling, 26.4.96). This construction of Scottish values as 'aspirational' was developed when he continued that: 'even in its more virile days . . . [the] stagnant egalitarianism of the old socialist political culture . . . [was] in contention with one of the most powerful and consistent instincts of the Scots, the spirit of enterprise. Thrift, commerce, work creation, these are quintessentially Scottish characteristics'.

So as to support this aspirational/entrepreneurial construction of Scottishness, Forsyth argued that the Scots' concern with the underdog was not manifested in collectivism: 'real concern for the underdog has traditionally been translated into practical terms by Scots in works of philanthropy. Hand in hand with the wealth-creating enterprise went good works. Philanthropy fuelled by enterprise is a classic Scottish preoccupation'. However the climax of Forsyth's account came with the entrance of a now familiar figure:

Extract 19

It is one of the most universal unifying characteristics of our people. When most of Europe was illiterate, the lad o' pairts *giving evidence of talent to the local dominie would find a place at university. He would set off from home, armed with the bag of oatmeal to sustain him for the duration. Don't worry, it's not a hint of future policy! Hard work won a place in society. The school system meant that talent was tolled from all parts of the country. This in turn led to social mobility, in every generation, the brightest pupils from humble backgrounds have an avenue to self-betterment and to success.*

(Michael Forsyth, Conservative MP, speech, Stirling, 26.4.96)

In this context, our hero is a hero of enterprise, one whose individual efforts render both state intervention and collective support redundant. In other words, this figure of Scotland is a figure of Conservative values.

A rather similar argument was used by another Conservative MP, but rather than relying on the *lad o' pairts* he referred more directly to the interlinked Scottish institutions of church and education. The values enshrined in these institutions shaped the national psyche in a distinctive way. Thus, when we asked whether it was possible to talk of a Scottish character, he replied in the affirmative. That character, he argued, made Scots model Thatcherites – where Thatcherism was defined as: 'good old fashioned Presbyterianism, living within your means, an honest day's work for an honest day's pay'. More specifically, he traced the Scots character as follows:

Extract 20

[It] goes back largely to a traditional Presbyterian outlook on life, that hard work is to be encouraged, that we're put on this earth really not to enjoy ourselves but to make the best of a bad job. . . . Calvin's teachings and Knox's teachings are still very alive today and not just in the Presbyterian population, but even in the Roman Catholic population in Scotland is Calvinist in that aspect. Education I think still matters in perception terms to more Scots than elsewhere. You go to school, you get your 'O' grades, you get your Highers, you know, and that's very much alive today. And you don't enjoy yourself at the weekend, I think that's still there in a lot of older Scots.

(Conservative MP, interview 14)

This is the rhetorical equivalent of matching one's opponents and raising the stakes further. Not only is one account of education matched with another, but religion is also thrown into the pot on the side of Conservatism. Well, all can play at that game, and indeed all do play. So we can see how the SNP could construe Scottish ecclesiastical institutions so as to support their characterization of the Scots as radical. Indeed, whereas the Conservative MP cited above invoked the Presbyterian tradition to ground his claim that the Scots were Thatcherites, his SNP opponents argued that this tradition acted as a bulwark against Thatcherism. The following is taken from the magazine *Liberation*, which describes itself as 'a left nationalist quarterly' and which clearly supports the SNP:

Extract 21

Cultural factors also contributed to Scotland substantially ignoring the new right agenda. A tenement society is based upon co-operation. The democratic Presbyterian tradition, every believer an equal before God, needing no priestly interlocutor with him, able to dispute theology with the minister (himself no priest but a well-educated member of the priesthood of all believers) led to Melville's harsh judgement on James IV – 'Ye are nocht but God's silly vassal'. Such traditions, holding Kings in scant regard, sit uneasily with deference and individualism.

('The Left, Democracy and the National Question', in *Liberation*,
issue 2, p. 14–15)

However, the argument did not stop there. As our next extract shows, even if one were to accept the Conservative MP's argument that the Presbyterian church valorized 'hard work', this does not necessarily imply that Scottish values and norms imply support for the Conservatives. The following shows that such a valorization of hard work could be used to imply that the norms and values that constitute their collective identity entail the belief that people have a 'right to work':

Extract 22

I think certainly there is a strong work ethic. I think people believe that you ought to be given the opportunity to work, you ought to have the right to work and when you are given that right to work that you ought to work hard to earn a living and again I think that's something that probably the churches have encouraged.

(Labour MP, interview 27)

Here is further evidence for the danger of viewing identities in terms of traits without examining the context in which those traits descriptions are uttered. The MPs cited in Extracts 20 and 22 concur in ascribing the trait 'hard-working' to the Scots. They also concur in tracing the trait back to the influence of the churches. But they use the term in an entirely different sense and to entirely different ends. The latter's usage has to do with a collective right and a collective struggle to achieve that right. The former's usage has to do with individual progress and the need to leave individuals unencumbered by outside intervention. In the previous section we saw how both the 'activist' and 'idealist' notions of Scotland can be argued for using the same words; earlier in this section we saw how both notions could be argued for using the same institution; now we see how they can be supported through the use of the same terms which are rooted in the same institution. In all three cases, the important message is that institutional and character descriptions should not be taken at face value nor treated as the end-point of enquiry. Rather, it is necessary to look at their strategic use in reifying different forms of social practice as constituting the national identity.

Nonetheless, the temptation still remains to try and resolve arguments about the nature of Scottishness by inspecting the reality of Scottish experience. Where one is faced with competing definitions of Scottish culture or Scottish institutions, and hence of Scottish identity, perhaps one could compare their degree of correspondence with reality and so adjudicate between them? However, this is to underestimate the degree of argumentation concerning the Scottishness of contemporary Scotland. Just as people advance different constructions of what it is to be Scottish, so they also argue about the degree to which particular features of reality really represent the nation.

Take, for example, the arguments as to whether Scotland's schools are actually Scottish. Often, we found those wishing to construe Scottishness as 'radical', 'egalitarian' and 'communitarian', grounding their constructions through reference to the relatively large proportion of Scottish children attending non-selective state 'comprehensive' schools. Thus one Labour MP argued that Scottish education 'is quite distinctive from south of the border,' and he continued, 'I think that it is egalitarian and more Comprehensive and I think that most people in Scotland, whether they have a lot of money or very little money, most people are quite content for their children to go to the nearest school and I think that that plays an important part too in Scottish culture' (Labour MP, interview 27).

Yet we found others arguing that not all schools in Scotland are Scottish. Some Conservatives argued that comprehensive schooling constituted a distortion, if not a subversion, of the Scottish tradition. For instance, one Conservative MP argued that 'comprehensivization represented the ultimate Anglicization of our school system' (Michael Forsyth, speech, Stirling, 26.4.96). Another asserted that anything that was Scottish about Scottish education had 'nothing to do with the Department of Education, St Andrews House [which houses the government ministry responsible for Scottish affairs] and secondary schools and so on. The love of learning and getting on in the world was self-taught or if not self-taught by the family certainly self-taught by the minister who was the dominie'. This same MP continued that 'we must again be self-taught. We must have individual schools. I see we're now threatened this very day that all individual schools in Scotland will be abolished and everything will be comprehensive which will destroy the unique independence of mind which is so important in Scotland' (Sir Nicholas Fairbairn, interview).

If the relationship between the conditions existing in Scotland and the 'authentic' Scotland is a matter of debate, it stands to reason that one could not settle the matter of identity by referring to any given set of conditions even if it were possible to agree on the significance of those conditions in the first place. One would still have to determine *when* Scotland was truly Scottish. In other words, one cannot avoid matters of history either by commission or by omission. For Fairbairn, in the above extracts, the true Scotland comes from an era before the structures of modern government had evolved when the teacher was the dominie and education was outwith the state. But history is not of interest purely for its own sake. The past is interrogated because of its links to the present and to the future. Fairbairn's particular narrative involves a past authenticity that has been lost in the present and which requires present action such that identity may be recovered in the future – his call is 'forward to the past!' In Fairbairn's own terms, a unique independence of mind is being destroyed through comprehensive schooling, and the Scots must again be self-taught for it to reappear.

Lest it be thought that such nostalgia is the unique preserve of conservatives – with either a big or a little 'C' – it is worth looking at another and similarly structured argument. An editorial in the liberal/left newspaper *Scotland on Sunday* of 10 April, 1994 dealt with the issue of racism. Through invoking Burns's dictum that 'a man's a man for a' that', the traditions of Scottish education and Scotland's history of providing 'a safe haven for refugees from Italy, Lithuania and Poland', it was argued that: 'Scottish society has long prided itself on its democratic instincts'. However, whilst defining the national identity in this way, the editorial also drew attention to the phenomenon of racism in contemporary Scotland: 'All over the country that most un-Scottish of instincts, xenophobia, is on the increase'. Hence the present was seen as a move away from Scots liberality and the future threatened its complete abnegation. One approach to this characterization of racism as 'in' the nation but not 'of' it, would be to construe it as typical ingroup bias: an example of the ways in which positive characterizations of the ingroup stereotype are maintained in the face of negative information (Hewstone, 1989; Hunter, Stringer & Watson, 1991). However, such an account would miss the strategic dimension. It overlooks the way in which this characterization of ingroup identity serves to promote future-oriented action for change. Most importantly, the definition of the ingroup identity as 'tolerant' is significant for the way in which it organizes action to bring about a 'tolerant' future. Not only is the end a rediscovery of the distinctive values of Scottishness, but the means are also distinctively Scottish as the editorial goes on to state: 'There is a good case to be made for Scottish schooling, based on its democratic intellect, to help young people understand that racial or political intolerance has no place in Scotland's variegated and constantly changing society' ('No place in Scotland for racial hatred', editorial, *Scotland on Sunday*, 10.4.94).

If the past helps make the future, it is too valuable a resource to be abandoned by anyone; Conservative, liberal, radical or whoever. If versions of identity can be given weight and inertia through their links to 'defining' moments in history or else through invoking a constant flow in time, then history becomes another technique of reification and hence another battleground. Indeed, it is probably *the* primary means for authorizing national identity and hence *the* primary ground of battle. It allows for many complexities in defining what the 'defining' moments of history are and in defining the meaning of moments once they are defined as 'defining'. It also allows for many narratives of the relationship between past, present and future. The next chapter deals with some of these complexities.

Conclusion

In previous chapters we noted the ubiquity of identity talk. We wish to make a similar point here. From speaker after speaker, interviewee after interviewee, we have heard talk about Scottish identity (or Australian identity or Danish identity or whatever). The difference between this and the previous chapters, of course, is in the aspect of identity with which we have been concerned. In this chapter, all the examples have addressed the content of identity. It could be objected that we have been selective and indeed we have. Every single one of the speakers we listened to – either in interview or speaking from a public platform – referred in some way or another to the distinctive meanings associated with being Scottish. Sometimes they referred to the matter repeatedly and at length. To have related all these examples would have been impossible. We had to select. But no one was exempt, left-winger or right-winger, prominent or less prominent, in public or in private.

How, then, do people describe the distinctive nature of national categories? We have noted once or twice that the question could be rephrased as: 'What is the nature of national stereotypes?' In fact everything we have covered could be translated into the language of stereotyping and hence the whole chapter can be seen as a critique of the psychology of stereotyping. This critique could be summarized in four associated points.

The first point is that stereotypic accounts are strategic and future-oriented rather than purely cognitive and present-oriented. All those we have listened to are not involved in giving neutral descriptions of the national group. Rather they are seeking to define the forms of social reality people should seek to defend or realize and hence the policies and parties they should support. Throughout the chapter, speakers construe a consonance between national identity and party policy such that their party is seen to realize national identity. Where descriptions of national identity bear little relation to reality it is not because the speaker has an insufficient grasp on reality, is subject to bias, or whatever. Quite often speakers show an explicit awareness or even choose to stress the discrepancy between current reality and stereotype. Their whole point is to use that discrepancy in order to argue for a change such that the two are once more brought into relation. These are graphic and powerful examples of the point that the whole concept of 'bias' only makes sense as long as one sees stereotypes as purely perceptual and ignores the strategic dimension.

What we find throughout are arguments over the nature of identity as a means of mobilizing people to create the future. If we are suggesting that there will be multiple versions of identity, it is because of the assumption that identity should be singular. Speakers only argue about identity because of that assumption. Otherwise they would be merely speaking to themselves. When people propose an egalitarian or else an entrepreneurial version of Scottish identity, it is never to speak only to egalitarian or entrepreneurial Scots, it is to address everybody and to solicit support from all. Even where people do acknowledge different types of national identity, it is to claim that these are contradictory strands – the good and bad faces of the national identity – which are shared by everybody. This has fundamental implications for our understanding of stereotype consensus. Consensus has always been important in the stereotyping literature. After all, the original point of studying the phenomenon was because it seemed to provide a basis for understanding common patterns of social action. Consensus was therefore counterposed to difference. We have argued that the two should be viewed as complementary rather than contradictory. It is the key assumption, shared by all our speakers, that nationals should act on a common national identity, that raises the stakes in the struggle to determine the distinctive meaning of the nation. As we have phrased it, borrowing the terms if not the conclusion from Haslam, Oakes, Turner, McGarty and Reynolds (1998), consensualization and dissensus are two sides of the same coin.

Our third point moves us from identity processes to the form in which identity content should be understood. In fact, the two issues are interlinked and our reconceptualization of the former has implications for how we conceive of the other. Traditionally, stereotypes are treated as a set of trait terms. As much as anything else this is a methodologically rather than theoretically driven choice. It is easy to measure trait terms on Likert scales, easy to determine differences between the perceptions of different groups and easy to determine changes in the perception of any one group from context to context. However, perhaps one of the most striking points to emerge from this chapter is the way in which the same terms, even the same phrases and sayings, can be used to mean fundamentally different things, to suggest fundamentally opposed notions of social relations as central to the national identity and to mobilize support for fundamentally incompatible political parties and projects. Theoretically, we have argued that identities need to be conceived as models of self-in-social-relations if we are to understand how they are related to practice – both in the sense of organizing our practices and of being changed through practice. The evidence of this chapter now lends empirical support to this way of understanding stereotype content. The different versions of identity we have come across have always been different versions of the forms of social relations in which group members should live – both at an intra- and inter-group level – even if these versions sometimes share the same trait terms.

This takes us to our fourth and final point, which has occupied us for most of the chapter. Ingroup stereotypes are offered with the intention of obtaining maximum ingroup consensus, but with the result that there is dissensus about the 'true' stereotype and hence where that consensus should come to rest. It therefore becomes increasingly necessary to naturalize one's own version such that it is no longer just one amongst many but becomes the only version worth considering. We have examined a wide range of resources which are used to naturalize identity and we have argued that, if we take them at face value, then we ourselves succumb to their hypnotic charms and take contingent creations for natural kinds. If we take character ascriptions as the nature of stereotypes rather than reifying ways of talking about them, if we take stereotypes as descriptions of reality rather than accounts designed to make reality, then we have already been hypnotized. This is what we mean when we suggest that the conventional psychology of stereotypes runs the danger of being ideology rather than ideology critique.

6 Lessons in National History

Heroes

Every nation has its heroes. Those exemplary figures who we are taught about in school, whose exploits are summarized in well-known tales, whose characters are exemplified in singular feats: Sir Francis Drake playing bowls as the Armada advances; Robert the Bruce watching the spinning spider; George Washington indulging in the single sin of chopping down a cherry tree. Their grave and graven features are known to us all: staring at us from portraits, towering over us as statues, commemorated on bank notes. We are led to believe that we know them so well, and that by knowing them we know ourselves. For these heroes become icons. Their character becomes the national character. The way they are defined defines how we should be. For those who have followed our argument thus far, the twist in this particular tale should already be obvious: because the character of these heroes is assumed to be a given and because it is acknowledged to characterize national identity, they constitute a primary resource through which different versions of the nation and different projects for the nation are fought out.

The place of heroic individuals in the grounding of particular constructions of the national community may be discerned in the attention paid to them by the state in situations where the organization of collective action is particularly pressing. Indeed, this attention illustrates the point that a hero's status is itself constructed. For example, Zionist propagandists, and subsequently Israeli state representatives, conscious of the need to organize collective sentiment, have made much of Yosef Trumpeldor. Trumpeldor was one of a few Zionist pioneers heavily outnumbered in a skirmish at Tel Hai in the Northern Galilee area of Palestine in 1920. The pioneers' resistance and Trumpeldor's last words – 'it is good to die for our country' – were seized upon to define the emergent Israeli identity. He was even linked with the long-dead Jewish heroes of antiquity and, many years after his death, was depicted as intervening in contemporary matters. In all of this Trumpeldor was the example of heroic self-sacrifice, which all were enjoined to emulate. Although this definition of national values was communicated to generations of school pupils in the form of celebrations of Tel Hai Day, an increasingly war-weary public has come to question such values. As a result they have also come to question the version of Trumpeldor's actions and character in which these values are grounded. Some suggest that rather than the Hebrew words 'tov lamut' ('it is good to die') gracing his dying lips, it was the Russian 'iob tvoiu mat' ('fuck your mother'). With this construction of his death Trumpeldor is transformed from a heroic icon who served to induce equal sacrifices in others, into a 'reluctant victim' who broke into profanities (Zerubavel, 1994: 115).

The controversial status of Trumpeldor in Israel is matched by the controversy surrounding Jan Palach in Czechoslovakia, though this time the state sought to dismantle and not to erect his heroic reputation. Palach, a student in Prague, set himself on fire to protest at the Soviet invasion of 1968. For the protesters, Palach's burning was reminiscent of the fate of the Czech hero, Jan Hus, burned at the stake in 1415. Like Hus, Palach was a national hero who had sacrificed himself in order to inspire others to resist a foreign onslaught. His was a particularly noble and distinctively Czech gesture (Holy, 1996). The Czech communist authorities of the time were particularly sensitive to the potential power of this account in mobilizing dissent against their regime. They therefore set out to rebut the charge that the Communists represented foreign powers and, more importantly, that Palach was appropriate as a patriotic icon. They characterized him as an unstable character who was obsessed with an alien Buddhist philosophy (as evidenced by a Buddhist book which was found in his apartment). Consequently his self-immolation was construed, not as something typically Czech, but rather as being driven by his idiosyncratic interest in a culture which was totally alien to the Czechs (Holy, 1996).

Palach is not only controversial in his own land. Like many heroes, his character has been appropriated by many movements in many countries. Thus Wallace, who, with Bruce and Burns, stands virtually alone in Scotland's pantheon of heroes, has been used in places as far apart as Nyasaland and Italy. Ash (1990) describes how participants in the Black nationalist revolt in the highlands of Nyasaland came, through their contact with Church of Scotland schools and ministers, to cite Wallace in their justification of their revolt against white oppression. More recently it has been noteworthy how Wallace has featured in the contemporary arguments of the 'Padanian' nationalists of the Northern League in Italy. Insofar as they conceive of themselves as the descendants of the Celtic tribe of the Longobardi, Padanian nationalists distance themselves from the south of Italy through identifying with a north-western Celtic culture. Their leader, Umberto Bossi, has repeatedly referred to 'our Scottish brothers' in his speeches and apparently identifies himself with Wallace (*Scotland on Sunday*, 12.1.97). For all this, however, Wallace and Bruce are a far firmer and more constant fixture in the political discourse of Scotland than of anywhere else. Take just three examples spanning three centuries. The first, a pamphlet authored by Scottish supporters of the French Revolution in 1796, asked if Wallace had died 'in vain' (cited in Scott, 1992: 223). The second occurred on the eve of the 1992 election when *The Sun* made a dramatic appeal: 'After 1,000 years of history, let us finally forge the dynamic nation that Bruce fought for, Burns wrote for and Wallace died for. Now's the day and now's the hour.' (*The Sun*, 8.4.92). The third, a cartoon published just after the 1992 General Election in the 'nationalist' magazine, *Siol*, showed a newspaper headline ('Election special – Scottish people reject freedom') and featured Bruce asking Wallace: 'Why the hell did we bother Sir William?' In case there was any ambiguity the cartoon was subtitled 'Men like Bruce and Wallace fought and died for Scotland's freedom – what have you done?' (*Siol*, issue 11, 1993: 6). The roll-call of national heroes would be familiar to any Scot, and the use to which they are put would be familiar anywhere.

Sir William Wallace and King Robert the Bruce are both famous for their roles in the thirteenth and fourteenth century battles which led to Scotland's independence. Whilst Bruce led the military victory at Bannockburn, Wallace had won another strategically important battle at Stirling Bridge and, when finally delivered into the hands of the English, met a death of ritualized barbarity. The exploits of Wallace and Bruce have been commemorated in all manner of media. In poetry, Wallace's exploits were popularized in Blind Harry's fifteenth century epic, *The Acts and Deeds of Sir William Wallace*. Those of Bruce were celebrated in *The Brus*, written by John Barbour in the fourteenth century. Both heroes were also celebrated in the construction of public monuments, most notably the Wallace memorial tower near Stirling and the statue of Bruce at Bannockburn. More recently, their exploits were popularized in film. By far the most successful of these was *Braveheart*, the script of which was based on Blind Harry's *Wallace*. It played to packed cinemas throughout Scotland. It became the fifth biggest grossing movie in the UK in 1995. And Scotland, which normally provides just 8 per cent of the UK audience, this time provided 28 per cent (Edensor, 1997).

If every Scottish schoolchild can recite the exploits of Bruce and Wallace that does not mean that there is consensus about the uses to which they are put. Certainly the SNP took advantage of *Braveheart* and of its portrait of Wallace. They leafleted cinema audiences who were leaving the film. Inevitably the veracity of Mel Gibson's filmic portrayal of Wallace was disputed in the letters columns of the Scottish press. For example, one questioned 'whether the SNP should be so eager to endorse an oversimplified version of history. If their vision of 14th century Scotland is so blurred, some might conclude that their economic forecasts for Scotland today are equally out of focus!' (*The Scotsman*, 20.9.95). However, others argued that criticisms of the film's historical inaccuracies were to miss the larger point. Rather than questioning whether Wallace really did have a romantic fling with the Princess of Wales, the film was to be judged in terms of a wider history of national struggle. Thus it was claimed that, whatever the inaccuracies of historical detail, the film 'recreates as drama – not as historical documentary – the essential truths of Wallace's life and beliefs' and that drama 'does not deal with primary sources, but with emotions and the broad sweep of history' (SNP spokesperson, Mike Russell, *The Scotsman*, 20.9.95). Indeed, such was the extent to which the film came to be the reality of Wallace (and Wallace the reality of Scotland) that when a 30 ft-high stone carving of Wallace was set in place for the 700th anniversary of his victory at Stirling Bridge, the face was modelled on the *Braveheart* film star, Mel Gibson. When some in the Wallace Clan Trust complained that the real Wallace was 'taller, bearded, and, to be honest, not as good-looking' (cited in *The Guardian*, 10.9.97), the sculptor argued that whilst Gibson may not look like Wallace, his film performance had embodied Wallace's spirit and courage. Consequently, the modelling of Wallace on a short, handsome Australian with a dubious accent was entirely appropriate. The sculptor continued, "I think the fact it is an actor rather than the man does not detract from the spirit of it . . . *Braveheart* was inspiring . . . When we think of Wallace we see Gibson in full battlepaint, crying out 'freedom' at the top of his lungs'.

Above all, the SNP read *Braveheart* and the life of Wallace as indicating the necessity of independence, and they sought to ridicule any other interpretation. In his address to the 1995 SNP Annual Conference, Alex Salmond described how both the Conservative Secretary of State for Scotland (Michael Forsyth) and his Labour shadow (George Robertson) looked 'a bit on the pale side by the end of the film':

Extract 1

Perhaps they are starting to realize the power of the story of Wallace on the big screen. They were certainly having trouble explaining away the message. Michael said that Wallace was a fighter for Scottish 'interests'. George said he fought for Scottish 'identity'. Notice this difficulty with the 'i' word. The one word they didn't want to mention was INDEPENDENCE, which is what Wallace was actually fighting for. So we don't intend to allow Unionist politicians to tell us how we should commemorate William Wallace.

(Alex Salmond, SNP MP, SNP Annual Conference, Perth, 1995)

Salmond was not content merely to question his opponents' use of this history. Rather he sought to dramatize their reaction in the very terms of the historical narrative. Forsyth and Robertson thus became villains and traitors in the national drama. As Salmond put it in the same speech: 'George and Michael should also be worried because now, as anyone knows the story and has seen the film will know, the real villains are not the English but the establishment leadership of Scotland who bought and sold their country for personal advancement. Oh how little things change!' In a similar vein, Salmond used this history to construe his political project as uniquely consonant with the spirit of Wallace: 'At the battle of Stirling Bridge I would have been on Wallace's side and at least Forsyth would know he wanted to be on the other side. But Labour would have been in a quandary. I can safely say Wallace wouldn't have been in favour of devolution' (reported in the *Sunday Times*, 3.9.95).

However, Wallace has not only been invoked by those favouring independence. In the nineteenth century he was largely seen through the lens of laissez faire liberalism (Finlay, 1997). More specifically, the aspiring middle classes picked up on Wallace's status as a commoner who governed and protected Scotland not because of his birth but because of his ability and talent. Accordingly, the nineteenth century celebration of Wallace was bound up with articulating the rising political claims of the middle class. As Finlay puts it, 'liberty from oppression and the concept of freedom had little to do with anti-Unionism or anti-English sentiment as such, but everything to do with mid-Victorian laissez faire' (Finlay, 1997: 115). In fact, this celebration of Wallace took place at a time when Bruce was hardly referred to at all. Whilst it was Bruce the king who actually led the victorious army against the English at Bannockburn, the fact that it was Wallace the commoner who won the veneration is seen by Finlay as illustrating the degree to which the past was interpreted through the meritocratic, individualistic and anti-aristocratic thinking of the time.

There is more to it than that. Wallace has been invoked by unionists in direct opposition to a separate Scottish state. When the Wallace Monument was inaugurated by the Earl of Elgin in 1856, the Earl argued that it was due to Wallace's role in the fight for independence, alongside that of Bruce, that Scotland had gained the strength to enter the Union. Because of this, it shouldn't just be the Scots who celebrate these heroes. Indeed, he declared, all of England owe: 'to Wallace and Bruce a debt of obligation only second to that which is due to them by Scotland' (cited in McCrone, Morris & Kiely, 1995: p. 199; see too Morton, 1996).

In the twentieth century, as the balance of social forces changed, so has the interpretation of Wallace. As the Labour movement developed in the early decades of this century, Wallace was recast as striving to free the common people from oppressive barons. Thus, Scottish communists marching against unemployment in the 1930s were to be found parading with placards of Wallace alongside Marx (Marr, 1992: 12) and the famous Scottish Labour leader Tom Johnston was to be heard characterizing Wallace as a radical: 'If at bottom Wallace's revolt was not a last effort to cast off feudalism from Scotland, why did the Scoto-Norman nobles hate him so?' (cited in Finlay, 1997: 116). In similar vein, most of the prominent left-wing home-rulers of the early twentieth century construed Wallace as a proto-socialist, with one – the Reverend James Barr – claiming that the English saw him as 'almost a Bolshevik' (Milligan, 1995/6, p. 5).

In talking of a changing balance of forces, we should, however, remember that we are referring to a relative shift. Relations may change but a diversity of forces are ever present. Hence, here, as in the other domains we have surveyed, differences exist as much within any given period as between periods. This reflects itself at all levels, including the characterization of national heroes as they are put to use in shaping collective action. Consider the words of the SNP activist and parliamentary candidate, Dick Douglas, at the SNP's annual rally at Bannockburn. Standing a short distance from the imposing statue of Robert the Bruce seated on horseback, he argued that:

Extract 2

the challenge before us is not to live in the past as we stand in the shadow of Bruce, but rather to live up to the past. That's the challenge that we've seen. Let's spend just a minute or two trying to put our minds back to all those centuries ago and the decisive battle that was fought here. It was a decisive battle. But battles don't resolve things for all time. There are no final battles. Each new and oncoming generation has to rediscover and surmount its own problems. To realize their own potentialities. Bruce won a decisive battle but he wouldn't really have completed the case and struggle for independence had he not won the hearts and minds of the Scottish people and we must never forget that because each generation has to face new and different challenges.

(Dick Douglas, SNP candidate, speech at annual SNP Bannockburn rally, 26.6.93)

The call to emulate Bruce is unambiguous. More significant, however, is the definition of exactly what Bruce was doing and hence what such emulation consists of. For Douglas it means fighting and continuing the fight to realize national potentialities, it means struggling for independence and it means winning the hearts and minds of the Scottish people. Later in the speech, when he addressed the coming 'battle' for jobs at the Rosyth Naval Yard (which was threatened with closure), Douglas (himself a former Labour MP) explained more clearly what 'winning hearts and minds' actually signifies: 'The only way of winning that battle is to vote time and time again for Scottish National Party representatives. That's the only way. And that's so hard, I can tell you. This wee fellow here knows it's a hard and difficult lesson to learn. I know perhaps more than anybody else, but that's a lesson that we've to get over to the Scottish people. That's what winning the hearts and minds of the Scottish people means. And that's what you've pledged yourselves to do today. To keep in your mind the memory of Bruce. To remember the past but to live up to the past. That's the challenge.' Used in this way, the tedious business of party political canvassing is transformed into a modern Bannockburn, and each canvasser is a contemporary Scottish hero in the mould of Bruce.

Others portrayed a very different Bruce and put him to work for an entirely different cause. Michael Forsyth, the Conservative Secretary of State for Scotland, started one of his speeches as follows:

Extract 3

In their disparate characters, backgrounds and destinies [Wallace and Bruce] *epitomize the contradictory strands of the Scottish identity. Wallace was a heroic failure. Bruce was a spectacular success. A loser and a winner. It is Wallace which is in fashion today. That must tell us something about the contemporary Scottish people.*
(Michael Forsyth, Conservative MP, speech, Stirling, 26.4.96)

Forsyth does not dispute the heroic stature of Wallace, nor his relevance to the Scots character. However the distinction between character strengths and character flaws allows him to dismiss Wallace as a model. It is Bruce who alone stands for what is good about Scotland. It is Bruce alone who should be emulated, and Bruce-like characteristics which should be nurtured. What these characteristics are becomes clearer as Forsyth develops his account, an account which draws on the same statue of Bruce at Bannockburn to which Douglas earlier referred in Extract 2. In contrast to Wallace:

Extract 4:

The graven image is majestic and monarchic: less Braveheart than Lionheart; no bedraggled, woad-daubed outlaw, but a European sovereign in chain mail, seated high upon his caparisoned horse, battleaxe poised to strike for Scotland and his own royal rights. He personifies the motto of the ancient Scottish monarchy: 'No one assails me with impunity'. We would do well to take that image to heart and acknowledge it as our own. Scotland strong. Scotland confident. Scotland victorious. Too often the grievance politics of the Scottish Left have depicted us as exploited, impoverished and supine. That is demeaning and an inaccurate representation of a great nation and we must repudiate it.

(Michael Forsyth, Conservative MP, speech, Stirling, 26.4.96)

The elision of Bruce and Scotland in this account is absolutely explicit as is the call on Scots to embrace and emulate this fused character. The traits that are listed – strength, confidence, success – serve to repudiate the notion of a Scotland that is oppressed or down-trodden in any way. They are organized to repudiate a 'left' which includes Labour and the SNP. By this account, the notion that Scots fare badly in the Union or that they have to recover their potential is a misrepresentation of and an insult to the real Scottish identity. It implies that Scots have been assailed and that the assailant has got away with it. So, whereas 'strength, confidence and success' are fairly ambivalent terms on their own, in context they clearly serve to make calls for independence, or even for increased state support, unacceptable. As the speech progresses further, the terms are also developed such that their consonance with the Tory project becomes yet clearer. Scottish power and confidence are translated into an economic sphere. Forsyth claims that 'thrift', 'commerce' and 'wealth creation' are 'quintessentially Scottish characteristics' and that the 'Scots have always been instinctive entrepreneurs'. Finally, he concluded his speech with the following call for the recuperation of this distinctively Scottish 'entrepreneurial' identity: 'If we can shake off the rusty shackles of corporatism and give free rein to our genius for wealth creation, whilst retaining our spiritual values, the new Millennium will be for Scots a golden age. Let us turn our backs on all that is inward-looking and our faces to a brilliant future.'

Thus far we have limited our analysis to the ways in which Wallace and Bruce are used as national heroes, accepting that they are seen as such. It is certainly true that they probably have more call on this status than anyone else, but that does not mean that it is impossible to question their heroism or whether it is national. So, in response to all the uses of Wallace, one Labour MP made public his dissent:

Extract 5

It is depressing that in 1995 there should be any who think that a long-dead medieval warlord held to anything that represented freedom as it is understood today. Sir William Wallace would have been the principal beneficiary of any change of government in Scotland wrought by his military actions. He would have headed a state where the monarch ruled supreme and the people remained subject to the feudal system. For the Scots nothing would have changed, since none would have known any freedom. The romantic view of Wallace may have gained currency through Hollywood but realism drives Scottish politics. That realism says that every adult Scot has a vote and at every election the Scots overwhelmingly reject the SNP's separatist prospectus.

(Norman Hogg, Labour MP, letter to *The Times*, 28.9.95)

Wallace, then, was no hero. He was not sacrificing himself for the Scottish people. He was only seeking to ensure that it was him rather than anyone else who would be in a position to oppress the people. Having said that, Wallace is still retained as a model of sorts. Having punctured nationalist idealism, Hogg uses the individualistic pragmatism of the dead warlord as a stick with which to beat SNP policy. Others go further. They not only reject these medieval figures as national heroes and nationalist models but as any sort of hero or any sort of model. That is not to say that they are entirely innocent of using heroism to their own ends. Allan Massie, a well-known supporter of the Union drew a parallel between Wallace and the Serb General Miladic (condemned for genocide in Bosnia). He asked, does 'it really serve us well to identify as our national hero a man who however brave and honourable he may have been, had his hands red with English blood?' (*Scotland on Sunday*, 3.9.95) Answering in the negative, he suggested as a more appropriate and meaningful model a figure like David Livingstone, the famous Scottish explorer from the nineteenth century heyday of British imperialism.

From another part of the political spectrum, a left-wing Labour MP also questioned whether Bruce (along with a fellow hero from the romantic casebook) was to be held up as a model Scot, or indeed whether he was in any real sense Scottish. However, when it came to alternatives, he introduced a very different cast of characters embodying a very different set of values allied to a very different political project:

Extract 6

Bruce was a French or Norman noble with very little appreciation of what it meant to be Scottish. Similarly, Bonnie Prince Charlie was an Italian exile who came to Scotland. No, the Scottishness that I take great encouragement from is the kind of Scotland that emerged in the eighteenth and nineteenth centuries through the industrial revolution. . . . I take my identity and I identify with the people like John Maclean and Jimmy Maxton, and see that as being Scottish and having a distinctively socialistic contribution to make.

(Labour MP, interview 38)

Thus it seems that even those who argue against the use of particular national heroes do not refrain from using heroes to define the national character. One can argue about who the heroes should be, one can argue about the significance of any given hero, but the use of national heroes in order to ground national identity seems to go right across the political spectrum. That this should be so reveals much about the concept of the 'nation' and the way in which the national imagination entails and necessitates a particular approach to history. It is to such issues that we now turn.

Identity and history

Nations, however young, have an old history. They are not necessarily 'as old as history' as Walter Bagehot once claimed (Bagehot, 1873; cited in Connor, 1978), but there is much at stake in characterizing them as such and there is more than one way of doing so. Already it should be apparent from several of the examples in this and the previous chapter that history may be frozen into a critical moment which is presented as the moment in which the nation was truly itself. Whatever happened subsequently, and however the nation appeared in practice, that moment existed outside historical flux as the measure of identity. All this is summed up in the term, 'defining moment'. However, as we hinted in our introductory chapters, there is another way of creating a national essence that is outside history and that, paradoxically, is by looking at the nation in history. Holy (1996) puts it thus: 'It is precisely by speaking of the nation as having historical experience that we construe it as such and imagine it as an entity which moves through time' (p. 116). Citing Wright (1985), he continues that it is this image of a supra-individual entity moving through time that creates that 'imaginary collective subject – a transhistorical national identity going by the name of "we" – that allows "us" to see ourselves as participants in an ongoing national drama, and, so utter (as the Czechs do) such sentiments as, "We have suffered for three hundred years"' (p. 117).

But history doesn't just create us as a collective entity, it creates us as a particular type of collective entity. It is by showing that entity as staying constant through the flux of history that one creates an essence which itself is timeless. If the 'we' of tomorrow and today is the same 'we' as of all our yesterdays, then what we have is a constant identity across all time. The issue, of course, is how one defines the various moments of the historical narrative and what one abstracts as the unchanging essence through time. However, once done this provides a formidable device for mobilizing people in the name of, or else in defence of, the named element. In 1943, British survival depended on keeping society mobilized at all levels to fight against the Axis. In that year, a book was published with the title *England is Here* (Hanchant, 1943). It was comprised of extracts from speeches by British Prime Ministers from Walpole to Churchill. The theme of the book was explained in the Introduction and summarized by a poem which ended that Introduction:

> It is not to be thought of that the Flood
> Of British freedom, which, to the open sea
> Of the world's praise, from dark antiquity
> Hath flowed, with pomp of waters, unwithstood . . .
> That this most famous Stream in bogs and sands
> Should perish. (Hanchant, 1943)

Lest poetry be too indirect, the introduction was preceded by a 'Calendar of Liberty', a list of 67 events starting in 1215 with 'Magna Carta: the bold and broad foundation of English liberties' and ending in 1942 with 'Publication of the Beveridge Report on Social Insurance and Allied Services, 20 November: a plan to secure freedom from want'. The thing to note about the Calendar is the way in which all the events were characterized as exhibiting the same essential quality of British freedom and how, together, they constituted not just a flow but a flood whose ending would be inconceivable to British people. Hence they were enjoined to act in defence of their country and against the German-led threat.

This is a particularly elaborate example, mirroring, perhaps, the seriousness of the times. Much more usual is a move to establish continuity by showing a commonality between two points distant in time, the one characteristically in 'dark antiquity' and the other in the present. In doing this one establishes both the essential character of identity and the status quo as an expression of that identity. This serves then to defend the status quo against the challenges to it. Such usage is well illustrated by both sides in the Iran–Iraq War which ran from 1980–8 – a near total war which, like the Second World War, required the mobilization of the whole population on both sides in a sustained war effort.

Two elements were necessary in order to achieve such a mobilization. The first was to establish a common collective identity which could unite a population who could otherwise be thought of as highly heterogeneous on religious and cultural dimensions. A second was to define this identity in such a way as to support the war effort. On the Iraqi side, the key means to the first of these ends was the celebration of a peasant folklore which portrayed *sunni* Muslims, *shi'i* Muslims and Kurds alike, as sharing a national culture which had its roots in an ancient Mesopotamian past (Davis, 1994; Dijkink, 1996). This was pursued through all manner of media, from museums (Davis, 1994) to the imagery on the humble postage stamp (Reid, 1993). The importance ascribed by the regime to this project is apparent from the amount of money poured into archaeology; Dijkink (1996) cites the director of the Babylonian excavations as having told an American journalist in 1979: 'Whatever we want, we get . . . Not just a million or two, but anything we wish, without restrictions!' (cited in Dijkink, 1996: 121).

If history was used to establish a common category, it was also used to characterize the category in ways that placed the population in fundamental opposition to the Iranian enemy. Most strikingly, the Saddam Hussein regime constructed a parallel between the 1980–8 war and the historic battle of Qadisiyya in 637, which itself was characterized as a war between the Arabs (Iraqis) and the Persian Sassanids (Iranians). Saddam Hussein's characterization of the 1980–8 war as the 'second Qadisiyya' or 'Saddam's Qadisiyya' functioned to construe it as but one phase of an ongoing ancient Arab national struggle (Reid, 1993). Once again, the political significance of the parallel is illustrated by the efforts and resources that were devoted to propagating it. Zemzemi (1986) reports that a film commemorating the battle of Qadisiyya was produced with a budget of 7.5 million dollars, and images that mixed elements of the 'first' and 'second' battles were reproduced in such diverse forms as wall murals and postage stamps. For example, one postage stamp, entitled 'The First Qadisiyya Battle', portrayed horsemen wielding swords and the image of both Saddam Hussein and Sa'ad Ibn Abi Waqas (the leader of the Arab army in 637). Indeed, the image of the latter took the form of the shadow cast by Saddam himself (Reid, 1993).

While Saddam Hussein used Qadisiyya to define the Iraqis as the Arab descendants of ancient Mesopotamia struggling against Persian aggressors, his Iranian foe was to be found using the same battle to advance a very different set of categories for contemporary self-definition. Zemzemi (1986), in a tract that reproduces the Iranian position, contests the categorization of antagonists at Qadisiyya as Arab and Persian. He argues that Arabs were to be found on both sides and that 'since the principal characteristic of one side was Islam, whilst on the other it was a matter of hate of Islam' it was more meaningful to view the battle as one between Muslims and non-Muslims (1986: 190). This being the case, the 'second Qadisiyya' (that is, the contemporary Iran–Iraq War) should be seen as pitting those who apply Islam to every aspect of their life (i.e. the Iranians) against those who do not (i.e. the Iraqis). Once the categories were changed from Arab/ Persian to Defender/ Enemy of the faith, so too the ways in which individuals fitted into those categories had to shift. So, where Saddam Hussein represented himself as the victorious Arab, Sa'ad Ibn Abi Waqas, Zemzemi (1986) now placed him as a figure on the losing side, the defeated Zaid Ibn Bahish, who, as an ally of the Sassanid Persians, had broken all treaties signed with the peace-loving Muslims.

These two versions of history tie the present to the same mythical event and each seeks to appropriate the heroic mantle of the victor for themselves while casting their opponent as the inglorious loser. In order to do this, they dispute the very nature of the categories that are involved. Saddam Hussein would have both past and present as the Arabs (which he represents) against the Persian foe. It is worth noting that, in doing so, he does not only provide a basis for uniting his own population but also for calling on the support of other Arab states in the conflict. The Iranians, by contrast, would have both past and present as the True Believers (which they represent) against the Apostates. Here too, such categories invoke the support of other states, but this time Muslim states in support of the Iranian side.

In other contexts there may be less argument about precisely which categories are relevant. However, even if there is agreement on the centrality of a particular (national) category, this does not mean that its history is 'non-controversial'. On the one hand, as we have intimated, there is the question of 'what history?' What events should be used as the key to the national psyche? On the other hand, there is the question of what meaning should be ascribed to those events and therefore what exactly do they tell us about the national psyche. So, for instance, debates about Belgian identity construe periods as far apart as the Roman era and the industrial mining past as central to the identity. From the Roman era, what is often remembered are Julius Caesar's words. These have achieved the ultimate accolade of being included in an Asterix book (*Asterix and the Belgians*) where Caesar is shown saying: 'The Belgians are not barbarians! Of all the peoples of Gaul, they are the most brave'. However, as contemporaneously recorded, what he said was: 'The most brave of these three peoples are the Belgians, because they are so distant from Rome and from the refinements of civilization' (all quoted in Decharneux, 1995: 27). The least one can say is that the preferred collective memory is open to dispute!

These processes are summed up by Holy who comments that national history 'is a history of rewriting its history' (1996: 118). Sometimes, this is a matter of protagonists each writing their own history and over-writing that of the other. An example can be found in Holy's account of the history of Czechoslovakia. On the one hand, Czech Communists sought to bolster their regime through constructing a specifically *Czech* revolutionary tradition which legitimated the Communist regime's claim to national authority (Holy, 1996). Of particular significance in this history was the fifteenth century Hussite movement (in which the Czech theologian Jan Hus challenged Papal authority). The Communists construed this as the first social revolution in a Czech revolutionary tradition. Indeed, the Hussite movement was to provide the regime with much of its symbolism: most strikingly the heraldic shield in the pre-Communist state's coat-of-arms was replaced with the Hussite shield on which the lion of the Bohemian kings was surmounted by a red star. Opponents of the regime rejected this history, and wrote another which showed the Czechs to possess a distinctive national tradition of democracy. The fact that Czech history had experienced many periods in which there was a marked absence of democracy did little to undermine such a construction of Czech identity. This was not, as Holy observes, because such periods were somehow obliterated from memory. Rather such dissonant experiences were 'declared to be anomalous discontinuities in Czech history' (1996: 84), and as such were excluded from the construction of the Czech tradition and identity. In fact, the mismatch between the image of the democratic Czech character and the non-democratic reality of totalitarian state rule was used to define the Communist regime as 'non-Czech' and motivate action which could bring about a new Czech reality.

At other times, the re-writing of history occurs from one period to the next. This is more directly in line with what Holy himself intended, but is probably best illustrated not by Czechoslovakia but by one of its erstwhile neighbours, the German Democratic Republic. For many years, East German Communist Party historians had sought to establish the regime's 'national' legitimacy through linking the GDR with a radical German past. The obvious impediment to this, and the figure which looms over all contemporary attempts to define German identity, is the Nazi experience. How can a radical definition survive such a reactionary weight? The answer was to claim that the GDR had its roots in the history of anti-fascist struggle and that this, in turn, represented the 'true Germany'. Just weeks before the regime's collapse one historian was to be found arguing that 'the history of the anti-fascist Resistance belongs to the best traditions of our state: it is . . . a kind of prehistory of the GDR' (cited in Koonz, 1994: 269). After the collapse of the regime such histories were notable for their absence. A new nation demands a new history.

If key events are sometimes forgotten, there are other times when forgotten events are remembered. Zerubavel (1994) traces the fate of Masada which, until the nineteenth century, was a relatively obscure event, largely ignored in the Talmud and medieval Jewish literature. However, for the Zionist movement, the resistance of Jews to the Romans came to symbolize a heroism and love of freedom which, they argued, had been lost during the period of exile and which they sought to recover in action. The cult of Masada grew until, after 1948, it became the site for the swearing in of the Israeli defence forces. The excavation of Masada by Yadin became a key piece of nationalist iconography and Zerubavel quotes Yadin on the link between past and present:

> We will not exaggerate by saying that thanks to the heroism of the Masada fighters –
> like other links in the nation's chain of heroism – we stand here today, the soldiers of a
> young-ancient people, surrounded by the ruins of the camps of those who destroyed us

. . . We, the descendants of these heroes, stand here today and rebuild the ruins of our people. (cited in Whitelam, 1996: 17)

More succinctly, Zerubavel cites a famous dictum by A.B. Yehoshua: 'Masada is no longer the historic mountain near the Dead Sea but a mobile mountain which we carry on our back anywhere we go' (ibid). As Zerubavel explains, this linkage of past to present is hardly innocent, since it silences any Palestinian claim to the past and therefore to the land. Once again, the new nation is served well by its new history.

If the Czech example differs from the East German and Israeli ones in terms of whether the argument is synchronic or diachronic, in all three cases the argument is about the same thing: what events are historical? But, as we saw in the Belgian example that came before, one can agree on the relevant events but differ when it comes to their interpretation. Such is the case in Scotland. Just as there is considerable (even if not total) agreement concerning the national heroes, so there is considerable (but not total) agreement over the key moments of Scottish history. What is more there was a clear link between the two. Listening to Scottish political activists, whether we interviewed them in cars, bars and hotel rooms, or listened to them addressing audiences around the country, we heard the same events, dates and names time and time again. More than any other they were the events of the so called Wars of Independence against the English which began with Wallace in the late thirteenth century and culminated in Bruce's victory at Bannockburn in 1314 and which were consolidated through the Declaration of Arbroath in 1320.

This is well illustrated if we turn to two very well-known Scottish politicians. The first asserts that her party can 'offer you a worthy vision of the future. We can offer you a future worthy of our past'. The second declares that 'We owe a duty to our homeland. We have a destiny to fulfil. The name of Scotland must be writ large again in the annals of mankind'. Both therefore agree that the future must be guided by the past. Both agree on what past – Bannockburn. However, there the agreement ends. The first speaker, SNP MEP Winnie Ewing, tied Bannockburn to future independence (speech at SNP annual Bannockburn rally, 20.6.92). The second speaker, the Conservative MP, Michael Forsyth, contrasted the glory of Bannockburn to 'petty chauvinism or the fabrication of pygmy senates' – that is, an independent Scotland. Instead he called for 'the re-affirmation of our identity through spiritual regeneration and material achievement' (speech at Stirling, 26.4.96).

Let us take another equally prominent pair: the Conservative Secretary of State for Scotland before and after the 1992 election, Ian Lang, and the SNP Deputy Leader during the 1992 election, Jim Sillars. In a pre-election public meeting in Falkirk, one of the sites of battle during the Wars of Independence, Sillars produced one of the most elaborated parallels between 1314 and the present:

Extract 7

Now whether we are blessed or cursed this generation, I don't know. I believe that we should be blessed, that we are going to have on our shoulders – this generation alone

> *and the people at this election have on their shoulders – the sole responsibility for deciding what is the future of Scotland. We are going to decide. This is an historic election and every one of us individually and collectively is on the spot in 1992. Just as in 1314 the political/military circumstances put the nation on the spot at Bannockburn. This is the modern Bannockburn. We're not talking about crossing swords, we're talking about crossing a ballot paper. But the essential issues are exactly the same. There was no way off the Bannockburn field in 1314. You either stood or you ran away. It's exactly the same in 1992. We either stand up and face our responsibilities or we bow the knee to power south of the border.*
>
> (Jim Sillars, SNP MP, speech, Falkirk, 26.3.92)

The important thing here is not just that the parallel with Bannockburn is built up through many layers, but that, at each point, the characterization is one of opposition and conflict with the English. The choice of vote becomes a challenge, electoral mobilization has a weight akin to military mobilization, even the mundane act of voting becomes an act of battle. Thus a refusal to vote for the SNP and independence is no longer a choice but a weakness, not a difference as to the interests of the nation but an act of desertion and a surrender to the English foe. Everything depends upon portraying present social relations as the same as those some seven hundred years earlier. However, there is a different way of invoking Bannockburn. It becomes no less important in defining current reality. In this other version, Bannockburn determines the present by changing social relations and transcending the antagonism between countries. When Ian Lang was asked to choose any event in Scottish history to witness at first hand, he settled for Bruce's victory at Bannockburn. The consequence of the victory was that Scotland could enter the Union as an equal partner:

Extract 8

From then on as a nation, we have never looked back. So much so that it was our king James IV who succeeded to the throne of England in 1603; and it was his great grand-daughter – another Scot – who oversaw the Union of the nations of Scotland and England in 1707. This is the real legacy of Bannockburn and it is one of which I am very proud. That is why I would like to have been there in 1314.

(Ian Lang, Conservative MP, interview, reported in *The Scotsman*, 27.11.93)

If this argument seems familiar, it is because it echoes the use of Wallace and Bruce in the Victorian era which we described in our section on national heroes. It will be remembered that the Earl of Elgin on inaugurating the Wallace monument lauded both men as giving Scotland the strength to enter the Union as an equal. In words that are even closer to those of Lang, the Earl went on from leaders to events and spoke of Bannockburn itself:

> If the Scottish people have been able to form an intimate union and association with a people more wealthy and more numerous than themselves, without sacrificing one jot

of their neutral independence and liberty – these great results are due to the glorious struggle which was commenced on the plain of Stirling and consummated on that of Bannockburn. (cited in Morton, 1996)

So much for Bannockburn. Consider now the Declaration of Arbroath. This declaration was the diplomatic dispatch to Rome which carried the news of Bruce's assumption of the Scottish Crown and is itself an interesting piece of political rhetoric redolent with the invocation of history in the definition of identity. Written at the time when authority was to be claimed through notions of 'lineage', the Scottish nobles drafting the document rejected English claims upon Scotland through invoking a different history (and hence another lineage) to that advocated by the English. More specifically, whereas English claims on Scotland were typically based upon the argument that Brutus the Trojan had founded Britain and divided the kingdom between his three sons, the Scottish nobles claimed that the Scots were descended from Gathelus the Greek who had married Scota, daughter of Pharaoh. According to this alternative history, when God drowned Pharaoh's troops in the Red Sea, Gathelus and Scota went to Spain and then to Ireland and Scotland. Thus the Declaration asserted that the Scots came from Greater Scythia, via the Pillars of Hercules, to Spain

and thence coming, 1200 years after the setting forth of the people of Israel, they won for themselves by victory after victory, and travail upon travail, the abodes in the west . . . Within their realm have reigned one hundred and thirteen kings of native royal stock, never an alien on the throne. (cited in Marr, 1992: p. 11)

The importance of this history is illustrated by the amount of effort that went into identifying the uninterrupted line of 'one hundred and thirteen kings of native royal stock'. For example the first principal of Aberdeen University – Hector Boece – took it upon himself to fill in the gaps in this supposedly unbroken lineage by inventing 39 fictional kings. Even as late as the sixteenth and seventeenth centuries political authority was claimed through reference to this lineage with the Dutch painter, Jacob De Wet, being commissioned to provide these kings' portraits to be displayed in Edinburgh's Holyrood Palace (Bruce and Yearley, 1989).

By 1992, there was little reference to the Scots' supposed middle-eastern roots or this unbroken royal lineage. However, the words of the Declaration of Arbroath continued to be invoked. Most notably the Declaration's qualification upon Bruce's authority has achieved the status of a rhetorical commonplace. More than that, it has even achieved T-shirt slogan status:

Yet if he should give up what he has begun, and agree to make us or our kingdom subject to the King of England or the English, we should exert ourselves at once to drive him out as our enemy and a subverter of his own rights and ours, and make some other man who was well able to defend us our King: for as long as but a hundred of us remain alive, never will we on any conditions be brought under English rule. It is in truth not for glory, nor riches, nor honours that we are fighting, but for freedom – for that alone, which no honest man gives up but with life itself.

We can appreciate the use of the above words in the context of contemporary political mobilization by looking at an SNP eve of poll rally held in the modern town of Arbroath:

Extract 9

In the year 1320 after the birth of Our Saviour, in this town of Arbroath, our ancestors met to consider and declare upon the issue of Scottish freedom. Their words reach out to us over the centuries in a ringing, confident declaration of self-government. 'For as long as one hundred of us remain alive we will never submit to the domination of the English. We fight not for honour or glory or riches but for that freedom which no true man gives up but with his life.' There is no arrogance there, there is no hatred, there is no jealousy, no attempt at all to do others down but only a massive reaffirmation of Scotland's rights and an assuredness about our place in that wider world. Nation or region? That is the challenge before all of us at this General Election.

(Andrew Welsh, SNP MP, speech, Arbroath, 8.4.92)

Welsh uses the familiar text to promote the SNP agenda. First of all the Declaration is treated as a mandate for independence. It illustrates that Scotland is a nation and has the confidence to assume nation-state status. Secondly, the Declaration is used to fend off pejorative accounts of nationalism. It is not negative nor does it promote negativity as the opponents of the SNP argue. Rather it is a positive thing, a sign of quiet self-confidence and a clear sense of selfhood.

Others, however, use the Declaration to promote alternative agendas. One senior Labour activist we interviewed, a person heavily involved in the campaign for a Scottish parliament, described the Declaration of Arbroath as 'one of the most important documents in Western historical thought' (Labour activist, interview 34). According to him it challenged the divine-right of kings and set out a distinctive Scottish approach to power. As 'there was no such thing as the King of Scotland, there was only the king of the Scots' and the Declaration asserted that 'if he fails us or he betrays us, then we reserve the right to turn him out and to have somebody else', he stressed issues of democracy and advanced the claim that Scotland had a distinctively democratic tradition. In fact, in the immediate aftermath of the election, the government's authority was frequently questioned through invoking this history. Speaking at the 1992 Scottish Trades Union Council's congress, Canon Kenyon Wright of the Scottish Constitutional Convention (a cross party campaign for a developed Scottish parliament) argued that:

Extract 10

Scotland has a tradition of saying to those in power you have no mandate unless the people give it to you. In the Declaration of Arbroath in 1320 they said to Robert the Bruce you have no mandate unless the people give it to you; in the Claim of Right of 1689 they said to King James you have no mandate unless the people give it to you. In

the Claim of Right in 1842, the Church said to the state that you have no mandate unless the people give it you, in the Claim of Right in 1989, which began the constitutional convention, we said to the government, you have no mandate unless the people give it to you, and today again in the election and again with a united voice the people must say to this government again, you have no mandate unless the people give it to you.
(Canon Kenyon Wright, Constitutional Convention, speech to STUC, Perth, 24.4.92)

We have one more point to make in relation to 1320 and 1314. In introducing these moments of history, we noted that, just as with Scottish heroes, their key national status was acknowledged by a wide consensus – but that the consensus was not total. As with Wallace and Bruce, so with Bannockburn in particular, there were those who saw it as saying little about the Scottish nation. One Labour MP who was very active in supporting constitutional change (and who was very prominent in the cross-party campaigns to secure a referendum on constitutional change) observed that he felt 'absolutely nothing about Bannockburn':

Extract 11

You know a triumph of a branch of the ruling elite over another branch of it more than 600 years ago is virtually by definition meaningless to me as a working-class Scots- Irish-man in the 1990s and it is one of the barriers, this kind of fetishism of the unimportant aspects of Scottish history which has provided a barrier I think for the Labour movement people to accept the validity of nationalism in Scotland . . . One of the odd things is the complete failure of the nationalist movement, other than its very far left, to commemorate occasions in Scottish history which are much more recent and much more important. For example, the 1820 rising with its socialist and nationalist platform and motivation.
(Labour MP, interview 36)

In this respect, the MP cited above on Bannockburn is very much like the Labour MP cited in Extract 6 on Bruce. He might argue that the battle was about class rather than national interests, but his aim is to supplant one national history with another – and thereby one version of identity with another – rather than to dispute the significance of national history in itself. His words stand as testimony to Holy's observation that 'nationalism can be seen as a discursive agreement that history matters without necessarily agreeing on what that history was and what it means' (1996: 118). For these Labour MPs, history matters as a means of imparting a socialist flavour to their nationalism.

Here, though, we must acknowledge a point of some importance. Throughout this chapter we have been examining how constructions of national identity are made, how speakers attempt to give unique weight to their versions and how that makes the basis for those attempts – whether it be environment, culture, the use of national heroes, national institutions or of history – a source of argument. We have shown how nothing is beyond argument and that grounds can be found for virtually any idea of the nation and hence nationalist authority can be given to virtually any form of action. However, before we conclude, it is important to acknowledge that the fact that anything is arguable does not mean that all arguments have equal weight. Undeniably, some positions have more resonance than others and seem more convincing than others. For instance, some may want to replace Bannockburn with the 1820 uprising and Bruce with John Maclean as national icons, but there is little doubt that, if most were asked to name a Scottish historical figure or event, then Bruce and Wallace and Bannockburn would easily take precedence over MacLean and 1820 and that they would be seen as far more significant to the national identity.

This contrast can be illustrated geographically as well as psychologically. There exist three small monuments to the 1820 uprising, which frequently fall into a 'sadly dilapidated' state and which are periodically renovated (Halliday, 1993). By contrast, we have already referred several times to the many imposing monuments to Bruce and to Wallace. Indeed, in the appendix to a recent edition of *Blind Harry's Wallace*, originally written by William Hamilton of Gilbertfield in 1722 (Hamilton, 1998), a map is provided with 83 Wallace place names on it. This reminds us that identities are not simply expressed in words but inscribed in the full range of human practices and artefacts. From the vantage point of the School of Psychology at the University of St Andrews it is a point that is impossible to miss. The building stands in an ancient courtyard and overlooks the School of Divinity on the other side. It was built at a time when St Andrews was at the eye of religious conflict in Scotland, as a counter-reformation statement. This was reflected in the French baronial style of the building, topped with the fleur-de-lys. The very stones that are seen through Psychology's windows were deliberately shaped to proclaim Catholic identity.

One way, therefore, in which the argument over identity becomes unequal is through the differential power of participants to instantiate their constructions in the fabric of our everyday lives. Thus Alonso observes that decisions as to the naming of streets and buildings allow the state to undertake a 'vast iconic structuring of "public" space' and so make a particular history 'palpable in every-day life' (1988: 41). The history of the Mexican revolutionary figure General Francisco Villa testifies to the range of state strategies that may be adopted in the pursuit of this end. Initially the Mexican state had characterized Villa as an aimless mercenary and force for disorder. However, Alonso describes how later, through the transformation of his house into the Museum of the Revolution, the regional and popular Villista history was brought into line with the 'official' history of the revolution and Villa re-incorporated into the pantheon of 'official' national revolutionary heroes. In Alonso's words, Villa was 'appropriated by the state for the nation' and the meanings of Villismo were 'cannibalized, re-valued and incorporated into a historical bricolage from which a hegemonic ideology has been built . . . The Mexican state has 'eaten' Villa and "regurgitated" his rehabilitated image' (Alonso, 1988: 43).

Perhaps the most potent image we have of categories and category relations constantly being reconstructed by the state is George Orwell's *Nineteen Eighty-*

Four. Orwell is quite aware of the centrality of malleable histories to this process. As he famously warns: 'who controls the past controls the future' and 'who controls the present controls the past' (1950: 38). Nonetheless, the power of the state, or of any other powerful agency, is not unlimited. Opponents to the state may organize their own alternative practices around their own alternative identities and state-initiated practices may cut against the realities of civil society and interpersonal relations. Continuing with her culinary metaphor, Alonso observes that 'official cuisine is not always to popular tastes' (1988: 47). The point of this observation, however, is less to do with alternative practices than with the need for histories to have internal coherence and cultural resonance amongst the intended audience. It is always perilous to employ resources whose meaning is either unknown or which invite alternative readings.

Both these provisos – practical and ideological – can be seen in a cautionary tale from Northern Ireland. At one point, one of the most prominent 'loyalist' groups, the Ulster Defence Association, sought to mobilize the Protestant populations through invoking the history of the 'Cruthin' – an ancient 'race' which they construed as the ancestors of an 'Ulster people'. One of the UDA's activists commented ruefully on the failure of this attempt: 'We tried to educate them. We did night classes on history but they weren't fuckin' interested. Outward bound and arms training, no bother at all, but getting them to read anything or think, you just couldn't do it' (quoted in Bruce, 1992, and cited in Finlayson, 1996: 100). What is more, the idea of the Cruthin 'called to mind the wrong national traditions . . . [because it] seemed to articulate with a Gaelic/Celtic past rather than a specifically protestant one' (Finlayson, 1996: 101).

This isn't to say that loyalists eschew history in general. Quite the opposite in fact. One only has to consider the importance of the Battle of the Boyne when, in 1690, the Protestant King William defeated the Catholic King James and established the Protestant Ascendancy. Each year, the Orange Order celebrates the victory with 18 parades. As either active participants or else as onlookers, these parades unite a large proportion of Ulster's Protestants. Their importance in consolidating identity is not just about the historical memory they evoke but also in the ways they are organized. On the one hand they are highly militarized in style, with the groups of marchers organized like regiments, each wearing identical uniforms and led by their officers. On the other hand, there is a structure of egalitarianism with all the marchers as equals in a fraternity of brethren (Jarman, 1997).

What, then, does the Battle of the Boyne have that Cruthin did not? First of all, it has a set of practices which articulate with other identity practices: they are masculine, military and egalitarian unlike the rarefied intellectuality of studying an ancient 'race'. Secondly, they are unambiguously Protestant rather than running dangerously close to Celtic ideas. More generally, these examples show that there is no monopoly of the state or the powerful in the use of history or the construction of identity. People are not a blank slate upon whom new pasts and new futures may be written at will. The powerful and the powerless alike have to pay attention to the understandings which people hold and the mundane structure of their lives. They have to demonstrate a wit – or rather witcraft (Billig, 1987) – through which their constructions articulate with these concerns. So while there may be an asymmetry between the powerful and the powerless, and while at any given moment in time some constructions will undoubtedly have more impact than others, those who pay sufficient attention to these various factors, may, in the future, change our histories. To be more concrete, and to return to the point from which this discussion sprang, it may be that, for now, 1820 is less central to Scottish history than 1314. However, by allying an astute rhetoric to the creation of monuments and practices of commemoration, it could play a place in rallying a radical sense of Scotland and support for radical policies. To the extent that it helps put those who advocate such policies in power, then the balance of resources through which the different histories gain prominence will itself change. If a new Israel can take Masada from obscurity to prominence, who knows what a new Scotland could bring?

Conclusion

The past, it is sometimes said, is a foreign country. The point of this chapter has been to argue that we can never allow the past to be foreign to us, for to do so would be to cede it to others and thereby cede them a key advantage in shaping reality. As a consequence, versions of the national past are as numerous as ambitions for the national future.

Yet for all that there is variation there remains the commonality of the past. As Brow puts it 'in the struggle for community, re-visions of history are as pervasive as they are endlessly contested' (1990: 5). Indeed, if this chapter illustrates anything it is that nationalism 'makes history a necessity and generates thinking in historical terms' (Holy, 1996: 117). In an important sense, this talk of history is crucial for the construction of an enduring 'national' 'we' which spans historical time. However, if this historical imagining is crucial, it is also remarkably ahistorical: in many ways the identity which is imagined is 'outside' historical contingency and 'timeless'. Again, this stands as testimony to the significance of the concept of character in the imagining of the nation. Indeed, it is because of the concept and its idea of an unchanging 'essence' that we are continually drawn to history for it is in the past that this 'essence' is to be found made palpable. Of course, the way in which the past is itself represented is also important. The past is powerful in defining contemporary identity because it is represented in terms of a narrative structure which invites those in the present to see themselves as participants in an ongoing drama. This narrative structure is all the more potent because it is typically construed in a most personalized form: the activities and achievements of individuals who embody the nation's qualities.

The invocation of these events and people is of course selective. Not all events nor all historical figures are nationalized. Indeed, one often finds whole periods of time 'excluded' as 'national' history. For example, Lofgren (1989) describes how, after many years of Danish rule and a union with Sweden, a distinctive Norwegian identity was established through reference to the history of the Vikings. As he remarks, the choice of a historical period up to 1300 (and before Danish rule) should occasion little surprise: the claim that the Norwegians were above all Vikings was an ideal way of establishing distinctiveness vis à vis Denmark and Sweden. In similar vein, Dijkink (1996) observes that there is 'no age limit' on the dates which may be invoked in such histories and that the neglect of the recent past should not be too surprising. Writing of Serbian nationalism, he explains that if one conceives of five centuries of Turkish rule 'as a gap in national history' one 'rapidly ends up in medieval Greater Serbia' (1996: 112). These examples make it clear that it is only those events which are construed as contributing towards explaining who and what 'we' are, that are included as 'national' history. And as different projects are contingent upon different definitions of the collective 'we', it follows that 'our' history is inevitably a site of contestation. Thus, just as people may argue about the Scottishness of contemporary Scotland, so too may people argue about the Scottishness of the past such that what one identifies as a period or event which stands as testimony to the 'real' nature of Scottishness, others construe as an anomaly.

The real significance of these arguments lies in their action-orientation. It is practical politics – the organization of collective action through the grounding of strategically organized identity constructions – which shapes these speakers' forays into the past. The nation's history is always written from a perspective, it is always organized to construct a transhistorical 'we' with timeless qualities which are to be realized in a speaker's political project. It is for this reason that the stakes are high and the arguments often conducted with much more than words. In South Africa, for example, the Neo-fascist Eugene Terreblanche and the Afrikaans Resistance Movement disrupted a conference (March, 1979) at which a leading South African historian was to deliver a paper which critically interrogated claims surrounding the Covenant. Not content with voicing their vision of the past, they proceeded to tar and feather the speaker (Thompson, 1985; cited in Archard, 1995). Indeed, even those histories that now seem so established and uncontested have, on closer inspection, a history of verbal and physical contention. Thus Gillis (1994) describes how in Philadelphia, the place where American Independence was declared, there was, until the 1850s, little consensus on how to commemorate the event. Rival groups paraded their different interpretations in the streets and were often to be found pursuing their arguments with fists as well as witcraft. If the Scots that we have heard throughout this chapter were physically restrained we should not downplay their passion. Their ability to win support was contingent upon their successfully grounding their definition of the collective and the passionate attention given to the past reflected this significance.

7 Representing the National Community

Titles and entitlement

When Denny Mendez was crowned Miss Italy in 1996 the *Guardian* newspaper reported that she was received by whistles of disapproval from the audience. The headlines in the Italian press gave some indication of the basis for her rejection. *Il Giornale* declared that 'Miss Italy is Dominican' and *La Stampa* declared that 'Denny Mendez is the first Miss Black'. In other words, despite the fact that Ms Mendez was an Italian citizen and had an Italian father it seems that whatever category she did represent, it was not the Italian nation. Indeed, her credentials were explicitly challenged by an Italian fashion photographer who argued that she could never be Miss Italy since 'she does not represent the beauty that is typical of Italy' (the *Guardian*, 9.9.96).

If Denny Mendez suffered from disapproval, at least she kept her crown. Lejla Sehovic was less fortunate. In 1998, Lejla was elected Miss Croatia. However subsequently the jury reversed its decision, took the title away from the Muslim contestant and bestowed it on Ivana Petkovic, described as an 'ethnic Croat'. According to the *Guardian*:

> the contest is highly popular in Croatia, but in a state where Muslims are not considered 'real Croats', the pageant turned political, with the media reporting that many people were unhappy with the jury's original decision. Croatia's Nacional magazine quoted Ksenija Urlicic, the head of entertainment at Croatian television and with close links to the ruling nationalist HDZ party, as saying: 'I don't intend to walk around the world with a Muslim.' (the *Guardian*, 27.10.98)

Much has been written on the gender politics of beauty pageants but, it seems, they can also be touchstones of nationalist politics (cf. Cohen & Wilk, 1996; Rahier, 1998). Even when it comes to a satin sash and tinsel crown, the choice of representatives reveals much about how the nation is conceptualized, who counts as a member of the national community and therefore who can bear the national title. Who is an Italian or a Croatian? Is it a matter of where one lives and what one chooses? Is it a matter of place of birth, one's parents' place of birth, or even some longer ancestry? Are there ethnic or racial criteria which determine nationality irrespective of how long one has lived within or without a national territory? Conversely, are there certain traits, characteristics or beliefs that must be held in order to be a true national? These are questions concerning the meaning of the category and the degree to which a category member, especially one who is held to represent the category, expresses the group's distinctive qualities. For instance, does Denny Mendez display 'the beauty which is typical of Italy' and, if not, can she represent Italian beauty?

Of course, these two types of questions can be, and often are, interlinked. One can be held to lack national characteristics because one lives elsewhere, was born elsewhere or is supposedly of different stock. It is reasonable to infer that Denny Mendez was condemned for her alien looks because she was perceived as a racial other. Conversely, intimations of racial otherness can be the result of failing to display the right characteristics – ideological as well as physical. Thus Peukert (1987) shows how anti-semitism functioned in Germany's Third Reich not only against so-called 'community aliens' but also to police the so-called 'national community'. In this latter respect the difficulty of defining who was Jewish and the absurdity of those physical measurement techniques used to achieve an 'objective definition' served as a positive advantage. It allowed for anyone who failed to deliver the requisite forms of conformity to be accused of not living up to the terms of the national community and thereby to be placed under suspicion as an alien – with all the terrible consequences that would ensue.

In a short time we have moved a long way from the comparative levity of beauty contests. Debates over nationality can mark the line between exaltation, exclusion and even annihilation. As the example of Louis XV shows, no one, however powerful, is immune. In 1776, Louis challenged the authority of the *Parlement de Paris* and asserted that no nationwide body of parliaments could be 'the organ of the Nation, the protector of the Nation's liberty, interests and rights'. Rather, he asserted that only he could represent the nation. In his words, the 'rights and interests of the nation, which some would make a body separate from the monarch, are necessarily joined with mine, and rest entirely in my hands' (cited in Miller, 1995: 29). The parliamentarians responded by arguing that the French nobility were not really French at all. The monarchy in particular was foreign and hence had no right to reign over France. Thus, Sieyes, in his celebrated pamphlet '*Qu'est-ce que le Tiers Etat?*' (written in 1789), proposed that the nation should be identified with the Third Estate and that 'it is impossible to find what place to assign to the caste of nobles among all the elements of a nation' (cited in Miller, 1995: 29).

This characterization of the nobles as alien was particularly potent because it drew upon a belief that that the nobility were the descendants of the Franks who had conquered Roman Gaul in the fifth and sixth centuries whilst the *Tiers Etat* were descended from the Gallo-Romans (Leoussi, 1997). As Leoussi explains, this ethnic differentiation was 'politically explosive'. It allowed Sieyes to urge the 'real nation' to 'send all these families . . . back to the forests of Franconia' (cited in Leoussi, 1997: 60) and so, as Leoussi points out, added an ethnic justification to the French Revolution's assault on absolutism. We now know that the arguments of Sieyes and others triumphed over those of Louis. Like Denny Mendez and Lejla Sehovic, Louis lost his crown. Denny and Lejla shed tears. Louis, alongside much of the nobility, shed much more.

What these examples show is how the criteria for nationality are open to debate and how the national prototypicality of any individual, or set of individuals is connected to such debates. However, while they are intimately linked, these two issues are not always dependent upon each other. For instance, rather than explicitly working on the criteria themselves, claims to prototypicality may take the criteria of inclusion for granted and work on the way in which the individual (or group) fits those criteria. In this chapter, then, we will look at the issues of category boundaries and category prototypicality independently, as well as address the connections.

As ever, though, there will be more to our analysis of category definitions than that. On the one hand, our focus will be on category argumentation and reification – although if, in earlier chapters we tended to focus on the ways in which speakers seek to stop the argument through the invocation of nature, culture and history, in this and the next chapter we balance that through a focus on the complexity of argumentation, counter-argumentation, counter-counter-argumentation (Billig, 1987) . . . and more besides. On the other hand, we will continue to analyse category definitions as the parameters of collective mobilization. Our aim is to investigate how definitions of category boundaries relate to who one is trying to mobilize as support and how definitions of prototypicality relate to who one is trying to mobilize support for. Should projects of mobilization differ in either regard, we would expect to find corresponding changes in the relevant aspects of category definition. This is most obvious if we consider the differences between speakers and between parties at a given point in time. As we will see in the next chapter it is also true if we consider what is said by the same party or even the same person at different points in time.

Drawing the boundaries

We have already discussed the numerous quests to determine a universal set of criteria by which nationhood may be defined. In Chapter One, we concluded that such quests are not simply futile but actively misleading. Bauman summarizes the argument eloquently. He insists that any attempt to produce an 'objective definition' of what constitutes a nation is problematic because it

> obliquely legitimizes the nationalistic claims that it is the sharing of certain attributes that 'makes a nation' . . . rather than exposing the fact that the 'commonality' itself (of land, of language, of tradition) is always an artefact of boundary-drawing activity: always contentious and contested, glossing over some (potentially disruptive) differentiations and representing some other (objectively minor) differences as powerful and decisive separating factors. (Bauman, 1992: 677)

We have also considered some of the characteristic forms this boundary-drawing activity takes. In particular we noted a distinction between the legacy of Herder and the legacy of Montesquieu; between the 'German' and the 'French' models; between 'ethnic' and 'civic' conceptions of the nation. However these are better viewed as analytic categories than as neat boxes into which different nationalisms can be divided. The example of Louis XV shows that even in France itself, the civic model does not apply unambiguously and that the ideological tradition of

1789 did not exclude ethnic elements. In the context of an analysis of Turkish nationalism, Poulton (1997) notes that mixed models tend to be the rule in terms of national ideologies and nationality laws. Thus, when it comes to citizenship, most nation-states advantage those born within the national territory over those born without. But, especially amongst the latter, they also advantage those of national descent over those without national ancestors.

The Turkish case is particularly interesting in its shifting mixture of the ethnic and the civic or territorial. Under the Ottoman Empire, the term 'Turk' was used almost as a term of abuse to refer to ignorant and backward Anatolian peasants. However, with the break up of the empire, a way had to be found of defining and defending the boundaries of the new state and winning the allegiance of its population. At one level, the founders – Mustafa Kemal (Atatürk) in particular – were explicitly pragmatic. Atatürk mocked President Wilson's ethnic definition of the nation, saying: 'I defended boundaries which Turkish bayonets had already defended and laid down. Poor Wilson, he did not understand that lines that cannot be defended by the bayonet, by force by honour and dignity, cannot be defended on any other principle' (cited in Poulton, 1997: 93). On the other hand, he was clearly aware of the need to devise a formulation of the nation which would mobilize the forces necessary to achieve this pragmatic project, but without inciting them to more dangerous enthusiasms.

Firstly, given the predominance of Islam within the population and its importance as a form of self-definition, defining the Turks as Muslim had clear attractions. However, it both failed to differentiate Turks from other Muslims and also had the danger of handing authority from secular to religious authorities. Secondly, an ethnic definition of the Turkish nation in terms of a Turkic people (so called Turanism) also promised to integrate the population. However such a definition was in danger of being both over- and under-extensive. It was over-extensive in the sense of including Turkic peoples outside Turkish boundaries and hence encouraging a destabilizing irredentism. It was under-extensive in the sense of excluding significant groups within Turkey, most notably the Kurds. Thirdly, it would be possible to have a straightforward territorial definition of Turks as those residing within Turkey's national boundaries. However, on the one hand, that would be to exclude the advantages of well-established Islamic and (to a lesser extent) Turkic ideologies. It was also to include groups, such as Christians, whose allegiances were claimed elsewhere.

The solution, as Poulton documents, was a hybrid whereby the Turks were defined as the Muslim population of Anatolia. Initially, within this formulation, Turks and Kurds were identified separately as brothers united by a common Islamic bond within the Turkish nation. However, not only did this leave open the theoretical possibility of separate ethnic mobilizations, Kurdish rebellion was a reality in the south east of the country – notably the Sheikh Said revolt of 1925. This led to a shift in category definitions. Henceforth an ethnic dimension was added to the existing brew. Turks were Turkic, Islamic and resident. However, a Turkic history thesis was elaborated according to which the Turks, or Turanians, were the oldest and noblest of races. Turks and Kurds were both Turanians, even if under the Ottoman Empire the Kurds lost their language and sight of their origins.

They were, in Atatürk's phrase, actually 'mountain Turks'. Hence, by reconstruing the boundaries of ethnicity, an ethnic dimension to Turkish identity could incorporate Kurds within the nation and render illegitimate appeals to independent nationhood. As Article 41 of the programme of the ruling party put it in 1935:

> Our party lays an extraordinary importance upon citizens knowing our great history. This learning is the sacred essence that nourishes the indestructible resistance of the Turk against all currents that may prejudice the national existence, his capacity and power, and his sentiments of self-confidence. (cited in Poulton, 1997: 113)

Both in its original construction and in its later mutations, such an example shows clearly the link between categorization and mobilization. It shows how categories are designed to achieve just the right level of mobilization – not so wide as to provoke unwanted forces to action, not so narrow as to exclude wanted forces from the mobilization. It also shows how definitions are designed so as to exclude potential rival mobilizations, whether they be Islamic, Kurdish or whatever. If such strategic considerations determine the process of boundary drawing, they help us understand when given criteria are or are not likely to appear within a given definition. We can illustrate this in regard to the criterion that is, perhaps, most often placed highly by those who chase the rainbow of objectifying nationhood; we are referring to language.

Consider the fact that early Catalonian nationalism placed great emphasis upon language but that early Basque nationalism did not (Conversi, 1990). Indeed, the famous Basque nationalist Sabino Arana went so far as to argue that language was just a means of keeping Basque people and 'foreigners' separate from each other. If, as he put it, 'our invaders were to learn Euskara, we would have to abandon it, carefully archiving its grammar and dictionary, and dedicate ourselves to speaking Russian, Norwegian or any other language, as long as we are subject to their domination' (cited in Conversi, 1990: 58). However the status of language in Basque nationalism relates less to the ability of 'foreigners' to speak it than the inability of most of those in the Basque country. In contrast to Catalan, Euskara had become a minority language. To mobilize on the basis of a linguistically defined category would be to exclude most of the population. Arana's skill was to take the established idea that the Basques had their roots in a community of noble families and rework this concept of 'collective nobility' in the light of the modern idea of 'race' to produce a racialized definition of Basqueness (Conversi, 1990). However, the strategic advantage of such a racialization was short-lived. Migration and the increasing focus of political activity on electoralist politics rendered this racialized definition problematic because it excluded many who formed part of the electorate. More recently, a territorial definition of national belonging has been developed which has had enormous strategic advantage in allowing the creation of a broad front in relation to Madrid (Linz, 1985).

In Spain as in Turkey, the category–mobilization link (more fully, the link between criteria of national inclusion and the constituency from which mobilization is sought) is clear. What makes it particularly transparent is the ways in which the definition of category boundaries change along with the nature of the population to be mobilized. This is true in two senses. Firstly, as the nature of the audience changes and categories alter in the proportion of that audience which they encompass, so the category definitions change. Secondly, as political strategy changes and hence there is a change in who amongst the audience one seeks to mobilize, so the category definitions also change. The obvious distinction is between strategies, such as electoralism, which depend upon gaining the maximum possible support from all sections of the population, and alternative strategies which rest on particular sections of the population.

At this point, it is necessary to elaborate a point we made in Chapter Three. There we argued that national categories should not be taken as givens but rather as means by which one can appeal to an entire population within a given territory. Hence they are particularly attractive to those seeking office through universal suffrage. Those who are content with sectional mobilizations may use alternative categories – class, gender or whatever. However, to argue that sectional identities cannot mobilize the whole population but national identities can does not mean that national identity is *necessarily* aimed at all. As we have seen, whether it does or not depends upon the criteria which are used to define the national community. Consequently, while one might expect electoralists to find national categories particularly appealing, they are not alone in doing so. We would, however, expect a difference in the criteria by which national categories are drawn between those appealing to the electorate as a whole and those pursuing sectional strategies (though, of course, it is possible to reconcile an electoral strategy with non-inclusive definitions of the nation if, say, the franchise is likewise limited as in Apartheid South Africa, or if one's use of elections is to achieve a platform rather than overall power). The variants of Welsh nationalism bear out this contention.

According to census returns, about 20 per cent of those living in Wales may be characterized as Welsh-speaking. However, this figure masks considerable geographic variation in the proportion speaking Welsh (ranging from 2.5 per cent in Gwent to 61.2 per cent in Gwynedd; cited in Bowie, 1993) and this variation has posed enormous problems for the establishment of a common Welsh identity. In the words of Dafydd Elis-Thomas – an MP and President of the electoralist and 'nationalist' party Plaid Cymru – the issue of language was 'divisive and was used as a negative reason for not supporting the Party of Wales' (cited in Borland, Fevre & Denney, 1992: 56). However, if some were concerned to downplay the language issue so as to allow a construction of the nation that could allow the 'Party of Wales' (i.e. Plaid Cymru) to appeal to all of those entitled to vote in Wales, others could be found arguing that such a strategy would entail the surrender of much that was important and of significance. For example, one activist argued that whilst Welsh was not needed for purely functional communication it fell to the Welsh language to be 'the only means of saving the separate identity of the Welsh people . . . its only possible special task now is the structural one of saving the separate identity of the Welsh as a People' (J.R. Jones, 'Need the language divide us?', 1967, lecture, reproduced in *Planet*, 1980; cited in Osmond, 1988: 149). This logic has been important in developing alternative conceptions of the national community and its interests and has been of particular significance in the thinking of those associated with a group named Meibion Glyndwr. This group – The Sons of Glyndwr (named after Owain Glyndwr, a nobleman who in the fifteenth century briefly succeeded in uniting Wales as an independent country) – advocates the politics of direct action, which, in its most extreme forms, has included burning the property of 'English incomers'.

In the 1980s, increased electoral support for Plaid Cymru was matched by increased activity by Meibion Glyndwr. Whilst at first sight it might be tempting to view this latter as an extension of the former, and explain both in terms of a common factor (e.g. a 'nationalist' rejection of Thatcherism), Borland, Fevre and Denney (1992) argue that the two groups' successes were bound up with their appealing to rather different understandings of Welshness. Whilst the electoralist Plaid Cymru's inclusive definition of Welshness (unrestrained by the ascribed status of language or place of birth) may have succeeded in building electoral support for their programme, others, with more exclusive conceptions of who is to count as being 'of the community' and the interests associated with that community were left feeling that such interests were inadequately represented and turned to Meibion Glyndwr.

If such examples are suggestive, let us now use the Scottish case to look more systematically at the link between category boundaries and the scope of mobilization. Who is a Scot? How are the answers to this question implicated in the arguments of those participating in electoralist and non-electoralist politics? It is with the latter that we begin.

National boundaries and non-electoral politics

As the Sons of Glyndwr stand to Plaid Cymru in Wales, so Scottish Watch stand to the SNP in Scotland. 'Scottish Watch' was formed shortly after the 1992 Election to campaign around issues concerning English migration into rural Scotland. The group's analysis of Scotland and its predicament may be illustrated through considering the arguments articulated at several public meetings and through its pamphlets and leaflets.

At a public meeting in the coastal town of Anstruther (28.4.94), the group's Highland organizer argued that Scotland's politicians: 'had betrayed their principles by refusing to recognize that ordinary Scots were being deprived of access to jobs and housing in rural areas by a massive influx of English incomers'. He went on to say that: 'the English control the economy', that they exploit a system 'designed to make the rich richer and the Scots poorer' and that the situation had reached crisis-point: 'We are the native people of this country and we must organize ourselves to resist these new Scottish Clearances. If we don't then there'll be no future for the Scots in Scotland. No future for our children and nothing left to call Scottish. That is what the English have strived for for hundreds of years' (Scottish Watch, Anstruther, 28.4.94).

The reference to the Scottish Clearances is important here. This refers to the eviction of Highland crofters from their lands by landlords eager for the increased profits to be had by turning the land over to sheep farming. Whole areas, indeed whole regions, were depopulated and the crofters were often forced into emigration.

Characteristically the evictions were brutal and, even if the crofters were rarely killed directly by the landlords and their agents, the Clearances are often seen as genocidal in the sense of destroying the social being of a people. As Lynch (1992) records: 'there are few issues in Scottish history which arouse such deep feelings as the Clearances' (p. 367). To talk of Clearances then is to invoke both an understanding that the very survival of the Scots is at stake and the passions associated with such an understanding. Not surprisingly, then, the reference was not an isolated one. Indeed, one of the pamphlets issued by Scottish Watch was called *The New Scottish Clearances*. It portrayed the Scots as 'most likely to be found in decaying urban labour camps – our cities and industrial towns'. By contrast, the English are 'most likely to be found enjoying the good life in the country – our country. Scotland is divided up on ethnic lines – the Scots are getting the left-overs' (p. 6).

At the heart of this analysis is a definition of 'the English' living in Scotland as an alien and insidious presence. Being foreign, their appropriation of resources characterized as Scottish – 'our' jobs, 'our' cities, 'our' country – is rendered illegitimate. 'They' are taking what is not rightfully theirs. This argument clearly involves the rejection of a territorial definition of nationality, since mere presence is not enough to make incomers Scots – quite the opposite. They are the scourge of the Scots. So how is nationality defined?

At one point in the *The New Scottish Clearances* it is argued that Scottishness is not to be defined in terms of 'race, colour, ethnic origin, creed or culture' and that it 'is entirely up to each individual to define his or herself as a member of a national group, for example a Scot, if he or she chooses to do so' (p. 10). However, the pamphlet also argues that 'while it is accepted that place of birth is not always the truest guide to nationality, it is the best indicator provided by the state and will apply to the vast majority of people' (p. 4). In other words, it is presupposed that background underlies choice to the extent that it can be presupposed that those without Scottish birth will choose to be foreign. Thus the pamphlet takes incomers as a homogenous English outgroup who constitute an 'enemy within'. Indeed: 'All the armies England sent against us were never as powerful as the present-day army of New English Settlers.'

For Scottish Watch, birth easily slips into birthright. It is ancestry not personal history which defines nationality and hence the English are a distinctive ethnic group with distinctive interests that personal experience can do little to alter. According to *The New Scottish Clearances*: 'Most settlers vote Tory for it is against their interests to do otherwise. As a foreign ethnic group with the right to vote, they are forming a political barrier to independence. With the greed and cunning of true colonialists the English know they will be culturally isolated and financially depleted by a return to Scottish self-government. Would an independent Scotland really tolerate the presence of a wealthy and powerful non-native ethnic-group within its borders?' (p. 9).

Elsewhere the ethnic otherness of the English was achieved through their description not simply as settlers but as 'White Settlers' (see, for instance, the Scottish Watch leaflet *The Struggle for Scotland*). Such a formulation also has the attraction of deflecting accusations of racism despite using a racialized construction. By claiming to be a victim, claims are made to anti-racist sensibilities. As Jedrej and Nuttall (1995) observe, the Scots are equated to black natives suffering from colonial domination by cosmopolitan Britain or metropolitan England. The added advantage of this anti-colonialist discourse is that it can dismiss objections to nationalism as merely the powerful seeking to deny the means by which they can be opposed. In *The New Scottish Clearances*, Scottish Watch argue that only nationalism 'can unite a social or cultural group in the war against the imperialism of economic theories and dogma' (p. 2). Indeed, they go further and suggest that cosmopolitanism is not so much a general imperialist ploy, but a specific invention of the English: 'The false modern values of liberal cosmopolitanism are based upon an essentially Anglo-Saxon mercantilism' (ibid).

As we will see further on, this form of argument, in which one simultaneously forwards one's own construction and recuperates alternatives in terms of one's own categories, is relatively common. In the present case, an ethnic definition of nationality is advanced, and objection to these terms is represented as itself a demonstration of ethnically based national values. Anti-nationalism, or cosmopolitanism, becomes Anglo-Saxon mercantilism. For Scottish Watch, then, even to question their definitions renders one suspect of being prey to alien influences if not being alien oneself. Since only a proportion of those in Scotland are actually Scottish, and since the alien is also an oppressor, then to court the entire population necessarily means conceding to the enemy. Hence Scottish Watch argues that the electoral approach of the SNP renders their nationalism bogus. Scottish interests can only be pursued by eschewing the ballot box and undertaking a programme of direct action. Such was the message in a speech by the organization's most prominent spokesperson:

Extract 1

We are here to take up issues that other organizations and political parties are afraid to take up. One would think that a national party in Scotland would exist in order to protect its people. But when you get involved in electoral politics, whether it be the Labour Party, the Liberal Democrats, the Conservative Party, you compromise your principles and the Scottish National Party is so afraid of losing the English vote here in Scotland that it is not prepared to defend the interests of its own people in rural communities, which are facing unfair competition in terms of money, income and resources. Now that political party should be ashamed of itself for taking that particular viewpoint and it is only Scottish Watch, we're taking an awful lot of stick for it, that's been prepared to stand up

(Ian Sutherland, speech, Scottish Watch, Coupar Angus, 15.3.94)

National boundaries and electoral politics

Scottish Watch are not the first to construe Scottishness in ethnic or racial terms. Indeed, Scotland was far from immune from the rise of 'scientific' racism and the upsurge of racial categorization in the nineteenth century. The anatomist Robert

Knox (famous for his purchase of fresh corpses from Burke and Hare) implied that 'races' and 'nations' were virtually synonymous (Miles, 1993). Writing in 1850, Knox claimed that 'in human history race is everything'. His followers and contemporaries were to elaborate these ideas so that the rise and fall of nations was seen as determined by 'race' and the problems of 'racial' degeneration.

When most Scottish writers and institutions of the late nineteenth and early twentieth centuries referred to issues of racial purity, racial mixing and racial degeneration, the concern that really preoccupied them was Irish immigration. For example, a Church of Scotland committee responded to the 1918 Education (Scotland) Act (perceived by some as giving certain advantages to Catholic schools), by stating that the Irish were a distinct race which could not 'be assimilated and absorbed into the Scottish race' (cited in Miles and Muirhead, 1986: 120). Further, the Irish were seen as 'having an unfortunate influence in modifying the Scottish habit of thrift and independence' and showing 'little inclination to raise themselves in the social scale' (ibid, p. 122). In similar vein, an early SNP document entitled *Scotland's Dilemma* (1937) argued that 'unless measures are taken to arrest and control immigration and to put into the hands of the Scottish people the key to the racial destiny of their country, there will be inevitably a race-conflict of the most bitter kind' (cited in Marr, 1992: 78).

Finn (1991) traces this concern with the Irish to Scotland's status as a stateless nation and its consequent reliance on social institutions – particularly the Scottish Presbyterian Church – in order to proclaim its nationhood. The equation of Scottishness with Presbyterianism meant that many Protestants could not see Irish-Scots as 'genuine Scots who happened to adhere to a different form of worship' (Finn, 1991: 374). If Protestants from Northern Ireland emigrating to Scotland were typically construed as little different from the indigenous Scots, Catholics seeking to make that transition found things far more difficult. They were the religious and racial other through which Scottishness was defined.

Whether such considerations have ever impacted upon the selection of Scottish beauty contestants we do not know. However these factors did place a question mark over the ability of those of Irish descent to represent Scotland at football – another domain in which the stateless Scots could express their nationhood. After all, in the absence of a separate government, Scotland did at least have its own football team. In 1887 the *Scottish Athletic Journal* replied to a reader who had asserted that those born in Scotland of parents born in Ireland were Scots. The paper objected: 'This is a mere quibble. They are Irishmen, all the same, by descent' (cited in Finn, 1991: 376). Of course sentiments have changed over the last 100 years and the status of Catholics in Scotland and in Scottish football is generally accepted – but not by all. Rangers football club, a bastion of Protestantism, sees itself and its supporters as 'the moral exemplars of Scottish society' (anon, cited in *Scotland on Sunday*, Spectrum, 9.8.98). When, in 1989 Maurice Johnston became the first Catholic to be signed by the club, there was widespread opposition. As the *Scotland on Sunday* article observed of the controversy: 'underpinning all this were the assumptions that the club was very Scottish and very Protestant, and now here was Johnston, in the vernacular of some, "a wee Catholic toerag", coming to sully this purity'.

The tradition of sectarianism in Scotland therefore leaves a complex legacy. Events still arise to focus that legacy, and not only in symbolic domains such as sport. In 1995 the death of the sitting Labour MP for the Glasgow constituency of Monklands led to a bitterly fought by-election. The constituency had a long history of sectarian dispute and the SNP leader, Alex Salmond, accused Labour of using that history to smear the SNP. Labour itself has been viewed as pro-Catholic. Certainly the evidence shows it to be the party favoured by Catholics (Bennie, Brand & Mitchell, 1997). However it could be argued that this reflects the poverty of Irish immigrants and the traditional sympathy of the Labour Party towards the poor. Later on we will see arguments from party speakers which seek to portray Labour as representing Scotland in general and not sub-categories of Scots. For the moment, however, we are concerned with Salmond's charge that Labour, especially when canvassing amongst the Catholics of Monklands, tried to portray the SNP as having a pro-Protestant bias. More particularly, we are concerned with how he dealt with the charge.

Clearly, the Labour charge had some resonance, hence Salmond's need to challenge it. We have already quoted the 1937 SNP document which expresses hostility to Irish Catholics as a racial group. However, in 1937 the SNP was exactly as old as was Scottish Watch in 1995. It was formed in 1934 out of a merger of the National Party (which itself had only formed in 1928) and the Scottish Party. While candidates did stand for election, they tended to do very badly and certainly had no prospect of election. Many in the party were not wedded to electioneering or indeed to any practical politics. Somewhat harshly, Marr (1992: 74) describes the early SNP as 'extreme and eccentric' and as 'cavorting in a faintly ridiculous tartan ghetto'. However he does bolster such criticism with the words of Lewis Spence, the first 'nationalist' by-election candidate (for the Scottish National Movement) in 1928. Spence characterized those in the 'nationalist' parties as follows: 'Every month produces its harvest of new 'poets', critics, and theorists, political and literary, until the mind reels before the kaleidoscopic confusion displayed by their multi-coloured and frequently absurd doctrines' (Marr, 1992: 75).

By the 1990s, poets had given way to professionals. The SNP had become a serious political force with pretensions (albeit unrealized) to being Scotland's principal political party. Independence was to be won through a strategy of winning a majority of the seats in a parliamentary election and sectionalism would have been the death knell of such an approach. In his 1994 speech to the SNP Annual Conference, the leader, Alex Salmond, explicitly confronted the charge of religious sectarianism:

Extract 2

The Presbyterian tradition left us with the legacy of egalitarianism and democracy and a passion for education. The Catholic view of social justice informs our attitude to inequality in Scotland and internationally. These traditions have jointly helped forge our national identity. We are all a part of all that experience. In this party we seek to add the extra dimension of national independence which will provide for the best

> *expression of what is best about being Scottish. That is why we reject totally all of those who would seek to divide Scotland to set friend against friend. The Scottish National Party needs all of Scotland and all of Scotland needs the Scottish National Party.*
>
> (Alex Salmond, SNP MP, speech, annual SNP conference, Inverness, 23.9.94)

Three aspects of this extract should be noted. The first is the shift from talking about religion as a racial characteristic that inheres in individuals, to religious traditions as cultural legacies that inhere in groups. The second is that Scottish identity is characterized as an amalgam of the various traditions. All, not some, both inform and can claim Scottishness. Thirdly, the SNP reflects that plurality rather than any section of it. But, for all this, the argument is in serious danger of dumping the SNP from the frying pan into the fire.

In the context of an accusation that one favours Presbyterians over Catholics, it might make sense to argue that one represents a Scotland that is made of both. However to define national identity in terms of such traditional variants of Christianity is still a partial formulation. Moreover it leaves one open to the charge of being racist. Indeed Miles (1987, 1989, 1993) notes how often racism is portrayed as a secondary, dependent and derivative ideological form of nationalism. Miles himself takes issue with this equation. Like ourselves, he argues that it fails to take account either of the various forms that nationalist ideology can take, or of the ideological specificity of nationalist and racist ideologies. Moreover, if all nationalisms are racist, attention is removed from the means by which they are constituted in racial terms. We lose the possibility of investigating those political arguments and practices by which racism and nationalism are articulated.

Of course this is not to deny that nationalism is very frequently formulated so as to be racist. Miles himself is moved to write that 'racism is the lining in the cloak of nationalism which surrounds and defines the boundaries of England as an imagined community' (Miles, 1987: 38). Perhaps the most notorious example of this in recent years was Norman Tebbit's 'cricket test'. According to Tebbit, a Conservative Cabinet minister, national identity could be measured by which cricket team one cheers for – the clear inference being that those black inhabitants who cheered for the West Indian, Indian or Pakistani teams could not be English. It may be that post-war Scottish politics has not been racialized to the same extent (Miles and Dunlop, 1986). However, to the degree that such constructions come to shape people's conception of the nature of nationalism, they stand as an obstacle to those typically characterized as *the* nationalists. If Salmond's 1994 Party Conference address had dealt with the charge of sectarianism, his 1995 address took on this more chronic charge of racism:

Extract 3

No one should be asked to sacrifice their identity to be part of Scottish society. After all when Scots go overseas they are not asked to sacrifice their Scottishness – on the

> *contrary, they enhance it. In the same way no minority should be asked to give up their culture or badges of identity to be fully accepted as Scots. There will be no cricket tests in a free Scotland. We see diversity as a strength not a weakness of Scotland and our ambition is to see the cause of Scotland argued with English, French, Irish, Indian, Pakistani, Chinese and every other accent in the rich tapestry of what we should be proud to call, in the words of Willie McIlvanney 'the mongrel nation' of Scotland.*
>
> (Alex Salmond, SNP MP, speech, annual SNP conference, Perth, 1995)

The passage is obviously a retort to those, particularly the Conservatives, who accuse the SNP of racism. It is they with their cricket tests who are the racists. Unlike them, Scotland includes West Indians, Pakistanis, Indians and others besides. Far from defining Scottishness in terms of ethnic purity, its defining quality is ethnic mixture. McIlvanney's splendid formulation bears repetition: Scotland has no ambitions to being pure bred; it is a mongrel nation in which all have their place.

So far so good. The evidence we have produced seems to bear out the contention that those seeking support from the entire electorate use inclusive national categories, whereas those who do not are freer to use either sectional definitions of the national community or else definitions of sectional identities. However those with long memories will recall from Chapter Four the ethnic account of Scottishness provided by the Conservative MP, Nicholas Fairbairn (see Extract 13). Indeed, so strict were Fairbairn's criteria for being a Scot that virtually no one qualified at all. As a reminder, consider the following two quotes from two different public meetings just before the 1992 election. In the first, Fairbairn criticized the SNP's proposals for Scottish citizenship. In the second he questioned the SNP leadership's Scottishness.

Extract 4

All the Scots worldwide who happen not to have been born in Scotland and not to be resident have no say in the affairs of Scotland. But everyone who is born in Scotland, be he Greek, Tasmanian or the bastard child of an American serviceman, or the tenth child of an Englishman, qualify to vote in Scotland.

(Sir Nicholas Fairbairn, Conservative MP, speech, Perth, 3.4.92)

Extract 5

I went round an elderly people's home today, sheltered housing, and out of the 20 or so people that I met, two were Scots and 18 were from England. So let us not forget that it is not the Scots who live in Scotland. It is the British who live in Scotland and far more Scots live in England than live in Scotland and the majority of Scots live all over the world and those who are being captains of the Scottish National Party have only been in Scotland with their families since the 1920s whereas some of us have been here for 1500 years.

(Sir Nicholas Fairbairn, Conservative MP, speech, Invergowrie, 31.3.92)

For Fairbairn, ancestry has to go a long way back before one can qualify as a Scot. Given that the exact figure lies somewhere between 70 and 1500 years, it is certain that not only first-generation immigrants, but that most second- and third-generation immigrants and more besides would also be excluded. Choice is irrelevant in this account; it is stock that matters. If that seems to make an absurdity of Scottish identity, that is precisely the point for Fairbairn. As we argued in Chapter Four, Fairbairn seeks to rubbish the definition of a Scot in order to rubbish the notion that the electorate in Scotland can be appealed to in terms of the Scottish nation. In other words, his definition of Scottishness is not designed as a basis on which to appeal to the electorate but rather to undermine the use of Scottishness by his SNP opposition. In political terms, it seeks to rip the rug from under the SNP.

Such was Fairbairn's status that his claims reached the front pages of the Scottish press. Their potential significance is indicated in the response of SNP speakers. For example, one SNP activist chairing a pre-election meeting in Brechin welcomed the audience with these words: 'Fellow Scots! It gives me great pleasure to welcome you all here tonight. And when I say fellow Scots I include all those categories excluded by Sir Nicholas Fairbairn. And I also include all of our English friends who live among us and who have chosen to throw in their lot with us. More than a few' (Chairperson, SNP meeting, Brechin, 7.4.92).

Another argued in interview:

Extract 6

Scottish nationalism could not be racist if it tried because there just isn't such a thing as a pure Scot. I mean what is a pure Scot? Somebody that doesn't have any ancestry from outwith Scotland? But you'd be down to, what? One per cent of the population?

(SNP activist, interview 2)

At first sight, this interviewee may seem to be saying much the same as Fairbairn. Both agree that using criteria of lineage, the true Scot would be an endangered species. However they draw diametrically opposed conclusions from this. Fairbairn takes the criteria of nationhood as self-evident and therefore presents the idea of a Scottish nation as absurd. The interviewee above takes the existence of Scots as self-evident and therefore assumes the criteria to be absurd. It was in a tone of incredulity and derision that he spoke the words 'one per cent of Scots'. He then proceeded to use the alternative criterion of subjective self-definition to show that more rather than less people than ever were Scots. Even Asian and black people saw themselves as Scottish and he stressed the word repeatedly: 'As Scottish and not as British. As Scottish. To me that is fantastic evidence that whatever it is, there is a Scottish identity'.

Such interchanges are a further indication, if any is needed, that category constructions take place in arguments. They are designed as much to counter the bases of rival mobilizations as to achieve one's own. It is only if one ignores this that one misses the strategic implications of Fairbairn's words or that they seem to work against our arguments concerning electoralism and breadth of category boundaries. Indeed, viewed in context it could be said that they actually illustrate a corollary of this argument. That is, to the extent that broad electoral mobilizations are dependent on inclusive definitions of the nation, then the best way to counter such mobilizations is to redefine the boundaries on which they rest as narrowly as possible.

If we are right in tracing Fairbairn's definition of Scottishness to the specific context in which he seeks to disrupt SNP mobilizations, we would expect his criteria of nationhood to alter as that context alters. Consider, then, two further extracts from the two interviews we held with Fairbairn. The first occurs in the context of a discussion about the SNP and repeats the arguments with which we are now familiar:

Extract 7

Only a comparatively small proportion of those who live in Scotland are of Scottish descent. I mean those who are trying to take us back to the reign of 'Scotland the Poor', the reign of the Stuart Queen Anne, er, very few of them can trace their ancestry in Scotland back beyond the reign of the Hanoverian King George V. Salmond and Mrs Ewing, and the other fellah, Sillars, their grandparents came here in the reign of King George V. They're Irish. They're nothing to do with Scotland. But they sense a Scottishness.

(Sir Nicholas Fairbairn, first interview)

The next extract arose when Fairbairn was asked for his comments on the views of Scottish Watch. He replied that he found them 'absolutely appalling' and based upon a false concept of racial purity:

Extract 8

Most people who live in Glasgow, or the huge majority, are Irish anyway. So to say that they're Scottish on the basis of a sort of blood test, you would find that most people who live in Scotland failed it. And the idea of turning the English out of Scotland, apart from the fact that it's a horrendous concept of intolerance and envy and hatred and contrary to 'we're all Jock Tamson's bairns', it has some very serious implications of 'master races'. . . . Once you speak with a Scottish accent you think you're a Scot. After all, none of us asked to be conceived or chose our parents, and the fact they were from Ireland or from England was irrelevant. And once you speak with a Scottish accent, certainly by the second generation, wherever you came from, you're a Scot.

(Sir Nicholas Fairbairn, second interview)

This argument is more like that of the SNP activists cited in Extract 6 than Fairbairn's own pronouncements in relation to the SNP. The criterion of lineage is raised at the start, but the fact that it would exclude most of the population is used to reject it, not to endorse it. By contrast, an inclusive civic criterion is used in place of anything that might smack of race or ethnicity. This rejection of 'race' when discussing Scottish Watch is explicable on two grounds. First of all, the controversy surrounding the organization was all to do with its racism. It therefore became all the more important to avoid any affinity with their views in order to avoid the charge of being racist oneself. Secondly, since Scottish Watch sought to mobilize on the basis of an ethnically defined Scottishness, the best way of undermining their arguments was to dismiss such a form of categorization. If a Scot is defined by choice as opposed to descent than the very notion of an incomer and of the Scots usurped by the English loses its sense.

Taking this evidence into account, we are now in a position not only to endorse, but to enrich our understanding of boundary drawing. In quotes throughout this section we find people seeking to define the criteria which determine who is part of the nation. We have found many forms of definition which combine the ethnic, the civic and the territorial in complex ways. We have seen that these definitions are argued over and, as Billig (1987) insists, category claims only make sense when viewed in terms of what they are arguing for or against. Finally, for all the variability of definitions, we can still see a regularity in the link between category boundaries and intended mobilizations. In advancing their own position, speakers set category boundaries so as to include all those they seek to mobilize. The wider the desired mobilization, the more inclusive the criteria of category inclusion. Conversely, when countering the position of others, speakers seek to render the categories on which their opponents depend as narrow as possible – even to the extent of dismissing these categories altogether.

There is one other theme that can be found repeatedly in the extracts we have provided, but which we have not commented upon. That is, in defining what makes a category member and hence who belongs in the category, speakers constantly ensure that they exemplify the category prototype whereas their opponents lie outside the category and have no right to speak for it. This is perhaps at its clearest in Extract 7 where Fairbairn casts 'Salmond and Mrs Ewing, and the other fellah, Sillars', the leaders of the SNP, as Irish. How can those who have nothing to do with Scotland purport to represent the Scots? As we shall see in the next section, these questions of prototypicality and the right to lead admit of no easy answers.

Representatives and representation

As one might expect, the topic of leadership has attracted an enormous amount of research. Stogdill's Handbook of Leadership (Bass, 1990) alone lists getting on for 8,000 references. Most of the psychological research can be fitted to the familiar taxonomy of individualism, situationalism and interactionism. After a long and forlorn search for general traits or general behaviours which mark out leaders from others, there was a not quite as lengthy but equally futile attempt to define effective leadership in terms of contextual features. The obvious compromise was to argue that certain types of individual are more likely to be leaders than others, but that their effectiveness will vary as a function of setting. Fiedler and House (1994) suggest that most recent models are of this type, which are commonly known as contingency approaches. Fiedler's own contingency model (Fiedler 1964, 1971) is probably the best known of all. Briefly, Fiedler argues that individuals can be divided into those who focus on relationships with others (relationship motivated) and those who focus on getting the job done (task motivated). One can look at work situations in terms of three factors: the quality of the relationships between the leader and others; the level of leadership power; and the degree of task structure. For Fiedler, when the level of all three factors is at either extreme – either very high or very low – the task-motivated leader will be most effective. However when the level is intermediate the relationship-motivated leaders will come into their own.

If Fiedler's approach is somewhat more nuanced than its predecessors and if considerable experimental evidence has been accumulated to support it (cf. Strube & Garcia, 1981) nonetheless it seems still to be a rather sparse edifice with which to capture all the subtle variations of leadership behaviour – a point endorsed by Peters, Hartke and Pohlmann's (1985) meta-analysis of the available studies. Perhaps more tellingly, there is something strange about these models of leadership which insist on relating leader to situation but which forget that the key context within which leaders operate is that of the group. Nowhere is there any sight of the group members whose endorsement is what constitutes effective leadership. Still less is there any analysis of the interdependence between leadership and followership. As one indication of the complexity of this relationship, let us borrow from Haslam (2001) who cites Bonar Law, who in turn was plagiarizing Ledru-Rollin, prominent in the French Revolution of 1848, when he declared of his supporters: 'I must follow them; I am their leader'.

These concerns are the starting point for recent analyses of leadership in the terms of social identity and self-categorization theories (Haslam, 2001; Hogg, 1996; Platow, Hoar, Reid, Harley & Morrison, 1997). As outlined in Chapter Two, self-categorization theory supposes that group members will seek to act in terms of their social identity. They will therefore seek out and conform to the position which best exemplifies that identity – the ingroup prototype. However, this prototype is not fixed as traditional models of categorization suggest. Rather it is a function of what minimizes intra-group differences compared to intergroup differences and therefore will be a product of the comparative context. In simple terms, if one compares a centrist party to a right-wing party the prototype will be more to the left and when the comparison is to a left-wing party, the prototype will be more to the right (Haslam, 2001; Turner, 1991; Turner, Hogg, Oakes, Reicher & Wetherell, 1987).

Applying this to leadership, it is argued, firstly, that the extent to which an individual matches the group prototype will be an important determinant of leadership effectiveness, especially when group membership is salient (Fielding & Hogg, 1997; Hains, Hogg & Duck, 1997); secondly, that conforming to the group prototype in one respect will enhance the ability of a leader to influence group members on other issues (Platow et al., 1997); thirdly that the more leaders are distinguished from other group members the less effective their leadership will be (Haslam, 2001); and, fourthly, that the criteria for effective leadership will co-vary with prototypicality according to the comparative context (Haslam, in press).

Drawing these various findings together, Haslam (2001) concludes that what makes a leader are not fixed characteristics of the individual, nor features of the situation nor even a combination of the two, but rather those features of individuals which render them representative of a contextually defined social category. The crucial point to observe here is that this goes beyond the interaction of the independently defined terms 'individual' and 'situation' by suggesting the terms themselves are transformed in a social process. As Haslam puts it:

> leadership, then, is a process of mutual influence that revolves around a partnership in a social self-categorical relationship. It is about the creation, co-ordination and control of a shared sense of 'us'. Within this relationship neither the individual nor the group is static. What 'us' means is negotiable, and so too is the contribution that leaders and followers make to any particular definition of 'us-ness'. (2001)

What is striking about this quotation is that, while Haslam's own work tends to either define the group prototype explicitly or else infer it as given by features of the comparative context, he acknowledges the process of negotiation and argument by which both context and categories may be defined. That is precisely the focus of our work and our argument, both as regards social categorization in general and as regards leadership – especially national leadership – in particular. We accept that individuals will gain the potential to influence a category by virtue of being represented as exemplifying that which renders the group special in contrast to other groups (to borrow further from Haslam's terms). Of course, as Haslam recognises, this doesn't mean that the match between leader and group-in-context is passive, fortuitous or a matter of serendipity. Our stress is therefore on the active process of construction whereby individuals work on the representation of self and of category (or of party and nation) in order to achieve a relationship of consonance between the one and the other.

There is a sense in which much of the material we have already addressed is, in fact, oriented to this point. When politicians and activists construe the content of national identity so as to make it consonant with their party projects, they are equally construing their party as consonant with national identity. The construction of national stereotypes and the construction of party prototypicality are often two sides of the same coin. When, in 1952, Eugene McCarthy characterized 'McCarthyism' as 'Americanism with its sleeves rolled up' was he defining the national ideology or nationalizing his own ideology? The question, of course, is absurd. He was doing both.

However, to argue that prototypicality can be asserted through the way in which one constructs the content of national identity is not to say that this is the only way, or even the principal way, by which politicians claim the right to represent. The argument can be conducted in many domains; it does not always turn simply on words but can turn on something that is seemingly as trivial as the colour of the booklet in which one's words are printed. Just after the 1992 Election, the Conservative government published a report defending the constitutional status quo (*Scotland in the Union: A Partnership for Good*). When it was debated in Parliament, one Labour MP observed that: 'It is interesting that the document was published in a blue cover, the colour of the Tory party, whose supporters amount to a small minority of the people of Scotland – a minority becoming smaller because of the Government's attitude.' (Tom Clarke, Labour MP; Hansard, 9.3.93: 804). Inevitably, the Conservative Secretary of State for Scotland, Ian Lang, rose to answer his critics. He returned Clarke's jibe with interest: 'The colour of the White paper is the blue of Scotland – the blue of Scotland in the Union. I believe that the presence of Scotland in the Union is a partnership for good.' (Hansard, 9.3.93: 804).

As we will shortly demonstrate, no domain is intrinsically more important than any other in the quest to appear prototypical. Indeed the art and the theatre of leadership is all about creating a performance where consonant relations are achieved across as many dimensions as possible, from forms of dress to forms of address. But, as the interchange between Clarke and Lang demonstrates, it is just as important to construe one's rivals as atypical of the nation – and hence unable to lead – as it is to construe one's personal and party self as prototypical. In the remainder of this chapter we shall look at attempts to claim prototypicality, and hence leadership, and how such claims are contested. However, we shall start off with dress before moving on to address.

Contesting representative status

In the long struggle of the Palestinian Liberation Organization (PLO) to win recognition for its claim to represent the will and interests of the Palestinian people, one of the few things to remain constant has been the headcovering, or *kufiya* worn by the PLO leader, Yasser Arafat. As Swedenburg (1990) explains, the *kufiya* is actually specific to peasants and Bedouin who constitute only a small proportion of the Palestinian population. If it is now hard to imagine Arafat without it, it is appropriate to consider its symbolic significance in both depicting the community that is to be stood for and in supporting and sustaining Arafat's claim to stand for the Palestinian nation. The Palestinian peasantry occupies a central place in the national iconography. This is not because the iconography functions to rally an actual peasantry to the national cause. Rather, it serves to identify the nation with the land, the land with the nation and thereby lays claim to this land. As Swedenburg suggests, identification with the peasant (or *fallah*) allows a scattered population to acquire a sense of itself as a community with roots in a specific place. Thus, although only 30 per cent of the Palestinian population is involved in agriculture, it is the peasant rather than the worker that symbolizes the nation, and, through signifying an imagined reintegrated nation, 'refigures present-day disfiguration' (Swedenburg, 1990: 24).

So, Arafat's *kufiya* is not merely hiding a bald patch from the glare of the Middle Eastern sun. Rather it is highly charged symbolically. On the one hand it helps to constitute the character of the Palestinian nation, on the other hand it confirms the wearer as embodying that nation. Given the barriers of geographical distance brought about by the PLO's long years of exile and the barriers of class and lifestyle that have separated this leadership from its constituency, Arafat's adoption of the *kufiya* links him with the masses and asserts his ability to 'stand for' the nation. It is a highly visible strategy to overcome that distance which Haslam shows to be so subversive of the leader's authority.

Arafat is not alone in employing dress to claim prototypicality. Mohammed Ali Jinnah, the Quaid-i-Azam, the Great Leader of Pakistan, employed headwear and more besides in order to help him create an idea of Pakistan and an idea of himself as Pakistan. In the country, Jinnah is revered. According to Ahmed he is viewed as 'the very symbol of the state, the father of the nation, the saviour of the Muslims' (1997: xix). Indeed, Ahmed claims that in Jinnah 'we are looking not at a biography but at the definition of a people' (1997: 87). This status would surely surprise an observer only acquainted with Jinnah's early political life. This was spent fighting for a united India. So, how was this 'liberal, Anglicized, seemingly secular politician' (1997: 62), who could not even speak Urdu (the language he claimed as the national language of the Muslims), able to transform himself into the champion of a Muslim Pakistan? According to Ahmed, one of Jinnah's skills resided in his use of clothing to create a modern Muslim persona, which could represent the subcontinent's Muslim nation. More specifically Jinnah adopted items of clothing worn by Muslims from different parts of India. Thus he wore the *karakuli* (a black sheepskin cap) as worn by Muslims in North India, the *sherwani* (knee-length black coat) as worn by those from Aligarh, and the *shalwar* (baggy trousers) characteristic of the faithful from the lands that would form West Pakistan. Wearing this unprecedented combination of previously local fashions allowed Jinnah to develop a common identification between geographically disparate communities and, in turn, present himself as representing all (and not just a particular group). Indeed, when, on 7 August 1947, Jinnah first arrived on the soil of an independent Pakistan, and descended the steps of his aeroplane wearing the *sherwani*, *shalwar* and *karakuli*, he simultaneously established the idea of a national dress (which remains today), constituted the disparate inhabitants of Pakistan as members of a single nation, and signalled his prototypicality of the nation. Quite a performance!

If all national dress, like all nations, needs to be invented, one does not need to be the inventor in order to reap the benefits. Whatever the origins of the kilt, most would now accept it as a sign of Scottishness. The kilt bestows a multitude of benefits upon the wearer. According to the novelist, John Masters (1948), the kilt is 'an unrivalled garment for fornication and diarrhoea'. Whilst some politicians may well be drawn to the kilt for the reasons cited by Masters, we suspect that most are moved by the kilt's communicative function. Thus, one Conservative candidate observed that 'I love to wear the kilt when I'm at dinners in London, not because I'm a raging exhibitionist or anything like that, but just because it's my own personal stamp of 'I'm a Scot and I'm proud of being a Scot'' (Conservative candidate, interview 7).

To the degree that the kilt is a national symbol it follows that to wrap oneself in the kilt is almost literally to wrap oneself in the national flag. Certainly the Conservative MP, Bill Walker, implied as much when he bared his legs in the

House of Commons. The occasion was his introduction of a Parliamentary Bill which would make constitutional change for Scotland virtually impossible. Walker may have hoped that his wearing of the kilt would help in representing himself, and hence his measure, as speaking for Scotland. However the gravitas of his gesture was somewhat punctured by the subversive intervention of a backbench colleague. Shortly after Walker had drawn attention to his Scottishness (announcing 'I stand before you, Madam Speaker, wearing the dress of Highland Scotland'), Sir Nicholas Fairbairn, (who else!) suggested that Walker's Scottish credentials were not all that they seemed. Catching the Speaker's eye, and making reference to the viewpoint that 'real' Scotsmen wear the kilt unencumbered by underwear, he intervened: 'On a point of order Madam Speaker. My Hon. Friend the Member for Tayside North suggested that he was in highland dress. He is in nothing of the kind. He misled the House and I have reason to believe that he is wearing little red pants under his kilt' (Sir Nicholas Fairbairn; Hansard 9.2.93: 825).

Whilst it may be rather rare to suffer such attacks from one's own colleagues and while literal references to underwear may be somewhat infrequent, metaphorical references were relatively common as a means of suggesting that the outward appearance of national identity was contradicted by the inner reality. Consider the SNP leader Alex Salmond's attack on the Labour Party's Scottish spokesperson, George Robertson: 'He's Scottish on the outside, British on the inside. Tartan ties, Union Jack underpants' (Alex Salmond, SNP MP, speech, Inverness, 23.9.1994). However, if this constitutes further evidence for the significance of dress in establishing or challenging claims to being a national representative it also points to a key limitation. Dress is superficial. It is easily chosen and can be donned without either membership or commitment to the causes that are expressed. Even the kilt, however properly worn, is no sure sign of Scottishness. Consider Salmond again, this time on the offensive against the Conservative Secretary of State for Scotland, Michael Forsyth. Forsyth was pictured wearing a kilt to the premiere of Mel Gibson's epic of the Scottish independence wars, *Braveheart*. Salmond responded with: 'just a wee personal note of advice to Michael. There is more to being Scottish than dressing up like a shortbread tin. If you want to lead Scotland then get elected by the people not selected by England's Tory Prime Minister' (Alex Salmond, SNP MP, speech, Perth, 1995).

Something more enduring than dress is often needed to claim nationhood. As noted above, a short lineage can be used to deny such claims – Salmond and his fellow leaders cast as Irish rather than Scottish. The converse is to use a long lineage to establish them. We have already seen how early monarchs tended to trace their descent past Kenneth MacAlpin, first King of a united Scotland, back to Gaythelus (Gael), a Greek Prince married to Scota, daughter of Pharoah, and thereby to the mythical foundations of the Scottish people (see Chapter Six). In this way, they establish not only their own pedigree but that of a country nobler and older than England. As Mackie puts it: 'It has been said that the first "international" was a lying match, and that the Scots won easily; but the long pedigree tells not only of ardent pride but of a determination to claim a distinct nationality' (1991: 46–7).

Such use of pedigree to establish prototypicality is not confined to a distant past. Those figures who may have used Scota, become figures to be used as they themselves merge into an immemorial past. The 1997 Election in Scotland provided a graphic example of this. Just before polling day the residents of North East Fife received a newsletter from the Conservative candidate seeking to unseat the incumbent Liberal Democrat MP. This candidate was described as coming from a family that were 'the oldest living descendants of King Robert the Bruce' and he himself was depicted in a large photograph wearing a kilt and holding what was described as the 'the broadsword of Robert the Bruce, handed down through generations of the Bruce family'. The analogy between past and present, candidate and ancestor, was underlined in the photograph's subtitle: 'In 1314 King Robert the Bruce defeated the English against all the odds. In 1997 Adam Bruce has only the Liberals to beat. Help him do it . . .' Modern Bruce, like mythical Bruce, stood as a defender of the Scots. Scots were enjoined to rally to the Bruce flag in the fight for Scotland. Lest anyone missed the point, the headline ran 'Fighting for Fife, Fighting for Scotland'.

The connection works because every Scot from their school days onwards, learns to know that Bruce was the original champion of the Scottish interest. That is non-negotiable. Hence, to hitch oneself to the Bruce bandwagon is to show that one also acts to the same ends. Lineage, then, is one way of claiming to represent the national interest. The former is the means to the latter which establishes one's right to lead. However it is not the only means. Indeed often the matter of who does, and does not, advance the national interest is debated more directly. Moreover, if the claim to do so is necessary for the mantle of leadership, so the claim that another does not would be fatal to their chances. More wounding still is the accusation that claims to act in terms of the national interest are mere covers for advancing one's own interests.

One of Samuel Johnson's most renowned and most repeated aphorisms is that 'patriotism is the last refuge of a scoundrel'. However the words are often quoted out of context. Boswell, in his *Life of Johnson*, provides that context:

> Patriotism having become one of our topics, Johnson suddenly uttered, in a strong determined tone, an apophthegm, at which many will start: 'Patriotism is the last refuge of a scoundrel.' But let it be considered, that he did not mean a real and generous love of our country, but that pretended patriotism which so many, in all ages and countries, have made a cloak for self-interest. (1934, II: 348)

According to Colley (1992), Johnson had the English radical John Wilkes in mind when he uttered these words. Wilkes sought to mobilize opposition to the government by arguing that he was defending the birthright of free-born Englishmen against those who sought to subvert the constitution. His protests were replete with symbols of Englishness. A typical Wilkite demonstration involved assembling at a tavern named after William of Orange before setting out under banners of the Magna Carta and the Bill of Rights (Colley, 1992). Such agitation landed Wilkes in jail, but even so he declared that: 'In this prison, in any other, in every place, my ruling passion will be the love of England' (cited in Colley,

1992: 108). The point of Johnson's aphorism, then, was precisely to puncture such grandiloquent claims to put the national interest before one's own interest by suggesting that the opposite is true: one's own interest is pursued under the cover of national interest.

Such is the power of Boswell's taunt that it has achieved wide currency. It can still be found in many places and in many forms. Consider for instance the following claim by the SNP that, whatever their lofty pronouncements, the reason why certain politicians oppose the policy of independence stems from much baser motives:

Extract 9

The very notion of Scots opting for Independence in Europe sends London's political leaders bananas. Even more, their Scottish placemen and women who tamely punt the London line. For it puts their *careers at risk. That's why it's up to us, to change things now* for a better life. Us, the Scottish people. Not the careerists. If *we don't, they won't.* No way.

(SNP 1992 election leaflet, *Scoring with the SNP*: emphasis in the original)

If this is not wounding enough, there is one way of upping the stakes still further. It is to claim that one's opponents are not merely acting in their personal interests rather than those of the nation, but that they are actually serving the interests of national foes. In other words, the opposition are more than scoundrels, they are traitors. Perhaps the most famous traitor in the British political lexicon is the so called 'Lord Haw-Haw', an Englishman who broadcast from Berlin during the Second World War. To brand people with Haw-Haw's name is then to accuse them of mounting a similar attack on the nation – though, as the following example shows, that nation need not necessarily be Britain. Thus in a speech to his annual party conference in 1996, the SNP activist Alex Neil applied the insult to the Scottish Labour leader: 'Lord Haw-Haw was an Englishman employed by Nazi Germany with one sole task: to sap the morale of his own people and undermine their confidence. We in Scotland have a new Lord Haw-Haw. His name is George Robertson.'

Lest it be thought that only 'nationalists' deal in the currency of betrayal, it is necessary to note that the SNP could also be on the receiving end. One of the key Scottish figures used by the SNP to promote its policy of independence was Sean Connery, possibly the world's best-known Scotsman and perhaps even better known in his screen persona of James Bond, Secret Agent 007. Connery had joined the SNP in early 1992 and frequently figured in SNP leaflets and broadcasts. When the Scottish *Sun* newspaper supported the SNP during the 1992 election with the front page slogan, 'Now or Never' (17.3.92) it was Connery's face that accompanied the headline. So did Connery represent the Scots and should Scots take notice of his views and support the SNP? Obviously his opponents needed to undermine him. One way was to portray him as deserting Scotland by emphasizing his Spanish residence. Thus Conservative MPs took to belittling Connery's political interventions by referring to him as 'the honourable member for Marbella' (*Dundee Courier and Advertiser*, 21.11.96). Another line of attack was exemplified by Bill Walker's words at a public meeting during the 1992 campaign:

> ## Extract 10
>
> *It's about time we began to realize what prominent Scots, leading members of the Scottish community have been saying. Now I'm not talking about Sean, you know the Suntory Scot. The one who exports jobs in the Scotch whisky industry. He's the one who's been telling us what we should be doing. Look at what he's doing to our whisky industry! He's promoting their biggest competitor. Well I'm not talking about him. No, no. I'm not talking about James Bond. I'm talking about real people. I mean people who live here, pay our taxes and are part of our community.*
>
> (Bill Walker, Conservative MP, speech, Glamis, 23.3.92)

There is much to this extract, but at its heart is an attempt to deny Connery's status as a national icon who can speak for the nation by stressing his betrayal of the country. He does not only threaten a Scottish industry, he threatens what might be considered as the fundamental symbol of Scotland. Connery, the man who advertises 'Suntory' Japanese whisky and who puts 'Scotch' under threat: what more base treachery could there be than that? The 'Suntory Scot' jibe therefore manages to use a referent with distinctively national cultural resonance in order to accuse the other of betraying the nation. In this sense it trumps the Haw-Haw reference. However, when referring to Scottish culture, the reader will be aware by now of how the figure of Burns towers above all else. And Burns provides a particularly valuable resource for those who wish to make accusations of betrayal. In one of his most famous poems, he lambasted those members of the Scottish parliament who had voted for Union with England in 1707 as a 'parcel of rogues' who had sold Scotland for personal gain:

> What force or guile could not subdue
> Thro' many warlike ages,
> Is wrought now by a coward few,
> For hireling traitor's wages.
> The English steel we could disdain,
> Secure in valour's station;
> But English gold has been our bane –
> Such a parcel of rogues in a nation!
> (Burns, 1909, vol IV p. 73)

If history repeats itself as farce, perhaps poetry is doomed to being repeated as doggerel. Witness the response by the Labour MP Dennis Canavan to the refusal by Conservative Secretary of State Ian Lang and his parliamentary colleagues to commemorate Burns with a national holiday in Scotland:

> ### Extract 11
>
> *Does that negative, disappointing reply have anything to do with the fact that Burns was an ardent supporter of a Scottish Parliament and a fierce critic of the Unionists, who used treachery, bribery and skulduggery to destroy Scotland's last Parliament?*
>
> > *Why are the Tories' prospects dim?*
> > *Could it be the reputation*
> > *Of Ian, Allan, Hector and Jim –*
> > *Such a parcel of rogues in a nation!*
> >
> > (Hansard, 25.1.95: 348)

If Burns provides a powerful resource, his is also an ambivalent resource. So Lang, facing an attack based on Burns, was also able to use Burns in his defence. Using a typically rich insult, he first described Canavan's words as those of 'a rhyming, ranting raving billie'. He then went on:

> ### Extract 12
>
> *As to Burns being a supporter of a Scottish Parliament, I remind the Hon. Gentleman of his words in* The Dumfries Volunteer:
>
> > *Be Britain still to Britain true*
> > *Amang oursels united*
> > *For never but by British hands*
> > *Maun British wrangs be righted*
> >
> > (Hansard, 25.1.95: 348)

Far from opposition to a Scottish Parliament being a betrayal of the Scottish interest, as buttressed by the separatist Burns, Conservative support for Scotland in Britain is a championing of the Scottish interest, as endorsed by the unionist Burns. Implicitly at least, this is turning defence into attack. For, if Union represents Scottish interests, then opposition to Union is an attack on the Scottish interest. Those who support it thereby subvert rather than represent the nation. So the accused becomes patriot accusing the accuser of betrayal. An argument that is simultaneously parry and counter-thrust has clear rhetorical attractions and, not surprisingly, the implications are often made quite explicit.

In 1919 the American President, Woodrow Wilson, observed that 'Sometimes people call me an idealist. Well, that is the way I know I am an American. America is the only idealistic nation in the world' (speech, Sioux Falls, 8th Sept, 1919). In the space of just three short sentences, Wilson took the charge that he was out of touch with reality (and hence could not pursue the 'real' interests of the nation) and turned that charge to his advantage. At one level his critics were right. He was an idealist. But idealism did not mean a distance from the material world but rather was a value which embedded him firmly in the reality of the nation. Crucial to this transformation is a reinterpretation of the accusatory term so as to turn it from a relationship of dissonance to a relationship of consonance with national interest and national identity. A similar shift is frequently used when not only turning attacks to one's own advantage but also turning them to the attacker's disadvantage.

For the Conservatives, SNP 'separatism' meant separating Scotland from the Union which, for them, was the source of Scottish wealth, influence and prestige. Note, then, how the SNP MP, Andrew Welsh, turns the term around:

Extract 13

'Separatism' is exactly what we've got at the minute. Scotland is separated from decision making. Scotland is separated from her wealth. Scotland is separated from the wider international community. Independence would end that separatism and allow Scotland to rejoin the world which is something in our history, our culture and the natural inclination of Scots, something we would want to do.

(Andrew Welsh, SNP MP, speech, Monifieth, 6.4.92)

With these last examples we have moved away a little from the theme of self-interest and betrayal. However, we do not have to look too far to find the turning around of one's opposition's attacks buttressed through the counter-accusation that such opponents are self-interested. For example consider the response of the Conservative Deputy Prime Minister, Michael Heseltine, to the charge that the Tories' resistance to devolution exemplified their distrust of the Scots. Just as the SNP speaker above gave 'separatism' a new meaning, so Heseltine gave 'devolution' a new meaning. Note too how this meaning was buttressed by the charge that, if anyone's proposals were driven by self-interest, they were those of Labour.

Extract 14

We want for the Scottish people an opportunity – wider for them – enhanced for their children and secure from generation to generation. When I say the Scottish people, I mean the Scottish people. Not Scottish local authorities. Not Scottish Trade Unions. Not the talk-Scotland-down brigade. Not that grubby army – fudging the figures, cooking the books, writing Scotland off – that is the stock and trade of every party in Scotland other than the Conservatives. Our devolution is to every individual in Scotland . . . Let no one hijack the language. We stand for devolution of real power to the people. The Labour Party stands for the devolution of power to assemblies, councils, unions, committees, working parties, pressure groups. They mean devolution of power to themselves. I mean devolution of power to you!

(Michael Heseltine, Conservative MP, speech, Edinburgh, 7.4.92)

In both of the above cases the opposition is attacked for acting against national interests. In both cases the policy under attack is re-presented as representing the national interest. And in both cases, those making the accusation are represented as the real enemies of the national interest. In Heseltine's case this is done twice. The first comes in the argument concerning 'devolution' which, as we have highlighted, runs through the extract. The second lies in the phrase 'the talk-Scotland-down brigade'. This encapsulates a common argument, used by all parties. In this case, the argument does not reconstrue the nature of the accusation but rather reconstrues the target of the accusation. Thus an attack on the party is taken as an attack on the nation and can be used to turn on the accuser as truly unpatriotic. An example can be found in another pre-election speech by one of Heseltine's fellow Tory ministers, Peter Lilley:

Extract 15

I have never once heard Gordon Brown, John Smith, Donald Dewar or any other Labour MP in Westminster pay tribute to the achievements of the Scottish economy in recent years. They know that what is good news for Scotland is bad news for Labour. So they rubbish success and trumpet failure. They put party before country. Think how well Scotland will do with more Conservative Members of Parliament trumpeting Scotland's strengths, achievement and opportunities.

(Peter Lilley, Conservative MP, press conference, 30.3.92)

The argument is also used by SNP speakers who portray attacks on the viability of the SNP independence policy as an attack on Scottish competence. Indeed Alex Salmond draws a distinction between attacks on the Party and attacks on the nation, the better to denigrate attackers once their challenge can be represented as targeting the latter rather than the former:

Extract 16

I don't mind attacks on the Scottish National Party. That is part of the stuff of democratic debate. But I'll tell you what I mind. And what I mind very much indeed. I mind political attacks which are not attacks on the SNP but are attacks on the Scottish nation. An attempt to denigrate and belittle the abilities of the Scottish nation, because that is what is going on.

(Alex Salmond, SNP MP, speech, Dundee, 19.3.92)

By now, we hope to have adduced sufficient evidence to convey something of the ceaseless ebb and flow of argument around prototypicality. Claims to prototypicality are countered by accusations of treachery; accusations of treachery are turned back to reassertions of action in the national interest; accusations of treachery are themselves transformed into evidence of treachery which in turn needs to be defended against. So the circle stays unbroken. As Billig stresses, there is no natural resting place and every attempt at closure presents the opportunity for new openings.

Conclusion

This chapter has been all about national inclusion and exclusion; about how subjects are related to categories both through defining the category boundaries and through defining the nature of individual and collective subjects: persons, parties and social movements. There is a sense in which this, more perhaps than any of the other themes we have dealt with, is central to the process of collective influence and mass mobilization. This is because it is necessary to constitute an audience before it can be appealed to, and to define one's (personal or collective) self before one is in a position to influence them. What we have tried to demonstrate, then, is how issues of boundary definition (and hence the constitution of people as group members) and claims to prototypicality are at the very core of politics.

As this chapter has illustrated, the question of where the nation's boundaries are placed has many implications. Their definition affects who may be appealed to, the characterization of the nation's interests, who may speak in the name of the nation and more besides. Given these important consequences it follows that anything in the social scientific analysis of group processes which implies that group boundaries are non-problematic 'givens' is itself deeply problematic. Indeed, to the degree that boundary definition is strategic, anything which contributes to the naturalization of the socially constructed is ideological.

Lest it be doubted that the definition of category boundaries is bound up with strategic matters, it is appropriate to reconsider some of our examples. Many of the concerns relevant to boundary definition were bound up with the organization of electoralist politics. Whereas those outside the electoral process worked with narrower conceptions of who was to count as a member of the nation, those working within the electoral process typically worked with more inclusive definitions of the national community, such that all those entitled to vote could identify with their party and its project. However, we also found exceptions to this picture which illustrate something of the diversity to be found in speakers' strategic considerations. Most notably we found Sir Nicholas Fairbairn, a candidate standing for election, advancing a highly restrictive definition of category membership which not only undermined his opponents' claims to Scottishness but also mocked the very idea that there was a substantial constituency in Scotland that could be mobilized as Scots in pursuit of constitutional change. Indeed, he concluded that the only category able to capture the reality of contemporary Scotland was one which defined its inhabitants as British. Yet another piece of evidence for the inherently strategic nature of boundary definition comes from the variation which may be found within a single speaker. Once again the clearest evidence was provided by Sir Nicholas Fairbairn. If he sometimes sought to pull the rug from under the SNP's feet by so narrowing the boundaries of Scottishness as to render it meaningless for political mobilization, he was also to be found pulling the rug from under the feet of those (associated with Scottish Watch) who sought to use a narrow conceptualization of who was to count as Scottish for another (non-electoralist) project. If, at first sight, this variation seems meaningless, as soon as it is interrogated in relation to the speaker's strategic concerns all is made clear.

Far from random, such variation is meaningfully related to strategy. Of course the wider significance of this evidence is that no definition of category boundaries should be construed as 'neutral' or without strategic purpose. All must be analysed in context and all must be interrogated for the strategic work that they do and for the projects that they support and sustain.

If the question of category boundaries has received relatively little thought from social psychology, the topic of leadership has, as we have seen, attracted massive attention. It has preoccupied theorists throughout the history of psychology from Le Bon and Freud onwards. It is one of the domains in which one might expect the application of psychology to make history, not simply to describe it (cf. Moscovici, 1981). However, since Le Bon's unashamed activist orientation, which was more concerned with mystifying leadership so as to preserve its fascination rather than identifying its ideological contingency (Reicher, 1996), most models of leadership have rendered the matter more and more passive: leadership inheres in individual traits or in situational characteristics or in some contingent relation between the two. In none of these suggestions is there any sense of the leader as agent. Even the self-categorization perspective – which acknowledges that leadership is a partnership in a social categorical relationship, that it is about the creation of a sense of 'us-ness' and which thereby acknowledges in principle the importance of including an agentic dimension – nonetheless tends in its research practices to establish the leader–group relationship as either consonant or dissonant and then look at the consequences, rather than examine the means by which such relationships are actively established in order to gain influence. The point is that leadership tends not to alight upon an individual but is actively sought. The practice of leadership is about the strategic creation of personal and collective realities so as to merge the two (or separate them in the case of one's rivals). To examine leadership while setting the terms of identity is to examine a craft in the showroom and not in the workshop. We may see the finished article but we cannot see how it is fashioned.

8 Changing Categories and Changing Contexts

New categories for new contexts

One of our constant themes has been that the relationship between context and categorization is a two-way street. Or, in relation to our present concerns, nationalism creates nations but nations also create nationalism. We have diagnosed the failure of psychology to address this reciprocal relationship as, in part at least, due to the omission of an historical dimension from most analyses. To understand that category definitions are as much about becoming as about being it is necessary to examine how things develop over time: how the nature of social practice at one point in time feeds into the way we categorize things at another point in time and also how our categorizations at a given moment mobilize people to reorganize the nature of social practice at another moment.

For all our protestations, however, it is not entirely clear that we have practised what we preach. Certainly we have stressed how a world organized along national lines (or at least certain forms of activity in the world that are so organized) leads to the invocation of national categories. We have also examined the various ways in which constructions of nationhood are oriented to the process of mobilization and the creation of new national realities. But hitherto we have tended to look at these as separate moments. We have not put them together. We have not seen how the world affects the category constructions which in turn reorganize the world and how this new world in turn impacts on the categories that are employed – and so on in a never-ending spiral. In this chapter we aim to take a first faltering step towards such an integration. We wish to look at the historical development from before to after the General Election of 1992 in Scotland. We want to show how categorization fed into the electoral process and how the outcome of the electoral process provided a new terrain allowing for new mobilizations that were reflected in new category constructions.

The first half of this task is, in effect, what we have been doing for the past five chapters and therefore need not detain us for too long. However, in those past chapters – and especially in Chapter Seven – we have generally looked at the claims of politicians concerning their own party or a single rival. To conclude our analysis of how politicians seek to make of themselves and their policies an enactment of the national identity (and hence a realization of the national interest) we will show how they construe themselves as uniquely blessed in this respect and how all their rivals are uniquely damned.

Such multi-lateral argument is best investigated in a context where several parties jousted for support from a single platform. One such event occurred shortly before the 1992 Election in the parliamentary constituency of Dundee East. The seat had been won by Labour from the SNP in the 1987 Election with a small majority (Labour, 19,539 votes; SNP, 18,524 votes; Conservatives, 5,938 votes). As a swing of little more than 1 per cent was all that was needed to overturn Labour's most marginal Scottish seat, it was clear that the campaign would be vigorously fought and the *The Herald*'s review of the local campaign (published just 7 days before polling) claimed that 'as well as being one of the most interesting contests in Scotland, Dundee East also has established itself as one of the most acrimonious' (02.04.92).

Dundee has a history of vigorous and acrimonious political contests. For 14 years Winston Churchill held a Dundee seat, but in 1922, at the age of 47, he found himself roundly rejected by the electorate. Recovering from a stint in hospital, the future Prime Minister recorded that: 'In the twinkling of an eye, I found myself without an office, without a seat, without a party, and even without an appendix' (cited in James, 1970: 149). During the campaign, his meetings had attracted furious opposition from the left. In one case the police used their batons on the crowd as Churchill faced what Dundee's local paper, *The Courier*, described as a 'howling mob' straining to produce 'a perfect rabble of vocal discord' (James, 1970). Ironically, though, Churchill was defeated not by a left-winger but by the Independent and Prohibitionist candidate, Edwin Scrymgeour. Scrymgeour won with a majority of over 10,000. The shock of this defeat sent reverberations throughout the political establishment. Churchill received a note from Buckingham Palace reporting that 'His Majesty is very sorry about the Dundee Election . . . the Scotch Electorate is rather an incomprehensible body!' (cited in Gilbert, 1975: 891). T.E. Lawrence put it rather more bluntly: 'I'm more sorry about Winston than I can say . . . What bloody shits the Dundeans must be' (cited in Gilbert, 1975: 890).

Seventy years on, the tone of the debate had changed little. The Conservative candidate had been a Labour member of Dundee District Council for 11 years before joining the Tories in 1987. He was held in personal contempt by many of the Labour members in the audience and, in his opening comments on the night, he returned that contempt, attacking the sitting Labour MP for not having made 'one positive contribution in his four years as a Member of Parliament towards this city'. Yet, for all this hostility, the assaults remained verbal. The police had no cause to use their truncheons. No candidate felt the need to emulate Churchill's example of having a detective sleep across the door of his hotel room to guard against attack.

The format of the meeting allowed each of the candidates to make an opening statement, followed by debate involving the audience. The Conservative spoke first, followed by the SNP, followed by the sitting Labour MP. What follows is one extract from each of these three statements:

Extract 1

This election, ladies and gentlemen, is not just about political parties and political policies. It is about responsible representation and the question is: 'Who on this platform tonight should represent Dundee East in Parliament?' At present Dundee East has a

Labour Member of Parliament and I say to the people of Dundee tonight that a vote for the SNP is a failed option. You tried that last time round and look what you got. You got a Labour Member of Parliament who, in my opinion, has not made one positive contribution in his four years as a Member of Parliament towards this city. His disgraceful leading of the Poll Tax campaign certainly did not do this city's image any good whatsoever and I do not believe that actions like that are the actions of responsible men . . . In Dundee the SNP are a mirror image of the Labour Party. Mr Coutts votes 99.9 per cent of the time with the Labour party. Both have said that they are socialists, Mr McAllion and Mr Coutts . . . Now we come to one of the issues that is going to be very important in this coming election and that is the constitutional question. I have to ask this question. Are the people of Scotland as uncertain about their future as the media tends to make out? I would suggest they're not. The media say that Scotland is at a crossroads. I say that if Scotland is at a crossroads, there is no middle road they can take. They must either decide the one way or the other, on UK or independence. It is time to bite the bullet, ladies and gentlemen. It is time to make your mind up. You cannot sit on the fence. You can stay, in my opinion which would be the best way, on the tried and tested road as part of the United Kingdom or you could go down the rocky road to independence and isolation, with the inherent problems that would bring to Scotland, job losses, the lack of inward investment etc. But I think what you also must realize is this: if you go down that particular road then there is no coming back.

(Steve Blackwood, Conservative candidate, Dundee, 7.3.92)

Extract 2

The one difference between myself and the three other candidates on the panel is that they will peddle the attributes of the Union between Scotland and England and I stand firmly in this election with the campaign for independence for Scotland . . . We've got members from the Labour Party, the Conservative Party and the slowly disappearing party, [i.e. the Liberal Democrats] *trumpeting round Scotland fiddling the facts and trying to undermine the Scots. There are placemen and placewomen from all these parties telling us that the Union is great. And this is like a meeting of Dundee District Council with all the Labour faces in the audience: you too are responsible and stand accused of the disinformation, the innuendo, the secrecy, all telling us that Scotland can't do it.*

(David Coutts, SNP candidate, Dundee, 7.3.92)

Extract 3

My message to the voters in Dundee East is really very simple, and it's this. If they really want to see this Tory Government defeated in the election, and if they really want to see a Scottish Parliament re-established in our country after nearly 300 years, and if they want to see a start made in building a new and modern Scotland, then they should vote for the Labour candidate because the Labour Party is the only party which is capable of taking on and defeating the Tories in this election . . . The SNP cannot win these seats. Though they claim they will be, they are really lying through their teeth. And of course

> *they can improve on their present position. They can advance in a parliamentary seat, here and there, across Scotland. But the price that will have to be paid for that will be to undermine the only party in Scotland that is capable of taking on and defeating the Tories.*
>
> (John McAllion, Labour MP and candidate, Dundee, 7.3.92)

In each of these extracts the speaker works on the categories at two different levels. Firstly, the parties are characterized such that the ingroup is distinctive from the opposition, who belong together. Secondly, the ingroup category is construed as representing the national interest, while the outgroup category (and hence all the rival parties) is construed as negating the national interest. To take them in turn, the Conservative construes the Labour and SNP speakers as identical in being socialists and in lacking responsibility – most notably by playing games with a tried and trusted constitution and insouciantly setting off down a road to perdition. Clearly, the responsible Conservatives don't imperil the nation's future unlike their irresponsible opponents. The SNP speaker retorts by grouping Conservatives and Labour (and Liberal Democrats) as defenders of the Union, with only the SNP and its independence policy as placing faith in Scottish abilities to succeed. Finally, the Labour candidate puts Conservatives and the SNP in the same boat by arguing that, whatever their theoretical differences, in practice both block Labour's attempt to give Scots economic prosperity and political choice.

Thus each speaker chooses different dimensions with which to look at the array of similarities and differences between parties and thereby comes up with different notions of who is similar and who is different: support for the status quo versus support for change in principle; support versus opposition to the Union in principle; ability to change the status quo in practice. Depending upon which dimension is chosen the ways of categorizing the parties (and their relationship to the nation) turns out very differently.

The US educator and historian James Harvey Robinson (1923) articulated a common complaint when he observed that 'Partisanship is our great curse. We too readily assume that everything has two sides and that it is our duty to be on one or the other'. From the foregoing argument it should be clear that we both endorse this claim and view it as having the potential to be seriously misleading. On the one hand, for the purposes of mobilization, categories are frequently constructed in a binary fashion such that the ingroup is uniquely representative of the intended audience and all those in the outgroup are equally unrepresentative. On the other hand, these sides are far from self-evident. Rather they are complex argumentative accomplishments – both in the sense of their binary nature and in the precise identity of the two sides.

For us, then, if anything counts as a curse, it is not so much that we take sides but rather an amnesia about how these sides are produced. The result of such amnesia is that we reify categories either as natural across all contexts or, at least as natural within a given context. At that point we slip into the one-sided illusion that categories make people. In losing sight of how people make categories we equally lose sight of how they may be unmade and we must thereby take responsibility both for producing antagonisms and for confronting them (Hopkins, Reicher & Levine, 1997).

The importance of these issues is compounded by the fact that defining category structure goes a long way towards determining category choice. We have seen that during the 1990–1 Gulf War, those supporting the military action to re-take Kuwait construed the war in terms of 'civilization' in general standing up to the barbarism of Saddam Hussein. By contrast, those opposing the war saw it as prosecuted by a political/business elite with scant regard to the consequences for the mass of ordinary people. As we concluded from this evidence: 'The answer to the well-known question "Which side are you on?" depends on the answer to a prior question: "What are the sides?" (Herrera & Reicher, 1998: 993). Thus, to pre-suppose the dimensions along which similarity and difference are investigated may turn out not only to be an act of reification but also to be an act of propaganda.

All in all, our three pre-election speakers in Dundee do not just provide a fine example of the way in which speakers seek to mobilize support for their party by construing that party as alone in advancing the national interest, as uniquely in tune with the national identity and hence as the only party able and deserving to represent the national electorate. They also provide a remarkably succinct and eloquent illustration of the fact that categories do not derive from inherent similarities and differences between stimuli, as well as of the dangers (both intellectual and political) of assuming that they do. Similarities and differences can only be computed once the relevant dimensions have been chosen. Relevance, in this respect, refers to who one is trying to mobilize and in support of what. As we have shown: different parties, different projects; different projects, different dimensions; different dimensions, different categories.

But perhaps we are overplaying our hand. Perhaps this ability to select different dimensions to create different categories and hence render the ingroup both unique and uniquely representative of the wider category derives from the abstract nature of the issues at hand. Perhaps if we were dealing with more concrete matters it would be far harder for each party to claim a unique ability to represent the Scots and we would find that objective features of context would determine the nature of category definitions. Indeed, where parties claim to represent the national population, there would seem to be a very simple and incontrovertible way of settling the matter. Just look at the figures. Of course, one has to take care that the counting takes place properly, but as long as the procedures are sound, numbers appear to have an objectivity that transcends strategic debate. Or, as the American writer Rex Todhunter Stout (1966) once observed: 'There are two kinds of statistics, the kind you look up and the kind you make up.'

In consequence, much play is made of figures in political debate. But the more one looks at the figures, the more one realizes that they serve more as a domain of argumentation than as a way of settling arguments. Indeed, just as with the uses of history, it is precisely because numbers are seen as being objective and decisive that they are so ferociously contested. The contestation can take many forms. The most obvious and the most mundane is simply to pick and choose the figures one wants. It is virtually a truism that politicians believe in polls when they are ahead and become instant atheists when they are behind. Polls such as that published early in the 1992 Election campaign that showed support for independence as running at over 50 per cent were so widely used by the SNP that one correspondent to *The Sunday Times* castigated them for using: 'an opinion poll lampost in similar manner to a drunk . . . more for his support than illumination' (letter, *The Sunday Times*, 22.9.96). Adding a personal gloss, he went on to contend that if the SNP: 'continue clutching that lampost for much longer, even little dogs will be doing it on them''. Yet, when later polls gave the SNP diminished support, the deputy leader, Jim Sillars, attacked them as tools to 'undermine the pride and self-confidence of our people'. He continued:

Extract 4

Can I just say about opinion polls, I am a very particular politician: I don't bother about them at all. I shock the folk on English television when they say things to me like, 'Look where you are in the opinion poll.' And I say to them, 'You wait and see what it's like on the morning of the 10th April. I'm no' worried about your opinion.' And that comes as a shock to The Times, *newspapers and that. I say, 'Oh come on, firstly, nobody reads you up here, and secondly, you haven't got a vote up here, and thirdly, I don't care about your opinion. I ken what's happening on the streets' level; what's happening in the streets, and the works, and the homes of Scotland is that people are discussing our nation's future.'*

(Jim Sillars, SNP MP, speech, Falkirk, 26.3.92)

This is a rich passage in which Sillars asserts his personal and party prototypicality and uses each to buttress the other. Thus he slips into the vernacular in two places ('I'm no' worried about your opinion' and 'I ken what's happening on the streets' level') in order to stress his Scottishness and his knowledge of what counts in Scotland. As a Scot, he understands that what really matters are not the pollsters' figures (which the pollsters themselves would claim to be the opinion of Scots but which Sillars turns round as 'your opinion' – the opinion of an English media) but the informal discussion occurring amongst Scots.

There are, however, less obvious and more interesting ways of contesting the figures. Even if one agrees on which figures to use, they can still be employed to very different ends and to draw very different conclusions about what the population actually supports. This derives from the fact that the neutrality of numbers is only apparent. All counting, including the numbers that 'you look up', is contingent upon the identification of criteria for categorization. The very act of counting presumes a particular criterion for recognizing an instance alongside others. Or, as Hacking puts it, counting is 'hungry for categories' (cited in Urla, 1993: 829). The fact that decisions about such criteria have to be made before the counting can take place is not always obvious and there are many examples of the ways in which the presentation of quantitative material may work to 'naturalize' those criteria such that they do not require explicit elaboration or justification. Indeed, it is for precisely this reason that Hacking (1982) and Urla (1993) argue that it is in the sorting and dividing of the social world into groups that statistical practices have their effects upon the social construction of reality and the definition of the social context.

One can therefore contest poll figures by taking the numbers who assent to different response options but then, using different categories, combine them in different ways in order to draw different inferences about who supports what. Consider the use of non-responses. Do these indicate support for one position, for another, for neither, or indeed is it possible to infer anything from them? Perhaps the most famous use of non-responses is to be found in US President Nixon's phrase 'the great silent majority' by which, in 1962, he characterized those who failed to oppose the Vietnam War as supporting his own pro-war stance. Rather than being a neutral description of the evidence, the purpose of this phrase was quite clearly to define a normative position and to define Nixon as representing US opinion. As Rosenberg and Converse (1970) put it, Nixon's talk of the 'silent majority' is 'more important for the reality it creates than the reality it describes. Whether or not there was a silent majority before [Nixon's] speech, his use of the term goes a long way to making the silent majority real' (p. 19).

Edelman (1977) argues that non-responses are particularly prone to such rhetorical uses. He suggests that the 'silent majority' can be moulded to Nixon's ends because the meaning of absence is indeterminate and it is therefore harder to adduce evidence that challenges his construction. As he puts it, the function of the 'silent majority'

> was to evoke a reference group other than the plainly visible and nonsilent one for the large numbers of people who were torn or uncertain regarding their position on the war . . . for such a purpose a 'majority' that cannot be observed because it is 'silent' is ideal. For anyone looking for a reason to support the President and the war, the 'silent majority' serves its purpose even if it does not exist. (Edelman, 1977: 30)

While we would stress the importance of creating the groups one inhabits rather than talk of groups as something other to which one refers, we would not dissent from Edelman's claims about the uses of absence. We would, however, argue that presence (or, in this context, actual responses) can equally be put to use in creating categorical realities by the skilled rhetorician. In simple terms, different responses can be grouped together in different ways to create different notions of what is representative.

There are many forms such arguments can take but, for the present, two examples will have to suffice (we will return to this issue in more detail later in this chapter). The first is provided by an SNP candidate who, in the course of a 1992 pre-election meeting, was using an opinion poll on the question of constitutional change: how many supported the status quo, how many supported a devolved Scottish Parliament in the framework of the UK and how many supported independence. The candidate argued that the figures showed that the SNP's independence policy was clearly representative of Scottish opinion, but, in doing so, he added those choosing the 'devolution' option to those choosing independence. Whilst others would construe these options as falling into distinctive (indeed mutually incompatible) categories, he argued that people were using devolution as a staging post on the road to a fully independent Scotland. Hence, both options constituted part of a single independence category. In his own words, when those ticking the devolution box were asked: 'Do you think this will lead to independence?', 'a lot, a majority, and these are poll figures, say "yes" they do. And they don't seem particularly worried about that. There is a huge consensus in Scotland for independence' (David Roche, SNP candidate, speech, St Andrews, 31.3.1992).

Our second example is taken from the speech of a Conservative MP to the House of Commons. This speaker combined the options into categories in a radically different manner. In response to a Labour member who asserted that the Scots wanted devolution of the sort proposed by the Constitutional Convention (a body comprising representatives from the Labour Party, the Liberal Democrats, the churches, trades unions etc.), the Conservative made reference to an opinion poll which showed that support for independence and the status quo stood at 50 per cent and 19 per cent respectively. He combined these figures into a single 'anti-devolution' category and hence concluded that the figures 'showed that 70 per cent of Scottish people oppose the proposals of the Scottish Constitutional Convention' (Allan Stewart, Conservative MP, Hansard, 7.2.92: 612).

So, positive responses (as opposed to non-responses) do not settle the matter of 'support'. Rather, they provide a terrain on which the would-be representative has to manoeuvre. By disputing which figures do (or do not) represent support for one's position it is possible to transform apparent disaster into triumph. Numbers that might look unpropitious for the representativeness of one's own party can be combined with others so as to establish party prototypicality. Conversely, figures that apparently look propitious for the representativeness of other parties can be combined so as to reject the prototypicality of these rivals. The flexibility this affords makes it a particularly useful means of manoeuvring.

We can sum up the first half of our argument – that relating to the pre-election period – in two points. The first is that there is no objective set of criteria which can be used to decide how to categorize political parties, their distinctivness, their relationship to the nation or the extent to which they represent the nation. Indeed, the notions of 'objective' and 'subjective' criteria are more rhetorical resources than ontological differences. The more a criterion is conceived to be 'objective' the more valuable it is if adduced in favour of one's construction. The second point is that, in this pre-election period where all the parties are seeking to mobilize the largest possible section of the electorate in their own favour, everyone seeks to make their own party uniquely representative of the nation. Whether in qualitative or quantitative terms, they add things together such that they and they alone support and have the support of the nation. But that, as we say, is before the votes are counted.

Category shifts

In the lead up to the Election, the polls suggested a narrow Labour victory. In the event, the Conservatives retained their overall parliamentary majority on 41.9 per cent of the popular vote. In Scotland the position was rather different. Of the

72 seats, Labour won 49 (68.1 per cent) on 39.0 per cent of the Scottish vote; the Conservatives won 11 (15.3 per cent) on 25.7% of the vote; the Liberal Democrats won 9 (12.5 per cent) on 13.1 per cent of the vote, and finally, the SNP won 3 seats (4.2 per cent) on 21.5 per cent of the vote. Given the complexity of these results, all were faced with Macbeth's oft-cited question: 'Stands Scotland where it did?' – and, we might add, if not, where exactly did it stand?

Any reader who has made it this far will quite rightly anticipate that there is no such thing as an uncontroversial answer to this question. This is because part of the process of determining where Scotland will come to stand derives from how one answers the question of where it currently stands. Indeed, all the arguments which were used before the election to suggest that parties are representative in the sense of having the support of the electorate were equally used afterwards. Voting figures, like opinion poll figures, might be important resources to be used in those arguments, but they were not by any means simple determinants of the outcome. Consequently, each party could challenge the representativeness of rivals however encouraging their results and could maintain the claim to being representative themselves even in the face of apparently discouraging results.

Lest anyone think that Labour were the obvious winners in Scotland with most votes and most seats, it could be argued that votes themselves are irrelevant and what counts is power. Hence the very electoral success enjoyed by Labour was a sign of the failure of their position since, despite all the votes in Scotland, they remained impotent before a Conservative Government. As the SNP's Winnie Ewing put it, speaking to the annual Bannockburn rally:

Extract 5

The Labour party had a victory as far as Scotland was concerned. But they didn't regard it as a victory and they turned their victory into a defeat, because the only victory that they are interested in is not a Scottish victory, but a British victory . . . They're just going on and on under Tory government after Tory government, impotently dreaming of running somebody else's country and not caring who runs their own.

(Winnie Ewing, SNP MEP, annual SNP Bannockburn Rally, 20.6.92)

Lest anyone thought the SNP had done well, by achieving a clear third place in terms of votes and pressing the Conservatives for second place, one could also argue, as did one of our Conservative interviewees, that votes are not the key criterion, although in this case an alternative criterion to power was invoked as truly authentic:

Extract 6

I think that you've got to look at the psychology of the change: what the impressions people take of it and the deductions that the political leaders take from it. And you will find, I found in fact, that the SNP have become much lower key. They started to fight among themselves ... The fact they're fighting among themselves meant that they got a psychological blow ... If you put the numbers up against the wall and look at them analytically, the change has not been that great. So it's a change in climate rather than change in numbers.

(Conservative candidate, interview 23)

Another strategy was to acknowledge the size of the SNP vote but deny that it could be used as a measure of SNP support. Thus, for one Labour MP, the SNP vote did not indicate support for their key policy of independence or even for the party itself. In fact, it was a purely negative vote:

Extract 7

The Nationalist vote is a curious animal anyway, which is now being demonstrated in the cities where Militant [a 'left' alternative to Labour] are picking up a lot of what was the Nationalist vote but are now diametrically opposite on the constitution. And you know, it's a lumpen vote. It's a dispossessed vote and again, the Labour Party is the establishment and they want to vote against the, you know, want to register some sort of protest. So it's got nothing to do with that [i.e. independence]. And in rural areas, you know, a lot of people vote tactically ... So it's a much more complex vote than even to say, you know, 25 per cent voted for independence.

(Labour MP, interview 35)

Those favouring constitutional change could play a similar strategy of divorcing 'support' from 'vote' to produce the opposite effect. Thus they were to be found combining the votes of the SNP, the Labour Party and the Liberal Democrats in order to produce a strong majority for a Scottish Parliament. For instance, at a rally held in Edinburgh just ten days after the election, the 'official' leaflet circulated amongst the crowd argued that:

Extract 8

We as Scots committed to the cause of democracy, recognize that rule by the consent of the people is at the heart of our nation's history and identity, and of all legitimate government. On April 9th 1992, three quarters of the Scottish electorate voted for parties supporting a Scottish Parliament. In the light of this, we call for a referendum on the establishment of a Scottish Parliament and make common cause to work together for the democratic Scotland that is the key to all our hopes for the future of our nation.

(*Democracy for Scotland/Common Cause* leaflet circulated at rally, Calton Hill, Edinburgh, 19.4.92)

This was not the only way of combining the votes. Indeed, perhaps the most common way of construing and contesting the meaning of the election results (and hence of determining 'where Scotland stands') was through defining the basis on which the different votes were to be counted together or apart. Thus, both for those on the more anti-constitutional change wing of the Labour Party and for the Conservatives, it made no sense to put those supporting devolution and those favouring independence together in the same category. For example, the Labour MP cited in Extract 7 argued that there was no sense in 'lumping together nationalism with constitutional change within the UK and calling it all part of the same thing'. Indeed he went further, saying, 'the electorate makes that sharp distinction':

Extract 9

I mean 50 per cent voted for unionist parties and 25 per cent voted for separatist parties and the two are, not only are they not going after the same, but they are mutually exclusive. So any attempt to tie them together is artificial and has got no basis in popular support.

(Labour MP, interview 35)

Likewise, Ian Lang, the Conservative minister, claimed that: 'The reality is that on the Opposition benches one finds unionists, federalists, separatists, devolutionists, don't knows and don't cares. That adds up to 75 per cent of nothing' (Hansard 9.3.93: 792). However, while fragmenting the 'change' coalition, Conservatives created a different coalition of their own by adding up the votes for the Conservative, Labour and Liberal Democrat parties which all opposed independence and therefore could be described as unionist in some sense. Thus, one Conservative MP responded to the argument that 75 per cent of the electorate had voted for constitutional change through arguing: 'Well I could turn that round and say that eighty per cent of Scotland voted for parties who are to a greater or lesser extent totally committed to the maintenance of the United Kingdom. That's the other argument' (Conservative MP, interview 7). In a post-election interview, a Conservative cabinet minister developed the basis for this argument by stressing the fundamental commonality between the parties:

Extract 10

What was interesting was that the Labour Party, the Liberals, and ourselves, all started off not only from a basic unionist background but from a continuing belief in the continuing validity of the Union. Now there may have been different views about how best to preserve the Union, but it's interesting that the Labour and Liberal parties, in putting forward their own constitutional proposals, did not say, yes this will weaken the Union and we're delighted, that's what we are trying to do. They said, no on the contrary, our proposals will strengthen the Union, will guarantee its continuation, whereas the Conservative Party will weaken it. We had a debate, an ongoing debate about whose proposals were likely to achieve the desired effect, but there was less debate about the desired effect than the means of achieving it.

(Conservative MP, interview 12)

What is striking is that, in the pre-election period, this same MP had argued that Labour and the Liberal Democrats were to be categorized alongside the SNP. In his words: 'The Conservatives are the party of unity. All the others, whether piecemeal or outright, offer only separation, division and disunity' (Conservative MP, press release, 6.4.92). The two extracts are not contradictory in a logical sense. Thus, it could be argued that Labour and the Liberal Democrats belong with the SNP in terms of the actual effect of their policies, but they belong with the Conservatives in terms of the desired effect (and why the electorate support them). What we wish to underline, however, is precisely the shift in dimensions of similarity/difference. Pre-election, actual effect is employed in order to make the Conservatives seem unique in comparison to the other parties. Post-election, desired effect is employed in order to marginalize the SNP and to contest the marginalization of the Conservatives. Far from the election constituting a failure for them, it constitutes them as at the core of the Scottish mainstream.

Here, then, is some preliminary evidence that shifts in mobilization, from fighting an election to fighting independence in this case, occasion shifts in categorization. That categories should shift in order to maintain a consonance with the project of mobilization is, of course, precisely what we are looking for in order to sustain our analysis. Nonetheless, there is a level at which the shift is relatively minor. In virtually all the examples used in this section, the speakers are still trying to defend the representativeness of their party albeit with different resources provided in new circumstances. As with the use of opinion polls in the pre-election period, when voting figures for one's own party are combined with those of others it is not to advance the claims of rivals but rather to suggest that one's own party is the true representative of the coalition and hence of the country at large. Yes, 78 per cent of the population voted to maintain the Union, but whatever others intend, only the Conservatives would deliver what the people want. Indeed, one Conservative MP was quite explicit in this claim. Countering the adding together of the votes to obtain 75 per cent voting for change with the argument that '78.8 per cent of people in Scotland voted to retain the Union', he continued that if one listened to the views of those who claimed that 75 per cent had voted for change (and introduced devolution) it would take no time before tensions between Edinburgh and London rent apart the Union with the result that 'we would have let down 78 per cent of the electorate if you listen to these people' (Conservative MP, interview 20).

There are, however, a set of more radical shifts which are foreshadowed by Extract 8. It is true that, for many, the day after the election was the first day of the next election campaign and hence there was no pre/post election periodization which could allow the common categorization of Liberal Democrats, Labour and SNP. For example, the Labour MP Brian Wilson, writing in *The Herald* newspaper of 15 April, mocked the 'myth that Scotland is conveniently divided into Tories and anti-Tories, the latter motivated by large common purpose'. Citing one constituency result where Labour's candidate had failed to oust the Conservative Michael Forsyth, he pointed to the constituency's relatively large SNP vote and declared that those urging common cause 'cannot have their cake and eat it. Having preserved Mr Forsyth for the nation, they cannot also proclaim themselves part of a common front against everything he stands for! . . . it is preposterous to claim that all non-Tory votes can now be totted up and counted as one.' For others however, 10 April 1992 marked a new context. However much the Conservatives had been rejected in Scotland, they retained power in the UK as a whole through their English vote. Thus ordinary party politics could do nothing to represent the will of the Scottish people. What was needed was an alternative politics wherein party difference was set aside in order to allow Scots to decide their own future – whether that be the status quo, devolution or independence. The argument is expressed clearly in the *Scottish Miner* (the Scottish Area newsletter of the National Union of Miners). Scotland was tired of politicians:

Extract 11

who put the narrow sectarian aims of party and position before the needs of the nation. Scotland is crying out for unity of the anti-Tory forces. Anyone or any party which impedes that unity in what is Scotland's darkest hour in 50 years, will face the wrath of the Scottish people. Scotland expects every anti-Tory party to do its duty. For 13 long years the people of Scotland have overwhelmingly put their trust in the opposition parties. That trust must be repaid with unity and action. Unity is the key, everything must come second to unity. . . . It is a message which politicians ignore at their peril.

(*Scottish Miner* no. 22 (new series), April, 1992)

If the politics shifts from party to a cross-party social movement, then one would expect a series of categorical shifts in response to the new project. Firstly, it is the movement rather than party that should be made prototypical of the nation. Secondly, erstwhile party opponents who have become movement allies should shift from being characterized as unrepresentative to being representative of the nation. Thirdly, in order to win party support for the movement, party identity, movement identity and national identity should all be construed as consonant.

From parties divided to Scotland United

The Election was on a Thursday. In the early hours of Friday 10 April, the Labour MP, George Galloway, interviewed on TV about the incoming election results, argued that there was a need for a 'patriotic front' which united the non-Tory opposition in Scotland. In Edinburgh, a non-stop vigil was established outside the building designated as the likely venue for a future parliament and within sight of the Government's Scottish Office. On Sunday, 12 April, and again on Sunday, 26 April, Glasgow's George Square saw speakers from a range of parties and groups address audiences (of approximately 4,000 and 5,000 people respectively) under the banner of the cross-party campaign group, 'Scotland United'. Subsequently, 'Scotland United' took its call for a cross-party campaign for a multi-option referendum on Scotland's constitutional future all around Scotland (including the SNP and Scottish Labour annual party conferences).

Campbell Christie, the General Secretary of the Scottish Trades Union Congress, opened the first George Square rally with the following declaration:

Extract 12

Hello! Welcome to Glasgow! Welcome to this demonstration to tell the nation, to tell the Conservative government and to tell everyone throughout the world, that we in Scotland are not prepared to accept the election results. We representing the 75 per cent in Scotland, we representing the 2.2 million electors in Scotland who voted for constitutional change, are not prepared to allow the 25 per cent, the 750 thousand Tories to rule us.

(Campbell Christie, STUC General Secretary, Scotland United Rally, Glasgow, 12.4.92)

For Christie, then, it is quite clear that the rally, that is Scotland United, rather than any individual party, represents the nation. The opposition of Scotland United to the election results thus becomes what 'we in Scotland' wish to communicate. Indeed, as Christie continued (once again making his voice the voice of the rally which in turn became the voice of the nation), it is only as Scotland United that the wishes of the nation can be fulfilled. Parties, whatever the party, can only stand in the way of the national interest: 'The message from the people of Scotland to the politicians is: "get your act together! Fight together! And then we'll win." No longer do we want to have a situation where we're fighting each other and the Tories are going into power and taking power. So therefore we have to bury our differences!'

The writer William McIlvanney likewise spoke of the rally as a metonym for the nation. Having dismissed the role of individual parties in securing a voice for Scotland ('if ever there was a time when we in Scotland should say let party politics be in suspended animation, it is now'), he used the very fact of the rally to suggest that Scotland was still fighting for its voice. Likening the event to 'a good Scottish wake' he told the rally that 'we are mourning a chance that is gone and we are here to celebrate the chance we're going to create and generate . . . it's a vague message and it's still an uncertain message, but if there's one message that should go from this place today, it is to tell Westminster, do not hold the funeral for the death of Scotland yet. You're too premature. To quote not Karl Marx, but Groucho Marx, reports of our death have been grossly exaggerated. Scotland lives!'

But of all the attempts to make Scotland United stand for Scotland as a whole, undoubtedly the most flamboyant came from David Hayman, director of the radical Scottish Theatre group 7:84, speaking to the second of the George Square rallies. Hayman engaged the audience in a dialogue of question and answer. In a voice gradually rising to a crescendo, he engaged all in establishing the meaning of the election (the audience response is given in brackets):

> ### Extract 13
>
> *On Thursday April 9th, did you vote Conservative?*
> *(No!)*
> *On Thursday, April 9th, did you vote for the destruction of our health service?*
> *(No!)*
> *On April 9th did you vote for the dismantling of our industry?*
> *(No!)*
> *Did you vote for the decay of our educational system?*
> *(No!)*
> *Did you vote for greed?*
> *(No!)*
> *Did you vote for selfishness?*
> *(No!)*
>
> (David Hayman, Scotland United Rally, Glasgow, 12.4.92)

Then, as a climax, Hayman delivered his verdict. With dramatic emphasis, he flung his arm out to point South, and declared:

> ### Extract 14
>
> *The English did. For the fourth election in a row, the people of England have voted for greed and self-interest and I'll tell you something; there's nearly fifty million of them and only five million of us, so we don't stand a snowball's chance in hell of ever having a parliament we deserve unless we have our own. Right?*
> *(Yes!)*
> *Right?*
> *(Yes!)*
>
> (David Hayman, Scotland United Rally, Glasgow, 12.4.92)

By establishing a contrast with an English 'they', Hayman establishes himself and his audience as constituting a Scottish 'we'. Moreover, the inherent conservatism of the English is likewise contrasted to a natural Scottish radicalism. The logic of numbers implies that the Scottish identity will never be translated into reality so long as Scotland is yoked in Union to an alien England acting on alien values which reflect an alien English identity. The use of a dialogical perspective establishes such a view as consensual rather than Hayman's own idiosyncratic opinion. Thus the voice of Scotland (United) is made to propose the programme of Scotland United as the sole possible expression of Scottish identity.

'The essence of a country is a series of art works' claims Debray (1994: 26) and the previous quotations certainly bear out the power which artists bring to the cause of nationalism. They clearly show how the common movement rather than individual parties represent the nation. However, these speakers – writer, actor, trades unionist – may have been saying similar things before the elections. Thus such words cannot be used as evidence of change, only that different strategies of mobilization demand different categories. Consider, then, what party representatives had to say at the rallies. First, Fiona Hislop, speaking for the SNP, echoed much of what Christie and McIlvanney and Hayman had been saying. It is Scotland United, rather than any party on its own, who represented Scotland by the content, but also by the form, of its politics: 'We are here not just because we're anti-Tory or anti- the Union. We're here together, as Scotland United, because above all we are pro-Scottish and pro- a Scottish Parliament. Scottish politics has always been deeper and wider than the political parties that represent us. It's always acted best when it's been on a local and mass basis. That's what we must make Scotland United' (Fiona Hislop, Scotland United Rally, Glasgow, 26.4.96).

Second, consider the speech of John McAllion MP to the first rally. Before the election, in the Dundee East meeting, McAllion had sought to construe Labour as unique in contrast to a common category comprising both Conservatives and the SNP. After the election, and from a Scotland United platform, he addressed his audience as follows:

Extract 15

This meeting is about unity and comrades in unity. It's absolutely pointless to speculate who won the General Election here in Scotland last Thursday. The Tories certainly didn't win it. But neither did the Labour Party. We may have won 49 out of Scotland's 72 MPs but we only won 39 per cent of the support of the Scottish people. The SNP certainly did not win it. They only won 21 per cent support of the Scottish people and 3 MPs. The Liberal Democrats didn't win it: 13 per cent support was all they had. And the truth of that election is that we are all minorities now and that we have to stand together united if we are to secure a majority for the Scottish people [applause] . . . *There were two banners I saw when I first came onto this platform which have up until now been on opposite sides of the political debate in this country. One at the back said, 'Scotland Free or a Desert'. One over here said, 'Irvine Trades Council, Unity is Strength'. It is time to bring those banners together because it is only through unity will we stop Scotland becoming a desert* [applause].

(John McAllion, Scotland United Rally, Glasgow, 12.4.96)

The contrast is stark. This time Labour is not unique but is similar to the other parties in being a loser. Indeed McAllion goes out of his way to choose a dimension (votes rather than seats) which diminishes the representativeness of his party and which renders them a minority like every other party. Thus it is only together that Scotland and Scottish interests can be represented. The final part of the quote concretizes that notion by drawing on a banner bearing a Labour Movement slogan ('Unity is Strength') and a banner bearing an SNP slogan ('Scotland Free or a Desert') in order to insist that it is only in their combination that the Scots will be served.

McAllion was not the only Labour representative to play down Labour support in order to gain support for Scotland United. Another Scotland United supporter drawn from the ranks of Scotland's Labour MPs ridiculed those who did believe that Labour stands for Scotland. During an interview he described the Party as 'like the Communist Party in the Soviet Union but without the Marxism'. This, he explained, is due to the belief that 'only it can do things. Only it can govern Scotland. And the absurd belief that Labour represents the Scottish people rather than 37.8 per cent of them' (Labour MP, interview 36). If this MP sought to diminish Labour, a fellow Labour MP sought to aggrandize the Conservatives in the course of another interview:

Extract 16

The Tories did remarkably well in Scotland. From a party which was supposed to be wiped out, which I think was unrealistic anyway, they gained two seats, the share of the vote was up and in a place like Stirling and Ayr where the constitutional issue was firmly put and you were going to lose, for example in Stirling, the most despised politician of a generation; he won with an 87 per cent turnout. The Tories came out of the woodwork. . . . [Such] trends make the Scottish scene not similar to the UK but not dissimilar in many respects.

(Labour MP, interview 29)

The significance of this quote stems from the conflict within the Labour Party concerning support for Scotland United. Whilst other Labour MPs (such as McAllion, cited in Extract 15) were heavily in favour, this latter was strongly against. In arguing that the Conservatives did well he is arguing that an anti-Conservative alliance cannot represent Scotland, and in arguing that Scottish politics is like English politics he is defining the context in such a way as to blunt the call for cross-party extra-parliamentary campaigning. In short, just as the Labour MPs supporting Scotland United do Labour down, not to be anti-Labour but to do Scotland United up, so the Labour MP cited in Extract 16 plays the Conservatives up, not to be pro-Conservative but to do Scotland United down. In either case, the argument is different from that used pre-election and in both cases it relates to a new form of mobilization. The commonality is that the target of mobilization is Scotland United rather than the party. The difference is that the one seeks to mobilize for the movement and the other seeks to mobilize against. However, these shifts support our first contention: issues of national prototypicality may involve mention of parties but only to address the status of the broader movement.

Moving on to a second issue, we also argued that individuals who were seen as un-Scottish when they were party rivals would be considered Scottish once they became movement allies. Before illustrating the point, let us continue a short while in the same vein as above by noting an obvious corollary: erstwhile party comrades who were previously seen as Scottish should be considered to be un-Scottish when adopting a different position concerning Scotland United. Thus, in the same interview as he defended the Tory performance, the Labour MP cited in Extract 16 put the national credentials of the prominent Scotland United activist and Labour MP – George Galloway – in question. Galloway, he remarked: 'is never in the country long enough to develop much of a Scottish perspective' (Labour MP, interview 29). If the attack came from a party colleague, it was left to a party rival to restore these credentials. In his address to a Scotland United fringe meeting at the Labour Party conference, the Liberal Democrat Dennis Sullivan spoke of Galloway in these terms:

Extract 17

When I told people in my party that I was going to sit on that platform with this man here [pointing to the Labour MP, George Galloway] – *they said to me 'I would sup with the devil but* anybody *but George Galloway'* [laughter and applause]. *I too will sup with the devil,* including *George Galloway* [laughter]. *So what I say to you is this. Very, very simple. I come from a large family, I should tell you this I come from a large family, six boys and a girl. I have one photograph of my family together. . . . In the photograph we're standing in a line and my daddy's at one end and my mammy's at the other and my daddy's got his hand at my biggest brother's mouth, my mammy's got her hand in mine and I've got mine in the pillar next to me and* [inaudible due to laughter and applause]. *Because it's a family put in the room. Seven opinions and six fights. That's what happens in this country. What I'm suggesting to you is that we put our hands in each other's mouth and that we do things together. The only way we will succeed in bringing the kind of justice that you want is to do it together.*

(Dennis Sullivan, Liberal Democrat activist, speech to Scotland United fringe meeting at the annual Labour Party conference, Inverness, 13.3.93)

Here we see family metaphors employed once again – only this time to define relations within Scotland and not between Scotland and other nations. The argument serves to establish Galloway (along with the Labour Party and the Liberal Democrats) as part of a common Scottish family. Indeed the antagonism between Galloway and those in the Liberal Democrat party is evidence of their proximity as category members. Moreover, both his behaviour and their behaviour is typically Scottish.

Support for Labour members of Scotland United came not only from their erstwhile foes in the Liberal Democrats, but also those who endorse the SNP. Billy Kay, a well-known SNP supporter, spoke the following words from a Scotland United platform that he shared with John McAllion MP:

Extract 18

I've great admiration for John McAllion. Labour Unionism, it's so anti-Scottish in a way. They think they hold the high-ground of the left in Scotland, whereas if it was given to me, a choice between the likes of Donald Dewar and John McAllion as the people who continue the great tradition of the Labour movement in Scotland, of Keir Hardie, of John Maclean, of John P. Mackintosh, I bet you it would be the majority who would say that it was McAllion and not Donald Dewar.

(Billy Kay, speech, Scotland United public meeting, Newport-on-Tay, 1.9.92)

The important point to note here is that Kay does not suggest that all Labour Party members are prototypically Scottish. Indeed he identifies a clear tendency in the Party which is anti-Scottish. By contrast there is a genuinely Scottish tradition in the Labour movement which, Kay claims, is represented by McAllion rather than Dewar. The contrast between the two is clear on a couple of dimensions. Firstly the inauthentic tendency is unionist whereas the alternative, by contrast, must endorse constitutional alterations to the Union. Moreover, the contrast between McAllion and Dewar is obviously also between more and less support for constitutional change. Thus McAllion is praised as an authentic Scot not simply in his capacity as a Labour member but as a Labour member who is within Scotland United.

However, Kay's argument is not simply an endorsement of McAllion, but also a claim that McAllion represents the genuine traditions of the Labour Party in Scotland. Dewar and his ilk might claim to represent the left and to be heirs to those traditions, however in fact McAllion truly represents those positions. Thus, any genuine Scottish Labour Party member must be characterized by a rejection of Unionism and an endorsement of McAllion's support for Scotland United. In this sense, the Kay quote (along with that of Sullivan) does not only illustrate our second point concerning party rivals who are movement allies being described as national prototypes. It also leads into our third point concerning the attempt to construe a consonance between party, movement and national identity when seeking to recruit party members to Scotland United's campaign to win over the Scottish people as a whole. Further and clearer illustration for this point can be derived from a Scotland United fringe meeting at the 1992 SNP Annual Conference.

The first address came from a member of the SNP, Mike Russell. Russell began by asserting his Party credentials: 'Many of you know me well. You know that for four years I was the publicity Vice-Convenor of this party, you know perfectly well that I have been a nationalist for many years'. He then took out his Party membership card and asked the audience to reflect on their own:

Extract 19

If you take it out and read it you can see what's written on the back of it: 'The aims of this party: self-government for Scotland. That is the restoration of Scottish National sovereignty by the establishment of a democratic Scottish parliament within the commonwealth, freely elected by the Scottish people whose authority will be limited only by such agreements as may be freely entered into by it with other nations or states or international organizations for the purpose of furthering international co-operation and world peace.' I believe that today as strongly as I believed it in 1974 and I'm sure that everybody in this hall believes that that must be achieved. But there's a 'b' on the card. A second point: 'The furtherance of all Scottish interests'. And both of those things are not just written on the card to fill up the space. They are actually things that we are enjoined as nationalists to do. . . . I see Scotland United as a nationalist campaign, very much so, I'm not ashamed to say it. It is a campaign to get Scotland the right to choose

*and if we work on it in that way and if we work with others in that way, we will get
Scotland the right to choose. We will challenge the legitimacy of the Tory government
and if there was ever a nationalist issue that is the issue. There is no legitimacy in the
Tory Government in Scotland.*

(Mike Russell, SNP activist, speech to Scotland United fringe meeting at the
annual SNP conference, Perth, 24.9.93)

The argument is sufficiently clear as to require little comment. That which is written
on the Party card is, by definition, the core of party ideology, a formalization of its
criterial attributes. To the extent that Scotland United embodies what the card
requires, and what the card requires is defined as realizing what the nation needs,
then being a member of the party is clearly consonant with being in the movement,
which is consonant with national identity. One can put it more strongly: SNP
members are 'enjoined' to work within Scotland United to realize the Scottish
interest.

Russell's ability to sustain this argument clearly revolves around his ability to
play his party card (both literally and figuratively) with the audience. Another
speaker was the Liberal Democrat, Dennis Sullivan. One might reasonably consider
that he would be less convincing in defining SNP identity for an SNP audience,
and hence to establish a convincing case for Scotland United before them. Indeed,
when he had spoken at the SNP's annual Bannockburn rally earlier in the year
(20.6.92) and claimed that he was a 'nationalist', Sullivan had been widely
barracked by SNP members, enjoined to '*join the party*', and one activist had
approached the makeshift platform proffering him an SNP membership card.
Insofar as he could not and would not use that card, Sullivan had to use a different
strategy. That is, he played a different card. His whole argument was structured
around the statement of goals written on the Scotland United 'supporter's card':

Scotland United is a campaigning organization founded by concerned individuals who
believe that the future form of government for Scotland can only be decided by the
Scottish people themselves, voting in a free and fair multi-option referendum. Scotland
United exists to give a united voice to that belief and to organize the people of Scotland
to demand and achieve such a referendum.

Sullivan began by asking two rhetorical questions: why should his audience
work alongside people like himself and what sort of party is the SNP? He then
sought to answer the latter in order to answer the former. In brief, he so construed
the SNP as such that, not one, but every one of its core dimensions coincided with
those of Scotland United and all of these dimensions had to do with representing
the Scottish nation. The consequence was that it became incumbent for SNP
members to stand together in a movement for Scotland. He concluded that past
foes had become present allies. The contrast from the pre-election period in which
each Party construed itself as a lone voice for the nation could not be more absolute.
If Russell was clear, Sullivan was forced, against potential mistrust, to spell his
message out even more clearly. Although lengthy, it provides an eloquent note on
which to end this analysis:

Extract 20

[The SNP is] *a political party but it's also a campaigning organization and you've got a really distinguished record of campaigning. In most recent times the Poll Tax, but even earlier campaigns, oil, steel; a distinguished campaigning organization. Who founded you? Patriots. Certainly, patriots. But they were concerned people living in Scotland. Who carried you on? You are concerned people at this moment in time. What do you believe to take up the point that you made? You believe that Scots and people living in Scotland can run their own affairs and do it properly and well. And you believe that the Scottish people should be allowed to decide that. Are you democratic? You've rejected the Westminster model of democracy where first past the post gives you, gives a minority, absolute rule. You've eschewed that type of political chicanery. You favour PR and you accept that you might not rule Scotland if there was an independent Scotland, proving your democracy. So why do you exist? You exist to give a united voice to your beliefs. You exist to organize the Scottish people. You exist for them to demand what you believe. That's my analysis of the SNP.* [Speaker takes out his wallet] *Incidentally, I'm not making a donation in case you think the wallet's out for that reason. What's in the wallet is my supporter's card for Scotland United. Let me read from that supporter's card for Scotland United a very simple statement of what we believe in Scotland United. We are a campaigning organization. As you are. We are founded by concerned individuals. As you are. We believe that only the Scottish people can decide the governance of Scotland. As you do. We believe that that can be achieved by voting in a fair and free multi-option referendum. As you do. We in Scotland United exist to give a united voice to that belief, to organize the people of Scotland, to demand and achieve that referendum. Therefore, I am not surprised when I go the length and breadth of this country to find everywhere I go that the Scottish National Party is well represented and is active in the ranks of Scotland United. So as an old political adversary I say to you that in this venture we are friends and allies and you should join us now.*

(Dennis Sullivan, Liberal Democrat activist, speech to Scotland United fringe meeting at the annual SNP conference, Perth, 24.9.93)

Conclusion

In many ways this chapter has continued themes established in the previous one. Once again we have been exploring the construction of prototypicality. However, we have sought to emphasize the strategic dimension to such construction through exploring the variability that may be found in constructions of category representativeness. The first form of variability concerned the way in which different people not only advanced different characterizations of prototypicality but sought to undermine those of their opponents as each sought to be 'king' of the self-same 'castle'. The second form of variability was diachronic. This showed that when there is a shift in the forms of mobilization – when support is sought for a broad movement uniting disparate parties – so one sees matching shifts in category constructions. So as to recruit support for a new organization and form of activity (e.g. Scotland United) party friends become movement foes and party foes become movement friends. In turn those who were characterized as representative of the nation become described as unrepresentative or even as traitors, just as traitors metamorphose into patriots. The mark of any model lies in its ability to explain patterns of variability. Our ability to account for these twin patterns of variability – synchronic and diachronic; across parties and across time – is a strong argument in favour of our own.

The model, of course, has to do with the construction of self-categories in order to take advantage of their social cognitive consequences. We have devoted much time to the model and so there is no need to repeat it here, except to reiterate two key meta-theoretical points which have arisen with particular clarity within the analyses covered in this chapter. The first has to do with the irreducibly strategic aspect of human social perception and action. Most directly, we have stressed and stressed again that our use of categories is not the outcome of intra-psychic computations based on the features of an existing social reality. Rather we need to look at the ways in which categories are actively produced in order to create future social realities. The second is that our examination of the active construction of categories must include reference to the structures and social institutions in which people are located, for the practices associated with these structures necessarily impinge upon the projects that are possible. Thus, if the recategorization of pre-election foes as movement allies is testimony to the active construction of dimensions of similarity/difference, it is also testimony to the ways in which political projects (and hence category construction) are shaped by structural factors.

Before closing this chapter it is appropriate to observe that the importance of including a constructive and strategic dimension to our analyses is not limited to matters narrowly related to self-categorization but applies to a whole range of social psychological phenomena. In previous chapters we have made such points in relation to stereotyping, social influence and leadership. Let us make them in relation to the way in which popular support for one's position is conceptualized – what social psychology often calls 'consensus estimates'. We have seen the issue arise repeatedly before the election. In the first part of this chapter, we found much talk concerning opinion poll evidence and found it construed so as to maximize support for the speakers' projects and marginalize that for their opponents. In the second half we found that even the evidence of the ballot box was not beyond dispute. If, for some, the 'fact' that 78 per cent had not voted SNP indicated a victory for Unionism, for others the 'fact' that 75 per cent had not voted Conservative indicated the strength of support for constitutional change. So what determines people's estimates of support for a position they hold and to what degree can social psychological theories of consensus estimation explain our activists' estimates? According to much work in social psychology, people have a tendency to over-estimate the extent to which others share the same position as themselves (e.g. Marks & Miller, 1987; Ross, Greene & House, 1977). One explanation suggests that this is because our own opinions are more salient or cognitively available to us. Consequently, alternative positions are less likely to be considered and hence reflected in our judgments of others' views. Another explanation suggests that people seek out similar others, and through their increased association with like-minded individuals, are led to underestimate the numbers holding contrary views. A third approach identifies various 'motivational' factors bound up with a need to 'promote a sense of certainty about the correctness of one's position' (Marks & Miller, 1987: 83), these needs being activated particularly in situations of uncertainty.

Despite their differences, all three explanations proceed from the assumption that consensus estimation is a computational process subject to bias. They only differ as to the source of that bias – whether it is cognitive, interactional or motivational. None of this makes any sense of what we have found. Here it seems clear that consensus estimates are strategic. They are made in order to constitute the post-election social field and hence the issues of the day. They are made so as to constitute those to whom one must appeal in particular ways. They are made in order to elide one's project with mass opinion and so claim representativeness. Most crucially then, rather than simply measuring support, such estimates are organized to construct an ingroup relationship of consonance and so win support. Indeed, this strategic dimension explains why, in certain situations, party members should play down the level of support their party enjoys. This goes against basic presuppositions of the conventional literature. It makes perfect sense when seen in terms of weaning the party off a 'go-it-alone' strategy and winning party support for a wider coalition.

More and similar examples could be provided, however to do so would go beyond the limits of this chapter and begin to draw general conclusions relating to the book as a whole. There is a similar danger in raising our next and final point – a point that we also encountered in the previous chapter. If, as we are arguing, mobilization depends upon the ways in which categories are construed, and if, more specifically, the ability to claim representative status depends upon the relationship of the subject to the nation, then once again there is more than a theoretical issue in forgetting the strategic dimension and seeing categories as automatic products. Such reification inevitably serves to privilege certain constructions over others and hence to advance certain claims to representativeness over others. Psychology thereby begins to serve as part of the process of mobilization rather than allowing us to understand that process. Wittingly or unwittingly, we are again moved from a psychology of politics to a politics of psychology – or, in the present case, from a psychology of nations and nationalism to a nationalist psychology. The contrast is sufficiently pressing that, in reverse order, it provides the basis for our final and concluding chapter.

9 Nationalist Psychology and the Psychology of Nationhood

A choice of sides

Throughout this book we have sought to develop and to illustrate a psychological analysis of nations and nationalism. At the same time we have repeatedly encountered psychological concepts and psychological models as part of the phenomena which we have been analysing. This is no coincidence. In part, our motivation for developing a psychology *of* nationhood has been motivated by the uses of psychology *in* nationhood.

The talk of our politicians and the rhetoric of our activists has been replete with psychological claims which serve to fix who and what a people are or are not, what the people can and cannot be and do, how they should, should not or even cannot relate to others. Psychology plays an important part in the construction and the reification of national categories; it is used strategically but it is used so as to deny the constructed and strategic nature of identity processes. In this sense, the nationalist use of psychology is used against a psychological understanding of nationhood. By looking at these uses we can see both the problems with certain psychological ideas and also the importance of avoiding them.

Such clarity is made all the more difficult and all the more essential by the fact that nationalists are not necessarily misusing or distorting ideas that exist in the academic domain. In this area, as more generally, there is a complex and mutually sustaining relationship between popular common-sense and professional knowledge (Wetherell & Potter, 1992). On the one hand, the conceptual vocabulary that we academics employ is shaped by a wider 'common-sense'. On the other hand, as Moscovici's analysis of the filtering of psychoanalytic concepts into popular consciousness illustrates, academic theorizing may come to inform and shape 'common-sense' (Moscovici, 1961).

Given this two-way relationship, we must both attend to the ways in which psychology serves as nationalist ideology and we must also be alert to the ways in which the nationalism that permeates contemporary common-sense results in a psychology which is itself 'nationalized'. Indeed, at various junctures throughout our text, we have warned against a failure to appreciate the strategic uses of identity and other psychological constructs. We have challenged the refusal to see that they are as much about making as about perceiving the world. We have argued that such failures and refusals would lead us to see these constructs as singular (as relating to the singular present) rather than multiple and variable (as relating to our manifold possible futures) and that this would turn them into a mirror of nationalism rather than a tool for analysing it. In this, the final chapter of our book, we will start by turning from the hypothetical to the actual. We will provide concrete illustrations of how psychological constructs are used by nationalists in order to promote their preferred nationalisms.

We do this partly to complete our analysis of how national identity is constructed and reified – for part of our point is that psychology is every bit as powerful a resource as history, culture, environment and other domains besides in naturalizing particular versions of nationhood and international relations. We do this also as a cautionary tale for psychologists and as illustration of how important it is to acknowledge the dimensions of strategy and of 'becoming' in the construction of national identity. Having looked at psychology in the service of nationalism and having discussed the implications of what we find, we then move on in the second part of the chapter (and the concluding part of the book) to consider how far we have got in developing an alternative and critical psychology of nationhood. We will address what the study of nationhood has brought to our understanding of psychology and what the study of psychology has provided in terms of an understanding of nationhood.

Psychology in the service of nationalism

By far and away the most obvious and the most widespread manner in which we have found psychology to be invoked within nationalist rhetoric has had to do with the notion of national character. In a world divided into nations, the attempt for each to claim a unique and distinctive identity has typically been achieved by claiming a distinctive set of character traits. These are notions that were the focus of analysis in Chapter Five but which arose insistently in the context of other issues. It is true that on occasion there were those who would insist that it is spurious to insist on some unifying trait or set of traits for the whole nation, and that diversity rules the realm. However this was usually in the context of an argument against the use of a particular national category in the first place (and often in the context of seeking to substitute another rival set of national categories). As we saw from Condor's work on Englishness (Condor, 1997, 2000a, in press), it is also true that a refusal to identify or promote the national character may, in certain circumstances, be a way of expressing a non-nationalistic nationhood against a background where nationalism can be equated with imperialism, racism and bigotry. Nonetheless, when embracing a national category, when seeking to define the nation and, above all, when invoking the national imagination in order to mobilize its population, the use of psychological trait terms was as commonplace in the mouths of politicians as it is in psychology textbooks.

Such is the ideological grip and the ideological power of such usage that the notion of a unitary national character can sometimes be asserted in theory even as it is being denied in practice. Perhaps the most compelling illustration of this comes from politicians who repeatedly invoke the construct as unitary but who define it in multiple ways as a function of different contexts and the different uses to which it is being put. The point is sufficiently powerful to warrant one more example in addition to those we have already provided. It is provided by an SNP MP. We first heard him speaking at an eve of poll rally in his home constituency. When he was asked why the local electorate had 'been able to overcome its fears and elect an SNP member?', he attributed success to the constituency's Scottish character. He first referred to the numbers from the area who, some 700 years before, had marched with Wallace and Bruce. Then he asserted that the local people's sense of self could be summarized in a set of self-descriptions: ' "I've been thrawn" and "I've been independent" and "I've been Scottish". . . . . The people here are very independent.' Such prolonged continuity therefore served to establish a timeless character centred on the attribute of independence – and which was represented by a party with political independence as its defining policy.

We spoke to the same MP just after the results of the election were known and it was clear that the SNP had performed far worse than they had hoped and expected. His explanation went as follows: 'Something very Scottish happened at that election. We called canny. Don't know if you know the expression but we tend to not to go to the extreme. We tend to, if there's a risky solution we tend not, like our banking system, that is well respected because it's very conservative with a small 'c', tends to be absolutely rock solid, we call canny, we take it easy. And therefore people I think at the election said yes, we'd like independence, but let's go for the easier option of devolution. And I think that's precisely what happened: we called canny. It's the cautious part of the Scottish nature' (SNP MP, interview 47).

The same category. The same MP. The same assumption that there is a national character. And yet what different constructions of that character! In the one, the Scots are a bold independent people who would march to war and risk even their lives to fight for their cherished freedom. In the other, the Scots are a cautious breed who would not even risk a vote for independence for all that they believe in it. Even if one wanted to claim that there is no overt contradiction here – the Scots could be independent on the one hand and yet sensible and cautious on the other – the focus changes entirely. Caution receives no mention earlier but takes centre stage later. At the very least, the attributes which are foregrounded in defining national identity undergo a fundamental change. What remains constant, of course, is the way in which the characterization protects the speaker's claim to be prototypical of the people from whom he claims support as the context shifts from pre- to post-election. The fact that people did not vote for the SNP does not mean that they don't really support the SNP. Rather, their character prevents them from expressing their fundamental agreement with the party.

Further evidence for the extent to which the idea of a unitary national character has a hold on our imagination comes from those who purport to challenge it – or at least to challenge some of the more crass ways in which national character is described and used. Even in the midst of their attacks, they find it very hard to avoid slipping back into similar usages and simply replacing one set of traits with another. One of the most powerful instances of this relates to debate in Britain concerning the consequences of German Unification for Europe and for international relations within Europe. In March 1990, Mrs Thatcher, her Foreign Secretary and six 'distinguished authorities' met to discuss the German 'national character'. The confidential memorandum drawn up by a government official (later leaked to the press) identified certain national characteristics which were identifiable in the past and so could be expected in the future. With regard to past events, the report observed that it was 'easier – and more pertinent to the present discussion – to think of the less happy ones' and listed their attributes as including 'their insensitivity to the feelings of others', 'their obsession with themselves', 'a strong inclination to self-pity', an 'aggressiveness, assertiveness, bullying, egotism, inferiority complex', and 'sentimentality'. The memo continued to explain that there were two further aspects of the German character which caused concern for the future: 'a capacity for excess' and 'a tendency to over-estimate their own strengths and capabilities' (the *Independent on Sunday*, 15 July 1990). The clear, if unstated, message was that German 'insensitivity', 'egotism' and a 'capacity for excess' constituted an unchanging national essence and that history must of necessity repeat itself. Nicholas Ridley, a government minister, went a step further by stating the implicit premise on which these claims were based. He collapsed German aspirations in the EU with those obtaining during the Second World War and, as McDonald (1993) puts it, argued that where the Germans had previously failed in military terms, they were now seeking to win 'through economically dominating displays of their insensitive rationality' (McDonald, 1993: 230).

If Thatcher and her distinguished advisors paid no price for their crassness, Ridley was forced to resign for explicating their logic. However, our point is that even in the midst of the furore surrounding his comments, even those most opposed to Ridley failed to find any alternative to the language of national character. They might dispute the terms of his description, they might also dispute his automatic equation of the Nazi era with the present, but they did not dispute the notion that Germans, like other nationalities, act on the basis of a single set of character traits. McDonald summarizes the debate by saying that: 'even the most optimistic who tried, with a post-Second World War or new "European" consciousness, to talk of possibilities of change in Germany, found themselves tied up in rhetorical dialogues about whether or not a "national character" was changeable' (McDonald, 1993: 231).

In fact there are two ways in which national character was taken for granted within the debate. On the one hand, all accepted the idea that past atrocities could be explained in terms of a pathological character. On the other, all accepted that Germans still had a national character and only differed on whether or not it remained pathological. This connection between character and pathology is not restricted to the German case. Indeed just as the notion of character and character disorder or else personality and psychopathology are connected in the psychological literature, so the use of character constructs in order to establish the pathogenic nature of certain nations, certain forms of international arrangements or certain forms of national being, is widespread within nationalist rhetoric. Indeed it adds to the strategic power and the strategic appeal of 'national character'. There is no more powerful way of regulating national relations than by invoking pathology to determine what is legitimate and what is illegitimate.

Thus far, our examples both of national character and of pathology have been at the simplest possible level. They involve a mention of descriptive traits, either desirable or undesirable. Sometimes, however, speakers produce far more elaborated constructions of the national character which invoke complex notions of process and of psychodynamics. It is within these versions that notions of pathology become both more frequent and more elaborate and are applied to one's own nation as well as to others. None of this should surprise us.

Once the body politic is likened to the individual body and collective identities are likened to individual characters and selves (cf. Handler, 1994; Jenkins, 1996) then, conversely, models of individual character and selfhood will come to inform our understanding of national phenomena. According to Charles Taylor (1989), modern Western thinking about the self offers an image of people as having unique inner depths which they have a calling to express. Where this 'core' is neither singular, coherent nor whole, or where it is denied full and proper expression, then it is assumed that we are faced with pathology. As Macdonald observes, much traditional psychotherapy is conceived of as facilitating access to such inner depths, healing these disturbances, and so allowing the self a 'healthy' unencumbered expression (Macdonald, 1996: 5). She observes that if this discourse of healthy individual development is applied to nations the results are striking: 'just as individuals might find their identities lost or confused through amnesia or not having come to terms with their childhood, so too might societies or peoples suffer identity crises if they lost hold of their history or roots' (Macdonald, 1993: 8).

So, once one elaborates models of national character and one acknowledges that there may be several inter-related layers, then the question of integrity comes to the fore. Once the question of integrity is posed, it necessarily introduces the possibility of disintegration and hence of pathology. Moreover, once the account of character becomes multi-layered and it becomes possible to acknowledge that one's national character is not a static entity that is either good or bad but rather a system in which health is always precarious, then the spectre of pathology can be used to regulate how the nation should be and what it should do: what 'we' propose serves to promote the healthy over the malignant, while 'their' policies encourage the malignancy to spread over the body politic.

Perhaps the most basic and the most frequent example of such usage is the distinction that is drawn between reason (associated with one's own position) and emotion (associated with that of others). Take, for instance, the construction of a tension between the Scottish 'head' and the Scottish 'heart' as invoked by one Conservative MP. He first observed that there was 'some form of idealism which clouds' the Scots' judgment such that the Scots 'allow their hearts more to rule their heads perhaps more than people in England do'. He illustrated this by reference to the enthusiasm with which SNP supporters sang the unofficial Scottish national anthem, 'Flower of Scotland'. He concluded that the Scots were prey to 'some sort of romanticism' which was divorced from 'hard political reality' (Conservative candidate, interview 11).

A different Conservative MP, on being asked if he could identify any negative aspects of the Scots' character, argued that: 'there are times that the Scottish people respond to the emotional argument. And you know they are quite happy to stop at that'. He continued that the Conservatives 'should actually be going out and hammering far more positively, a sound rational, commercial, business, political argument to combat that. You cannot run a country on emotion' (Conservative MP, interview 16). Still another Conservative MP, responding to our inquiry about the growth of interest in constitutional change, characterized both the SNP's project of independence and the Scots themselves as 'sentimental'. To be more precise, he described the support for independence in the following terms: 'This sentimental idea that this jolly little taxhaven nation, Ruritanian, you know, "Here's tae us wha's like us, gui few an' they're a' deid", mascot of the world, universally popular, whisky-driven, bagpipe-led, you know, it's got a sort of Harry Lauder ring to it which appeals if it isn't studied. The Scots are sentimental' (Sir Nicholas Fairbairn, interview). The reference to Harry Lauder is especially telling. Lauder, a popular entertainer who was famous for his tartan clothing, was equally famous for transforming the symbols of Highland Scotland into a Tartan Kitsch music hall joke (McCrone, 1992).

Such diagnoses are not new. Nor are they the sole preserve of political protagonists. Writing in 1919 the critic G. Gregory Smith argued in his *Scottish Literature: Character and Influence* that there was a peculiarly Scottish 'racial' propensity to alternate between a dour matter-of-fact realism and unrestrained fantasy (so convinced was he of this tendency that he gave it a specific name – the 'Caledonian Antisyzygy'). Given the contemporary examples used above, it may be tempting to believe that such a dichotomy would typically be drawn upon to pathologize support for independence. However, this is not inevitably so. Whereas the Conservative MP cited above attributed support for independence to the Scots' sentimental attachment to a 'whisky-driven, bagpipe-led' Tartan Kitsch, several commentators have maintained that this degraded culture reveals a deeper malaise in the Scottish psyche which impedes the cause of constitutional change.

Paterson argues that the principal legacy of tartanry is 'a cancerous national inferiority complex: the quite unmistakable psychological end-product of two centuries of tawdry palliatives – of escaping from social problems into wishful fantasy' (1981: 71). One of the most eloquent explorations of what Paterson refers to as 'our tartan pseudo-identity' (1981: 71), is advanced by Tom Nairn (1977). He suggests that, whilst 'normal' national development typically results in a harmonious relationship between the head and the heart, Scotland's development has been such as to render it 'a sort of lunatic or deviant, in relation to normal development' (Nairn, 1977: 164). Rather than locating the source of Scotland's difficulties in some 'racial' propensity to swing between realism and wild fancy, Nairn's analysis places considerable emphasis upon the economic experience of Scotland's nineteenth century bourgeoisie. Conscious of its economic interests, its sentimental leanings and its capacity for 'romantic' nationalism, the Scottish bourgeoisie of the time was forced to 'repress' or 'sublimate' its nationalist 'impulse' (Nairn, 1977). This meant that any romantic impulses were kept separate from practical politics. For these commentators, the tartan-wrapped figure of Harry Lauder and the entire culture of tartanry (which Nairn refers to as the 'Tartan Monster') is testimony to a distortion of identity. It reflects, and in turn, is responsible for, the failure to embrace demands for increased political autonomy.

This diagnosis has become so common amongst advocates of constitutional change that McCrone ironically observes that 'to be "normal" (not neurotic) you'd be advised not to think of Scotland at all'. As he puts it, their analysis is 'replete with "monsters", with "neuroses", with "split personalities"'. And it was, after all, a Scotsman, Robert Louis Stevenson, who invented Dr Jekyll and Mr Hyde' (McCrone, 1989: 166). It should be abundantly clear, then, that the division between 'head' and 'heart' does not map onto a particular political position. Rather, it provides a resource through which any position can be advanced by the way in which it is mapped onto reason as opposed to unreason. Thus Scotish unionists see Union as reason undermined by unreasoning nationalism, while Scottish 'nationalists' see independence as reason undermined by an unreasoned reluctance to break the Union. For each, their politics serve the mental hygiene of the nation.

This argument stands whatever the nation, and so we find that it is not only in Scotland that nations are spoken of in terms of health versus psychopathology and medical disorder. Sometimes these diagnoses of the national condition may be quite light-hearted. Brendan Behan ('Richard Cork's Leg') once famously observed that 'other people have a nationality. The Irish and the Jews have a psychosis' (1978). Sometimes the diagnosis may be rather more heartfelt as in the attempts of Spaniards to come to terms with the humiliating loss of Cuba to the USA in 1898. Medical and psychological concepts were commonplace when analysing Spain's 'degeneration' and its prospects for 'regeneration'. For example, Angel Ganivet's *Idearium español* (1897) explained 'the problem of Spain' through reference to a medical-psychological term ('abulia') which originally signified 'spinelessness, apathy or "paralysis of the will"' (Richards, 1996, p. 154). Gavinet's belief that Spain suffered from this condition on a national scale came to permeate Spanish literary works of the time and was given renewed status as a diagnosis of Spanish ills when, in the early 1940s, the state party publishing house reprinted Gavinet's works. In this way, the aggressive militarism of Franco's fascist Spain became a measure of healthy Spanish identity.

If the uses of psychopathological terms are global and not just Caledonian, we shall nevertheless finish our analysis of how psychology is used in the service of nationalism by using two further Scottish examples. They are particularly elaborate, they are particularly rich in their use of psychological constructs (although the one uses terms that might be familiar from the 'New Age' and 'alternative' shelves of a bookstore while the other uses the language of psychoanalysis) and they perfectly illustrate the strategic use of such talk.

Our first example is taken from the writings of William Woolfe, a former leader of the SNP. It might be entitled 'the head, the heart and the solar plexus', for, if others make a simple distinction between reason and passion, Woolfe employs an altogether richer taxonomy. This is laid out in two pamphlets which diagnose the Scottish psyche, identify the source of its pathology, and plot out a path towards healthy development. *You Are My Sunshine* was published in March 1992 and *A Look at the Scottish Psyche* was published in September of the same year. Woolfe starts by arguing that there is a puzzling contradiction between 'the reputation of Scots for courage and hardihood' and their 'inability to achieve progressive social and economic changes in defence of Scottish interests' (*You Are My Sunshine*, 1992: 1). The puzzle is resolved by suggesting that the Scots are held back from action by a series of repressed emotions – especially 'shame'. As he put it during a subsequent interview with us, people are constrained by an 'emotional fear of independence which they don't know they have . . . the majority of the people accept the intellectual arguments for their self-government. They know it in the head. The majority of the people in Scotland know it in a sentimental way, in the heart. They love Scotland, they would love it to be independent. Oh, but you can see we are afraid, we are afraid. And they don't know why they are afraid and they are afraid because it's shame shutting it off'.

According to Woolfe this 'irrationality' in the Scots psyche was not to be attributed to the malfunction of either the Scottish 'head' or its 'heart', but (and here the 'New Age' discourse is most readily apparent), in the 'solar plexus':

Extract 1

The effect of repressed shame is to close off the person's powerhouse of action, which is the solar plexus. That is why we talk of people not having the guts to do something courageous. They may know it in their minds that they ought to do a thing, they may feel in their hearts the desire to do it, but if the solar plexus is closed off, they have not the guts to do it.

(A Look at the Scottish Psyche, 1992: 3).

For Woolfe, a key event in the aetiology of this shame was the 1707 Treaty of Union with England. Until this date the Scottish people had on innumerable occasions (he specifically mentions the example of William Wallace) exhibited a confidence in themselves as Scots. However, with the Union this confidence was lost:

Extract 2

Defeat without battle of a nation in which the ideals of freedom and of courage in warfare had been upheld with honour for centuries was a devastating shame, and as invariably happens, the repression of it was followed by cover-ups to drive consciousness of the shame out of sight and out of feeling. . . . We are still affected by the shame of 1707. That is what must be healed for us to regain independence.

(A Look at the Scottish Psyche, 1992: 2).

Such arguments allow Woolfe to shrug off any possibility that electoral failure means that the SNP are out of touch with Scottish identity. Quite the opposite in fact. The policy of independence realizes the deepest aspirations of the Scottish people, both known and felt (they 'know it in the head' and desire it 'in their hearts'). The failure to vote for independence and the disappointments of the 1992 General Election stem from those factors which pervert Scottish identity, which undermine the ability of Scots to express their desires and interests, and of which they themselves are largely unconscious.

What is more, once a certain feature of the present can be seen as a perversion of identity, then changing this element can be seen as a return to the pure and unchanging essence of the nation. We have frequently encountered such arguments whereby the present is dismissed as an anomaly in the nation's history. To characterize the anomaly as a matter of pathology gives added potency to the argument since it then becomes essential to survival that the change takes place. The anomaly does not just distort 'true' identity, it threatens to consume it. Thus, the year of Union, 1707, does not only mark a political discontinuity but a psychological discontinuity. It is impossible for Scots to have psychological ease until the political roots of their dis-ease are pulled up and thrown out. In Woolfe's words: 'If our national identity is denied, or is spurious as in the case of many Scots, then personal fulfillment is incomplete. The commitment of individuals to their own identities is assisted by their commitment to national identity, and to identity with all of humankind. These add up to being fully human' (*A Look at the Scottish Psyche*, 1992, p. 5).

It is not just that notions of pathology render change necessary for identity to be safeguarded, it is also that these notions serve to define what one needs to change to – or, to make the same point in different terms, they locate the points where identity was fully and authentically expressed. For Woolfe, this was not just the period before Scots had betrayed themselves through Union, it was the noble point where Scots were willing to fight to gain independence. It was represented above all in William Wallace who 'exemplifies that quality of total confidence' (*A Look at the Scottish Psyche*, p.2) lacking in the damaged Scottish psyche. Woolfe's prescription for a return to health therefore includes a: 'vision for the future, grounded in an understanding of our unsatisfactory present, with the courage and determination of William Wallace to achieve it' (ibid., p. 6). The effect of this construction is to make not only support for independence but also confidence in the success of independence prototypical of Scottishness. Therefore the fact that the SNP oppose a pessimistic streak that is rife amongst contemporary Scots does not merely fail to dent their own prototypicality but actually serves as further evidence to buttress it.

The SNP therefore establish their representativeness by the process of purging shame and not only by leading the Scottish people to independent nationhood. Woolfe asserts that: '*We* have to deal with the shame so that its effects are *healed*: and we ought to learn how to use psychology to maintain confidence and destroy the *sham* of confidence in a Union which is destroying our personal and national identities.' He goes on to argue that people need to 'overcome the inhibiting effects of repressed emotions which prevent them from being the people they truly are' (*A Look at the Scottish Psyche*, p. 3, emphasis in the original). Indeed, he maintained that the SNP's task was to facilitate that change for 'the battlefield is here, in the psyche of the electorate' (ibid.).

Taken as a whole then these references to the body and psychology, to health and identity, to personal development and empowerment, work to construe personal self-realization and national self-realization as intimately related and as contingent upon the adoption of the poltical project of independence. The talk of 'health' and 'pathology' is used to construe unionists as the merchants of disease and the SNP as the agents of cure. Not quite 'just what the doctor ordered'. More like 'just what the therapist ordered'.

So much for our first example. Given his many contributions throughout this book, it is only fitting that our final voice should be that of an MP able to describe himself in his *Who's Who* entry as (amongst other things) a painter, poet, dress-designer, landscape gardener, *bon viveur* and wit; a man who listed his recreations as 'loving beauty and beautifying love'. The voice is unmistakable. It is that of the late Conservative MP, Sir Nicholas Fairbairn. Perhaps it was this range of experience that equipped him so well for the witcraft of politics. However, his adept deployment of psychological concepts in political argument probably owes more to the fact that his father was W. Ronald D. Fairbairn, a key figure in the development of what came to be known as the 'British object-relations' school of psychoanalysis.

As we sat discussing the complexities of the Scottish–English relationship, Sir Nicholas spent some time detailing the complex relationship between a child and its parent: 'As the child grows up having been anxious for the protection from the parent, it resents the protection of the parent and pushes the parent away again and then it takes a surrogate parent in the form of marriage. And then it hates the parent whom it loves in marriage because of its subconcious resentment of the fact it was rejected in the first place. It also rejects the re-tying of the umbilical knot.'

After this account of the child's psychological relationship with its parent, he turned to one of the authors of this book and observed, 'You'll know all that' (to which the hapless interviewer could, rather sadly, only give a weak smile). He then proceeded to characterize the Scots as feeling 'dependent and impotent as the child to the parent, the little one to the big one' and to attribute them with feelings akin to those which psychoanalytic theory ascribed to children in their relations with their parents. Crucially, the whole thrust to this psychoanalytically informed diagnosis of the Scottish psyche was to construe support for the SNP as some sort of 'infantile disorder' which spoke more about the irrational perceptions of an immature psyche than about 'reality'. For example, after detailing how the child's perception of the parent is coloured not just by love but also by resentment, he turned to the Scots and explained in like terms how they misperceive the English:

Extract 3

Mummy smashes your toys like your steel works and your coal industry and your things and she just tells you to shut up. The fact that she throws you sweeties in the form of vast subsidies which the English don't get, which mummy doesn't enjoy, just reinforces the psychological idea that she's trying to keep you quiet when your resentments are justified. It's a very fundamental psychology about that. But, unfortunately psychology does not lead, the resentments of psychology when given their rein do not lead to a solution of the trauma and they create, they will create a new trauma of isolation and loneliness and deprivation. This is what happens when the child breaks away, it has to live in a garret doesn't it? But the motivation is psychological, the search for separate potency.

(Conservative MP, Sir Nicholas Fairbairn, interview)

For us, the significant point here is not so much the difference between Woolfe's idiosyncratic psychology and Fairbairn's use of psychoanalysis but rather the commonalities between them. Fairbairn's diagnosis serves to pathologize Scottish discontent with England rather than the failure of the Scots to act on their discontent. In Fairbairn's psychology, the perception of England as powerful and as malign is a mark of immature identity and the achievement of a healthy psyche depends upon transcending such perceptions rather than doing anything that might seem to validate them. In fact, were the Scots to act upon their infantile resentments it would compound rather than resolve their trauma. Just as the rejection of the parent brings pain and suffering, so independence would create ' a new trauma of isolation and loneliness and deprivation'.

In our second interview with Fairbairn, he underlined the dangers of Government attending to Scottish demands. According to him, such pandering (say, 'throwing money at the Scots'), could only add to the problem due to the psychology involved:

> no child who's spoilt reacts well to its parents . . . we set up Scottish this and Scottish that, the government does it because it thinks it's complimenting them and therefore they will vote for us. But it has the opposite effect because you are merely emphasizing the fact that the children are being spoilt.

So, for Fairbairn as for Woolfe, the apparent opposition to their own policies is down to defects in national identity, such defects are pandered to by opposition parties and their own policies serve as the royal road to a fully integrated and renovated national identity. In Fairbairn's case, the flexibility of these psychological accounts is illustrated by his ability to characterize a range of policies, from constitutional to fiscal, in such terms. Psychology is thereby used to impel us towards a unique set of relations between nations and a unique set of policies within nations as the only healthy way of national being – which also just happen to be the policies of his own party.

There is nothing new in this, of course. This theme has been our constant refrain. What is distinctive about the analyses in this section is the way in which psychology is explicitly used as the resource through which particular arrangements are naturalized and the way in which the more elaborate the psychological model, the richer the way in which it underpins the given project. A one-dimensional psychology of traits may serve to promote the acceptance or rejection of policies as reflecting or undermining national identity. A multi-dimensional psychology which introduces the possibility of disintegration allows for many more things to be done simultaneously. It allows one to use a distinction between appearance and essence or even to counterpose appearance and essence such that apparent discrepancies between party and nation can re-emerge as the party rooting out malignancies in the national psyche. Equally, it allows one to reconstrue the easy popularity of one's opponents as reflecting the way in which they encourage rather than challenge such malignancies. It allows one to deal with more complex sets of social relations by the ways in which they mirror the complex dynamics of the psyche. But for all this complexity, our ultimate point remains equally simple whatever psychology is being used. Beware of any model which underwrites one particular definition of national identity, or, more broadly, which privileges one form of national being and which pathologizes all others. Note how these definitions and forms serve the purposes of those who offer them. Reflect on how the use of psychology to obscure the link between self-knowledge, collective action and the organization of social reality renders an understanding of those links all the more important.

Of course, that is the type of reflection we want to encourage but it is not the only reflection that might be provoked by the foregoing material. There are two other reactions which may, if anything, be more likely. The first, which we might expect from within the psychological community, is that the examples we have provided are completely alien to modern academic psychology and therefore have no implications for the conduct of the discipline. At one level, this is undoubtedly true. Few researchers nowadays entertain notions of national character. Within the psychology departments of our universities, Freud is rarely referred to and when he is, it is mainly to dismiss his views as unscientific and his therapies as producing no measurably positive effects. As for the solar plexus, well the least that can be said is that it would take uncharacteristic bravery to champion such ideas in any academic forum.

However, to draw comfort in this way would be to use the specifics so as to ignore the more general argument. As we hope to have made abundantly clear by this point – and therefore at the risk of sounding unduly repetitive – we would stress that the problem lies with any approach which fails to appreciate the two-sided relationship between psychological constructs and social relations – or rather, in the terms we have used above, which ignores the links between self-knowledge, collective action and the organization of social reality. The examples we have provided may well differ from academic usage, but they serve as a sort of magnifying glass. In their extravagance, they make the dangers of naturalizing identity and naturalizing specific ways of social being all too obvious. They therefore reveal dangers that may be more veiled in the academic case. Nonetheless they are still there for, as we have argued at some length, there is no doubt that mainstream psychology is no less restricted than our political practitioners in the way that psychology is related to reality.

The relationship is either ignored altogether or else viewed in a limited way. Even when there are attempts to relate identities and social relations, identity is still conceptualized in a way that obscures the link. As we have pointed out, the most advanced theoretical frameworks co-exist with the impression that identities are lists of traits rather than theories of the social world. Trait language and the assumption that people act in terms of a trait-defined identity is as common in psychology as in politics (even if psychologists stress that the trait definitions of others, which are peddled by politicians and endorsed by the populace, may be misperceptions). The failure to acknowledge trait definitions as tools of mobilization is equally as common in psychology as in politics and hence the politics of academic psychology may unwittingly merge with the use of psychology by political practitioners. In either case, taking categories and category relations as givens profoundly limits the types of social world that we may inhabit.

The second reaction, this time more likely to come from critical voices outside academic psychology, is to eschew all forms of psychological analysis. If psychology reifies the world, if it colludes with nationalists in denying people choice over the worlds that they wish to inhabit, then a plague on psychology in any guise! Yet it should also be clear by now that we consider this reaction to be just as erroneous as that of denying the problem. If nothing else, we need a psychological account to explain why limited constructions of identity should prove so consequential in limiting our horizons. If psychology is one of the ways by which nationhood is mythologized, we need to replace mythological psychologies with a psychology of mythologization (cf. Reicher, 1996). A failure to do so would simply leave us in the grip of that which is being deplored. Ironically, a condemnation of all psychology would protect the very thing which motivated the condemnation in the first place.

The proper response to the (mis)use of psychology by nationalists is therefore neither to dismiss any charges against academic psychology nor to dismiss academic psychology. It is to develop our psychological understanding of collective action through and for the analysis of nationhood.

Psychology and the analysis of nationhood

We have now devoted a considerable amount of space to showing how national identity is both organized by and organizes national structures of action. We have focused on how the various dimensions of identity relate to the various dimensions of action. We have analysed the ways in which each dimension is constructed and contested as a function of the forms of action which flow from it. We have examined the many attempts to reify these identity constructions so as to make the resultant actions appear as only too natural. We have even turned on ourselves and sought to demonstrate the power of psychology as a technique of reification. And so we have gone from a psychology of nationhood to a critique of psychology as it applies to nations and nationalism to a psychological critique of the psychology of nations as used by nationalists . . . It is clearly time to bring all this to a conclusion.

However, given that each chapter has already had its own conclusion in which we summarize the questions we have set and the way we have answered them, a conclusion of conclusions might both presume upon the patience of our readers and insult their intelligence. What is more, to protest so often that we have indeed answered the questions we set out to answer might lead the disgruntled reader to believe that we are protesting too much. The reader with an unduly long memory might even turn the quotation with which we began the book back on ourselves: if we manage to get people to accept the questions as we pose them, then we really cannot lose. Or, in slightly different terms, it may be that we only appear to solve the psychological problems of nationhood because we have set the problems so narrowly as to stack the odds in our own favour. In so doing, we could be accused of making one matter in particular disappear from view.

The trick, if it is a trick, was performed at the end of Chapter One, when we set up the criteria for an adequate psychology of nationhood. These revolved around the relationship between national identity and the forms of national being. Consequently, throughout the rest of the book our attention has been devoted almost exclusively to these matters. Our key message to psychologists has been that identity is a necessary component of the organization of human practice, but that we must introduce a historical dimension to this relationship. More particularly, whenever we consider identity (and, as we have seen, other forms of human understanding besides) we must always look at them in relation to the future as well as to the present. Much of what we have had to say is summarized by Paul Ricoeur when he states that: 'the identity of a community or of an individual is also a prospective identity. Identity is in abeyance. As a consequence, the utopian element is a fundamental component. That which we call "ourselves" is also that which we await and that which we are not yet' (1997: 407; translation by the authors).

Our key message to those interested in nationhood has been that national identity has to do with who is being mobilized, not what they are being mobilized for. Depending on the way in which a national identity is defined, it can be used to mobilize the population to any end, not only those which envisage a separate national state. Indeed, rather than seeing any given definition of the nation as more authentic than any other or representing any given political project as more authentically nationalist than any other, the task for the analyst is to examine how specific definitions relate to specific projects. It is in this task that psychology can prove its worth to the community of scholars who seek to understand national phenomena.

Yet, whichever way round we look at things and whichever message we focus upon, this attention to identity, to meaning and to action seems to omit the element of passion. Passion was something we acknowledged at the start of our first chapter. We quoted Ignatieff (1994) to the effect that nationalism is a language of the blood. We went on to reference Hooghe's claim that nationalism is often equated with psychological categories such as passion and sentiment (Hooghe, 1992). By the end of that chapter, however, these concerns seemed to have been all but forgotten. It might appear odd to elaborate a psychology of nationhood and to claim success for that psychology when it ignores the very issues which seem to suggest that psychology has some relevance to nationhood. Like characters who set out to conquer the world and end up as a tyrant in their own homes, we could be accused of a triumph that is contingent upon a radical curtailing of our own ambition.

One response to such accusations would be to reiterate Billig's claim that the power of nationhood lies in its recurrent banality and not in its occasional excess. There is much merit in this argument. However, it is not the strategy we wish to adopt. Rather, our claim is that issues of passion should not be seen as in opposition to issues of identity and meaning. Quite the converse in fact: emotion exists in relation to identity and cannot be understood separately from it. Therefore, before one can address the place of passion in the world of nations it is necessary, first of all, to put in place a model of identity which allows us to overcome the dichotomy between sense and emotion. Having spent so long on such a model, we are now in a position to wrap things up by returning to the passions of nationhood.

In fact, although we have not commented upon it at any length, we have repeatedly encountered issues of passion within our analyses: Conservatives pleading their national identity and expressing outrage at the notion that their unionism should put their Scottishness in question; the furious reaction to the selection of beauty queens who were considered as national outsiders; the wild cheering applause and cheering at a Scotland United rally as the English were denounced for voting in a government whose values were alien to the Scottish people. However, in order to introduce our explanation of such phenomena, it may help to recount the original impetus to our studies of self and nation.

In early 1982 we were watching the film *Gallipoli* on the television. The film focuses mainly on the disastrous campaign by Australian troops in the Dardanelles during the First World War. What struck us most was the fervour with which families and friends waved off the troop-ships which took the soldiers to die. How could people be so passionate about so futile a war? How could they regard the possible deaths of their sons and lovers for the cause of country as something to celebrate? It seemed something hard to imagine in the present – the sensibility of a lost past. Yet just a few weeks later we watched almost identical scenes on the television. This time, though, they were on the nightly news and they showed British troop-ships leaving port for the Falklands War. Once again, the quays were full of cheering crowds throwing streamers and waving flags, and full of enthusiasm.

The scenes were all the more bizarre for the fact that most of us had little idea of where the Falklands were prior to the spring of 1982; we had hardly heard of them and, if they had been in the news at all, it was because the nationality rights of the inhabitants had been removed by legislation the previous year. When Argentinian nationals landed on the nearby island of South Georgia at the start of the crisis there was much speculation concerning the way in which the relevant issues – and the relevant categories – should be construed. Was it a matter of seeking oil rights in the South Atlantic? Was it a matter of scrap metal merchants out for a quick but relatively meagre profit? Was it a consequence of a diminished British naval presence in the region? Should it concern us at all? Yet when Argentinian troops landed on the Falklands one dominant construction superseded all the speculation: Britain had been affronted, British territory had been invaded; British people were under the jackboot of a foreign dictator. The *Daily Express* of 3 April, 1983 devoted its entire front page to a picture of the 1,813 Falkland inhabitants and to an editorial under the banner headline: 'Our loyal subjects. *We* MUST *defend them*' (emphasis in the original). The second paragraph of the editorial read: 'The right of the Falkland islanders, people who are wholly British in origin, sentiment and loyalty, to remain British and to continue to live under British rule must be defended as if it were the Isle of Wight which had been invaded.'

So, an obscure island and islanders whose British nationality rights had been recently removed with virtually no objection – but once the phenomena had been construed so as to represent them as prototypically British and thereby to represent the attack on them as an attack on us, then suddenly the reaction was fury. A population was mobilized to enable the mobilization of troops and the population applauded as the soldiers and sailors went to war in order to regain national territory. Clearly there was emotion, but emotion was contingent upon the construction of events in terms of identity. Passion flowed once identity was engaged in the events.

Consider, now, a second example of emotion – one which is much more intimate in scale, but which is all the more intricate in its phenomenology for that. Just after the Second World War, in 1946, the city of Trieste was taken out of Italian administration and governed by the allies until 1954. In 1949, the great national bicycle race – the *Giro d'Italia* – returned to the city for the first time since the allies had taken over. The race was covered by the great Italian journalist, Dino Buzzati. He described matters in the following terms:

> Three years ago, the Giro had come to Trieste the very day before it became a Free Territory. Furthermore, at Pieris there had been the well known assault on the racers that brought the poignancy of that day to its highest point. There were extraordinary demonstrations in the city, a sort of farewell to the Fatherland, and those who were present narrate how even the most unfeeling people wept like children. (1999: 96)

So, where the event is construed as a symbol of nationhood, and where a loss of nationhood is involved, so the event becomes an occasion for weeping.

However, where the event remains a symbol of Italian identity, but where it portends a regaining of identity, then the emotion is equally strong but very different:

> Today, three years later, it was almost like a reunion for the people of Trieste, moments of tremendous joy and, at the same time, of bitterness because we went by like a whirlwind . . . Today, at about two o'clock, Trieste was stirringly splendid, with its delicate cobalt blue sea, a white-hot sun and waving flags as far as the eye can see: the red, white and green fluttering everywhere. It's been quite some years since we had seen such a sight. They shouted 'Hurrah for Coppi!' but it was something else they wanted to say, 'Hurrah for Bartali!' and it was something else they were referring to, and not to Bartali. 'Hurrah for the Giro's little guys, hurrah for Cottur, hurrah for Leoni!' they shouted, and it was always something else the people of Trieste referred to today, something that had more grandeur, that's felt more painfully, and that by now they had become accustomed to keeping well-hidden within themselves. And the racers, with numbers on their backs, understood they had all become equal, that they were only Italians and no longer champions, locomotives, human torpedoes; as one, they push forward amid all those powerful waves of love, forgetting they were enemies. (pp. 96–7)

The length of this quotation may, perhaps, be excused by the richness of the account. If Buzzati is right, it demonstrates not only that the race, as the symbol of national reincorporation, invokes joy in the audience. It also shows that once the mantle of nationhood falls on the race it alters the relationships and hence the emotions within it. An inherently hierarchical and competitive set of inter-individual relations become a horizontal community where hatred and rivalry are transformed into intimacy. Such transformations are derived once national identity is invoked; they are not contrived, as one final extract from Buzzati's account will illustrate.

Buzzati describes a discussion with a fellow journalist the night before. This colleague was dismissing the idea of patriotism and nation. He claimed to be a citizen of Europe for whom any injustice was distressing, whether it was done to 'Italy or Sweden or England, or even Persia'. His was a newer, nobler patriotism – that which embraced all humanity. And so, Buzzati relates how he observed the man closely as they passed through jubilant Trieste: 'his lips were pursed up oddly in a way I had never seen before. He put on large black glasses, which he usually did not wear. The citizen of the world, full of shame, did not want to be seen. He was weeping. I swear that he was weeping' (ibid. p. 98). Perhaps one might be ashamed of succumbing to national passions when one officially eschews them. However these enthusiasms – the support for one's own soldiers, the pain of national loss or the joy of national rediscovery – could all be seen as the more positive side of national phenomena. They are about the pride and pleasure that relate to national insiders. Let us therefore use one final example which relates to feelings about and actions towards those who are placed outside the national community. We refer not simply to enemies, but worse, to those insiders who are construed as serving the cause of the enemy. We refer to what happens when someone is named as a traitor.

Karpin and Friedman (1999), in their analysis of the murder of Israeli Prime Minister Yitzhak Rabin, provide a graphic illustration of how such accusations are constructed and just how severe their consequences can be. They seek to demonstrate that the murder cannot be put down to the aberrations of a single person – the assassin, Yigal Amir – but rather must be analysed in relation to a deep ideological divide in Israeli society. As Karpin and Friedman put it:

> on the one side of it stands a community that sees clericalism, messianism, and ethno-centrism as the continuation of the Zionist revolution toward a purer expression of 'authentic' Jewish values. On the other stands a community that sees the rejection of modernism, pluralism and pragmatism as a throwback to the ills that Zionism emerged to cure. (p. 53)

For those on the religious and nationalist right Israel was exclusively the land of the Jews and that land, as defined in the Bible, which stretched 'from the river of Egypt to the great river, the river Euphrates' (Genesis 15:17). Consequently, the signing of the Oslo Peace accords and the ceding of occupied territory in return for an agreement with the Palestinians, was seen as a betrayal of Jews and of Jewishness. In the words of Hillel Weiss, a spokesperson of the religious right, the 'peace process' was 'a mythological process of tearing down Jewish uniqueness'. Accordingly, Rabin (the actual signatory) was portrayed as betraying the Jewish people and as siding with their enemies. In demonstrations against the Oslo accords, a photomontage portrayed Rabin dressed in Nazi uniform. Other opponents spoke of him as 'the Judenrat [Jewish collaborators with the Nazis] putting us on the trains' (cited in Karpin & Friedman, p. 86). Most alarmingly, a number of radical activists and Rabbis began to invoke the Talmudic concepts of *din rodef* and *din moser* whereby someone who imperils the life or property of another Jew, or else who hands a Jew over to non-Jewish authorities may be killed. Rabin, it was argued, was endangering the life of those Jews in the territories to be ceded, he was handing over their property and he was handing them over to Palestinian authorities. When Rabbi Hecht was asked how he would feel if somebody drew the appropriate conclusion and murdered Rabin, Hecht replied, 'I wouldn't feel [at all] . . . Rabin is not a Jew any longer' (cited in Karpin & Friedman, p. 149).

Such is the strength of hatred against Rabin for being a traitor that it can obliterate not only the individual himself, but all the feelings one might ordinarily feel for the death of a fellow human being. Although the point, of course, is that in being a traitor he is no longer a fellow. He stands against the community of fellows rather than being part of it. If we empathize and feel for ingroup members this is an extreme example of the lack of feeling for outgroup members. Identity, in other words, relates to the suppression as much as to the intensification of feeling. However, the more general point we wish to make is that this example – like the others – shows how the frightening intensity and power of national emotions should not lead us to see them as something primordial and beyond reason. They depend upon the way in which phenomena are understood – or, more properly, upon the construction of social categories and the social relations and norms which they imply. In the Rabin case, there are at least three levels of construction which underlie the emotional tone. First of all, there is a particular construction of the Jewish community in messianic and biblical terms. Secondly, there is a construction of particular acts by Rabin as putting that community in danger. Thirdly, there is the interpretation of particular norms as allowing the murder of someone who is construed as endangering part of the community. Only once all these elements have been rhetorically accomplished does nationalism become a language of blood.

What all of our examples suggest is that our awareness of a relationship between events and identities has profound emotional consequences. The type of emotion that we have found depends upon the relationship that has been involved: the affirmation of an identity provokes joy, its denial provokes sadness, an attack on identity provokes anger towards the offending agent – and so on. Such a bold claim does, of course, have a considerable number of implications, of which we shall focus on just three. The first goes back to the traditional opposition between intellect and passion, or else between rationality and irrationality. It should be clear that our whole argument concerning identity served to undermine this opposition, even before we began with an explicit discussion of emotion. For us, self-interest cannot be defined without questioning the self and hence the rational pursuit of interest depends upon the nature of identity. This means that identity is neither rational or irrational but constitutes the grounds of rationality. It defines what we value, it provides a model of the social world which allows us to plan how to get what we value. If identity is that which allows us to have interests then it follows that identity acquires a value in and of itself. The extent to which it is validated or undermined affects not only our pursuit of particular interests but our ability to pursue any interest. It is not surprising, then, that there should be strong emotional reactions to events which impinge on our identities – especially when, as in the case of nationhood, those identities are so central to the way in which our actions and relations are structured in the world. Such emotions are not irrational. They may be arational, but even then one must acknowledge that they buttress the psychological structures which allow us to be rational actors.

The second implication of our claim is that, as with the relationship between identity and action, we need to distinguish between generic processes and specific outcomes. In arguing, say, that those who are seen to endanger the national self will be viewed with hostility – a generic relationship – we are making no general claims for how any given others will be viewed. As in the Rabin case, or in the case of how the Scottish view the English, we still need to consider the particular ways in which self, other, and the relationship between them is construed. Even then, we need to examine the local construction of collective norms which govern how those who offend against us should be treated. Our generic claims about emotions do not obviate the need for situated analyses of the rhetorical construction of national identity. Quite the reverse – the one demands the other. Emotion cannot be used as a back door through which to sneak in an essentialist view of identity.

Thirdly and finally, our argument suggests that the banality and the extremity of national identity should not be seen as counterposed, nor should either be seen as more fundamental than the other. Both derive from the taken for grantedness of particular constructions of national identity. Much of the time these identities remain in the background and we fail to see how they frame the ways in which we order our priorities, the ways in which we define the relevance of phenomena, the ways in which we relate to and evaluate others and – of particular interest to us – the ways in which others may order us about. Sometimes, however, events may be construed as putting our identities in question and so identity itself goes from ground to figure. At that point, our banal existence – our very ability to lead our day-to-day lives – is put in question. What we took as solid ground may turn out not to be so and therefore no step is a safe step. Little wonder that we can get so emotional about events that impinge on national identity precisely because national identity makes everyday life possible in a world of nations.

Conclusion

We have observed how it is the fate of books, however rich and however nuanced, to be remembered through a single quote (if they are lucky, that is; if not, they are recalled through a single misquote). In the forlorn hope of controlling the way in which this book is appropriated, understood and used, and also to make up with brevity for the length of what has gone before, let us finish by supplying the one quote by which we would like this book to be remembered: 'National identity is always a project, the success of which depends upon being seen as an essence'. Psychology has spent too long in essentializing identities. We hope that it will come to play an increasing part in explaining how identities realize projects. This book is intended as a nudge in that direction.

References

Ahmed, A.S. (1997). *Jinnah, Pakistan and Islamic identity: the search for Saladin*. London: Routledge.

Alexander, D. (2000). Old national stereotypes should be cast aside. *The Glasgow Herald*, 17 Jan.

Allport, G.W. (1954). *The Nature of Prejudice*. Cambridge, MA: Addison Wesley.

Alonso, A.M. (1988). The effects of truth: re-presentations of the past and the imagining of community. *Journal of Historical Sociology*, *1*(1), 33–57.

Altemeyer, B. (1988). *Enemies of Freedom*. San Francisco: Jossey-Bass.

Alvarez Junco, J. (1996). The nation-building process in nineteenth-century Spain. In C. Mar-Molinero & A. Smith (Eds.), *Nationalism and the Nation in the Iberian Peninsula: competing and conflicting identities* (pp. 89–106). Oxford: Berg.

Amir, Y. (1976). The role of intergroup contact in prejudice and ethnic relations. In P.A. Katz (Ed.), *Towards the Elimination of Racism* (pp. 245–308). Elmsford, NY: Pergamon Press.

Anderson, B. (1983). *Imagined Communities: Reflections on the origins and spread of nationalism*. London: Verso.

Anonymous (1989). Ethnicity and pseudo-ethnicity in the Ciskei. In L. Vail (Ed.) *The Creation of Tribalism in Southern Africa* (pp. 395–413). London: James Currey and Berkeley: University of California Press.

Anzulovic, B. (1999). *Heavenly Serbia: from myth to genocide*. London: Hurst.

Archard, D. (1995). Myths, lies and historical truth: a defence of nationalism. *Political Studies*, XLIII, 472–481.

Ascherson, N. (1988). The religion of nationalism. *The Observer*, 4 December.

Ash, M. (1990). William Wallace and Robert the Bruce: the life and death of a national myth. In R. Samuel & P. Thompson (Eds.), *The Myths We Live By* (pp. 83–94). London: Routledge.

Azad, A.K. (1993). Presidential address of Abul Kalam Azad, Ramgarh, December 1940. In M. Hassan (Ed.), *India's Partition: Process, strategy and mobilization*. Delhi: Oxford University Press.

Bagehot, W. (1972). *Physics and Politics*. London: Henry S. King.

Balfour, S. (1996). The lion and the pig: nationalism and national identity in Fin-de-Siècle Spain. In C. Mar-Molinero & A. Smith (Eds.), *Nationalism and the Nation in the Iberian Peninsula* (pp. 107–117). Oxford: Berg.

Balibar, E. (1991a). Racism and nationalism. In E. Balibar & I. Wallerstein (Eds.), *Race, Nation, Class* (pp. 37–67). London: Verso.

Balibar, E. (1991b). The nation form. In E. Balibar & I. Wallerstein (Eds.), *Race, Nation, Class* (pp. 86–106). London: Verso.

Balibar, E. (1991c). Is there a neo-racism? In E. Balibar & I. Wallerstein (Eds.), *Race, Nation, Class* (pp. 17–28). London: Verso.

Baron, R.A., Byrne, D. & Johnson, B.Y. (1998). *Exploring Social Psychology*. Boston: Allyn & Bacon.

Bar-Tal, D. (1993). Patriotism as fundamental beliefs of group members. *Politics and the Individual*, *3*, 45–62.

Bar-Tal, D. & Staub, E. (1997). Introduction: patriotism: its scope and meaning. In D. Bar-Tal & E. Staub (Eds.), *Patriotism in the Lives of Individuals and Nations* (pp. 1–19). Chicago: Nelson-Hall.

Bass, B.M. (1990). *Stogdill's Handbook of Leadership: a survey of theory and research* (2nd edition). New York: Free Press.

Bauman, Z. (1992). Soil, blood and identity. *The Sociological Review, 40*(4), 675–701.

Behan, B. (1978). *The Complete Plays*. New York: Grove Press.

Benedict, R. (1946a). *The Chrysanthemum and the Sword*. Boston: Houghton Mifflin.

Benedict, R. (1946b). The Study of cultural patterns in European nations. *Transactions of the New York Academy of Sciences, 8*, 274–279.

Bennie, L., Brand, J. & Mitchell, J. (1997). *How Scotland Votes*. Manchester: Manchester University Press.

Beveridge, C. & Turnbull, C. (1989). *The Eclipse of Scottish Culture*. Edinburgh: Polygon.

Billig, M. (1976). *Social Psychology and Intergroup Relations*. London: Academic Press.

Billig, M. (1978). *L'Internationale Raciste*. Paris: Maspero.

Billig, M. (1979). *Psychology, Racism and Fascism*. Birmingham: Searchlight Publications.

Billig, M. (1987). *Arguing and Thinking: A rhetorical approach to social psychology*. Cambridge: CUP.

Billig, M. (1995). *Banal Nationalism*. London: Sage.

Billig, M. (1996). Remembering the particular background of Social Identity Theory. In W. P. Robinson (Ed.), *Social Groups & Identities: Developing the legacy of Henri Tajfel* (pp. 337–357). Oxford: Butterworth Heinemann.

Billig, M. & Tajfel, H. (1973). Social categorisation and similarity in intergroup behaviour. *European Journal of Social Psychology, 3*, 27–52.

Blommaert, J. & Slembrouck, S. (1995). La construction politico-rhétorique d'une nation flamande. In A. Morelli (Ed.), *Les Grands Mythes de l'Histoire de Belgique, de Flandre et de Wallonie* (pp. 263–280). Brussels: Vie Ouvrière.

Blumer, H. (1969). *Symbolic Interactionism: Perspective and method*. Englewood Cliffs, NJ: Prentice Hall.

Borland, J., Fevre, R & Denney, D. (1992). Nationalism and community in North West Wales. *The Sociological Review, 40*, 49–72.

Boswell, J. (1934). *Life of Johnson (2 vols.)* London: Everyman.

Bowie, F. (1993). Wales from within: conflicting interpretations of Welsh identity. In S. Macdonald (Ed.), *Inside European Identities: ethnography in Western Europe* (pp. 167–193). Providence/Oxford: Berg.

Breakwell, G. & Lyons, E. (1996). *Changing European Identities: social psychological analyses of social change*. Oxford: Butterworth-Heinemann.

Brewer, M.B. & Crano, W.D. (1994). *Social Psychology*. St Paul, Minneapolis: West Publishing Co.

Broun, D. (1996). When did Scotland become Scotland? *History Today, 46*, 16–21.

Brow, J (1990). Notes on community, hegemony, and the uses of the past. *Anthropological Quarterly, 63*, 1–5.

Brown, D. (1999). Are there good and bad nationalisms? *Nations and Nationalism, 5*(2), 281–302.

Brown, R. (1965). *Social Psychology*. London: Collier-Macmillan.

Brown, R. (1986). *Social Psychology* (2nd edn.). New York: Free Press.

Brown, R. (1999). *Group Processes*. Oxford: Blackwell.

Brown, R. & Haegar, G. (1999). 'Compared to what?': Comparison choice in an internation context. *European Journal of Social Psychology, 29*, 31–42.

Brown, R., Vivian, J. & Hewstone, M. (1999). Changing attitudes through intergroup contact: the effects of group membership salience. *European Journal of Social Psychology, 29*, 741–764.

Bruce, S. (1992) *The Red Hand*. Oxford: Oxford University Press.

Bruce, S. & Yearley, S. (1989). The social construction of tradition: the restoration portraits and the Kings of Scotland. In D. McCrone, S. Kendrick & P. Straw (Eds.), *The Making of Scotland: Nation, culture and social change* (pp. 175–188). Edinburgh: Edinburgh University Press.

Burns, R. (1909). *The Complete Works of Robert Burns. Vol. 6*: New York: Bigelow, Brown & Co.

Buzzati, D. (1999). *The Giro D'Italia*. Boulder, CO: Velo Press.

Cannadine, D. (1983). The context, performance and meaning of ritual: the British monarchy and the 'invention of tradition' c. 1820–1977. In E. Hobsbawm & T. Ranger (1983), *Inventing Tradition* (pp. 101–164). Cambridge: Cambridge University Press.

Castells, M. (1997). *The Power of Identity*. Oxford: Blackwell.

Cheyne, W.M. (1970). Stereotyped reactions to speakers with Scottish and English regional accents. *British Journal of Social and Clinical Psychology, 9*, 77–79.

Cinnirella, M. (1996). A social identity perspective on European integration. In G. Breakwell & E. Lyons (Eds.), *Changing European Identities: Social psychological analyses of social change* (pp. 253–274). Oxford: Butterworth-Heinemann.

Cinnirella, M. (1997). Towards a European identity? Interactions between the national and European social identities manifested by university students in Britain and Italy. *British Journal of Social Psychology, 36*(1) 19–32.

Coakley, J. (1992). *The Social Origins of Nationalist Movements: The contemporary West European experience*. London: Sage.

Cohen, C.B. & Wilk, R. (with Stoeltje, B.) (Eds.) (1996). *Beauty Queens on the Global Stage: Gender, contests, and power*. New York: Routledge.

Colley, L. (1992). *Britons: forging the nation 1707–1837*. New Haven CT: Yale University Press.

Condor, S. (1996). Unimagined community: social psychological issues concerning English national identity. In G. Breakwell & E. Lyons (Eds.), *Changing European Identities: Social psychological analyses of social change* (pp. 41–68). Oxford: Butterworth-Heinemann.

Condor, S. (1997). Having history: a social psychological exploration of Anglo-British autostereotypes. In C.C. Barfoot (Ed.), *Beyond Pug's Tour: National and ethnic stereotyping in theory and literary practice* (pp. 213–253). Amsterdam and Atlanta: Rodopi.

Condor, S. (2000a). Pride and prejudice: identity management in English people's talk about 'this country'. *Discourse & Society, 11*(2) 175–206.

Condor, S. (2000b). *The taming of Tajfel*. Paper presented at the Annual Conference of the History and Philosophy Section of the British Psychological Society.

Condor, S. (in press). Temporality and the construction of entitativity: a study of national representation in talk. *British Journal of Social Psychology*.

Connor, W. (1978). A nation is a nation, is a state, is an ethnic group, is . . . *Ethnic and Racial Studies, 1*, 377–400.

Connor, W. (1994). *Ethnonationalism*. Princeton, NJ: Princeton University Press.

Conversi, D. (1990). Language or race?: the choice of core values in the development of Catalan and Basque nationalisms. *Ethnic and Racial Studies, 13*(1), 50–70.

Cornevin, M. (1980). *Apartheid: Power and historical falsification*. Paris: UNESCO.

Crick, B. (1993). Essay on Britishness. *Scottish Affairs, 2*, winter, 71–83.

Crick, B. (1995). The sense of identity of the indigenous British. *New Community, 21*(2), 167–182.

David, B. & Turner, J.C. (1996). Studies in self-categorization and minority conversion: is being a member of the out-group an advantage? *British Journal of Social Psychology, 35*(1), 179–200.

Davie, G. (1961). *The Democratic Intellect*. Edinburgh: Edinburgh University Press.

Davis, E. (1994). The museum and the politics of social control in modern Iraq. In J.R. Gillis (Ed.) *Commemorations: The politics of national identity* (pp. 90–104). Princeton: Princeton University Press.

Debray, R. (1977). Marxism and the national question. *New Left Review, 105*, 5–30.

Debray, R. (1994). *Charles de Gaulle. Futurist of the Nation*. London: Verso.

Decharneux, B. (1995). Les anciens Belges. In A. Morelli (Ed.), *Les Grands Mythes de l'Histoire de Belgique* (pp. 21–33). Brussels: Vie Ouvrière.

Diaz-Andreu, M. (1996). Archaeology and nationalism in Spain. In P.L. Kohl & C. Fawcett (Eds.), *Nationalism, Politics, and the Practice of Archaeology* (pp. 39–56). Cambridge: Cambridge University Press.

Dijkink, G. (1996). *National Identity and Geopolitical Visions: Maps of pride and pain.* London: Routledge.

Dixon, J. & Reicher, S. (1997). Intergroup contact and desegregation in the new South Africa. *British Journal of Social Psychology, 36*, 361–381.

Edelman, M. (1977). *Political Language: Words that succeed and policies that fail.* New York: Academic Press.

Edensor, T. (1997). Reading *Braveheart*: representing and contesting Scottish identity. *Scottish Affairs, 21*, 135–158.

Edwards, D. (1997). *Discourse and Cognition.* London: Sage.

Emerson, R. (1960). *From Empire to Nation.* Cambridge, MA: Harvard University Press.

Faber, R. (1985). *High Road to England.* London: Faber & Faber.

Farr, R. & Moscovici, S. (Eds.). (1984). *Social Representations.* Cambridge: Cambridge University Press.

Fiedler, F.E. (1964). A contingency model of leadership effectiveness. In L. Berkowitz (Ed.), *Advances in Experimental Social Psychology, 1*, 149–190. New York: Academic Press.

Fiedler, F.E. (1971). *Leadership.* Morristown, NJ: General Learning Press.

Fiedler, F.E. & House, R.J. (1994). Leadership theory and research: a report of progress. In C. Cooper & I. Robertson (Eds.), *Key Reviews in Managerial Psychology* (pp. 97–116). New York: Wiley.

Fielding, K.S. & Hogg M. (1997). Social identity, self-categorization and leadership: a field study of small interactive groups. *Group Dynamics, 1*, 39–51.

Finlay, R.J. (1997). Heroes, myths and anniversaries in modern Scotland. *Scottish Affairs, 18*, winter, 108–125.

Finlayson, A. (1996). Nationalism as ideological interpellation: the case of Ulster Loyalism. *Ethnic and Racial Studies, 19*(1), 88–112.

Finn, G. (1991). Racism, religion and social prejudice: Irish Catholic clubs, soccer and Scottish society – II Social identities and conspiracy theories. *International Journal of Sports History, 8*(3), 370–397.

Foley, C.A. (1996). *The Australian Flag: Colonial relic or contemporary icon?* Sydney: The Federation Press.

Forsyth, D.R. (1987). *Social Psychology.* Belmont, CA.: Brooks Cole.

Foster, J. (1992). Red Clyde, Red Scotland. In I. Donnachie and C. Whatley (Ed.), *The Manufacture of Scottish History* (pp. 106–124). Edinburgh: Polygon.

Fyfe, H. (1946). *The Illusion of National Character.* London: Watts & Co.

Gallagher, A. M. (1989). Social identity and the Northern Ireland conflict. *Human Relations, 42*(10), 917–935.

Gallagher, M. (1995). How many nations are there in Ireland? *Ethnic and Racial Studies, 18*(4), 715–739.

Geertz, C (1993). *The Interpretation of Cultures.* London: Fontana.

Gellner, E. (1964). *Thought and Change.* London: Weidenfeld & Nicolson.

Gellner, E. (1983). *Nations and Nationalism.* Oxford: Basil Blackwell.

Gellner, E. (1994). *Encounters with Nationalism.* Oxford: Blackwell.

Gellner, E. (1997). *Nationalism.* London: Weidenfeld & Nicolson.

Giddens, A. (1985). *A Contemporary Critique of Historical Materialism. Vol. 2.: The nation-state and violence.* London: Polity.

Gilbert, M. (1975). *Winston S. Churchill, vol. IV 1916–1922.* London: Heinemann.

Gillis, J.R. (1994). Memory and identity: The history of a relationship. In J.R. Gillis (Ed.), *Commemorations: The politics of national identity.* Princeton, NJ: Princeton University Press.

Gorer, G. (1948). *The American People.* New York: Norton.

Griffin, R. (1991). *The Nature of Fascism*. London: Routledge.

Grosby, S. (1995). Territoriality: The transcendental, primordial feature of modern societies. *Nations and Nationalism*, *1*(2), 143–162.

Guibernau, M. (1996). *Nationalisms: The nation-state and nationalism in the twentieth century*. Cambridge: Polity Press.

Hacking, I. (1982). Biopower and the avalanche of printed numbers. *Humanities in Society*, *5*(3/4), 279–295.

Hains, S.C., Hogg, M.A., & Duck, J.M (1997). Self categorization and leadership: effects of group prototypicality and leader stereotypicality. *Personality and Social Psychology Bulletin*, *23*, 1087–1099.

Halliday, J. (1993). *The 1820 rising: the Radical War*. Stirling: Scots Independent.

Hamilton, W. (1998). *Blind Harry's Wallace*. Edinburgh: Luath.

Hanchant, W.L. (1943). *England is Here: Selected speeches and writings of the Prime Ministers of England 1721–1943*. London: John Lane.

Handler, R. (1994). Is 'Identity' a useful cross-cultural concept? In J.R. Gillis (Ed.), *Commemorations: The politics of national identity*. Princeton: Princeton University Press.

Harvie, C. (1994). *The Rise of Regional Europe*. London: Routledge.

Haslam, S.A. (2001). *Psychology in Organizations: The social identity approach*. London: Sage.

Haslam, S.A., Oakes, P.J., Turner, J.C., McGarty, C. & Reynolds, K.J. (1998). The group as a basis for emergent stereotype consensus. *European Review of Social Psychology*, *9*, 203–239.

Haslam, S.A. & Turner, J.C. (1992). Context dependent variation in social stereotyping 2: The relationship between frame of reference, self-categorization and accentuation. *European Journal of Social Psychology*, *22*, 251–278.

Haslam, S.A., Turner, J.C., Oakes, P.J., McGarty, C. & Hayes, B.K. (1992). Context dependent variation in social stereotyping 1: The effects of intergroup relations as mediated by social change and frame of reference. *European Journal of Social Psychology*, *22*, 3–20.

Hayes, C. (1931). *The Historical Evolution of Modern Nationalism*. New York: Macmillan.

Heidegger, M. (1991). *Nietzsche (Vols. 3 and 4)*. San Francisco: Harper Collins.

Herrera, M. & Reicher, S. (1998). Making sides and taking sides: an analysis of salient images and category constructions from pro- and anti- Gulf war respondents. *European Journal of Social Psychology*, *28*, 981–993.

Hewstone, M. (1989). *Causal Attribution: From cognitive processes to collective beliefs*. Oxford, UK/Cambridge, MA: Blackwell.

Hewstone, M. & Brown, R. (1986). *Contact and Conflict in Intergroup Encounters*. Oxford: Blackwells.

Hewstone, M., Stroebe, W. & Stephenson, G. (1996). (Eds.). *Introduction to Social Psychology*. Oxford: Blackwell.

Hill, C. (1974). *Change and Continuity in 17th Century England*. London: Weidenfeld & Nicolson.

Hill, R. (1997). *We Europeans*. Brussels: Europublic.

Hiro, D. (1992). *Desert Shield to Desert Storm*. London: Paladin.

Hobsbawm, E. (1990). *Nations and Nationalism Since 1780: Programme, myth, reality*. Cambridge: Cambridge University Press.

Hobsbawm, E. (1992). Ethnicity and nationalism in Europe today. *Anthropology Today*, *8*, 3–13.

Hobsbawm, E. (1994). *Age of Extremes*. London: Michael Joseph.

Hobsbawm, E. & Ranger, T. (Eds.). (1983). *The Invention of Tradition*. Cambridge: Cambridge University Press.

Hogg, M.A. (1996). Intra-group processes, group structure and social identity. In W.P. Robinson (Ed.), *Social Groups and Identities: Developing the legacy of Henri Tajfel* (pp. 65–93). Oxford: Butterworth-Heinemann.

Hogg, M.A. & Moreland, R.L. (1995). *European and American influences on small group research*. Small groups preconference of the joint meeting of the European Association of Experimental Social Psychology and Society for Experimental Social Psychology, Washington, DC.

Hogg, M.A. & Vaughan, G.M. (1998). *Social Psychology* (2nd edn.). Hemel Hempstead: Prentice-Hall.

Holy, L. (1996). *The Little Czech and the Great Czech Nation: National identity and the post-Communist transformation of society*. Cambridge: Cambridge University Press.

Hooghe, L. (1992). Nationalist movements and social factors: a theoretical perspective. In J. Coakley (Ed.), *The Social Origins of Nationalist Movements: The contemporary West European experience* (pp. 21–44). London: Sage.

Hopkins, N. (in press). National identity: Pride and prejudice? Comments on Mummendy, Klink & Brown 'Nationalism and patriotism: National identification and outgroup rejection'. *British Journal of Social Psychology*.

Hopkins, N. & Murdoch, N. (1999). The role of the 'other' in national identity: exploring the context-dependence of the national ingroup stereotype. *Journal of Community and Applied Social Psychology, 9*, 321–338.

Hopkins, N., Regan, M. & Abell, J. (1997). On the context dependence of national stereotypes: some Scottish data. *British Journal of Social Psychology, 36*, 553–563.

Hopkins, N., Reicher, S. & Levine, M. (1997). On the parallels between social cognition and the 'new racism'. *British Journal of Social Psychology, 36*, 305–329.

Horne, D. (1984). *The Great Museum: the representation of history*. London: Pluto.

Hroch, M. (1996). Nationalism and national movements: comparing the past and the present of Central and Eastern Europe. *Nations and Nationalism, 2*(1), 35–44.

Hume, D. (1748). Of national characters. In *Three essays, moral and political*, Andrew Millar: Edinburgh & London. Reprinted in E.F. Miller (1987). (Ed.). *David Hume: essays, moral, political and literary* (pp. 197–215). Indianapolis: Liberty Fund.

Hunter, J. A., Stringer, M. & Watson, R.P. (1991). Intergroup violence and intergroup attributions. *British Journal of Social Psychology, 30*, 261–266.

Ignatieff, M. (1994). *Blood and Belonging*. London: Vintage.

Inkeles, A. & Levinson, D.J. (1954). The study of modal personality and socio-cultural systems. In G. Lindzey (Ed.), *Handbook of Social Psychology, Vol. 2* (pp. 977–1020). New York: Holt, Rinehart and Winston.

Israel, J. & Tajfel, H. (1972). *The Context of Social Psychology*. London: Academic Press.

James, P. (1996). *Nation Formation*. London: Sage.

James R.R. (1970). *Churchill: A study in failure, 1900–1939*. London: Weidenfeld & Nicolson.

Jarman, N. (1997). *Material Conflicts*. Oxford: Berg.

Jedrej, M.C. & Nuttall, M. (1995). Incomers and locals: Metaphors and reality in the repopulation of rural Scotland. *Scottish Affairs, 10*, winter, 112–126.

Jenkins, R. (1996). *Social Identity*. London: Routledge.

Jensen, J.V. (1977). British voices on the eve of the American Revolution: trapped by the family metaphor. *Quarterly Journal of Speech, 63*, 43–50.

Jinnah, M.A. (1993). Presidential Address of M.A. Jinnah – Lahore, March, 1940. In Hassan, M. (Ed.) (1993), *India's Partition: Process, strategy and mobilization*. Delhi: Oxford University Press.

Johnson, S. (1979). *A Dictionary of the English Language*. London: Times Books.

Jurt, J. (1992). L'identité allemande et ses symboles. Une identité mal assurée par l'histoire. *Les Temps Modernes, 550*, 125–153

Kamin, L.J. (1977). *The Science and Politics of IQ*. Harmondsworth: Penguin.

Karpin, M. & Friedman, I. (1999). *Murder in the Name of God: The plot to kill Yitzhak Rabin*. London: Granta.

Katz, D. & Braly, K. (1933). Racial stereotypes of one hundred college students. *Journal of Abnormal and Social Psychology, 28*, 280–290.

Kecmanovic, D. (1996). *The Mass Psychology of Ethnonationalism*. New York: Plenum Press.

Kedourie, E. (1960). *Nationalism*. London: Hutchinson.

Khan, S.A. (1988). *The Lahore Resolution: Arguments for and against*. Karachi: Royal Book Company.

Kinnock, N. (1992). *Thorns and Roses: Speeches 1983–91*. London: Hutchinson.

Kiss, C.G. (1992). La guerre des blasons dans l'Europe centrale. *Les Temps Modernes*, *550*, 117–124.

Kitching, G. (1985). Nationalism: the instrumental passion. *Capital and Class*, *25*, 98–116.

Kohl, P.L. & Fawcett, C. (1996). (Eds.). *Nationalism, Politics and the Practice of Archaeology*. New York: Cambridge University Press.

Kohn, H. (1965). *Nationalism: Its meanings and history*. Princeton, NJ: Hutchinson.

Koonz, C. (1994). Between memory and oblivion: concentration camps in German memory. In J.R. Gillis (Ed.), *Commemorations: the Politics of National Identity* (pp. 258–280). Princeton: Princeton University Press.

Kristeva, J. (1993a). Open letter to Harlem Desir. In J. Kristeva, *Nations without Nationalism*. New York: Columbia University Press.

Kristeva, J. (1993b). What of tomorrow's nation? In J. Kristeva, *Nations without Nationalism*. New York: Columbia University Press.

Labour Party (1984). *Report of the Annual Conference of the Labour Party 1984*. London: Labour Party.

Le Bon, G. (1894). *Les Lois Psychologiques de l'Évolution des Peuples*. Paris, Felix Alcan.

Le Bon, G. (1917). *Aphorismes du Temps Présent*. Paris: Flammarion.

Leoussi, A.S. (1997). Nationalism and racial Hellenism in nineteenth-century England and France. *Ethnic and Racial Studies*, *20*(1), 42–68.

Levin, J. & Levin, W. C. (1988). *The Human Puzzle: An introduction to social psychology*. Belmont, CA: Wadsworth.

Lindsay, I. (1997). The uses and abuses of national stereotypes. *Scottish Affairs*, *20*, summer, 133–148.

Linklater, E. (1934). *Magnus Merriman*. London: Jonathan Cape.

Linz, J. (1985). From primordialism to nationalism. In E.A. Tiryakian & R. Rogowski (Eds.), *New Nationalisms of the Developed West* (pp. 203–253). Boston: Allen and Unwin.

Llobera, J. (1983). The idea of *Volksgeist* in the formation of Catalan nationalist ideology. *Ethnic and Racial Studies*, *6* (3), 332–350.

Llobera, J. (1996). The French ideology? Louis Dumont and the German conception of the nation. *Nations and Nationalism*, *2* (2), 193–212.

Lofgren, O. (1989). The nationalization of culture. *Ethnologia Europaea*, XIX, 5–23.

Lowenthal, D. (1985). *The Past is a Foreign Country*. Cambridge: Cambridge University Press.

Lowenthal, D. (1994). European and English landscapes as national symbols. In D. Hooson (Ed.), *Geography and National Identity* (pp. 15–38). Oxford: Blackwell.

Luxemburg, R. (1976). *The national question*. New York: Monthly Review.

Lynch, M. (1992). *Scotland: a new history*. London: Pimlico.

Macdonald, S. (1996). *Europe's national baggage*. Paper presented to British Association for the Advancement of Science, 'Changing National Identities in a Changing Europe', September, Newcastle upon Tyne.

Macdonald, S. (1993). Identity complexes in Western Europe: some anthropological perspectives. In S. Macdonald (Ed.) *Inside European Identities: Ethnography in Western Europe*. Providence/Oxford: Berg.

Mackie, J.D. (1991). *A History of Scotland*. London: Penguin.

MacLaren A.A. (1976) An open society? In A.A. MacLaren (Ed.), *Social Class in Scotland: Past and present*. Edinburgh: Donald.

Macnaghten, P. & Urry, J. (1998). *Contested Natures*. London: Sage.

Mar-Molinero, C. (1996). The role of language in Spanish nation-building. In C. Mar-Molinero & A. Smith (Eds.), *Nationalism and the Nation in the Iberian peninsula: Competing and conflicting identities* (pp. 69–87). Oxford: Berg.

Mare, G. (1993). *Ethnicity and Politics in South Africa*. London: Zed.

Marks, G. & Miller, N. (1987). Ten years of research on the false-consensus effect: An empirical and theoretical review. *Psychological Bulletin, 102* (1), 72–90.

Marquand, D. (1995). After Whig imperialism? Can there be a new British identity? *New Community, 21*(2), 183–194.

Marr, A. (1992). *The Battle for Scotland.* London: Penguin.

Masters, J. (1948). *Bugles and a tiger: a Volume of Autobiography.* New York: Ballantine.

McCrone, D. (1989). Representing Scotland: culture and nationalism. In D. McCrone, S. Kendrick & P. Straw (Eds.), *The Making of Scotland: Nation, culture and social change.* Edinburgh: Edinburgh University Press.

McCrone, D. (1992). *Understanding Scotland: The sociology of a stateless nation.* London: Routledge.

McCrone, D. (1998). *The Sociology of Nationalism.* London: Routledge.

McCrone, D., Morris, A. & Kiely, R. (1995). *Scotland – The brand: the making of Scottish heritage.* Edinburgh: Edinburgh University Press.

McDonald, M. (1993). The construction of difference: An anthropological approach to stereotypes. In S. Macdonald (Ed.), *Inside European Identities: Ethnography in Western Europe.* Providence/Oxford: Berg.

McLaren, M. (1961). *The Wisdom of the Scots: A choice and comment by Moray McLaren.* London: Michael Joseph.

Miles, R. (1987). Recent Marxist theories of nationalism and the issue of racism. *British Journal of Sociology,* 38(1), 24–43.

Miles, R. (1989). *Racism.* London: Routledge.

Miles, R. (1993). *Racism after 'Race Relations'.* London: Routledge.

Miles, R. & Dunlop, A. (1986). The racialization of politics in Britain: why Scotland is different. *Patterns of Prejudice, 20,* 23–33.

Miles, R. & Muirhead, L. (1986). Racism in Scotland: A matter for further investigation? *Scottish Government Yearbook,* 108–136.

Miller, D. (1995). *On Nationality.* Oxford: Clarendon Press.

Miller, N. & Brewer, M. (1984). (Eds.). *Groups in Contact: The psychology of desegregation.* New York: Academic Press.

Milligan, T. (1995/6). Wallace the Bolshie? Almost a Bolshevik: The posthumous career of William Wallace. *Cencrastus, 53,* 3–6.

Minogue, K. (1967). *Nationalism.* London: Batsford.

Montesquieu, C. de S. (1977). *The Spirit of the Laws.* Berkeley: University of California Press.

Moreland, R.L., Hogg, M.A. & Hains, S.C. (1994). Back to the future: Social psychological research on groups. *Journal of Experimental Social Psychology, 30,* 505–533

Morelli, A. (1995). *Les Grands Mythes de l'Histoire Belge.* Brussels: Vie Ouvrière.

Morton, G. (1996). Scottish rights and 'centralization' in the mid-nineteenth century. *Nations and Nationalism, 2*(2), 257–279.

Moscovici, S. (1961). *La Psychoanalyse: Son image et son public.* Paris: Presses Universitaires de France.

Moscovici, S. (1972). *Introduction à la Psychologie Sociale.* Paris: Larousse.

Moscovici, S. (1981). *L'Age des Foules.* Paris: Fayard.

Mosse, G.L. (1995). Racism and nationalism. *Nations and Nationalism, 1*(2) 163–173.

Mugny, G. & Papastamou, S. (1980). When rigidity does not fail: individualisation and psychologization as resistances to the diffusion of minority innovations. *European Journal of Social Psychology, 10,* 43–62.

Mummendy, A., Klink, A. & Brown, R. (in press) Nationalism and patriotism: national identification and outgroup rejection. *British Journal of Social Psychology.*

Nairn, T. (1977). *The Break-Up of Britain.* London: New Left Books.

Nairn, T. (1997). *Faces of Nationalism: Janus revisited.* London: Verso.

No Sizwe (1979). *One Azania, One Nation.* London: Zed.

Oakes, P.J. (1987). The salience of social categories. In J.C. Turner, M.A. Hogg, P.J. Oakes, S.D. Reicher & M.S. Wetherell (Eds.), *Rediscovering the Social Group: a self-categorization theory* (pp. 117–141). Oxford: Blackwell.

Oakes, P., Haslam, S.A. & Turner, J.C. (1994). *Stereotyping and Social Reality*. Oxford: Blackwell.

Oakes, P.J., Turner, J.C. (1990). Is limited information processing the cause of social stereotyping? In W. Stroebe and M. Hewstone (Eds.), *European Review of Social Psychology, vol. 1*. Chichester, UK: Wiley.

Oakes, P.J., Turner, J.C. & Haslam, S.A. (1991). Perceiving people as group members: the role of fit in the salience of social categorizations. *British Journal of Social Psychology, 30*, 125–144

Orwell, G. (1950). *Nineteen Eighty-Four: A Novel*. London: Secker & Warburg.

Osmond, J. (1988) *The Divided Kingdom*. London: Constable.

Ostergard, U. (1992). Peasants and Danes: The Danish nationality and political culture. *Comparative Studies in Society and History, 34*(1), 3–27.

Paicheler, G. (1988). *The Psychology of Social Influence*. Cambridge: Cambridge University Press.

Parekh, B. (1995). Ethnocentricity of the nationalist discourse. *Nations and Nationalism, 1*(1), 25–52.

Paterson, L. (1981). Scotch myths – 2. *The Bulletin of Scottish Politics*, Spring, 67–71.

Peabody, D. (1985). *National Characteristics*. Cambridge: Cambridge University Press.

Pearton, M. (1996). Notions in nationalism. *Nations and Nationalism, 2*(1), 1–15.

Pennebaker, J.W., Rime, B. & Blankenship, V.E. (1996). Stereotypes of emotional expressiveness of northerners and southerners: A cross-cultural test of Montesquieu's hypotheses. *Journal of Personality and Social Psychology, 70*(2), 372–380.

Pennington, D.C., Gillen, K. & Hill, P. (1999). *Social Psychology*. London: Arnold.

Penrose, J. (1995). Essential constructions? The 'cultural bases' of nationalist movements. *Nations and Nationalism*, 1(3), 391–417.

Peters, L.H., Hartke, D.D. & Pohlmann, J.T. (1985). Fiedler's contingency theory of leadership: an application of the meta-analytic procedure of Scmidt and Hunter. *Psychological Bulletin, 97*, 274–285.

Peukert, D.J.K. (1987). *Inside Nazi Germany*. London: Batsford.

Platow, M.J., Hoar, S., Reid, S., Harley, K. & Morrison, D. (1997). Endorsement of distributive fair and unfair leaders in interpersonal and intergroup situations. *European Journal of Social Psychology, 27*, 465–494.

Poole, R. (1994). Nationalism, ethnicity and identity. *Journal of Area Studies, 4*, 30–42.

Poppe, E. & Linssen, H. (1999). In-group favouritism and the reflection of realistic dimensions of difference between national states in Central and Eastern European nationality stereotypes. *British Journal of Social Psychology, 38*, 85–102.

Potter, J. (1996). *Representing Reality: Discourse, rhetoric and social construction*. London: Sage.

Poulton, H. (1997). *Top Hat, Grey Wolf and Crescent*. London: Hurst.

Prat de la Riba, E. (1906/1986) *La Nacionalitat Catalana*. Barcelona.

Privat, E. (1931). *Le Choc des Patriotismes*. Paris: Felix Alcan.

Przeworski, A. (1980). Social Democracy as a historical phenomenon. *New Left Review, 122*, 27–58.

Rahier, J.M (1998). Blackness, the racial/spatial order, migrations, and Miss Ecuador 1995–96. *American Anthropologist, 100*(2), 421–430.

Reicher, S. (1984). The St. Pauls' Riot: An explanation of the limits of crowd action in terms of a social identity model. *European Journal of Social Psychology, 14*, 1–22.

Reicher, S. (1991). *Mad dogs and Englishmen: telling tales from the Gulf*. Paper presented to the British Association 'Science '91' meeting. Plymouth, August.

Reicher, S. (1993). On the construction of social categories: From collective action to rhetoric and back again. In B. Gonzalez (Ed.), *Psicologia Cultural* (pp. 37–50). Seville: Eudema.

Reicher, S. (1996). 'The Crowd' century: Reconciling practical success with theoretical failure. *British Journal of Social Psychology, 35*, 535–553.

Reicher, S. (1997). Laying the ground for a common critical psychology. In Ibanez, T. & Iniguez, L. (Eds.), *Critical Social Psychology*. London: Sage.

Reicher, S. (in press). *An Historical and Interactive Social Psychology*. London: Sage.

Reicher, S. & Hopkins, N. (1996). Constructing categories and mobilizing masses: an analysis of Thatcher's and Kinnock's speeches on the British miner's strike. *European Journal of Social Psychology, 26*, 353–371.

Reicher, S. & Sani, F. (1998) Introducing SAGA: Structural Analysis of Group Arguments. *Group Dynamics, 2*, 267–284.

Reichler, C. (1992). La réserve du symbolique. *Les Temps Modernes, 550*, 85–93.

Reid, D.M. (1993). The postage stamp: A window on Saddam Hussein's Iraq. *Middle East Journal, 47*(1), 77–89.

Renan, E. (1990). What is a nation? (1882). In H.K. Bhabba (Ed.), *Nation and Narration* (pp. 8–22). London: Routledge & Kegan Paul.

Reszler, A. (1992). L'Europe à la recherche de ses symboles. *Les Temps Modernes, 550*, 209–220.

Richards, G. (1997). *'Race' and Racism in Psychology*. London: Routledge.

Richards, M. (1996). Constructing the nationalist state: Self-sufficiency and regeneration in the early Franco years. In C. Mar-Molinero & A. Smith (Eds.), *Nationalism and the Nation in the Iberian Peninsula: Competing and conflicting identities* (pp. 149–167). Oxford: Berg.

Ricoeur, P. (1997). *L'Idéologie et L'Utopie*. Paris: Seuil.

Robinson, J.H. (1923). *The Mind in the Making*. London: Jonathan Cape.

Rose, S., Kamin, L.J., & Lewontin, R.C (1984). *Not in Our Genes: Biology, ideology and human nature*. Harmondsworth: Penguin.

Rosenberg, M. & Converse, P. (1970). *Vietnam and the Silent Majority: The dove's guide*. New York: Harper & Row.

Ross, L., Greene, D. & House, P. (1977). The 'false consensus effect': an egocentric bias in social perception and attribution processes. *Journal of Experimental Social Psychology, 13*, 279–301.

Royce, A.P. (1982). *Ethnic Identity: Strategies of diversity*. Bloomington: Indiana University Press.

Sabini, J. (1992). *Social Psychology*. New York: Norton.

Sabini, J. (1995). *Social Psychology* (2nd Edn.). New York: Norton.

Sani, F. & Reicher, S. (1998). When consensus fails: An analysis of the schism within the Italian Communist Party (1991). *European Journal of Social Psychology, 28*, 623–645.

Sani, F. & Reicher, S. (1999). Identity, argument and schism: Two longitudinal studies of the split in the church of England over the ordination of women to the priesthood. *Group Processes & Intergroup Relations, 2*(3), 279–300.

Schama, S. (1996). *Landscape and Memory*. London: Fontana Press.

Schlesinger, P. (1987). On national identity: some conceptions and misconceptions criticized. *Social Science Information, 26*(2), 219–264.

Schwarz, B. (1982). 'The people' in history: the Communist Party Historians' Group, 1946–56. In Centre for Contemporary Cultural Studies, *Making History: Studies in history writing and politics*. London: Hutchinson.

Scott, P. (1992). *Scotland in Europe. Dialogue with a sceptical friend*. Edinburgh: Canongate Press.

Seriot, P. (1992). La langue, corps pur de la nation. Le discours sur la langue dans la Russie brejnévienne. *Les Temps Modernes, 550*, 186–208.

Seton-Watson, H. (1977). *Nations and States: An enquiry into the origins of nations and the politics of nationalism*. West View: Boulder, CO.

Sherif, M. (1966). *In Common Predicament: Social psychology of intergroup conflict and cooperation*. Boston, MA: Houghton-Mifflin.

Shils, E. (1995). Nation, nationality, nationalism and civil society. *Nations and Nationalism, 1*(1), 93–118.

Shore, C. (1992). Inventing the 'People's Europe': critical approaches to European Community 'cultural policy'. *Man* 28, 779–800.

Sinko, K. (1989). Arpad versus Saint Istvan: Competing heroes and competing interests in the figurative representation of Hungarian history. *Ethnologia Europaea*, XIX, 67–83.

Smith, A. & Mar-Molinero, C. (1996). The myths and realities of nation-building in the Iberian peninsula. In C. Mar-Molinero & A. Smith, *Nationalism and the Nation in the Iberian Peninsula* (pp. 1–30). Oxford: Berg.

Smith, A.D. (1986). *The Ethnic Origins of Nations*. Oxford: Blackwell.

Smith, A.D. (1991). *National Identity*. London: Penguin.

Smith, A.D. (1995). Gastronomy or geology? The role of nationalism in the reconstruction of nations. *Nations and Nationalism, 1*(1), 3–23.

Spears, R., Oakes, P.J., Ellemers, N. & Haslam, S.A. (1997). *The Social Psychology of Stereotyping and Group Life*. Oxford: Blackwell.

Spillman, L. (1997). *Nation and Commemoration*. Cambridge: Cambridge University Press.

Steiner, I.D. (1974). Whatever happened to the group in social psychology? *Journal of Experimental Social Psychology, 10*, 94–108.

Stout, R.T. (1966). *Death of a Doxy*. New York: Viking.

Strube, M. J. & Garcia, J.E. (1981). A meta-analytic investigation of Fiedler's contingency model of leadership effectiveness. *Psychological Bulletin, 90*, 307–321.

Swedenburg, T. (1990). The Palestinian peasant: a national signifier. *Anthropological Quarterly, 63*, 18–30.

Tajfel, H. (1970a). Aspects of national and ethnic loyalty. *Social Science Information, IX*(3), 119–144. Section 1, p. 62.

Tajfel, H. (1970b). Experiments in intergroup discrimination. *Scientific American, 233*(5), 96–102. Section 1, p. 46.

Tajfel, H. (1978). *Differentiation between Social Groups: Studies in the social psychology of intergroup relations*. London: Academic Press.

Tajfel, H. (1979). Individuals and groups in social psychology. *British Journal of Social and Clinical Psychology, 18*, 183–90.

Tajfel, H. (1982). *Social Identity and Intergroup Relations*. Cambridge: Cambridge University Press and Paris: Maison des Sciences de L'Homme.

Tajfel, H., Flament, C., Billig, M.G. & Bundy, R.P. (1971). Social categorization and intergroup behaviour. *European Journal of Social Psychology, 1*, 149–178.

Tajfel, H. & Turner, J.C. (1979) An integrative theory of intergroup conflict. In W.G. Austin & S. Worchel (Eds.), *The Social Psychology of Intergroup Relations* (pp. 33–47). Monterey, CA: Brooks Cole.

Tajfel, H. & Turner, J.C. (1986) The social identity theory of intergroup relations. In S. Worchel & W.G. Austin (Eds.), *The Psychology of Intergroup Relations* (2nd edn.) (pp. 7–24). Chicago: Nelson-Hall.

Taylor, C. (1989). *Sources of the Self: the Making of modern identity*. Cambridge: Cambridge University Press.

Taylor, G. (1989). *Reinventing Shakespeare*. London: The Hogarth Press.

Taylor, P.J. (1991). The English and their Englishness: 'a curiously mysterious, elusive and little understood people'. *Scottish Geographical Magazine, 107*, 146–161.

Tehranian, M. (1993). Ethnic discourse and the new world dysorder: a communitarian perspective. In C. Roach (Ed.), *Communication and Culture in War and Peace*. London: Sage.

Telfer-Dunbar, J. (1981). *Costume of Scotland*. London: Batsford.

Thaiss, G. (1978) The conceptualisation of social change through metaphor. *Journal of Asian and African Studies, XIII* (1–2), 1–13.

Thompson, J.B. (1990). *Ideology and Modern Culture*. Oxford: Blackwell.

Thompson, L. (1985). *The Political Mythology of Apartheid*. New Haven & London: Yale University Press.

Torregrosa, J. R. (1996). Spanish international orientations: Between Europe and Iberoamerica. In G. Breakwell, & E. Lyons (Eds.), *Changing European Identities: Social psychological analyses of social change* (pp. 111–122). Oxford: Butterworth-Heinemann.

Trevor-Roper, H. (1983). The invention of tradition: the highland tradition of Scotland. In E. Hobsbawm & T. Ranger (Eds.), *Inventing Tradition* (pp. 15–41). Cambridge: Cambridge University Press.

Triandafyllidou, A. (1998). National identity and the 'other'. *Ethnic and Racial Studies*, *21*(4), 593–612.

Tudor, H. (1972). *Political Myth*. London: Pall Mall Press.

Turner, J.C. (1991). *Social Influence*. Milton Keynes: Open University Press.

Turner, J.C. (1999). Some current issues in research on social identity and self-categorization theories. In N. Ellemers, R. Spears, & B. Doojse (Eds.), *Social Identity*. Oxford: Blackwell.

Turner J.C., Hogg, M.A., Oakes, P.J., Reicher, S.D. & Wetherell, M. (1987). *Rediscovering the Social Group: A self-categorization theory*. Oxford: Blackwell.

Turner, J.C., Oakes, P.J., Haslam, S.A. & McGarty, C. (1994). Self and collective: Cognition and social context. *Personality and Social Psychology Bulletin*, *20*, 454–463.

Urla, J. (1993). Cultural politics in an age of statistics: numbers, nations and the making of Basque identity. *American Ethnologist*, *20* (4), 818–843.

Wachtel, A.B., (1998). *Making a Nation, Breaking a Nation: Literature and cultural politics in Yugoslavia*. Stanford: Stanford University Press.

Wallerstein, I. (1991). The construction of peoplehood: racism, nationalism, ethnicity. In E. Balibar & I. Wallerstein (Eds.), *Race, Nation, Class* (pp. 71–85). London: Verso.

Webber, M.W. (1967). Order in diversity: community without propinquity. In L. Wirigo (Ed.), *Cities and space* (pp. 29–54). Baltimore: Johns Hopkins University Press.

Weber, M. (1968). *From Max Weber: Essays in sociology*. New York: Oxford University Press.

Wetherell, M. (1996). Constructing social identities: the individual/social binary in Henri Tajfel's social psychology. In W.P. Robinson (Ed.), *Social Groups and Identities: developing the legacy of Henri Tajfel* (pp. 269–284). Oxford: Butterworth-Heinemann.

Wetherell, M. & Potter, J. (1992). *Mapping the Language of Racism: Discourse and the legitimation of exploitation*. Hassocks, Sussex: Harvester-Wheatsheaf.

White, R. (1981). *Inventing Australia: Images and identity 1688–1980*. St Leonards, NSW: Allen & Unwin.

Whitelam, K.W. (1996). *The Invention of Ancient Israel*. London: Routledge.

Williams, L. (1994). The elastic nation or when is a category not a category? In K. Cameron (Ed.), *The Nation: Myth or reality?* (pp. 39–49). Oxford: Intellect Books.

Wilson, J. (1990). *Politically Speaking: The pragmatic analysis of political language*. Oxford: Blackwell.

Wittig, K. (1958). *The Scottish Tradition in Literature*. Edinburgh: The Mercat Press.

Woolf, V. (1943). *Three Guineas*. London: Hogarth Press.

Wright, P. (1985). *On Living in an Old Country: The national past in contemporary Britain*. London: Verso.

Wrightsman, L.S. & Deaux, K. (1981). *Social psychology in the 1980s* (3rd edn.). Belmont, CA: Brooks Cole.

Zemzemi, A-M. T. (1986). *The Iraq–Iran War: Islam and nationalisms*. San Clemente, CA: United States Publishing Co.

Zerubavel, Y. (1994). The Historic, the Legendary, and the Incredible: Invented tradition and collective memory. In J.R. Gillis (Ed,) *Commemorations: The politics of national identity* (pp. 105–123). Princeton: Princeton University Press.

Author Index

Subject Index